Glasgow Media Group Reader, volume 1

The work of the Glasgow University Media Group has become a core part of many media and journalism study courses and has made a great contribution to our understanding of the relationship between the mass media and society. In recent years, the Group's assertion of the role the media plays in shaping audience understandings of current events has provided a crucial counter argument to theorists of postmodernity such as Jean Baudrillard.

These two Readers bring together key articles and new writings by members of the Group from the early 1970s to the present, making newly available for students material from the Group's classic books, *Bad News*, *More Bad News*, *Really Bad News* and *War and Peace News*.

This volume focuses on issues of news content, language and the role of visual images in news reporting. It includes case studies of media coverage of Greenham Common and the controversy surrounding 'the Church and the Bomb'. The Reader opens with two introductory essays in which John Eldridge surveys the Group's work over the past two decades and responds to critics of the Group, and it concludes with Raymond Williams' classic article, 'Isn't the news terrible?'.

John Eldridge is Professor of Sociology at the University of Glasgow and a founder member of the Glasgow University Media Group.

Communication and Society
General Editor: James Curran

Glasgow Media Group Reader, Volume 1

News content, language and visuals

Edited by John Eldridge

Bad News and *More Bad News* by Peter Beharrell, Howard Davis, John Eldridge, John Hewitt, Jean Oddie, Greg Philo, Paul Walton and Brian Winston

Really Bad News by Greg Philo, John Hewitt, Peter Beharrell and Howard Davis

War and Peace News by Lucinda Broadbent, John Eldridge, Gordon Kimmett, Greg Philo, Malcolm Spaven and Kevin Williams

London and New York

First published 1995
by Routledge
11 New Fetter Lane, London EC4P 4EE

Simultaneously published in the USA and Canada
by Routledge
29 West 35th Street, New York, NY 10001

© 1995 Routledge: the collection as a whole; John Eldridge:
editorial material; the contributors: their individual chapters

Typeset in Times by Solidus (Bristol) Limited
Printed and bound in Great Britain by
TJ Press (Padstow) Ltd, Padstow, Cornwall

British Library Cataloguing in Publication Data
A catalogue record for this book is available from the British Library

Library of Congress Cataloguing in Publication Data
A catalogue record for this book has been requested

ISBN 0–415–12729–7 (hbk)
ISBN 0–415–12730–0 (pbk)

Contents

Figures

Tables

Acknowledgements

It has been a privilege to have been involved with the work of the Glasgow University Media Group since its inception and I express my thanks to all colleagues who, over the past twenty years, have been part of this truly collaborative venture.

We were originally financed by a grant from what was then the Social Science Research Council. We are glad to express again our appreciation for that support and for subsequent funding from the Economic and Social Research council on more recent work, some of which is reported on in Volume 2.

Some of the research discussed in this volume on war and peace issues was funded by the Joseph Rowntree Charitable Trust and by UNESCO and renewed thanks are due to them for their timely support.

Special thanks are offered to Routledge who over the years have published much of our work. On this occasion I particularly want to mention, Rebecca Barden, Tamsin Meddings, Moira Taylor and Sandra Jones. Their support throughout the process of production has been invaluable. The series editor, James Curran, has been a constant source of encouragement and it is a pleasure to acknowledge his support for this venture. Finally, thanks to Rick Holliman for his efficient compilation of the index.

Chapter 1

Introduction: That was the world that was

John Eldridge

This is the first of two volumes of work by the Glasgow University Media Group. The first has a specific purpose. Much of the earlier work of the Group is no longer readily available. With the exception of the first essay, what follows is a selection of readings from four sources: *Bad News* (1976), *More Bad News* (1980), *Really Bad News* (1982) and *War and Peace News* (1985). The second volume draws upon some earlier material but also brings in new and unpublished work. The two volumes are intended to bring together examples of work done by the Group over the past twenty-one years. They can also be read in conjunction with other new work already published in *Getting the Message* (1993).

In introducing the first volume I want to outline the sequence in which the work was done and to comment briefly on the context in which it took place. I will then explain the rationale for the selection of readings that follows. Twenty-one years is a long time for an academic project to hold together, and the political and organisational changes that have taken place in British society over those years have been radical indeed. A new generation of readers interested in media studies may like to know something of the trajectory of our work, what it was rooted in, and the sense in which it has changed and developed in this period.

THE *BAD NEWS* PROJECT

The first work undertaken by GUMG was financed by the then Social Science Research Council on television news coverage of industrial relations. This was a two-year award, beginning in September 1974. We took the view that everyone actively involved in the study should be named as co-authors and we took the collective name of Glasgow University Media Group since this was our location. The name has remained through other projects, involving different combinations of people, and notwithstanding the fact that members of the Group move on to other positions away from Glasgow. Where appropriate, individual authors are named within the context of GUMG work, as in Greg Philo's *Seeing and Believing* (1990) and the collection of essays in *Getting the Message* (1993).

Television coverage of industrial relations was a matter of public controversy. On the Left of British politics there was a widely held view that news coverage was biased against the trade unions, even though, it should be recalled, a Labour government was in power at the time of our study. Furthermore, it had come into office because Edward Heath the Conservative Prime Minister, as a result of major conflicts with the trade unions, had gone to the country for a supporting mandate and had lost. From a left perspective, the Heath period was memorably lampooned by E. P. Thompson at the time in his essays on the power workers and the miners, later reprinted in *Writing by Candlelight* (1980). On the Right of the political spectrum, the view was often expressed that television was left-wing in its orientation to news and current affairs. This view was later to have spectacular consequences when Margaret Thatcher became Prime Minister in 1979, especially for the BBC. Much of this is well chronicled in *The Battle for the BBC* (1994). Barnett and Curry record an encounter which Denis Thatcher had with Marmaduke Hussey shortly after he became Chairman of the Board of Governors: 'Denis Thatcher came in and started talking to [Hussey] ... "You've got to do something about that place. It's a nest of vipers. A lot of bloody reds. You've got to get it back under control"' (Barnett and Curry 1994: 39).

What made television a particular focus of controversy? The beginning of widespread commitment to television viewing in Britain is usually linked with the coronation of Queen Elizabeth in 1953, so it was a relatively new growth industry with a large viewing audience. Laid upon both the BBC and the then Independent Broadcasting Authority (commercial television) were the obligations of impartiality in the presentation of news. Inscribed in the IBA Act of 1973 was the following:

> It should be the duty of the Authority to satisfy themselves that so far as possible the programmes broadcast by the Authority comply with the following requirements: That is to say ... that due impartiality is preserved on the part of persons providing the programmes as respects matters of political or industrial controversy or relating to current public policy.

This mirrored what was already required of the BBC. And in the BBC Handbook for 1977 we find a standard formulation: 'The licence requires the BBC to refrain from editorialising'. The criticisms from Left and Right were that they saw departures from these obligations. A conventional response at the time from the broadcasters was that since they were criticised from all sides, they probably had it about right. We argued that an extended study of TV news bulletins was a prerequisite of an informed debate on the subject and that is what we did for the first half of 1975.

There is a further contextual point to be made about the study. In April 1974, the Wilson Labour administration, with Roy Jenkins as Home

Secretary, set up a Committee of Inquiry on the future of broadcasting. Under the chairmanship of Lord Annan the report was published in March 1977. This was a far-ranging exercise and its terms of reference included the need 'to consider the implications for present or any recommended additional services of new techniques; and to propose what constitutional, organisational and financial arrangements and what conditions should apply to the conduct of all these services' (Annan 1977: 1.1). As far as the broadcasting organisations were concerned, such inquiries breed a measure of uncertainty. Some of the forebodings about the report within the BBC were borne out. The chapter on BBC organisation refers to the lack of self-confidence in the BBC and confusion about its objectives and priority. This is related to problems of internal organisation and, ironically given that it is the BBC, to lack of communication, for example between management and staff and between programme makers and programme schedulers. Reference was made to 'the bureaucratic fog which is said to envelop the upper slopes of the BBC' (ibid.: 9.25). Even so, this critique has to be put in perspective:

Despite the loss of loyalty to the BBC, we found far greater loyalty to it as an employing institution than we found in any commercial television company. Despite the failings in communication, we found that people were less resentful of management and saw the division between themselves and it less, by and large, than in the television companies . . . the ever present measure of profitability, so evident in ITV, and the need through success to hold down one's job, was not so evident in the BBC; and hence the tension in working there . . . was less.

(ibid.: 9.29)

Nothing could be taken for granted, however, before the report came out and it is significant that extended discussions took place as to whether the BBC should be divided. Five members of the committee indeed, a significant minority, thought that there should be two Corporations, one for television and one for radio.

More specifically, Annan came to the judgement that ITN's *News at Ten* displayed a livelier and more professional presentation than did the BBC news. But, in some respects both were found wanting: it was presented in too stereotyped a fashion, with not enough attention given to explanation:

Who would feel from watching BBC news that the BBC had a mission to show world events each day to the nation? There is too much coverage of minor home news and pseudo-events, and too little of foreign issues which can intimately affect the lives of all of us. News is particularly singled out by many experienced foreign observers as the one weak spot in an output for which otherwise they have the highest praise. The broadcasting organisations should concentrate more on strengthening and varying their television news programmes.

(ibid.: 17.53)

In coming to this conclusion, the Committee acknowledged that they were influenced by the evidence submitted by John Birt and Peter Jay. This had originally surfaced in a series of articles in *The Times* and pursued the argument that the bias in television news was a 'bias against understanding'. There was, they argued, too little attention to context, too many items with too narrow a focus and an unhelpful separation of news from analysis. Annan reported that broadcast journalists were not enthusiastic about the Birt/Jay proposals. ITN claimed that if analysis replaced information they would be failing in their duty to inform the public and also be in danger of boring them to death. The BBC response was to suggest that, if followed, the Birt/Jay proposals would lead to a 'bias against unadorned fact'.

Twenty years later, this disagreement has its own fascination, given that John Birt is now Director-General of the BBC and Peter Jay the economics editor of BBC News. In *The Battle for the BBC*, Barnett and Curry refer back to this period when John Birt was head of current affairs at LWT and Peter Jay was economics editor at *The Times*. They see their prescriptions as 'an uncanny portent of the radical shake-up that was to be imposed on the BBC' (Barnett and Curry 1994: 79). In 1975, the then Chairman of the BBC, Sir Michael Swann, had endorsed the Birt/Jay thesis, offering the view that the need for greater public understanding of the problems which beset us is so great that every effort should be made to do something about it. Swann arranged for copies of the Birt/Jay material to be distributed to all BBC journalists which, according to Barnett and Curry, was 'a gesture which was not universally welcomed by the staff. At one point, a bundle of the offending articles was hurled out of the window at the back of Broadcasting House and finished up liberally scattered over cars in the Duchess Street car park below' (ibid.: 79). Swann called Birt and Jay in for conversations at the BBC and there was some possibility that they might have been invited to put their theories into practice. However, this was resisted, not only by the journalists but also by the then Director-General, Charles Curran. He wrote a paper for the governors 'explaining that the theory of a bias against understanding was, in fact, a theory about the sociology of management and was therefore nothing to do with news. It seemed to do the trick' (ibid.: 79–80).

The Committee devoted a chapter of its report to news and current affairs and stated that they regarded it as one of the most important subjects they had considered; pointing out that it is the policy of due impartiality which differentiates the broadcasting information services from those of the press. Moreover, they were prepared to indicate what they understood by due impartiality:

We consider it to be composed of three elements. The first is that it should allow the widest possible range of views and opinions to be expressed. Broadcasters are not doing their job if they allow one view to monopolise their services. Nor have they fulfilled their responsibilities, if this view is countered by one opposite view, when in fact people want to discuss the issue in different terms from those in which it was originally posed. The second element ... is that the broadcasters must take account, not just of the whole range of views of an issue, but also of the weight of opinion which holds these views. Their duty to let the public hear various voices does not oblige them to give too much weight or coverage to opinions which are not widely held. While it is right that accepted orthodoxies should be challenged, equally it is essential that the established view should be fully and clearly put and that the status and implications of the challenge should be made clear. Thirdly, in their exercise of due impartiality, broadcasters have to recognise that the range of views and the weight of opinion are constantly changing. What may be an acceptable and justifiable approach to an issue at any time will not necessarily remain so for all time. In deciding how to bring together these three elements, a broadcaster needs to be knowledgeable and sensitive to issues, attitudes and changes in public life. Due impartiality should not be a shield behind which broadcasters shelter but a pass-key to open up public affairs.

(Annan 1977: 17.10)

This is as full a statement as one is likely to encounter on the issue of impartiality written at a time when, as they saw it, the concept itself was under siege. Whether or not one thinks that this complex version of the concept can be reasonably approximated in professional practice, in terms of public awareness it is important to try and understand what is being done in the name of impartiality. This is where empirical research comes in.

Many academics writing on media topics gave evidence to the Annan Committee. From Glasgow, we submitted some preliminary findings from our research and also met with a sub-group of the Committee, but since *Bad News* was published in 1976, the Committee was able to make use of that as well, and did so. In publishing the first of the two volumes so quickly, we did so with the deliberations of the Annan Committee in mind. This is one way of trying to make social science research relevant to public debates and political concerns. In the event our work was discussed in two respects. The first related to the reporting of industrial and commercial affairs. After discussing some of our findings on the coverage of industrial disputes, they came to the conclusion that while broadcasters were not guilty of deliberate or calculated bias, there were indeed problems with the reporting, because broadcasters had not fully thought it through. This was not, they concluded, just a matter of failing to deal with the complexities of industrial disputes, true though that was, but more fundamentally, of not representing adequately the industrial and commercial life of the country:

We do not suggest that they should play down the disputes which occur in industry. After all, the public as consumers have a right to be told that a disastrous dispute is costing the country, and therefore the public as taxpayers and ratepayers, hundreds of thousands of pounds or that a company is closing down a plant at the cost of thousands of jobs. Broadcasters must not enter a conspiracy of management and unions to conceal the damage. But how is it possible for people to put these disputes into context, or to have an understanding of that part of the country's life on which, after all, much of our main chance of prosperity and a better future depends, if other aspects of industry or commerce and the world of work as a whole are inadequately covered in the news, current affairs or documentary output?

(ibid.: 17.19)

The second element appeared in Annan's reflections on the question: do broadcasters set the agenda? This referred to the difference between academic views and those of the broadcasters. The academic views cited were those of Stuart Hall, James Halloran and the Glasgow Group. Thus, for example:

Mr Stuart Hall told us that in his view the media were not only continually opening a window on the world; 'they are adjusting, organising, deciding who should speak to whom; establishing the order of priorities'.... In explaining the purpose of their project the [Glasgow] Group commented that 'All the techniques used to convey information through complex multi-phase channels of communication involve manipulation and processing of the original raw data – which is then in turn selectively perceived and interpreted by the audience. All media presentations of reality are selective and are therefore impregnated with values, viewpoints and common-sense working assumptions.'

(ibid.: 17.27)

The next paragraph of the report went on to comment that such analyses of the agenda-setting activities had 'naturally raised resentment, not to say bewilderment, among the journalists in broadcasting with whom we discussed this outlook'. Both BBC and ITN views were cited on this. For example, according to the editor of ITN, the thesis of agenda-setting

while it had an element of truth in it created a wholly false impression of what news was like. News was not dictated by some subjective considerations of ITN; it was dictated primarily by events that had happened that day. In their written evidence, ITN told us that 'the first priority of a television news programme is to present the viewer with a plain unvarnished account of happenings, as free as humanly possible of bias, and making the maximum possible use of television's unique capacity to *show* these happenings.'

(ibid.: 17.28)

What did Annan make of this? The Committee had, it said, no quarrel with those who saw editors and journalists as gatekeepers. They do, after all, have to choose what will be news and what they believe will be of interest to their audience:

> In doing so, how can they not be influenced by their own cultural and social backgrounds, by the requirements of their organisation, by their professional experiences and by the assumptions of their profession? They must also be influenced no less by the logistics of news production and by their assessments of the comparative cost of collecting news stories. News cannot be some sort of objectively established entity.
>
> (ibid.: 17.29)

The Committee then added that it was important to understand what gatekeeper theorists assumed. If it was simply that broadcasters should have a greater awareness of what they were doing, it could be endorsed. But if it implied that they were so irresponsible in their agenda-setting that some other group should set the agenda, such a view should be rejected. In the end, they concluded: 'What protects the public against manipulation of news reporting is not the centralisation of editorial decisions. It is the variety of news outlets and of editorial judgments, both in broadcasting and in the press, which is maintained in the nation' (ibid.: 17.30).

What emerges from this period, I think, is something of the intensity of the debate between the broadcasters and their critics, not least because the Annan Report was expected to have significant implications for the future of broadcasting. We were, in the course of our work, no strangers to hostility from both the BBC and ITN. We could, I suppose, have used the standard defence broadcasters themselves used: we were attacked from both sides so we must have got it about right. Certainly we were happy to engage in public debate and also made efforts to disseminate the research findings in seminars and video presentations, not only to academic gatherings but to church groups, trade-union conferences, as well as people working in the media. Some of this conflict was referred to in our books. There were also exchanges in the letter pages of the press and some memorable personal encounters including a private visit to the Glasgow Group from Sir Michael Swann.

One illustrative story will suffice for present purposes in relation to this early work. Richard Hoggart, well known for his study *The Uses of Literacy*, and an influential member of the Pilkington Committee on Broadcasting, agreed to write a Foreword to *Bad News*. In one of his autobiographical volumes, *An Imagined Life* (1993), Hoggart recalls an incident that happened shortly afterwards:

> Walking up Regent Street, in early 1976, to a small meeting in the BBC, just outside All Souls, I ran into a friendly acquaintance from the Corporation. His greeting was unusually muted, as if to one previously

believed to be on our side but now revealed as a member of a terrorist cell. More amused than abashed, I went to the meeting, where the Chairman, also a staff member, had the same betrayed air. A few days later yet another Corporation executive repeated the reaction, and elaborated on it so far as to say I had allowed myself to be duped by a bunch on the far left. All three men were devoted servants of the Corporation, intelligent and honest.

(Hoggart 1993: 258)

For all his experience, Hoggart was surprised that the profession should be so deeply resistant to the view that what constitutes 'news' is a culturally conditioned construction, seeing it as an attack on their professional integrity. Commenting further on the professional response, Hoggart referred to a senior man in ITN who said to him, 'But the news is out there and we simply report it as accurately as we can.' On this Hoggart commented: 'That the very process of selection – "this is news, this is not" – were products of his time and place, not of illegitimate outside pressures but of all the unspoken assumptions of his class, of professional case-law and of society as a whole was, surprisingly, news to him and unacceptable' (ibid.: p. 259).

In the Foreword to *Bad News*, Hoggart referred to four filtering processes that affect the way 'the news' is selected. The first related to the constraints that affected what could be done because of the nature of the medium or the contingencies of the moment: matters such as time, resources or geography. The second was 'news values', which he believed television had largely taken over from the popular press without thinking through their relevance or irrelevance to television's own situation. Third, there were specifically 'television values' 'which related to professional judgements concerning the role of visual material and what makes 'good television'. Fourth, and for Hoggart the most important, since it partly contains the others:

the cultural air we breathe, the whole ideological atmosphere of our society, which tells us that some things can be said and others had best not be said. It is that whole and almost unconscious pressure towards implicitly affirming the status quo, towards confirming 'the ordinary man' in his existing attitudes, towards discouraging refusals to conform, that atmosphere which comes off the morning radio news-and-chat programmes as much as from the whole pattern of reader-visual background-and-words which is the context of television news.

(Glasgow University Media Group 1976: x)

What the practitioners call 'objective news' is, in Hoggart's view, what emerges through those filters. What we get as a result is 'a heavily-selected interpretation of events, one which structures reality for us, which shapes and frames a world for us to inhabit and accept as real and legitimate, one which sets the agenda within which – except by a positive effort at remaking – we are led to discuss the terms of our lives' (ibid.: x). Hoggart expressed the wish that the Glasgow study be scrutinised as a basis for discussing and moving forward with a more critical understanding of what 'news' is and how it comes to be constructed in the way it does. He urged broadcasters to respond to the work 'not in a mood of defensiveness so rancorous that they are unable to see the main drift of the argument, nor with an implicit urge to let niggles about this or that statistical point justify their resolute refusal to face the general case. The time is overdue for them to look steadily at that case' (ibid.: xi).

Hoggart then went on to a brief but interesting discussion of conspiracy theories about the media (which, for the record, he did not think applied to the Glasgow work). He distinguished between two types of conspiracy theories: 'low' and 'high'. The first referred to the proposition that what is or what is not shown as news is politically determined by the state in a direct way. Hoggart's point is not that such pressures do not exist nor that interventions are not attempted, but that as an explanation of what actually happens it is woefully lacking. The 'high conspiracy theory' is more subtle and more indirect in what it sees as taking place. News agendas are tightly framed by more hidden forces: there are firm, even if unspoken assumptions about how topics like strikes, race, or Northern Ireland are to be treated. Where there are implicit controls operating around agenda-setting, direct pressures are rarely needed. Again, Hoggart allows a role for this, seeing it as a line that can usefully be followed a long way. Indeed, he extends the point of this analysis by suggesting that these processes can be seen in all corporate states, including of course communist states where state control of the media was notoriously tighter than in the West. Yet neither low, high or a combination of the two conspiracy theories tell the whole story, because even when they carry some weight, the controls are not complete. What is needed, consequently, is a close analysis of how agendas are set up and the extent to which they are, or are not, preordained:

> From that we can move to what also and no less needs doing – to analysing what really are the relations, direct or indirect, explicit or implicit, between the television people and the authorities – government, business, the trade unions. These relations are tough and tender, strong and weak, and extraordinarily complicated; and they do not all run in the same direction. If we did work in depth on these two fronts we would at last be getting somewhere. The Glasgow Media Group would claim no more – and they have a right to claim it – that they are contributing, at a relatively early stage, to that sort of understanding.
>
> (ibid.: xiii)

The strategy adopted in the Glasgow study was to video all news bulletins for an extended period. We started on 1 January 1975, which began with news of the collapse of the Burmah Oil Company, and ended on 3 June 1975, the day the British people voted, through a referendum, to stay in the European

Common Market (as it then was). By collecting all the bulletins on what were then three channels, rather than sampling them, we were able to follow stories through and generate transcripts from them, as required. Although we were later to sample within that material for particular purposes, this did give us considerable research flexibility. This was valuable not least because we could not anticipate very precisely the volume of work which the analysis would entail, nor the possibilities for study which the material itself would reveal. Perhaps most importantly, this decision enabled us to work with the journalists' own category of 'the story'. We were able to trace through the way particular stories were presented, what themes were present, who was interviewed, what questions were asked, and what visual aspects were evident in a way that would not have been possible if we had simply sampled within that period. Thus it was even possible to show what editorial changes took place in the coverage of a story as between a lunch-time and evening bulletin, or to compare the way a story was told as between ITN and BBC.

No one should enter upon this kind of research task lightly. The amount of material collected can soon become overwhelming unless there is a group of researchers with the skill and the diligence to take it on. With the increasing sophistication and flexibility of video recorders and the development of micro-computers, the collection, storage, retrieval and analysis of data can be done more quickly and efficiently than was possible in 1975. Nevertheless, it is all too easy to underestimate the time and energy involved, with the potential danger that qualitative analysis gets squeezed out or marginalised because of the need to deal in the first instance with quantitative measures of coverage.

On the basis of the first three months of 1975, we used what we termed the primary log, that is the log of all news items on the bulletins not just industrial coverage, to generate information about bulletin profiles. This referred to such matters as the length of bulletins; the number and duration of items in each bulletin; the category profiles for each channel (industrial, political, foreign, and so on); the placement of items in the bulletin order; the technical and graphic inputs; and the use of interviews, including how many and with whom. This part of the work constituted a conventional, if detailed, form of content analysis. Methodologically it is a form of unobtrusive measure. The material, in this case news bulletins, is created quite independently of the research interest. It is then analysed in ways that do not influence what is being produced. This only happens once the findings are publicised and disseminated. In this study, it allowed us to examine how bulletins were structured and organised, which represented taken-for-granted professional routines at that time. The findings can sometimes surprise those whose work is being studied and, for that matter, the researchers. For example, a number of structural similarities in bulletin and category profiles emerged when the BBC and the ITN were compared. This was something we did not anticipate, not least because the two institutions were differently organised and saw themselves as being in a competitive relationship. But only in an oblique way does this suggest anything about news values. We get a little closer to this in the analysis of who was interviewed. We concluded that the choice of interviewees, their selective use in different story categories, and the frequency with which interviews were used revealed considerable stability through time and across channels. This still does not say anything about the meaning of the news text but it does raise questions in our minds about the significance of these patterned arrangements. What use, for example, is made of interviews in the explanation and interpretation of news stories? This would merit further exploration, but even the descriptive outline of bulletin and category profiles points to journalistic criteria that lead us to a sense of news as a constructed product which is organised in one way rather than another. This does not imply that such criteria are universal or unchangeable but it does provide a point of departure for further analysis and raise questions as to why it is the way it is.

Through the primary log, of course, we were able to locate the industrial and economic news which formed the basis for the video archive for the substantive part of the project. By a sequence of steps, we were then able to put the method of content analysis to several uses. First, we were able to identify all the news stories pertaining to particular industries and the number of reports concerning those stories. We could also establish an inventory of what those stories were. We were able to classify these reports and stories with reference to the Department of Employment's Standard Industrial Classification. From this we could describe the contours of industrial coverage over a five-month period. Just as we had shown that structural similarities existed between channels in bulletin and category profiles, so we were able to show that this was also the case for industry-by-industry coverage. Again, it should be noted, this does not say anything about the meaning of the content, it simply refers to its structural properties. Even so, when these industrial profiles were checked against the employment figures for each industrial category, it could be shown that there was certainly no direct relation between the amount of coverage given and its employed population. For example, in the case of the car industry, 2.1 per cent of the employed population received 24.4 per cent of industrial news reporting. By contrast, the distributive trades category, with 11.9 per cent of the employed population, constituted only 0.7 per cent of industrial news. In terms of journalistic criteria, we can still recognise that there may be good reasons for this, but in terms of data obtained on the basis of these unobtrusive measures, we are in a better position to ask why the coverage is structured in this way.

When we looked at the kind of stories that were covered by industrial news for the five-month period, we saw that just over a fifth of them were about strikes and this was so for all channels. However, strike stories tended to carry more reports than other industrial stories and, for each channel, this amounted to just under 40 per cent of the bulletin reports of industrial news, so that again the structural similarities between the three channels was evident. Moreover, in each case, between 70 and 80 per cent of the strike reports were concentrated in three Standard Industrial Classification categories – motor vehicles, transport and public administration – and even at this relatively disaggregated level, the similarities between channels remained close, especially for motor vehicles and transport. This does begin to suggest something about journalistic routines. By and large it was the same stories that were being covered and exclusive stories, when they did occur, tended to receive fewer reports than the shared ones.

Could it have been that these structural similarities and shared stories simply reflected the incidence of industrial disputes in the UK at that time? The only practical way of getting some external check on this was to make use of the Department of Employment's strike statistics for the period. This comparison showed that the car industry was highly strike-prone during that period and, in that respect, the reports reflected what was happening on the industrial scene. Yet, interestingly, it did not reflect what was happening in the shipbuilding industry, where stoppages per worker and working days lost per worker were even higher than for the car industry. This kind of comparison is a way of identifying not only what is present on a bulletin but also what is absent or infrequently referenced.

Once we have identified the contours of coverage, we do have a research rationale for analysing linguistic and visual aspects of particular stories. If, as we discovered, the car industry was the most frequently covered and if strike stories were the most frequently featured, then a case study of the news coverage of such a story is not an arbitrary choice. That is why, in *Bad News*, we looked at the two industry categories most in evidence on television news and showed how these stories were covered. In practical terms, this meant taking all the reports of the story on all channels and working with a transcript taken from the screen and with the accompanying visual material. From this we can show how the story is told and various questions can be posed. Which people are interviewed or offer comment? What questions are asked? Are there definable interviewing styles? What is the role of specialist corres-pondents? How do voice-over commentaries take the story on? What reference is made to 'experts' and who are they? Do the correspondents themselves sometimes get used as experts to the extent that they are interviewed by the newscaster? Are there any taken-for-granted or common-sense assumptions that may be located in the text? Is there a particular frame that is established wherein, for example, a problem is defined or an issue contextualised, or causes attributed or imputed? When we pursue these questions we are looking at professional routines and practices. It is through such devices that accounts of the world are filtered. This, in short, is a way of approaching the process of encoding. To follow through the implications of this is to realise the inadequacies of using a term like bias, as though there were a wholly objective account of the world that can be reproduced on a news bulletin instead of different ways of constructing the account.

Clearly, the analysis of output through the method of content analysis only one element in the study of the communication process. Before content is the production process: all the things that lead to the linguistic and visual encoding in one way rather than another. After output is reception. Because we can show that information is shaped in certain kinds of ways, that stories have certain kinds of predominating themes, and so on, we do not suppose, and never have, that those on the receiving end of these messages hear or see them in the same way. Yet, unless we have some method for analysing content, we have no basis for discovering what it is that people are responding to. But that is only one element in trying to understand the communication process, which involves looking at the sequences of production, content and reception and their complex interactions. In methodological terms, therefore, we saw content analysis not as an exclusive or superior form of communications research but as a bridge which could facilitate the analysis of the communications process.

By the time *More Bad News* was published in 1980 most members of the Group had moved from Glasgow to other academic posts and we might well have ended our collective work at that point. Moreover, in 1979 there was a change of government led by Margaret Thatcher and driven by 'New Right' thinking. Social science research was not encouraged and sociology was regarded with hostility. The Social Science Research Council came under particular government scrutiny and its title was changed to Economic and Social Research Council since, according to Sir Keith Joseph, then Secretary of State for Education, there was no such thing as social science. This was not a product of any epistemological debate but of political fiat. Indeed, leaked documents of correspondence between Sir Geoffrey Howe and Sir Keith Joseph indicated that they hoped the inquiry they had set up into the SSRC, headed by Lord Rothschild, would provide grounds for its closure. In this, at least, they were disappointed.

There was, however, one more publication in hand that was derived from the original project. This was *Really Bad News*, which was co-authored by four members of the original Media Group and was published in 1982. This was, in part, intended as an accessible summary of the two research volumes but it also contained new material, particularly relating to the coverage of the Labour party's leadership and deputy leadership elections in 1980 and 1981. These matters and the way political issues were subsequently dealt with on television news are covered by Greg Philo in Volume 2. However, it is worth noting that this period was one in which Margaret Thatcher proclaimed the end of consensus politics and the advent of the politics of conviction. In post-war British politics there was a measure of agreement across the parties about the positive value of Keynesian economics and the welfare state, whose architect was William Beveridge. This had been labelled 'Butskellism' after Butler and Gaitskell of the Tory and Labour parties respectively. No doubt this

Tweedledum and Tweedledee view of British politics was overdrawn. It masked differences within the parties and of course did not address the question of Europe which cut across party loyalties, as the referendum campaign of 1975 had clearly shown. But from the beginning of the 1979 Conservative administration it was clear that Keynesian economics was to be rejected in favour of monetarism, with Milton Freidman and von Hayek as the preferred authorities, and that the welfare state assumptions were to be challenged on the grounds that they had created a dependency culture. An enterprise culture in which market forces were sovereign was espoused. Full employment as a goal was subordinated to the conquest of inflation. *Really Bad News* referred explicitly to this breakdown of consensus politics and its significance for broadcasting:

> Public broadcasting ... is committed to an ideological perspective which is founded on the view of consensus, 'one nation' and 'the community', while having to report phenomena which cannot be fitted easily into this framework of understanding. The broadcasters attempt to relay ideas which are already more or less present and interpret them for what they mistakenly see as a 'mass' audience. But to secure this consensus they have to make sense of new and difficult social and economic trends like unemployment, investment collapse and inflation. This involves giving meaning to events, facts and figures by providing explanations, stating causes, and by editorial comment.
>
> The change in government to the Conservatives in 1979 is a good illustration of the problem the media face in maintaining a coherent, consensual view. This was difficult enough with the economics of Healey and the Treasury, but at least the Social Contract had a semblance of being an 'agreement' with something in it for everyone. But the BBC is distinctly unhappy with the politics of the new right and the rise of Thatcherism. However hard they try they cannot work out how to say 'we are pulling together' in the face of 3 million unemployed. Their natural territory is the right wing of the Labour party or the Social Democrats.... The policies of the new right, by contrast, are awakening the slumbering giant and raising demands for political alternatives that the BBC had long ago pretended did not seriously exist.
>
> (Glasgow University Media Group 1982: 134–6)

THE *WAR AND PEACE NEWS* PROJECT

As things turned out, despite the difficult political climate for social science research and the funding problems to which it gave rise, *Really Bad News* was not our final work. Instead, we took the opportunity to explore another subject of public and political controversy – defence and disarmament – with the aid of research funding from the Joseph Rowntree Charitable Trust and

UNESCO. In the early 1980s there were identifiable strains in the NATO alliance and the peace movement in Europe was growing apace, including the marked revival of the Campaign for Nuclear Disarmament in the UK. In the UK Edward Thompson and Dan Smith edited a widely sold Penguin Special, *Protest and Survive* (1980), urging determined and organised resistance to the government's policies. The Church of England, the established church, produced a well-publicised report, *The Church and the Bomb* (1982), which questioned the adequacy of nuclear deterrence as a basis for collective security and the morality of NATO's declared willingness, in certain circumstances, to use nuclear weapons first.

The original purpose of our research was to look at the way in which the United Nations Second Special Session on Disarmament was covered on television news. This event took place in June/July 1982. This was an example of what we termed set-event coverage. We knew when and where it would take place and could, therefore, video all the news programmes for that period and extract from them the relevant coverage. Moreover, it was possible to obtain copies of all the speeches made to the Special Session which were, of course, available to journalists. This provided us with a particularly clear way of identifying the selection process which television journalists (and indeed print journalists) employed. We could see what speeches were referenced, which extracts used, and the way they were presented and contextualised.

What were some of the salient findings? First, that there was no coverage at all of the speeches from the NGOs (Non-Governmental Organisations). This absence meant that speeches from such notable figures as Helder Camara, Lord Noel Baker, Philip Potter, Sean McBride and Rear Admiral Gene La Rocque were judged not to be newsworthy. This was also the case in the British quality press. Second, and this was also true of the quality press, none of the speeches from the seventy-six representatives from Third World or non-aligned countries was reported. Third, we noted that only five speeches were reported on British television: Herr Schmidt (West Germany); Mr Gromyko (Soviet Union); Mr Begin (Israel); President Reagan (USA); and Mrs Thatcher (UK). Only the last three named contained any examples of direct speech, as opposed to reports about the speech, and all of these were highly selective. So, by checking in an empirical way what was routinely available to journalists for this event, we were able to show, in a very straightforward way, what was present and what was absent in the coverage. This in itself gives us a clue as to which news values were operative.

For present purposes, one illustration will suffice to show how, once the selection of what speeches to cover has been made, the story is put into a frame. When President Reagan spoke, these were the headlines that signalled the nature of the speech on the main news channels:

> President Reagan has accused the Soviet Union of pursuing policies of tyranny and repression backed up by the biggest arms build-up in history
>
> (BBC 1, 17:40, 17 June 1982)

> President Reagan has accused Russia of pursuing a programme of aggression, repression and atrocities backed up by the biggest arms build-up in history
>
> (ITN, 17:45, 17 June 1982)

> President Reagan has accused Russia of aggression, repression, tyranny and atrocities in its actions round the world ... President Reagan said the Soviet Union had embarked on violence supported by the biggest arms build-up in history.
>
> (ITN, 22:15, 17 June 1982)

As individual members of a television audience, we may have agreed or disagreed with the reported sentiments of the President, but the similarity of the message is clear across the channels. Not only so, but when we examined the direct quotes from the speech used in this story we noted that, while there were variations in cutting and length, they all included the following:

> Soviet aggression and support for violence around the world have eroded the confidence needed for arms negotiations. While we exercise unilateral restraints they've forged ahead and today possess nuclear and conventional forces far in excess of an adequate deterrent capability. Soviet oppression is not limited to the countries they invade. At the very time the Soviet Union is trying to manipulate the peace movement in the West it is stifling a budding peace movement at home.

This then was the journalistic consensus on how to tell the story. However, BBC2's late night news programme, *Newsnight*, did find a different headline, which clearly had other resonances and connotations: 'President Reagan ignored a Soviet challenge to renounce the first use of nuclear weapons'. This sharply reminds us of the importance of headlines as a signalling device. Both sets of headlines could be justified with reference to the content of the speech but they operated with different criteria of relevance and significance. If at the end of these news stories anybody watching had been asked what proposals the President had for arms control or disarmament, they could not have answered, simply because the information was not given. Yet the text of the speech did contain some proposals. A four-point agenda was put forward: the elimination of land-based intermediate missiles; a one-third reduction in strategic ballistic missile warheads; a substantial reduction in NATO and Warsaw Pact ground forces; and new safeguards to reduce the risk of accidental war. Whatever the merit of such proposals, they were made. But they were not reported. What this and other examples derived from the analysis of the UN Special Session can show in a concrete way is the way in which stories are selected, filtered and framed.

When we analysed the news bulletins through June and July 1982, the UN Special Session on Disarmament was only a small part of what could be called defence and disarmament news. During this period President Reagan toured Western Europe and attended a NATO conference along with other heads of state. There were many visual treatments of the ceremonies, banquets and parades surrounding this. These were stage-managed media events. Although they gave the viewers a ring side seat to a situation they would otherwise never get near to, they were not in themselves very informative. The way such events are contextualised by journalists comes into the reckoning at this point. Journalists, if they choose, can show a critical awareness which they can share with their viewers. The BBC's Charles Wheeler exemplified this on *Newsnight* (9 June 1982). The television cameras drew back and showed us the world's press, the entourage of advisers and secret service personnel, which accompanied President Reagan on his visit to West Germany. Wheeler commented that Reagan was 'undeniably the least widely admired American President ever to tread on German soil'. He pointed out that 'there are no crowds on this trip – to catch a glimpse of their American visitor Germans must turn to television with its narrow view of a few carefully controlled events and non-events like arrivals and departures of the glamorous and the great'. This is an instructive example of an experienced reporter offering us his judgement on an event and also taking his audience behind the scenes in a reflective manner. He is indeed pointing out the collusive way in which the powerful and their public relations advisers can work with the media. In doing so he demystifies this process of impression management and for that reason provides us with a different perspective on what is taking place. The reference to carefully controlled events and non-events prompts the question: who is controlling them? In such ways does the issue of news management surface. Any journalist who is prepared to make visible the processes by which the news of the day comes to be defined and organised, including the struggles this can entail with powerful interests and groups, does democracy a service. When this is not made clear, we as viewers may not always appreciate that journalists and politicians can collude in ritual performances, whereby the routines of public life are stage-managed in media events. Now news as ritual may be regarded, I suppose, as something of a spectator sport, which we can judge according to taste or entertainment value but not as an aid to the understanding of great public issues. But, as stated in *War and Peace News*:

> We are not employing a reductionist argument here and implying that all news is simply to be understood as ritual. Rather, we suggest that news is a selective combination of ritual, rhetoric, factual claims and statements, informed (sometimes misinformed) speculations and interpretative comment. We find it difficult, indeed unhelpful, to assign labels like 'objective', 'impartial' or 'neutral' to such a manufactured product. The beginning of

wisdom is to recognise news for what it is and not what it claims for itself.
(Glasgow University Media Group 1985: 237)

Nowhere have questions of news management been raised more sharply in recent years than during the Falklands/Malvinas conflict. One of the most critical treatments of source–media relations was that of the journalist Robert Harris, who came to the following conclusion:

> The episodes which caused most disquiet, and which have been described in this book, were not necessarily unique to the Falklands crisis. The instinctive secrecy of the military and the Civil Service; the prostitution and hysteria of sections of the press; the lies, the misinformation, the manipulation of public opinion by the authorities; the political intimidation of broadcasters; the ready connivance of the media at their own distortion ... all these occur as much in peace-time Britain as in war.
>
> (Harris 1983: 151)

Because of our work on the defence and disarmament project, we had been recording all news bulletins since 1 May 1982. This coincided with the arrival of the British Task Force in the South Atlantic. The bulletins themselves were full of Falklands news, sometimes nothing else and often longer than normal. As battle was joined in the South Atlantic a parallel conflict broke out – a media war. This has been well described in *Gotcha!* (Harris 1983) and *The Fog of War* (Mercer, Mungham and Williams 1987). In particular, the BBC came under attack from the government and sections of the popular press, notably the *Sun* and the *Daily Mail*. *The Times* which, like the *Sun*, is owned by Rupert Murdoch, was also critical of the BBC. Referring to Peter Snow, one of the *Newsnight* presenters, John Page wrote of his 'superior tone of super-neutrality which so many of us find objectionable and unacceptable' (*The Times*, 10 May 1982). Conservative MPs, including members of the cabinet, expressed their dissatisfaction, sometimes amounting to anger, with the BBC, but not with ITN. In *The Fog of War* a member of the war cabinet was cited:

> At a war cabinet meeting there was a general hate of the BBC whom we reckoned to be biased and pro-ITN whom we reckoned were doing much better. One minster said: 'well, you know we give all this information to the bloody BBC and what do they do with it? We don't help ITN enough and we ought to help ITN more.'
>
> (Mercer, Mungham and Williams 1987: 134)

Given the seriousness and high public visibility of the 'media war', as it came to be labelled, we had to decide whether to make a research intervention. Given our slender research resources this was not easy but we chose to do so. Apart from anything else, it was an opportunity to see what happened to the concept of impartiality in time of war. Clearly, from the government's point of view it was not appropriate. The question was 'Whose side are you on?' and there was no doubt either that the BBC should speak for Britain, which, more precisely, meant the British government. As a result of extending our research activity to cover this 'crisis news', the first part of *War and Peace News* was devoted to this topic. We undertook a content analysis of some of the major themes of the conflict: the bombing of the Port Stanley airfield, the sinking of the Argentinian cruiser *Belgrano* by the British, and later of HMS *Sheffield* by the Argentinians; as well as the treatment of the diplomatic initiatives to end the war. The issues surrounding news management, with particular reference to the lobby system, were also highlighted in the first chapter of the book, 'Making good news'.

Our conclusion was that, notwithstanding government criticism of the BBC, both it and the ITN produced news that was heavily dominated by government and official sources. When, for example, the bombing of Port Stanley took place, the official reports that it had been successful and had made the runway inoperable became the accepted story. So, on 1 May 1982 a BBC correspondent refers to 'the fact that we've knocked out the airfield' and the BBC evening bulletin told us, unequivocally: 'Destroying the Port Stanley runway has cut off the Argentine garrison's life support system.' Similarly, the ITN news bulletin stated: 'The Vulcan's task was to pockmark the runway and it did it with 1000lb bombs, ten tons of explosives.' This report by the defence correspondent was accompanied by visual graphics which showed a clear line of craters going along the length of the runway. This theme of the successful raid, emanating from official sources, was sustained even after its accuracy was questioned in the British press, sometimes with reference to 'American sources'. In fact, the Ministry of Defence account was inaccurate and gradually the truth came out. This was ironically illustrated on ITN news on May 14 when, over film of a Hercules transport plane taking off from the runway, we were told: 'The Ministry of Defence now concedes that light aircraft can still use the runway.' This was a grudging concession since the Hercules was the largest in the Argentine airforce. Since the Argentine military obviously knew what was the case, the only people being misled by all of this were the British public.

Our research findings for that period were consistent with some of the views being expressed in the BBC's own News and Current Affairs Committee. For example, the day after the BBC's current affairs programme on the Falklands, which was strongly criticised by Conservative MPs for including dissenting views on the conflict, the minutes of the Committee tell us: 'the weight of BBC coverage had been concerned with government statements and policy. In their vilification of the BBC, the government seemed to have entirely overlooked this. The meeting endorsed this point' (11 May 1982). Despite the affinity with the government's general position which BBC news coverage showed, it would be a mistake to conclude that this was the result of a unified government information machine that determined output. In many ways the government's own information policy was haphazard and there were certainly conflicts of interest and approach between different sections of the state: the Ministry of Defence, the Foreign Office, the war cabinet, the military. Even so, the implications of the lobby system as a form of news management and self-censorship cannot be ignored. Sometimes those who are outside its structures can best judge its significance. Thus Leonard Downie of the *Washington Post* wrote:

> This was the system used by the British Defence Ministry to control through the lobby of defence correspondents most information about the Falklands war. Only those correspondents were allowed into secret briefings throughout the war, while the rest of the large body of newsmen covering the conflict from London were told little in public statements and press conferences. Few British newsmen sought to find out more from officials or senior politicians outside these government-controlled forums. The leading political correspondent for a respected British Sunday newspaper said he would not even try to contact members of Thatcher's inner 'war cabinet' because he doubted they would talk to him and he wanted to avoid 'doing anything that might endanger our boys'. As a result, it was left to an American newsman to report from sources in the war cabinet that it had unanimously made the decision to sink the Argentine cruiser *General Belgrano*, one of the most important military and political events of the war.
>
> (*Washington Post*, 20 August 1982)

ITN, as already indicated, was favourably regarded by the government for its coverage of the Falklands conflict. Indeed, after the war, while ITN's editor expressed regret that they had not indicated when material had been censored, its strictures with regard to the Ministry of Defence were about the inadequacies of the information flow. In its evidence to the House of Commons Select Committee on Defence, ITN stated that 'great opportunities were missed for the positive projection of single-minded energy and determination by the British people in support of the Task Force'. It could have been so much better. 'Flair in high places could have led to a nightly offering of interesting, positive and heart-warming stories of achievement and collaboration born out of a sense of national purpose' (House of Commons Defence Committee 1982: 76–7). But what was the evidence for this sense of national purpose? It was certainly part of the political rhetoric. Margaret Thatcher said: 'The spirit of the Falklands was the spirit of Britain at its best. It surprised the world that British patriotism was rediscovered in those spring days. But it was never lost' (Aulich 1992: 2). However, the empirical basis for this is not at all clear. This touches, among other things, on the problematics of opinion polls, which is discussed extensively in *War and Peace News*; some of which is included in the selections that follow.

'The most arresting image on television in recent weeks has been the stylish map of the world which introduces *Newsnight*. It does not show the Falkland Malvinas Islands'. So wrote Raymond Williams in 1982 (reprinted in Williams 1990). His short essay, 'Distance', was an incisive commentary at the time. A decade later we can scarcely say that distance lends enchantment. Yet it was an event that revealed the state of our political culture. The nation that begat the British Empire was reduced to scrabbling to recapture islands that few in Britain had ever heard of. The Argentinian invasion took place after the announcement that HMS *Endurance*, the only British naval presence in the South Atlantic, was to be scrapped. The Trident missile programme was proving very costly and this had clear implications for the distribution of the navy's budget. Such are the costs of dining at the high table of the nuclear powers. Although rhetorical and mythic appeals may be made to 'a sense of national purpose', there is something threadbare about it in the context of the Falklands conflict. We know that, after the war, the soldiers came back to a divided Britain, with mass unemployment. Many of them joined the dole queue. Some at least, and the families of those who perished, now answer in an uncertain voice the question: Was it worth it? The Tin-Pot General and the Old Iron Woman of Raymond Briggs's cartoon story have both departed the central arena. The terrible simplicities of that episode, with its *Boy's own* delineation of the conflict, have been superseded by the corruptions of the Gulf War and the desolation of the former Yugoslavia. We return to these later considerations in Volume 2 (Philo 1995).

THE SELECTIONS

The selections that follow are drawn from a number of previously published volumes. Apart from some minor editorial changes, the essence of the original essays remains intact. The illustrations are necessarily from the original texts and further reproduction has diminished their clarity even more. 'Ill news comes often on the back of worse' is an essay which first appeared in *Religion and the Media* (Arthur (ed.) 1993). I have included it here since it gives an accessible overview of the continuing concern we have had with the concepts of impartiality and objectivity. As well as touching on the way this worked out from the beginning of British broadcasting with John Reith, later Lord Reith, the essay draws upon material from both the *Bad News* project and the *War and Peace News* study and also comments briefly on more recent matters including government pressure on the BBC in the 1980s. However, this last is taken up more centrally and extensively in Greg Philo's (1995) work in Volume 2. The subsequent chapters, as already indicated, are all drawn from the *Bad News* volumes or from *War and Peace News*. We begin with 'Reviewing the news', which was the first chapter of *Bad News*. The opening sentence states its dissenting position: 'Contrary to the claims, conventions and culture of television journalism, the news is not a neutral product.' It continues: 'This study is an attempt to unpack the coding of television news.'

The chapter then goes on to explain what this involves and the sense in which it moves beyond an approach to news analysis based on the gatekeeper function.

'Measuring the news', the next chapter, was originally part of chapter 4 of *Bad News*. This summarizes the material on bulletin structures for the first three months of 1975. We argued that the results indicated that, given a range of stories from which to choose, they were contained within a clearly defined structure. To this we have also included the concluding section of chapter 5 of *More Bad News*, 'Who gets on?' where we conclude that 'the day-to-day production of news is based on the inherited wisdom of journalistic routines, assumptions about the audience and about the society that is being reported. This is what enables the journalist in the newsroom to "recognise" the newsworthy truth with apparent certainty.' And that is the context in which claims to objectivity and impartiality are made. When we turn to industrial coverage in the next chapter, 'Contours of coverage', this is a very detailed account. This was chapter 5 of *Bad News* and was the first time British television news had been subjected to such detailed scrutiny. We show which industries are covered, as well as the extent to which industrial disputes, industrial accidents, pay claims and wage settlements are reported. Considerable use is made here of statistics from the Department of Employment. We recognised and stated that official statistics pose their own problems of interpretation, but they did constitute an independently arrived at and publicly available set of data. We argued that the conceptual model and technical apparatus used in the production of these statistics, though not beyond criticism, did not pose any major theoretical problem. I have discussed the nature and construction of these statistics elsewhere (Eldridge 1968; Eldridge, Cressey and MacInnes 1991). Although our main interest was in television news, we did undertake a two-month comparison in January and February 1975, between television news and five national newspapers, together with the general wire service abstract of the Press Association. This is included here.

The next two chapters deal with news talk and news visuals respectively. Chapter 6, 'News talk', comprises chapters 7 and 8 of *More Bad News*. This is an attempt to show how information is organised. We were interested not only in the composition of the text as a series of more or less meaningfully related sentences but also in the devices of headlines, of boundary markers between one story and another, and the establishment of themes. We did not assume that the codes and rules we were seeking to identify were necessarily intentional, either for news talk or for news visuals. But we did suggest that unspoken, unacknowledged or unrecognised assumptions, practices or perspectives help to constitute what Goffman had called the 'primary framework', whereby news talk becomes meaningful. This does not imply that television viewers interpret the news in the same way. There may be differences in terms of basic comprehension of terms such as inflation or social contract. There may also be differences of judgement between viewers.

People may argue about what they have seen and heard on television news but disagree strongly with one another as to the appropriateness, the validity, the adequacy or the politics of what is being shown and said. This basic point should still borne in mind when we move on to the discussion of the visual components of news. This is drawn from chapters 10 and 11 of *More Bad News*, 'Halting the flow' and 'Good evening'. In *More Bad News* there were five chapters in all dealing with the analysis of the visual components of television news under the general title 'See it this way'. I suspect this has been somewhat neglected in commentaries on our work. This kind of analysis is difficult and arduous to undertake. As we made clear at the time, we had no wish to overstate the findings since the sample period was a short one. But it did cover total bulletins and not just the industrial news. A number of questions are addressed. What are the rules for opening and ending programmes? How are news presenters themselves presented? How are correspondents and reporters shown to the viewer? What visual rules govern interviewing? To what extent do the normative rules of film editing apply? There was at the time, and continues to be, considerable discussion as to whether television news was dominated by the 'visual imperative'. This, indeed, had been part of the Birt/Jay thesis on the bias against understanding. Our conclusion, one which surprised us at the time, was that it was not the case. What we documented was the extent to which the traditional role of correspondents had been taken over by television news and argued that this was a major factor in avoiding the visual imperative. It does provide a benchmark against which subsequent changes could be identified.

I have already indicated the role that case study analysis played in our work. Chapter 8 presents four of these. All of them have more to say about language and visual codes as they explore the way the news narrative is organised and presented. The first concerns the Glasgow dustcart drivers' dispute with the then Glasgow Corporation, in 1975. This was first discussed in *Bad News* but was developed and rewritten for *Really Bad News* and this is the version reproduced here. The second case deals not with a strike but with the coverage of pay negotiations between the National Coal Board and the miners (represented by the National Union of Mineworkers). How was this contextualised? How was the story told? The case was interesting at the time for various reasons. It reflected a particular kind of awareness of the history of industrial conflict in the mining industry. It was seen as a crucial case in relation to the Labour government's Social Contract policy and in a context of news coverage where all pay deals were routinely monitored. Considered twenty years later in the knowledge of what has happened to the British coal industry, its conflicts, closures and privatisation, we can as readers in the 1990s bring other connotations to the narrative which were then not available and, in some respects, scarcely imaginable. Further work which we did on the coal strike of 1984–5 is to be found in Greg Philo's *Seeing and Believing* (1990) and is discussed in Volume 2 (Philo 1995).

The other two cases are taken from *War and Peace News*, chapters 6 and 9. The first concerns the coverage of the women's peace movement, with special reference to Greenham Common and the peace camp that was established there at the gates of the American base where nuclear Cruise missiles were sited. Among the issues discussed are the treatment of public opinion polls and the coverage of violence. Both of these matters are topics which have come up at various times in our work, but particularly in *War and Peace News* in relation both to the Falklands conflict and the coverage of the peace movement. In relation to the Falklands, we showed that public opinion was not taken to be controversial or newsworthy. Consequently, public opinion polls were scarcely reported. We never heard, for example, that, during the conflict an ORC poll asked the following question: Do you support or oppose the idea that the United Nations should administer the Falkland Islands for an interim period during which Britain and Argentina negotiate about the future of the Islands? The response was: Support 76%; Oppose 19%; Don't know 8%. At the same time, when opinion polls *were* reported that were said to be supportive of the government's position, the full question was not shown, the answers were conflated and, for that reason, were misleading. In the case of the peace movement and Greenham Common, we noted the failure to cite public opinion polls that supported their opposition to Cruise missiles.

There is in *War and Peace News* a short Appendix on Theoretical Issues raised by Opinion Polling (pp. 305–8). The final paragraph reads:

> The opinion poll is a social invention which has its roots in market research and election studies. It has typically operated in the context of doing work for client organisations such as political parties, businesses, the press and broadcasting. When the polls are made public the reporting-back process through the media can be subject to various filters. From the original findings (with all their methodological problems that are usually left unremarked) more selection, simplification, compression and re-emphasis can take place. In this way we learn what 'the public', in which we are included, are supposed to think about this or that. It thereby plays a part in the social process, which it purports to describe and define; it becomes part of the social milieu within which issues are discussed and evaluated
>
> (Glasgow University Media Group 1985: 308)

The question of the representation of violence is and remains a controversial matter. In the case of Greenham Common there was the particular paradox given the women's commitment to an ideology of non-violence as part of their rationale for opposing the presence of nuclear weapons in a situation where first-strike use had not been ruled out by NATO. The demonstrations outside the base raised questions of violence against the women, in which police and sometimes soldiers were involved. Violence against the women and accusations against the police did not surface much in television news, although when a policeman was injured that did feature. Comparisons with the coverage in publications such as *Spare Rib* and *Outwrite* are noted in this case study. Again, I would draw attention to the way violence was covered in the coal strike of 1984–5, where similar kinds of selectivity could be identified. This is taken up in Volume 2 (Philo 1995).

The fourth case study covers the formal debate in the Church of England Synod, following the publication of its working party report *The Church and the Bomb* (1982). Since this was a set event we were able to anticipate and examine the press and television coverage that led up to it. The debate was televised live on BBC television, which is an indication of the importance attached to it. There was, after all, the possibility that the established church with its close connections with the state would find itself out of step with the government of the day. As far as the news was concerned, questions of framing and filtering necessarily arise, of the kind already discussed in relation to the UN Special Session on disarmament. The way this is done and its significance is discussed in the case study.

The penultimate chapter of these selected essays concerns the coverage of current affairs in relation to questions of peace and disarmament in 1983, from May onwards. The extensive study of current affairs programmes is still relatively neglected. Here the use of different formats is described and the content and organisation of information and opinion outlined. The issues around peace and disarmament were certainly controversial as this account makes clear, and questions of censorship, balance and choice of topic come into focus. We came to the conclusion that TV current affairs, documentaries and opinion programmes are the sites of considerable cultural and political struggle. We are used to describing societies such as our own as pluralist. In the context of the media, current affairs programmes can play an important critical role in looking at the issues of the day. The extent to which this is done, especially the coverage of dissent, is one indicator of the limits of pluralism. This is contested space and, in the context of recent developments, is at risk of becoming a shrinking space.

And finally ... The last chapter reproduced here is in fact taken from the last chapter of *More Bad News*. Here an attempt is made to summarise the nature and significance of the work we had undertaken, as well as somewhat robust reflection on the critics. This introduction will simply underline the concluding words which, while originally referencing the *Bad News* project, has continued to be our research objective: 'What has been offered up here is not a contribution to an unnecessarily small-minded debate, but a detailed and documented critique of the ideology and practice of current television journalism – a first step in the decoding of the all-pervasive messages of the electronic media' (Glasgow University Media Group 1980: 418).

There is a Coda. This is a piece by Raymond Williams, which was written as a review of *More Bad News* and also of Todd Gitlin's *The Whole World is Watching* (1980). Williams did much to encourage the development of media studies, not least with his own writing on communications and television. His concept of 'flow' in relation to the medium of television was and remains important. His preoccupation with the conditions under which a democratic communications could be accomplished was central to his writing. This, he was convinced, would be a continuing matter of political and cultural struggle to ensure that the space for diversity of opinion is ensured and extended. But he refused to succumb to versions of technological determinism or cultural pessimism which asserted that things could not be other than they are, or could move only in anti-democratic ways. This essay is reprinted here as a small tribute to his work and influence, not least on our own thinking.

REFERENCES

Annan, Lord (1977) *Report of the Committee on the Future of Broadcasting*, London HMSO, Cmd. 6753.

Arthur, Chris (ed.) (1993) *Religion and the Media*, Cardiff: University of Wales Press, pp. 146–61.

Aulich, J. (ed.) (1992) *Framing the Falklands War: Nationhood, Culture and Identity*, Milton Keynes: Open University Press.

Baker, John Austin (ed.) (1982) *The Church and the Bomb. Nuclear Weapons and Christian Conscience*, London: Hodder and Stoughton.

Barnett, Steven and Curry, Andrew (1994) *The Battle for the BBC*, London: Aurum Press.

Eldridge, J.E.T. (1968) *Industrial Disputes*, London: Routledge and Kegan Paul.

Eldridge, John, Cressey, Peter and MacInnes, John (1991) *Industrial Sociology and Economic Crisis*, Brighton, Harvester.

Gitlin, T. (1980) *The Whole World is Watching*, Berkeley: University of California Press.

Glasgow University Media Group (1976) *Bad News*, London: Routledge and Kegan Paul.

——— (1980) *More Bad News* London: Routledge and Kegan Paul.

——— (1982) *Really Bad News*, London: Writers and Readers.

——— (1985) *War and Peace News*, Milton Keynes: Open University Press.

——— (1993) *Getting the Message*, Eldridge, John (ed.) London: Routledge.

Harris, Robert (1983) *Gotcha! The Media, the Government and the Falklands Crisis*, London: Faber.

Hoggart, Richard (1993) *An Imagined Life*, Oxford: Oxford University Press.

House of Commons Defence Committee (1982), *The Handling of Press and Public Information during the Falklands Conflict*, London: HMSO, vol. II, p. xxxvii.

Mercer, Derrik, Mungham, Geoff and Williams, Kevin (1987) *The Fog of War*, London: Heinemann.

Philo, Greg (1990) *Seeing and Believing*, London: Routledge.

——— (ed.) (1995) *Industry Economy, War and Politics*, Glasgow Media Group Reader, vol. II, London and New York: Routledge.

Thompson, E.P. (1980) *Writing by Candlelight*, London: Merlin Press.

Thompson, E.P. and Smith, Dan (eds) (1980) *Protest and Survive*, Harmondsworth: Penguin.

Williams, Raymond (1990) *What I Came to Say*, London: Hutchinson.

Chapter 2

'Ill news comes often on the back of worse'*

John Eldridge

Living by proxy in the half light,
Items of news slip by like flakes of food in a fish tank.
Between the un-seating of a royal jockey
And the bland insincerities of talking heads
We see, for an instant, the awkward dead
Heaped carelessly at the corner of a street
Like brushwood piled for burning.
This wood is green, unsuitable for firing.
Sap still comes from the stricken limbs of striplings,
Broken boys and girls
With faces made anonymous by death.
Only a tear in the knee of a pair of jeans,
A shoeless foot unnaturally bent,
A rucked up sweat shirt revealing pitiful flesh,
Reminds us that they once possessed a singularity
Beyond the comprehension of the killers
Who stare at the camera lens with eyes
As blank as bottle tops.

('An Item of News', Ewan MacColl)

When we in the Glasgow University Media Group (GUMG) called our first three books on television news *Bad News* (1975), *More Bad News* (1980) and *Really Bad News* (1982), we were, of course, being a touch mischievous. The binary contrast good news/bad news is deeply embedded in our history and culture. We are all familiar with the injunction not to blame the messenger for the bad news. But in an age of mass media the messengers are typically contracted to powerful institutions in press and broadcasting. The stories they tell and the how, when, where and why of the telling are an important part of

*First published in C. Arthur (ed.) *Religion and the Media*, Cardiff, University of Wales Press, 1993, pp. 146–61.

our media culture. In scrutinising those stories, which are communicated to us day by day, we begin to learn about news values. The processes of creating, transmitting and receiving messages are not just a secondary feature in modern society, they are part of the warp and woof of it. What takes place in and through these processes is, therefore, not simply a comment on social reality but part of it.

The case of television news – a specific form of mass communication – was and remains an important site of study. The reason for this is that one particular value is formally required from news broadcasts: impartiality. Clearly, this is different from the press, where editorialising is built into the activity. Impartiality, by contrast, is typically seen as the cornerstone of good public service broadcasting, so far as news is concerned. The rationale for this is to resist the capture of this news medium by a particular interest group, so that it will not be regarded as partisan or propagandist. This, indeed, is seen both as the guarantee of its reliability and trustworthiness and also the source of its authority and objectivity.

However, I want to argue that the concept of impartiality is inherently problematic. Indeed, however worthy their motives, those who seek to base their claim to credibility by appeal to the concept of impartiality will constantly find themselves immersed in challenges and attacks. Seasoned broadcasters know standard ripostes to some of this: we know our own business and should be left to get on with it; or, since we are attacked from all sides, we have got it just about right. Moreover, to replace impartial, objective news with partial and subjective news would surely be to lose one's credibility at a stroke. I want to suggest that there is another way of coming at this which dissolves a spurious dichotomy.

What does adherence to the concept of impartiality mean in practice? Let us recall the way this impinged on John Reith (later Lord Reith) in the early pre-television days of the BBC. In his capacity as first Director-General of the BBC, he promoted the view that broadcasting could help to develop an informed and enlightened opinion on the issues of the day. His position, while clearly paternalist, was one which explicitly resisted the idea that the BBC was there simply to relay the instructions and views of the government of the day. That was precisely why he favoured the setting up of a public corporation rather than have it working under the aegis of a government department. He wanted the BBC to be free from state interference and political interference. But he also wanted it not to be subject to the normal commercial pressures. Within such a space and within these institutional arrangements, public service broadcasting could, he believed, flourish. So it was, he thought, that a public corporation could serve the public interest with the state's role being confined to the operation of the licensing system. In this regard the public interest was seen as the guiding consideration in contradistinction to private interests.

But from the beginning the worm was in the apple. The BBC was not immune from political pressure as *The Reith Diaries* make clear. In time of controversy and political conflict this is particularly so. At the time of the 1926 General Strike, Reith records that the government was going to set up its own newspaper, the *British Gazette*, edited from the War Office. According to Reith, the editor expected to see the BBC news as an offshoot of that, which Reith characteristically refused to accept. An argument developed within the cabinet with Winston Churchill insisting that the instrument of radio should be used to the best possible advantage by the government. This view did not prevail in straightforward propagandist terms. Reith's diary entry for 11 May shows a more subtle policy:

> The Cabinet were to make a decision at long last about the BBC. Davidson was going to it. I primed him up with all the arguments and he came to see me at 7.15. As he was smiling broadly I knew it was all right. The decision was not a definite one, but at any rate we are not going to be commandeered. The Cabinet decision is really a negative one. They want to be able to say that they did not commandeer us, but they know that they can trust us not to be really impartial. Davidson came around again at 9.15 and we were supposed to draft a notice defining the BBC position. I wanted the inconsistencies in our acts so far squared up, setting us right with the other side. Davidson, however, thought the Cabinet would only agree to a statement that we could do nothing to help the Strike since it had been declared illegal. This does not seem to me to be straight.[1]

As Reith pointed out, the BBC was in a very awkward position. He was clear that to turn the BBC into a propaganda arm of the government would have destroyed its credibility, and even more so if it had been commandeered. In seeking to resist that, he tried in vain to square the circle. His declared sense of loyalty to the Prime Minister cut across his uneasiness that impartiality was a cloak for supporting the government's position – at the very least by keeping other views off the air. What Reith had to come to terms with, albeit with a bad conscience, were the interests of the state in a moment of crisis. The decision on the part of the government as to how to play it was a matter of strategy and tactics.

What does happen when events that take place in the world are conflict-riven and controversial as so many are? We are given in the press and in broadcasting news stories about them. Let us remember that the journalists telling these stories on television share an occupational background with press journalists: they may even move from one medium to another. They attend the same press conferences and relate to one another's output. What emerges to count as the news of the day is itself a cultural construct. In the case of television news, a whole range of professional conventions in the presentation operate. These are not unchangeable, as archive film of old news programmes show, but there are established continuities. Let us recall some: the use of music and established iconic forms at the beginning and end of bulletins; the newscaster(s) as providing continuity (sometimes bringing to the programme their own celebrity status); the use of film to delineate the event or graphics to reference it; the use of correspondents to report, describe, interview and interpret what is going on; the use of experts to comment (which nowadays may incorporate the reporter: 'our economics/political editor, Peter Jay/John Cole'); the boundary markers – headlines and devices for turning from one item to the next; and the overall 'ordered' structure of the news bulletin.

These activities, complex though they are in terms of organisation and technology and often taking place with considerable time constraints, are grounded in professional routines and practices. Indeed, without such constitutive rules by which news of the world can be made meaningful to us – organised, encoded, framed – the daily production of news would be impossible. This output, its nature and significance, not least in relation to the values of impartiality and objectivity, is what we have attempted to examine in the *Bad News* and later studies. An important part of the research strategy was to consider, through quantitative and qualitative analysis, what these routines and practices produced to make up the product we know was television news and, more particularly, to look at the treatment of issues which were socially or politically divisive such as the state of the economy, industrial conflict, or questions of defence and disarmament.

In 1975, with a Labour government in power, we showed how television newsrooms adopted a number of strategies for concretising and dealing with economic affairs. Central to this was a constant and ongoing assessment of the government's agreements with the trade-union movement known, in the parlance of the time, as the Social Contract. This was an attempt by the government to set out guidelines for collective bargaining in the period following the previous Conservative administration's attempts to impose an incomes policy. Not only did this concept provide the thematic frame within which stories about the economy were covered, but the containment of wages was presented as the main instrument for the control of inflation. Thus many of the industry wage agreements signed during the first half of 1975 were reported on the news in terms of whether they were within or outside the terms of the Social Contract. In 1992 we do not routinely hear about wage settlements but in 1975 all the major settlements were reported within this frame. The identification of these matters as newsworthy is an interesting indicator of a particular social and political climate but it also tended to be from a definite perspective. Whether one agreed with that perspective or not, it was not value-free.

Take, for example, the case of a wage negotiation between the miners and the National Coal Board. As the reports of the negotiations developed, we had the BBC's industrial news reporter telling us that the deal was outside the Social Contract, even though the parties concerned said it was within the terms. And, at the end, the BBC newscaster summed up the position: 'The miners through their negotiators put the Coal Board out of its misery this week by accepting a large pay offer. After some haggling the offer crept pound by pound to the miners' own demands.' (BBC2, 18:50, 15 March 1975). Employers offered, workers demanded. The employers were put out of their *misery*. The pay offer was a *large* one. The story was told in a particular way. The pay negotiations were presented in the langauge of battle and as an 'acid test' for the Social Contract. Through the narrative we learn more about the journalists' assumptions regarding an agreement which saw the advent of a £3,000-a-year basic rate for some miners and £41 a week for surface workers. Analysis of the narrative showed that while some of the participants in the negotiations were able to comment, explain and justify, this was typically within highly structured conventions of interviewing. There were, moreover, more general assumptions about the role of trade unions and the nature of the economic crisis. Thus within the overall frame of the Social Contract was a series of strike stories. The connecting links were about workers and trade unions who were causing inflation, whose disruptive activities were the cause of our economic ills and therefore against the national interest.

The point to be made about this is that news is from a distinct perspective. In so far as this was the dominant tendency in the coverage of industrial and economic questions, not only did it represent a particular ideological view, but also effectively excluded other kinds of explanations – those which had to do with concerns about investment, the role of management, education, training and the structural problems of the economy in a world context, after the oil crisis of the early 1970s. Whatever our opinions of these stories, they are restricted accounts, given that other accounts were publicly available. In other words, our analysis concluded that news accounts were limited and narrow. Such restricted news was, we said, bad news. Not only did it present stories within a dominant interpretive framework, but it did so from a position that laid claim to impartiality.

In his review of *More Bad News*, Raymond Williams commented:

> Let us face it then: the news has been very bad lately. But it is very difficult to be sure how much of this badness has been in the events themselves, and how much in their intense and relentless interpretation by the authorities: a one-sided polemic which I cannot remember being at this pitch since the late Forties. . . . To be sure, we cannot draw any firm line between events and their presentation. A very large number of the events now presented are in fact interpretations, by a small group of highly privileged voices, directly transmitted or read out by hired celebrities. The privilege of such voices would matter less if it were not also, in the leading cases, the privilege of command of men and resources.[2]

He goes on to point out that as events become the subject of news reports, even when the evidence for their occurrence has been reliably tested, long-standing problems of narration remain, including the identity of the narrator,

5/29

his/her authority, point of view, assumed relationship to audience, and the possible wider purposes in selecting and narrating the events in the way chosen. In everyday encounters when we hear stories we learn to ask such questions.

> Yet it seems that we have only to ask them about a broadcasting service or a newspaper to produce outraged cries about an assault on professional competence and independence, or to provoke dark hints, which at least sometimes are surely projections, about a conspiracy to interfere with freedom of news and indeed to manipulate or censor it.[3]

There are, I think, a number of ways in which the media critic can respond to the media professionals who manifest such concerns. What can we reasonably expect from a television news service in a society that embraces democratic ideas? We expect the information to be reliable and accurate. This, after all, is the *sine qua non* of professional journalism and the touchstone of its integrity. At the simplest level, when the football results are given we expect them to be accurate and have good reason to think that they are. They can be corroborated by many witnesses, whatever their view of the outcome. Any mistake in conveying the results can be quickly corrected. It is helpful to take a simple example since it reminds us that issues of truth are involved. So while, for reasons already touched upon, objectivity in news narratives is problematic, the alternative is not an undisciplined subjectivity where anything goes and one account is as good or as bad as another. Why these facts should be reported raises quite other questions of their presumed significance to the audience. And once these facts become embedded in accounts of matches, then we are into a narrative which characteristically will have its judgements, interpretations and sometimes speculation.

If, as the adage has it, journalism is the first draft of history, we can appreciate that, as with historical study itself, selection and interpretation of facts will take place and we are dealing not with unassailable facts marshalled incontrovertibly together but with provisional accounts. Indeed, the epistemological basis on which these accounts rest can vary. We, as readers, hearers or viewers, will not necessarily be aware of this.

In their paper, 'Accidental news: the great oil spill'[4] Molotch and Lester describe how President Nixon visited the beach at Santa Barbara in January 1969 and stated that it had recovered from a massive oil spill. This was duly reported in the national media of the USA despite the fact that there was plenty of evidence, which the journalists could see and smell, that it was not so. In their view this was an example of professional news services being subordinate to political interests. If they are correct then this has the character of cover-up. Unless we are there and have direct experience of that situation – we can see and smell the oil slick – or unless someone, as it were, breaks cover or leaks an alternative version, we have no independent way of evaluating that story.

The above example, if typical, would fit in with a conspiracy view of the media – that they operate as servants of the powerful. As a general theory of the role of the media, I think this is unconvincing. But it does draw our attention to the issue of verification. For example, in the Falklands War, ITN lunchtime news showed some film taken by an Argentinian amateur cameraman. The defence correspondent worked on the assumption that all the film was taken on 1 May, when, according to the Ministry of Defence, no British planes were lost. This is what he said:

> But the attack had been concentrated on the airfield [i.e. Port Stanley] where it is assumed these pictures of wreckage were taken. This roundel is not in the colours carried by the British Harriers and may have come from an Argentine plane destroyed on the ground. The variety and totality of wreckage scattered around the airfield suggest British reports of inflicting severe damage to aircraft and military equipment were true. One piece of wreckage which had the word 'Harrier' on it was unidentifiable. Britain says she lost no aircraft during this raid though one Harrier was shot down three days later near the other airport at Goose Green. These would seem to be aircraft wheels, although it's not yet clear what type of plane they came from.[5]

The film actually showed the colours of the roundel which were unmistakably British, the unique undercarriage design of the Harrier, its name – Harrier – and its serial number. Because the correspondent believed it was Port Stanley and not Goose Green, he is unable to accept this evidence and actually uses British wreckage to stress the success of British bombing! Now this was not a cover-up. It was a mistake. Indeed, although there was no apology for it, the evening news used the same film with the following commentary: 'The cameraman was also taken to the Goose Green airstrip where a British Harrier jet was shot down last Tuesday. The Royal Navy roundel showed through the film of paint.'[6]

What was happening? It was difficult to get news let alone film out of the Falklands and there was in practice heavy reliance on Ministry of Defence briefings. They had been stressing the success of the bombing raids on Port Stanley airport. Part of the film ITN received was of Port Stanley and part of Goose Green. Given the success theme, the correspondent cannot believe the evidence before him and actually turns a failure into a success. Ironically, the success theme about the bombing of Port Stanley was to bring other news reporting problems to the surface. The Ministry of Defence stated that the bombing on 1 May had severely cratered the runway at the airport. BBC and ITN news embraced this account. ITN reported: 'The Vulcan's task was to pockmark the runway and it did it with 1000lb bombs, ten tons of explosives.'[7] This was accompanied by a graphic of the runway with the pockmarks circled along the length of it. Yet eventually this was shown to be inaccurate. Gradually another story emerges that the airport was still operational. It is not a simple matter of cover-up news. In *War and Peace News* we came to the following conclusion:

> Once having established a view of the Port Stanley raids – a destroyed runway and cut-off garrison – the news found it difficult to go beyond it. New facts and information were fitted into this framework. The constraint seemed to emanate from the need for broadcasters to maintain their image as purveyors of reliable, balanced and objective information. Journalists found it difficult to admit they had made mistakes. Following the ceasefire, TV news expressed surprise concerning the condition of the airfield. The subject was not considered in any detail. In *Task Force South*, a BBC production in August, viewers were finally told what British troops had heard before the final push on Port Stanley. In it we see shots of a briefing for troops. A soldier comments: 'The RAF missed the fucking runway ... bombs all around it but there are thirteen aircraft, some of which are definitely Pucara, parked on the aprons around Stanley airfield. There's also another report that they have managed to reinforce themselves from the mainland' (BBC1, 12 August 1982). This piece of film was absent from the pictures of the advances on Stanley which were first shown on British TV on 25 June.[8]

Our general conclusion about television news coverage of the Falklands War was that both BBC and ITN kept close to official sources. Where, we may ask, does impartiality figure in this? In some respects we get a re-run of the Reith difficulty, discussed earlier. So, the Director-General of the BBC told an internal meeting of the News and Current Affairs Committee that he anticipated the BBC would come under pressure, as it had during the Suez Crisis to 'conform to the national interest'. He accepted that there was a legitimate point in this but the difficulty was to define precisely what 'the national interest' was. Clearly, he argued, the BBC should be careful not to do anything to imperil military operations or diplomatic negotiations, but it should report accurately and faithfully the arguments arising within British society at all levels. This in practice didn't happen. The Director-General's remarks were made at the beginning of April; by 11 May the BBC's Political Editor was telling the committee that 'the BBC was most vulnerable to criticism over its limited coverage of the internal debate in the country, though many Tories would regard any coverage of this as pure speculation because the dissenting views were being kept so private'. Meanwhile another senior broadcaster 'reminded the meeting that the BBC was the *British* Broadcasting Corporation [italics in original]. It was now clear that a larger section of the public shared this view and he believed it was an unnecessary irritation to stick to the detached style.'

Nevertheless, as has been well documented, the Tory government was very critical of the BBC's coverage of the war.[9] BBC's *Newsnight* programme was criticised for giving the appearance of being too detached and an episode of the BBC's flagship current affairs programme, *Panorama* was the subject of heavy criticism from sections of the Conservative Party. This particular programme, broadcast on 10 May 1982, included some dissenting views on government policy, alongside those of Cecil Parkinson, a member of the war cabinet. Conservative MPs complained that some of the programmes on the BBC appeared to give the impression of being pro-Argentinian and anti-British, while others appeared to suggest that this was an issue over which the BBC could remain loftily neutral. A senior Conservative, Sally Oppenheimer, referred next day at Prime Minster's Question Time in the House of Commons, to the *Panorama* programme as 'an odious, subversive travesty in which Michael Cockrell and other BBC reporters dishonoured the right to freedom of speech in this country'. In her reply, the Prime Minister indicated that she shared the concern that had been expressed. She continued:

> I know how strongly many people feel that the case for our country is not being put with sufficient vigour on certain – I do not say all – BBC programmes. The Chairman of the BBC has assured us, and has said in vigorous terms, that the BBC is not neutral on this point, and I hope his words will be heeded by the many who have responsibilities for standing up for our task force, our boys, our people and the cause of democracy.

The difference between this situation and the Reith episode over the General Strike was that it was much more exposed to public view. The *Panorama* programme was called 'Traitorama' by the *Sun* newspaper (echoing some of the comments in the House of Commons). After a stormy meeting between the Chairman and Director-General of the BBC and the backbench media committee of the BBC, Alasdair Milne (then Director-General) told the *London Evening Standard* in an interview on 12 May 1982:

> The notion that we are traitors is outrageous. There is no one in the BBC who does not agree that the Argentineans committed aggression. But this is not total war. One day we will be negotiating with the enemy so we must try to understand them. We at the BBC have re-examined our broad policy and will not change it. We have no sense of guilt or failure.

What was also significant about this episode was the strength of feeling that was generated and how specifically government hostility was directed at the BBC. In *The Fog of War*, Mercer, Mungham and Williams cite a member of the war cabinet who told them:

> At a war cabinet meeting there was a general hate of the BBC whom we reckoned to be biased, and pro-ITN whom we reckoned were doing much better. One minister said: 'Well, you know we give all this information to the bloody BBC and what do they do with it? We don't help ITN enough and we ought to help ITN more.'[10]

What emerges from all this is not a conspiracy theory of the media but rather the consequences of a professional set of practices which, while valuing the principle of independence, relies heavily upon official sources for its news. In some respects the very mark of its professionalism is that it has access to these sources. The controversy over the *Panorama* programme was a sharp reminder of the tight limits on dissent that were regarded as permissible in time of crisis, which the Falklands conflict undoubtedly was. It was, after all, the government that had left the Falklands undefended in the first place and it was in jeopardy of falling as a result.

The government's hostility to the BBC was to have further ramifications. When the United States bombed Libya in April 1986, Norman Tebbit, then Chairman of the Conservative Party, produced a report of the coverage comparing the BBC unfavourably with ITN.[11] He accused the BBC of carrying Libyan propaganda uncritically. In his letter to the BBC accompanying the report, he questioned 'whether an increasingly confrontational style of BBC news coverage is appropriate for a public-service broadcasting system, funded by the taxpayer, required to emphasise impartiality, objectivity and factual reporting'. The BBC offered its own detailed reply. Nevertheless, Alasdair Milne had been forced to resign as Director-General by the end of 1987 by a board of governors that had become increasingly politicised. Before his successor was appointed, the offices of BBC Glasgow were subjected to a police raid. The government was unhappy with two programmes prepared by the journalist Duncan Campbell in a six-part series entitled *Secret Society*. One of these was on the procedures surrounding the financing of the Zircon satellite, which Campbell argued had been irregular; the other was on the operation of secret cabinet committees, which, among other things, produced evidence of the government's campaign against the peace movement in 1982–3. No charges or arrests were made but the pressure on programme producers and journalists was clear enough. The Zircon programme was eventually screened and the cabinet programme re-made for Channel 4. This is a sharp reminder that those in positions of power will certainly make attempts to control the media, but the concern for independence is a journalistic value that is genuinely striven for and embraced by many journalists, even while they are aware that they can sometimes be restricted, censored and constrained by the powerful.

But impartiality as a journalistic value becomes almost a will-o'-the-wisp phenomenon: now you see it, now you don't. In time of war or national crisis the governmental concern with broadcast (and other) news is not 'Are you impartial?' but 'Which side are you on?' If, in other instances, the broadcasters say we cannot be impartial about apartheid, they will find themselves criticised from the Right. Norman Tebbit, for example, in the report on the Libyan coverage, took a side-swipe at the BBC, because its Assistant Director-General had said that they could not be impartial over apartheid. The report stated that this was in breach of the BBC's constitutional duty.[12] This from the same Norman Tebbit who, in an Open University programme on the media, was to state that impartiality was very difficult and that the problem was of balance rather than impartiality. This, he pointed out, was a matter of judgement in practice.[13]

In the end, if we take account of the conditions under which news is gathered, it is difficult to apply concepts of objectivity or impartiality to it. The question of accuracy is and will remain a bedrock of credibility and trustworthiness. However, where there are grounds for doubt or uncertainty on factual accuracy, this needs to be indicated. In the Gulf War, Martin Fletcher of NBC spoke from Israel on the second night. Wearing a gas-mask he reported that Israel had been hit with a chemical weapon. This was relayed on BBC news where the source for the story was claimed to be NBC's monitoring of police radios in Tel Aviv. However, the BBC's veteran reporter in Washington, Charles Wheeler, urged caution: 'Everybody here's getting in a dreadful panic.' As the programme went on, more uncertainty about the missile attack seeped through. Towards the end of the bulletin we hear this exchange:

Martyn Lewis: So that report from NBC could well be wrong?
Charles Wheeler: A lot of reports could well be wrong.

It is precisely that kind of scepticism that is important and in my view is a more effective way to judge the quality of news reports than an appeal to impartiality. After that we can ask questions about the framework within which the facts are presented. To understand that these frameworks are not determined by the events themselves is the beginning of wisdom and incidentally provides a solid reason for media studies. The general point has been nicely made by Robert Manoff:

Narratives are organizations of experience. They bring order to events by making them something that can be told about; they have power because they make the world make sense. The sense they make, however, is conventional. No story is the inevitable product of the event it reports; no event dictates its own narrative form. News occurs at the conjunction of events and texts, and while events create the story, the story also creates the event. The narrative choice made by the journalist is therefore not a free choice. It is guided by the appearance which reality has assumed for him, by institutions and routines, by conventions that shape his perceptions and that provide the formal repertory for presenting them. It is the interaction of these forces that produces the news, and it is their relationship that determines its diversity or uniformity.[14]

So I want to suggest that television news, like other journalism, occupies a space that is constantly contested, which is subject to organisational and technological restructuring, to economic, cultural and political constraints, to commercial pressures and to changing professional practices. The changing contours of this space can lead to different patterns of domination and agenda-setting and to different degrees of openness and closure, in terms of access, patterns of ownership, available genres, types of disclosure and range of opinions represented. Although it is intrinsically difficult to theorise about the complexities which are implied in this formulation, the implications of the empirical outcomes of the struggle over this terrain are crucial for the ways in which they help or hinder the democratic process. For this reason journalists and their audiences when they first hear news should always ask the irreverent question: 'Says who?' This may be bad news for the official managers of society, but it will be good news for democracy.

NOTES

1   Lord Reith, *The Reith Diaries*, ed. C. Stuart, London: Collins, 1975, p. 96.
2   Raymond Williams, 'Isn't the news terrible?', in Raymond Williams, *What I Came to Say*, London: Hutchinson, 1980, p. 114.
3   *Ibid.*, p. 115.
4   Harvey L. Molotch and Marilyn Lester, 'Accidental news: the great oil spill', *American Journal of Sociology*, vol. 81 (1975), pp. 235–60.
5   ITN Lunchtime News, 12.00, 9 May 1982.
6   ITN News, 18.50, 9 May 1982.
7   ITN News, 21.55, 1 May 1982.
8   Glasgow University Media Group, *War and Peace News*, Milton Keynes: Open University Press, 1985, p. 91.
9   See, for example, Glasgow University Media Group, op. cit.; Robert Harris, *Gotcha! The Media, the Government and the Falklands Crisis*, London, Faber, 1983; Derrik Mercer, Geoff Mungham and Kevin Williams, *The Fog of War*, London: Heinemann, 1987.
10   Mercer, Mungham and Williams, op. cit., p. 134.
11   Conservative Party Central Office, *The American Raid on Libya: a Comparative Analysis of its Treatment on the BBC 9.00 O'Clock News and ITN News at Ten*, 1986.
12   *Ibid.*, p. 12.
13   Open University programme D103, *Society and the Social Sciences*.
14   Robert Carl Manoff, 'Writing the news (by telling the "story")', in Robert Carl Manoff and Michael Schudson (eds), *Reading the News*, New York: Pantheon, 1986, pp. 228–9.

Selections from previous volumes by the Glasgow University Media Group (1976–85)

Chapter 3

Reviewing the news*

Reluctance to display its codes is a mark of bourgeois society and the mass culture which has developed from it.

(R. Barthes)

Contrary to the claims, conventions and culture of television journalism, the news is not a neutral product. For television news is a cultural artefact; it is a sequence of socially manufactured messages, which carry many of the culturally dominant assumptions of our society. From the accents of the newscasters to the vocabulary of camera angles; from who gets on and what questions they are asked; via selection of stories to presentation of bulletins, the news is a highly mediated product.

This study is an attempt to unpack the coding of television news. It aims to reveal the structures of the cultural framework that underpins the production of apparently neutral news. At some common-sense level, television news has to appear neutral or its credibility would evaporate.

There is the agreement widely shared in our society that television news is more objective than the press. Indeed, most people still firmly believe that it is intrinsically more trustworthy. Historically, it is argued, the press is partisan, whilst broadcasting is more neutral. It is this illusion, this 'utopia of neutralism', that many of our findings deny. So thoroughly convinced are most media professionals and the public that television news is trustworthy that the basis of such beliefs must lie in the national culture. The public seem prepared to credit the national television organisations with a neutrality they would deny to others.

A BBC survey conducted in 1962 demonstrated that 58 per cent of the population use television as their main source of news, as against the 33 per cent who principally rely upon newspapers. Most significantly the survey showed that 68 per cent of the population interviewed believed that television

*This was first published in Glasgow University Media Group *Bad News*, London, Routledge & Kegan Paul, 1976, pp. 1–31.

news was the most trustworthy news medium, whilst only 6 per cent said this of the press.[1]

One perceptive critic, Trevor Pateman, has noted that whilst British audiences seem prepared to believe that foreign news services are faulty, biased or distorted, the same judgement is not accorded our own news services. He suggests that this privileged assumption that our news service is best and is reliable, rests upon an unstated nationalism which historically is only made credible by the BBC's role during World War II.[2]

In the post-war period television has come into unchallenged dominance as the prime medium of entertainment and news communication. Such news is bound by law, and convention, to be balanced and impartial. The news is produced on a day-to-day basis by a professional media elite who, whilst doing their best, embody in their routine practices ideological assumptions which reinforce certain stratified cultural perceptions of society and how it should and does work.

Much of the debate about the ideology of television production in general and news in particular would be unimportant were it not for the fact that television is now the front-runner medium eclipsing everything else bar face-to-face communication. In the UK most families spend four to five hours per day watching television, whilst on any given day around 60 per cent of the adult population hear or see at least one broadcast news bulletin. Moreover, until recent shifts in public attitudes, the objectivity of television news was highly regarded.

The most obvious feature of this huge audience is that it tunes in mainly between 17.30 and 22.30 each day, with the maximum number watching at about 21.00. This five-hour period includes five out of the eight weekday news bulletins. The main evening programmes of BBC1 and ITN therefore occupy commanding positions in the evening's schedule and each is regularly watched by about 17 per cent of the population, although this percentage falls during the summer months. For completing broadcasts such as the main and early evening bulletins, the audiences are about the same and there has been little change in recent years (see Table 3.1).

Seventy-five per cent of the viewers of an early evening bulletin will also watch one later in the evening. Since the main bulletin audience is larger, about 40 per cent of the audience of a 21.00 bulletin will have watched an earlier one. This degree of overlap is not acknowledged as a rule in the output. The easily noticed lack of reference back in the bulletins from day to day and week to week might indicate an assumption that the television audience is conversant with the general trends of the news; yet on a daily basis the repetition from bulletin to bulletin makes little concession to the overlapping of audiences.[3] Predictably, viewers of one channel are more likely to view that channel again than another, and the strength of the preference varies little for the three channels. Less predictably, Goodhart et al. found that the audience for news was no different in its viewing habits from the audiences of other programmes.[4]

Table 3.1 January–March weekday audiences amongst UK population (aged 15 and over)

		1965 %	1968 %	1971 %	1974 %
BBC1	22.15/21.00	18	22	18	17
ITV	21.00/22.00	20	18	18	17

Source: *Annual Review of BBC Audience Research Findings, 1973–4*

The half to two-thirds of the population who watch one or more bulletins on the average weekday are described by both the BBC's and the IBA's research organisations in terms of socio-economic groupings using a simple market research classification. The composition of audiences as measured by the BBC is shown in Table 3.2. BBC is watched by a considerably larger proportion of the numerically small A top socio-economic group than ITN. To a lesser extent the same applies to the B group. The picture is reversed in the C group, which has a larger following on ITN. This is confirmed in JICTAR research for the same period (March 1974), which shows that a majority of ITN's audiences was composed of viewers from lower socio-economic groups.[5]

Just as there is a larger proportion of ITN views among the lower socio-economic groups in the audience, so there is a difference in the way that the two organisations were viewed by those groups. In a 1970 BBC survey the

Table 3.2 Estimated audience composition for television news (Wednesdays, January–March 1974)

		Socio-economic group of persons aged 15 and over		
		A %	B %	C %
ITN	12.40	1	2	3
BBC1	12.55	1	1	1
BBC1	17.50	18	19	15
ITN	17.50	6	9	17
BBC2	19.30	1	1	–
BBC1	21.00	21	21	15
ITN	22.00	12	13	19

Notes:
A = the 'top' 6 per cent in professional and managerial positions
B = the next 24 per cent, mainly white-collar and skilled manual workers
C = the remaining 70 per cent
Source: *Annual Review of BBC Audience Research Findings, 1973–4*

C group nominated ITN as their 'main source' of news more frequently than either BBC television, radio or the press. The B group nominated BBC television more frequently than any other source. Only in the small A group was the press cited more frequently as a 'main source' than television.

Although high levels of interest were claimed by all socio-economic groups, this 1970 study showed that a greater proportion of the middle class were 'very interested' or 'extremely interested' in the news. Where above-average interest was shown, however, radio and newspapers were more frequently cited as a 'main source' of news. A comparison of these 1970 results with those of the similar survey in 1962 shows that, only 38 per cent cited BBC as their 'main source', 20 per cent ITN, 33 per cent newspapers and 17 per cent radio. In 1970 ITN had drawn level with the BBC. There has been a trend in favour of television news in general and ITN in particular.

The people interviewed in 1970 were also asked to say which source of news was 'most interesting'. Approximately equal proportions cited BBC and ITN (34 per cent and 35 per cent respectively), which again reflected a trend in favour of ITN since the 1962 study. But the most important result of these BBC surveys is to be found in what they reveal of the audience's perceptions on the accuracy and trustworthiness of news sources. Results in 1957 and 1962 indicated that when asked to judge the trustworthiness of different sources of news, viewers elected television news to a greater position of trust than either radio news or newspapers. These results were confirmed in 1970 (see Table 3.3). It is of course to be expected that the main selected source of news will usually be regarded as trustworthy. What is most interesting about this table is that even among those who claim that the newspapers are their 'main source' of news, far more thought television news, especially on the BBC, to be more 'accurate and trustworthy' than the papers they read. The supposed lack of editorial content on television news, the brevity of news

Table 3.3 The 'most accurate and trustworthy' news

| | Main source of news | | | |
	BBC TV	ITN	Radio	Newspapers
Most accurate and trustworthy source is:				
BBC TV	75	18	19	39
ITN	5	59	6	13
Radio	5	6	61	12
Newspapers	3	5	8	27
Undecided	12	12	6	9

Source: Annual Review of BBC Audience Research Findings, 1973–4

items, the widespread feeling that 'the camera never lies', and the lack of first-person statements, must all contribute to this result.

Trustworthiness is not, however, impartiality, and another slightly different question revealed that perceptions of the 'impartiality' of the television news have changed dramatically. BBC television news was thought to be 'always impartial' by 62 per cent in 1962 but only by 47 per cent in 1970. This trend was particularly marked among younger viewers. The BBC has suggested that this does not 'constitute proof of a decline in the BBC's standards of impartiality. It may be "society" that has changed, more people (particularly the young) taking a sceptical view of organisations seen as part of "the establishment"'.[6] This jaundiced view of the young cannot alter the fact that less than half of the sample interviewed believed the BBC was always impartial. To blame society for this is to argue without evidence that there is some platonic notion of truth obvious to and practised by the broadcasters, but that only the audience's increasing wilfulness prevents them from seeing it.

Concern at the absolute and relative decline in the standing of BBC news led to a further in-depth interview study in 1972 to determine the causes.[7]

At a general level, opinions of the news cannot be separated from opinions about each channel as a whole. The news is not normally seen in isolation from the rest of the output; news-watching is, according to these interviews and other studies,[8] habitual, often passive, and governed by behaviour patterns that have little to do with the news programmes themselves. These factors help to explain why public opinion emphasises stylistic differences; the BBC's formal, serious, humourless and establishment image, and ITN's interesting, friendly, human image. Among the attitudes to the BBC revealed in the 1972 study, the features singled out for criticism were a class bias in favour of the Conservative Party and management, unnecessary complexity of language, and a stiffness and formality in presentation. On questions of detail (including the balance of items, the use of film, etc.) there is less clear differentiation between channels in the minds of the interviewees. Where it does exist, it is more likely to arise from general attitudes towards BBC and ITN rather than for specific differences in news output.

Thus, for example, although BBC was thought to concentrate on more serious items and ITN to aim for a balance of serious and lighter items, this was a judgement about style rather than about selections or balance of items. But despite these perceptions and the fact that the channels are supposedly in competition, our study found few structural differences between them. The amount of time devoted to each category of news; how long the individual items last; how much film is used, all vary very little from channel to channel. The main differences are that ITN industrial items tend to be longer than the BBC's, possibly as a result of the different organisations within the two newsrooms. ITN has a team of three covering industrial and economic affairs, whereas during the period of our study the BBC had two correspondents independent of each other. BBC, with an education correspondent, covers rather more in that area than ITN. Aside from this, ITN uses more photographs than the BBC, and although they use about the same amount of film, ITN's film contains fewer interviews, fewer 'talking heads'. In fact ITN, certainly in *News at Ten*, covers a slightly greater range of stories rather more quickly than does the BBC. But none of this alters our fundamental finding that at a deep level, considering the range of journalistic approaches available, the bulletins are very similar. Out of the range of possible stories, they both make a closely corresponding selection day by day, often down to running the same joke human interest items at the end.

In view of our own findings that, in most structural essentials, BBC and ITN news bulletins do not differ, the 1972 survey is significant. What the broadcasters know of audience perception has allowed them to turn these questions away from themselves and place the onus on the viewers. Thus, the BBC claims 'balance is important to the news viewer, but different sections of the audience understand different things by it. This being so, it seems unlikely that one could produce a news programme which seems "balanced" to everyone who sees it.'[9] By implication the broadcasters here again separate themselves from society, which is too differentiated to perceive the balance the broadcasters achieve. The achievement of balance cannot thus be checked against perceptions. What it can be checked against is not suggested.

In view of the findings that television news is still widely regarded as an 'accurate and trustworthy' source, it is not surprising to discover that in this study, few people were concerned about bias or indeed believed that it existed. Those who did claim to detect deliberate or avoidable bias seemed to derive their views from an overall assessment of BBC and ITV rather than from a particular sense of bias in the news. Only some of the younger interviewees appealed to 'significant absences' as a source of bias, arguing that the lack of space given to the IRA or Vietcong points of view was evidence of a lack of objectivity.

Thus the BBC was able to dismiss the issue of bias as 'not really relevant', or at least as simply a question of style. At the surface level, the results of our own study tend to confirm that there is little to choose between the two sources of news on grounds of content, technical competence and consistency. Yet by the broadcasters' own findings, more than half the viewers see their news output as 'not always impartial'. Whether those viewers are young, extremists or otherwise, this change-around cannot be dismissed easily and has created what Anthony Smith, has termed the 'contemporary crisis in news credibility'.[10]

The news bulletins are becoming a contentious area. Yet it is in exactly this area that the appearance of credible neutrality is so crucial. For as Smith suggests, 'Credibility in the minds of the actual audience is the *sine qua non* of news. All else is propaganda or entertainment.'[11] Smith argues that the trade-union movement has mounted a steady campaign against news reporting which fails to satisfy what trade unionists may feel are adequate standards of neutrality. Smith overstates his position, for with few exceptions the complaints about trade-union coverage from unions are fairly informal and cannot be said to constitute a campaign. The notable exception to this is the pioneering study undertaken by the ACTT Television Commission in 1971. This study was an imaginative albeit limited attempt to assess the impartiality or otherwise of news and other programme coverage of industrial and trade-union issues. The researchers found that the BBC was erratic in its coverage, and tended to trivialise. It also suggested that on a number of occasions it had failed to maintain impartiality. This was said to be less true of ITN whose treatment, they found, 'evidences conscientious effort to maintain imparti-ality'.[12] It also criticised the trade unions for not being fully aware of the 'positive role they must play in supplying and checking television coverage of industrial affairs'.[13]

Smith remains convinced that the most likely outcome of a debate on any given area of news is that the 'news will in the course of time simply mop up the areas of discontent in order to regain credibility'.[14] However true this might be of the broadcasting institutions' on-going relationship with such bodies as the TUC or CBI, these political activities find little reflection on the screen. Smith appears to be wrong on both counts. The trade-union movement continues to pay surprisingly little attention to television news coverage and our own research reveals that many trade unions still aim their information at the press rather than television. On the second count, Smith was writing over three years before [i.e. 1973], yet there are often instances of the cultural skewedness of industrial reporting such as those given here and in *More Bad News*. Moreover, unless the changes in news coverage are to be merely the outcome of pressure from powerful interest groups, there has to be some process which provides safeguards for the less powerful.

It is an unfortunate lacuna in the work of social scientists who should be concerned with these important public issues that the job of monitoring and analysing media output has remained such an undeveloped area.

The literature to guide us in this area was virtually non-existent. The most relevant work was an American text, *Message Dimensions of Television News* by R. S. Frank who had videotaped and analysed seven weeks of American television news. This study, although very limited in scope and outcome, highlights some comparative findings which are worthy of attention; namely that network television news broadcasts reached a wider news audience than any other mass media source, and that television was described as the most important and credible source of news.[15] Frank explains this by virtue of the tendency of viewers to see television news as 'raw news' rather than as encoded or socially manufactured information. He was also able to demon-strate by comparing the airtime given to specific topics with Gallup Poll data that public concern with inflation and crime far outdistanced the amount of television news devoted to these topics.[16] The study concluded that whilst network news may not have necessarily changed or affected viewers' attitudes and values concerning specific issues, at the very least it reinforced perceptions of 'what is important'.[17] He therefore supports the long-held central thesis of much audience effects research, especially American, as to the prime media function.[18] But this ignores the crucial importance of the frames within which such reinforcement takes place. More recent work, both empirical and theoretical, has stressed the agenda-setting role of media as a clue to their importance as systems of social control.[19]

But it remains a commonly held notion that the media effect is reinforcing – rather than converting or causal. Academic psychology relies for its main causal explanations upon reinforcement theory, and demonstrates long chains of reinforcements can lead to changes in attitudes and behaviour. The further analysis of this paradox is essential if studies such as Frank's are to be of use.

The agenda-setting role, the ability to give certain events public prominence whilst ignoring others, is crucial in considering the news operation. Agenda-setting is not a value-free exercise, for as one academic has noted:

> Priorities in their [the broadcasters'] agenda tend to be set by the priorities assigned to topics or themes in the mass media. The informal daily education of the population is conducted by the mass media which tends to select some topics and ignore others, give precedence to some and not to others, and frame contexts and select content, all according to standards which perhaps owe more to custom than malevolent design, and more to unconscious synchronisation of decisions than to conspiracy.[20]

The professionals tend to deny that their professionalisation has any real effect on the nature of coverage, arguing that within the limits of time and money their coverage is objective. But such objectivity assumes that the 'facts' exist outside of a frame of reference.

The work reported here reveals that 'facts' are situated in dominant story themes; that such themes build upon basic frames of reference – basic assumptions about society viewed in particular ways – which often hinder the full and proper coverage of the events in question. Instead of admitting and attempting to overcome predilections for particular frames of reference, the television journalist tends to rely upon some notion of balance as a defence of objectivity. As one social scientist commented, 'by pairing truth claims or printing them as they occur on sequential days, the newsmen claim "objectivity"'.[21] It is this ritual bow to supposed balance which hides the fact that objectivity is not guaranteed by mere balancing acts.[22]

Our study indicates that professional and public faith in impartiality is indeed misplaced. The notion of cultural neutrality itself is only workable as an ideal, but in practice can never be achieved. The very process of cultural selection means that the news is not a mirror image of reality. The subtler and more routine assumptions of news production have rarely been subjected to the close scrutiny that this study attempts. The charge may be made that what is revealed via close study of the television news is merely that which is already known; that analysis of the output is really little better than the impressions which any careful viewer could carry away from the screen. Yet this study is not impressionistic. Indeed, amongst the research team as many impressions or prejudices were refuted as were confirmed. Until the constant flow of television output is stopped, reviewed and subjected to close scrutiny and analysis of the kind here outlined, then any charges of omission, slanting or bias are merely hot air about a cool medium.

This study is intended as a step along the path to the systematic decoding of one centrally important element of contemporary culture. Contemporary cultural codes allow the often taken-for-granted generation of specific basic frames of reference. Such codes or routine handlings are not always easily revealed. For although they exist and are used in constructing and manu-facturing news, they are so deeply ingrained as cultural assumptions that only occasionally, if at all, do they come up for questioning. It is only recently, for instance, that a public debate has emerged as to the proper length of the news bulletins. Whether news bulletins are readily comprehensible to most viewers remains a virtual unknown. A Finnish study revealed that even with help from the interviewer, 48 per cent of people questioned immediately after watching the news could recall nothing of the content.[23]

We would argue overall that many criticisms of the news offered up in the following pages are not easily resolved. There is much that is intrinsic in the social and normative coding of those messages we call 'news', which prevents the realisation of aims of neutral communication of information.

The code works at all levels: in the notion of 'the story' itself; in the selection of stories; in the way material is gathered and prepared for transmission; in the dominant style of language used; in the permitted and limited range of visual presentation; in the overall duration of bulletins; in the duration of items within bulletins; in the real technological limitations placed on the presentation; in the finances of the news services; and above all, in the underpinning processes of professionalisation which turn men and women into television journalists.

Erving Goffman has observed that:

> Obviously passing events that are typical or representative don't make news just for that reason, only extraordinary ones do and even these are subject to the editorial violence routinely employed by gentle writers. Our understanding of the world precedes these stories, determining which ones reporters will select and how the ones that are selected will be told.[24]

It is clear that across a whole range of academic commentators there is agreement on the selected and non-neutral nature of professional frames of reference.

Stuart Hall has argued that news values, and the apparent neutral ideology of news production, require that we examine the codes so that the ideology of news can be properly seen. Hall suggests that: 'News values appear as a set of neutral, routine practices: but we need also to see formal news values as an ideological structure – to examine these rules as the formalisation and operationalisation of *an ideology of news.*'[25]

The general claims of neutral news production are therefore undermined by much social science research. Indeed, the pioneering and perhaps most important of early American social scientists in this field, Lazarsfeld and Merton, wrote in 1948 that the net effect of the mass media was dysfunctional for social change, 'for these media not only continue to affirm the status quo, but, in the same measure, they fail to raise essential questions about the structure of society'.[26] Yet such arguments are not limited to social scientists. Former professional media men and social historians have made similar points.

In the UK, television is an industry that operates upon government licence. Stuart Hood, a former Editor of BBC News, argues that the financial control exercised by government is potent enough to force the BBC's policy into alignment with its general purposes. Government annually votes the proceeds of licence fees to the BBC and also retains the right to decide on the current size of that fee. Therefore, the overall ethos of the BBC within this political reality is an impartiality skewed as it were towards state policy – which makes sense of Asa Briggs's view, in his history of the BBC, that 'it is an organisation within the constitution'. Hood says 'in practice it is the expression of a middle-class consensus politics, which continues that tradition of impartiality on the side of the establishment'.[27] This ethos filters down as 'traditional wisdom' through the organisation, creating a situation where (in the case of news):

> a bulletin is the result of a number of choices by 'gate-keepers'. Each of the gate-keepers accepts or rejects material according to criteria which obviously, under no-system, can be based on individual whim but are determined by a number of factors which include his class background, his upbringing and education, his attitude towards the political and social structure of the country.[28]

To the extent that broadcasting institutions are trading on some taken-for-granted consensus, they are in the business of shaping public consciousness. The sources for this hidden consensus, as Stuart Hall has suggested, lie in the political culture of our society. The nature of the consensus is one bound up with parliamentary democracy. The prime values of British political culture become tied up with the institutions which legitimate its way of life. Perhaps it is for this reason that Lord Reith wanted the public broadcasting service to become a sort of value-free neutral administration, which is what indeed it has tried to become. But as Professor Tom Burns in his study of the BBC has indicated, the very 'rationale of the creation of a Broadcasting Corporation separate from the Government is that neutrality cannot be assumed in these regards. There is no culturally or normally neutral position to assume.'[29]

Historically this is particularly true with regard to industrial relations. After the 1926 strike John Reith, in a letter described by Asa Briggs as a document of basic importance, says: 'But, on the other hand, since the BBC was a national institution, and since the Government in this crisis were acting for the people, the BBC was for the Government in the crisis too.'[30] Reith goes on to say that: 'The only definite complaint may be that we had no speaker from the Labour side. We asked to be allowed to do so, but the decision eventually was that since the Strike had been declared illegal this could not be allowed.'[31]

Asa Briggs comments; 'There was no doubt, as an early message to the Station Directors put it, that there was a "certain natural bias towards the Government side". There was equally no doubt that the straight facts of working-class life were not well known to most members of the early BBC.'[32] Some researchers, such as Nicholas Garnham, have suggested that this 'natural bias' is a continuing reality.[33]

These tendencies have not gone entirely unnoticed by other researchers, and a recent work on *Television and the Working Class* concluded that:

> the political function of television has generally been to promulgate and reinforce conservative social values in a number of forms including industrial relations, race, political protest and so on. Its broadcasting staff have been over-reliant on journalistic stereotypes and news values for its presentation of news and current affairs.[34]

The notion that in representing some assumed consensus the BBC or commercial television is culturally neutral and does not serve to reinforce and shape some assumed consensus is a contradiction, as Burns so perceptively notes in his study. This view of television and television news as political production or as an outcome of processes which themselves are political, has emerged in social science. Yet some cultural questions in media sociology are still very unclear. If much of the consensus is ideological; if the dominant ideas are the ideas of some ruling class or elite; if the dominant means of communication produce 'ideology', why does that ideology prove so slippery and intractable when under study? The phenomenon of mass communications provides us with a severe challenge.

Ideology is not something out there – independent of its producers. In part, ideology is the common-sense awareness of social processes. Common sense serves to both reveal and obscure what is going on. Most of what we or anybody else does is so rooted in our everyday practical activity that it is difficult, if not almost impossible, to bring our common-sense routine assumptions into view. Now common sense, as the bedrock of social interchange, is the widest form of communication. It and public broadcasting systems are all subject to cultural and class stratification; but broadcasting is coupled with a professional ideology and is tightly circumscribed by legal and conventional requirements.

Communicative power is about the right to define and demarcate situations. When we look at cultural power in this context we mean the power to typify, transmit and define the 'normal', to set agendas. The power is used to reproduce highly selected events, and to manufacture news as if these events were the centrally important events of that day. In short, one must see the news as reflecting not the events in the world 'out there', but as the manifestation of the collective cultural codes of those employed to carry out this selective and judgemental work for society.

The year in which our study took place provides an interesting if rather crass indicator of the unquestioned cultural norms of our broadcasting institutions; for it was International Women's Year. Yet despite this, the national television news for all three channels was read either by one of 15 men or a person called Angela Rippon. This will come as no surprise to anybody, but it occurs in a nation where more than 50 per cent of the inhabitants are female. As with the news personnel so with news interviews: of the 843 named interviewees in the first 12 weeks of the year only 65, or 7.7 per cent of them, were women. The cultural conventions and codes of our society operate against a background of structures which regulate certain forms of cultural dominance. As the messages which television produces negotiate and pass through these structures, shaped by the relevant cultural codes, they cease to be neutral, free-floating information about the social world.

We have concentrated on television news in our studies because it is here that supposedly neutral cultural production reaches its largest audiences on an everyday basis. Television news is concerned with the reproduction of information within the realms of a dominant consciousness.

The project has therefore had to concern itself with the vexed questions of cultural power and the consensual legitimation of beliefs. Culture, especially mass culture, is always in the process of change; if one wishes to be more than a spectator to such changes one must identify and map out the nature and output of one of the prime sources of communication. The kind of cultural decoding that reveals the systematic structure of day-to-day productions is needed. This work of decoding is a prerequisite if any acceptable theory of cultural production is to be forthcoming.

Thus far theoretical analysis of the mass communications industry has revealed that critiques which simply stress commercialism are in themselves too limited. Enzensberger, in his book *The Consciousness Industry*, talks of 'immaterial exploitation'.[35]

Enzensberger suggests that if you buy a book you pay costs and profit; if you buy a magazine or newspaper you only pay a fraction of its costs; if you tune into radio or television your set is virtually free. Enzensberger's view is that the commercial exploitation of the media is not central and not intrinsic to it. According to him, the consciousness industry's main business is to sell the 'existing order': to maintain the prevailing hierarchical pattern of society.

Television news excludes that which falls outside of some assumed consensus and that to this extent it serves to render views outside of such an assumed consensus as irrational. Ralph Miliband has suggested that:

> The mass media cannot assure complete conservative attunement – nothing can. But they can and do contribute to the fostering of a climate of conformity – not by the total suppression of dissent, but by the presentation of news which falls outside the consensus as curious heresies, or even more effectively, by treating them as irrelevant eccentricities which serious people may dismiss as of no consequence.[36]

George Gerbner has said of mass communications that 'they are the cultural arm of the industrial order from which they spring'[37] – that is they reflect and reinforce the power structure of the society in which they operate. Thus they are *in all ways* political.

An important British study by Halloran *et al.* of the 1968 Grosvenor Square demonstration followed the preparations for the event itself in seven newspapers and in the programmes of BBC and ITV. They found that the event was anticipated as a stereotypically violent one and that the media borrowed one another's stereotypes. Moreover, the event was structured by the effect of the media on the demonstrators themselves, and most significantly on the police; and that even though the demonstration did not live up to its projected image as 'news', for it was relatively passive, the image of a violent demonstration persisted for many months after the event.[38]

The event achieves perceptual reality by being reported, while in addition consequences flow from the report which actually shape the original reality in accordance with the meanings given it by 'the news'.

Although, for instance in the buying of receivers and the paying of licences, it can be admitted that the mass media or the consciousness industry is in many areas highly profitable and is generally subject to the logic of commercialism, it does serve another and no less important function at the cultural level, a function which is unaltered by the private or public ownership of the medium.

This second function, the cultural legitimation of the consensus and the status quo, is not subject to the narrow confines of commercialism. It is the role of television as a front-runner medium of cultural legitimation that is served by institutions of broadcasting however funded, whether privately or state owned. Historically, broadcasting has always seen its role as one of entertaining, educating and informing within the confines of some unstated, taken-for-granted consensus. But as we have said, this debate has not been a central issue in mass communications research.

The dominant media research tradition can be divided into two types of activity: audience research conducted by broadcasting organisations themselves, chiefly for commercial or programming reasons; and second, academic research into production processes and output as well as audiences. The former tends to be extensive rather than intensive and is concerned with patterns of consumption rather than production. Unfortunately, ever since the BBC began systematic research in 1936, dominant interest has been to determine the size and the distribution of audiences. Today most of the resources of the Audience Research Department of the BBC and the commercial broadcasting equivalent JICTAR are taken up in this way, although general audience reaction studies are regularly carried out as well as some specialised studies of individual programmes, such as we have utilised above.[39]

Our project was designed against a social science research background which has, typically, concentrated on broadcasting personnel and their audience and has not usually examined, nor indeed developed the methodologies to examine television output itself. Since the screen reveals social communications of an extremely complex order, the creation of viable methods of analysis is a difficult but essential task; and one that can only be undertaken initially, we believe, by examining a very small area of output. What follows can be seen as illustrating the difficulties and potentialities of such an approach.

Our belief is that this approach ought to be at least as fruitful as previous work by social scientists which has concentrated upon determining the function and effects of broadcasting in our society. Unfortunately, broadcasting organisations have not been active in this sort of area themselves; nor have they been encouraging to outsiders.

The project undertook a scientific critique of contemporary news output. It is a positive critique, not in some arcane sense of limiting itself to checking or producing the facts, but rather it is an attempt to document and map out the codes utilised in the practice of television news production. In seeking to assess, reveal and demonstrate the results of this judgemental work, we should stress that we are not engaging in negative criticism; however, we are suggesting that by decoding, it is possible to show that the social and professional assumptions lead to particular frames of reference which are not neutral images of reality.

It is our assessment that most television journalists will readily admit that news stories, whether good or bad, are the result of much judgemental work. The positive contribution this study makes is by revealing some of the rules and structures governing the codings. The very notion of news values itself leads many researchers and commentators to question the inferential frames of news ideology. For behind these frames lies the task of interpreting and offering accounts of the central events of our days, months, and lifetimes. For instance:

Good evening. For the first time in many months we have some good news. In the City the value of shares went up by about two thousand million pounds when the financial index jumped by 19.9 points to close this evening at 217.

(ITN, 22.00, 24 January 1975)

What constitutes the definition of news or newsworthiness may well be a more important question than the debate as to whether the output is 'biased' or 'objective'. For cultural bias is inevitable; however, its scope and direction are not. Hall has suggested that the common-sense constructs of the professional journalists guide the moral order and meanings which their stratified world presents, and that news selection comes to rest upon an inferred knowledge about the audience and society which are limited by professional ideology.[40]

All of this is without prejudice to the defences of routine news practices normally presented. The duration of bulletins, the nature of the events included, and the technological and economic limitations are not set in opposition to the inevitable cultural bias we believe to exist but are an expression of choices made as a result of those 'common-sense constructs'. News values and the expertise utilised in applying them are the mechanisms by which events reach the screen in a skewed, mediated and highly selected fashion.

Galtung and Ruge, writing on the structuring and selecting of news, make the important point that 'the more similar the frequency of the event is to the frequency of the news medium, the more probable that it will be recorded as news by that medium.'[41] The orientation of television news is on a day-to-day basis. Events and actions which take time to develop and occur are likely to become news only at some culmination point. Halloran *et al.* in their previously mentioned study support the frequency observation by suggesting that 'a demonstration is a possible news event, while the development of a political movement does not have the correct frequency'.[42]

Frequency does not by itself explain the coverage of any particular area of activity on the bulletins. But with the other elements of the code it excludes or downgrades certain areas. Thus because of frequency, and basic assumptions about industrial life, the codes will contribute towards the newsworthiness of strikes rather than agreements, for example. But not all strikes will be covered equally. The process of selection operates to make some strikes more newsworthy than others. This newsworthiness is a function of the dominant view presented of the strike within the basic frame of reference which attaches to all strikes. The fact is that the sense of urgency engendered by professional practices leads to a spurious concentration on the immediate event. Today's news has no place for the 'late intelligences' that characterise the pre-telegraphic press. The result is that from day to day the bulletins seem to have been assembled by professionals who, while understanding broadly what events should be covered, are nevertheless rather amnesiac about the background and causes of any particular event.

Journalists insist that their professional integrity is based on a respect for 'hard facts', but definitions, within the newsrooms, of what constitute such facts are elusive. One major factor in determining 'facts' is the proven reliability of the source which increases the authenticity of the information in the mind of the journalist. Such sources would include the government, recognised experts and press agencies. In everyday practice, as our observation work inside the television newsrooms shows, the exigencies of journalism and the inherited wisdom of the profession make journalists uncritical of certain sources. But research and verification and constant warnings on the laws of libel and precinct are part of the professionalisation of the young journalist. Thus formal legal and professional constraints operate to discipline the use of incoming information. This is especially true of television newsrooms, where the dangers of editorialising, i.e. working without 'facts', are further enforced by the requirements of broadcasting Charter and Act.

The never easy definition of what constitutes 'fact' is further compounded in television journalism by the medium's ability to record actual events. Indeed, a premium is put on such 'events' as an alternative to the head talking to camera which is, we shall argue, most of the news. An 'event', i.e. a good piece of film with action, stands a far higher chance of inclusion in a bulletin than a weight of unvisualised 'facts'. Yet beyond this, as it were, implicit faith in the adage that the camera cannot lie there is no body of professional wisdom comparable to the checking of sources and the constraints of the law against which to check the 'hardness' of 'events' coverage. Thus 'events' material is selected and used in accordance with criteria that have more to do with entertainment than the circumscribed caution exercised by journalists in their use of hard 'facts'.

In the industrial area the source of 'facts', our research suggests, tends to be management, this being in line with a general tendency to obtain facts from official sources. The labour side is looked to for 'events' – although as often as not this resolves into film of factory gate, picket line, demonstrations, long shots of meetings and little else. The balance, often achieved, of getting 'both sides' on the air is thus too crude. Time allocation to each side in a dispute is no guarantee of balance and impartiality. The concept of 'both sides' is often itself too limiting, and the coverage afforded to each side tends to be of a different order. Labour disputes are thought to involve 'photogenic discord'[43] and the source of the discord is more often than not the workers.

It is not the case that everything that is photogenic is made into news or that there is a dearth of alternative fact to give more balanced accounts. The routine practices of the newsrooms tend to look for 'events' angles in one area and 'fact' angles in other areas. In the reporting of industrial life, these predilections are the result of the inferential frame used to account for the real world. Considering the complexity of television as a cultural form and in the light of the literature cited thus far, we reject any crude notion of bias. The problems of producing a supposedly 'neutral' ideology render such notions unproductive. The central question thus becomes: 'Does television news as presently constituted help explain, and clarify events in the real world or does it mystify and obscure them?'

To move at least some way towards a systematic answer to this, we distinguished three areas of possible analysis. We sought other records of events in the real world apart from the television and we examined the linguistic and visual components of the television's account. Industrial coverage within the news, as indicated already by the examples given, is an exceptionally rich area for this work.

Industrial news is of extreme public importance. One central dynamic in British society, especially over the last decade, has been the conflict between what are often termed 'the two sides' of industry. In a hierarchical and profit-based society, it is unlikely that the central value system is neutral as between labour and capital. Although the value system of the broadcasting institutions is not, except at moments of extreme crisis such as 1926, exactly co-terminus with society's central value system, yet it would square sufficiently in the industrial area for the problems of producing 'neutral' news to be high-lighted.

ACCOUNTS OF THE REAL WORLD

Much of the popular debate over television news has been concerned with the way in which it may distort, misrepresent and select or affect reality. Such questions are notoriously difficult to handle. Most claims of distorted presentation have been based on evidence that is circumstantial and subjective and therefore weak.

To try and avoid this we have taken the Department of Employment descriptions of industry in general and compared them to the television coverage. In particular, the strike record of various industries in the DE statistics is compared with the number of television news items devoted to such strikes. This reveals a highly distorted picture of UK disputes during the period of the study. Television news emphasised strikes in some areas and ignored them in others; it shifted its attention from one industrial sector to another irrespective of the continuing patterns of disputes in the first sector. Moreover the television news did not even cover all the disputes deemed to be of real significance by the Department of Employment.

Routine facts as to whether disputes are official or unofficial are rarely given, although most strikes are unofficial. Which trade unions are involved in a dispute is also not normally given. Another characteristic of industrial reporting is that despite the fact that the Department of Employment has a variety of causal explanations for industrial disputes, these rarely appear on the screen. Basically, for television, the explanation is usually assumed to be money. Again this is strange, for a glance at the government statistics – well used by the television industrial and economic correspondents for other purposes – would reveal that between one-quarter and one-third of industrial disputes are about matters other than money.

Perhaps more serious is the spurious causality that often is implicitly created by the range and form of the industrial and economic coverage. For instance, despite much academic evidence on inflation, which suggests wages contribute only a third to any price increase, the predominant assumption behind the coverage for our period was that of a wages-led inflation. We are not here arguing the merits of the case one way or another. We are simply pointing out that one interpretation is being used at all levels of news production to the virtual exclusion of others. The simple formula of demonstrating that price rises were being matched by pay increases during the period under consideration, conveniently ignores the fact that because of taxation, wage rises of 1.5 per cent are needed to match retail price increases of 1 per cent and that, in any case, the relationship is not necessarily causal.[44] The one-sided causal explanation of inflation is a feature created by the news services' own range of sources for viewing this, yet is often presented as if it were otherwise, for example, 'Big wage deals are again blamed for rising prices ...' (BBC1, 21.10, 29 April 1975); 'again' is the indicator of the narrowness of the range of views routinely presented. Much of this critique is of journalism itself and would apply at least in general to all media. So further work is presented which, by comparing the television coverage of industry with the press coverage, seeks to examine the reality of the particular constraints of television reporting. This is, as it were, a critique of the television journalists as journalists.

LINGUISTICS

The almost complete lack of convergence between the discipline of linguistics, the literary and stylistic criticism of texts, and the rag-bag of sociological content analysis provides an unfavourable climate for analysing news language. The pursuit of structure in texts by locating narrative units or episodes, and the distinction between form and content presupposed in most conventional content analysis have distracted from the importance of research on units of discourse larger than the utterance.

However, recent progress in conversational analysis has done much to show that the internal organisation of discourse, and the ways in which participants produce order in conversation, provide hope for a more systematic understanding. Ideally this is an understanding with a high degree of universality but at the same time a high degree of sensitivity towards particular contexts. The central questions in this kind of analysis are: How are successive utterances related? Who controls the conversation? How are speaker turns organised? How are new topics introduced and old ones brought to a close? What type of utterance can appropriately follow what?

There is no doubt that Sacks, Schegloff et al. can claim some success in achieving a naturalistic and observational discipline that can deal with the details of social action rigorously and empirically.[45] There is also some evidence that the framework derived from conversational analysis may be appropriately applied to non-verbal interaction.[46] What is less clear is the relevance of conversational analysis to other uses of language and to public messages in particular.

The problematic of naturally occurring conversations may well give rise to descriptive apparatus of greater generality, but there are features of this kind of interaction between participants of roughly equal status which make it a particularly difficult form to begin with, for example very rapid and apparently arbitrary changes of topic; digression and the questioning of the questioner; ambiguity; misunderstanding, etc. Naturally occurring conversations are the most complex, subtle and difficult rule-governed form of spoken discourse. In contrast, the language of news (in its simplest, scripted form) is one of the most concise, and obviously stylised forms – and deliberately so. But this does not prevent the language of news from obscuring many of the processes of its production and reproduction. There is no doubt that methods of conversational analysis are appropriate to broadcast interviews despite their highly specific context. What is less certain is that they can be extended without large amendment to scripted news material.

The work of sociolinguists has been directed mainly towards correspondences between variations in language and variations in social structures (e.g. class, ethnic or sex differences). It is rare to find socio-linguistic work which goes beyond a consideration of the competence of speakers to communicate in varying linguistic and social contexts. Phonetic, grammatical or lexical variations are correlated with social context; or a language code is related to structural variations. Stylistics has had a similar concern with the possibility of a large number of stylistic 'registers' named after the field in which they are used (advertising, newspaper, scientific English, etc.) and defined similarly by their grammatic and lexical features. Hence, for example, the 'register' of television commercials includes the following linguistic feature: the ratio of active clauses to passive clauses is 22:1.[47]

It is reasonable to suppose that news broadcasts have a register of their own which might have such features as: a high proportion of concrete nouns; a low adjective ratio; a greater than usual freedom in the use of pre-modifying nouns, e.g. 'The striking Newmarket stable lads' (ITN, 22.00, 20 April 1975). But this kind of work would suffer from a major limitation which is common in sociolinguistics as well as stylistics. A grammatical, lexical or phonological description of a text or series of utterances does not of itself show the function of the different elements in the discourse. Questions, for instance, need not only have an interrogative structure. They can also be imperative, declarative or moodless. According to Sinclair and Coulthard[48] this is only one of the aspects of language which indicates that the sentence, phrase or clause is not the highest order of unit which has to be studied.

For the moment let us return to Sack *et al.*, whose seminal work on the rules of conversational interaction provides us with a starting point for our own work on news talk. Sacks has called one such rule the *consistency rule* which is simply this: it holds that if some population is being categorised and if the category from some devices collection has been used to categorise the first member of the population, then that category, or other categories from the same collection, may be used to categorise further members of the population. For instance we can find examples of news talk that run as follows:

> The week had its share of unrest. Trouble in Glasgow with striking dustmen and ambulance controllers, short time in the car industry, no *Sunday Mirror* or *Sunday People* today and a fair amount of general trouble in Fleet Street and a continuing rumbling over the matter of two builders; pickets jailed for conspiracy.
>
> (BBC2, 18.55, 19 January 1975)

In this piece of news talk the category 'unrest' is used simultaneously to gloss such diverse phenomena as different strikes, short-time working, and a conspiracy case. The preferred hearing is clearly that we see (since we are talking of television) all of these as merely cases of 'unrest'. What this rule allows then is the following: that a hearer who uses the consistency rule, and most of us do as a matter of course, will regularly not even notice that there might be an ambiguity in the use of some category among a group. In other words, where the consistency rule is in operation, by and large although that category or sentence is ambiguous, the consistency rule will be used by hearers so that they will tend not to hear any ambiguity with regard to that category or sentence. Various membership device categories such as 'strikers', 'militants' and 'shop stewards' are ambiguous. Each can have several distinct and quite different referents, e.g. 'a militant consultant', is not the same in any way as a 'militant miner', not because of 'consultant' and 'miner' but by virtue of the fact that the category 'militant' has changed. The regular operation in the media of the consistency rule means that ambiguities are glossed. In other words it says: hear it this way rather than another and do not notice the problems in using this category.

These hearers' maxims are the taken-for-granted rules which allow members of a given culture to make sense of everyday talk. We may pay attention to category devices which serve this purpose very well and there are some which have this essential property, and which are often used in news talk; namely, they are *duplicatively organised*, so that when such a device is used, one counts not the number of 'ambulancemen', 'dustcart drivers' or 'electricians', but the number of 'Glasgow strikers'. That they are 'similar' by virtue of 'geography' or 'time' or that they often involve pay disputes then becomes the preferred causal explanation e.g. '*Still* in Glasgow, 350 corporation dustcart drivers began a strike over a pay claim two months after a *similar* strike' (ITN, 17.50, 13 January 1975; our italics). The ideological glossing here, reflected in the deep coding of news talk, really implies that strikes are directly caused by unreasonable pay claims – a standard interpretive or inferential framework which tends to apportion blame for disputes on to the side of labour. So although it might be the case that the workers in Glasgow are on strike for a whole variety of reasons, if one uses a sentence which turns upon a *duplicatively organised category device* which has as its centre 'Glasgow strikers', then the hearers identify any possible group of strikers as causal coincumbents. That is, duplicated categories are a case of devices in which the hearer's maxim is to hear it that way, rather than hear any ambiguity. Instances of news talk leading to spurious association and via such devices giving preferred and false causal messages are common and misleading, e.g. 'On a day when nearly 8,000 car workers were *made idle* by a *dispute* in the Midlands, the president of the motor manufacturers' society, Sir Raymond Brooks, has said no major British firm is making a profit' (ITN, 17.50, 1 May 1975; our italics). Competent hearers cannot really understand the above news sentence without taking for granted the assumed relationship or consistency between disputes and 'no profits'. One does not of course have to believe such an exclusive association however the news sentence has to be heard as constructed around such a preferred connection. If we avail ourselves of present work on language, we begin to observe and give instances of more general rules which are consistently followed and produced by television news. A central aim in the production of scripted news talk is to create preferential hearings which invite the competent listener to hear the talk as neutral. This often closes off any questions about evidence, about the problematics of such production, and frequently rests upon unexamined causal inferences.

The main BBC1 news for 3 January 1975 provides a clear example of how supposed neutrality works.

> British Leyland said tonight they shared Mr Wilson's exasperation at the series of futile strikes within the corporation – *and there was more trouble today.* Two thousand workers at the Cowley plant near Oxford were laid off because of a strike by 350 men in the tuning department
>
> (BBC1, 21.00, 3 January 1975; our italics)

The analysis of such talk requires little effort and almost no science. Especially if one remembers that Mr Wilson in his speech that day did not talk about 'futile strikes'. Rather he talked about 'manifestly avoidable stop-pages', blaming management and finance as much as the workforce for any dispute. This in later bulletins is a framework to interpret motor strike stories, which implies that they are irrational and caused by 'senseless' action on the part of the workforce.

Another rather different example can be given. We have found only one clear instance where a person demanding a wage rise was interrupted sympathetically. The person was Eric Moonman speaking for MPs. 'How much do you want?' asked Leonard Parkin. Moorman hastily replied that they hadn't had a rise for ages and that £1,000 was a minimum. He was going on to justify this when Parkin broke in with 'I would have thought that was very reasonable in fact' (ITN, 13.00, 7 March 1975). The lessons for researchers here are clear. If we wish to move beyond merely subjectively assessing such editorialising techniques as evidenced by the phrase 'more trouble', then we must learn to utilise the advances in sociolinguistics.

VISUALS

Our study does not support a received view that television news is 'the news as it happens'. The vast majority of the coverage consists of men reading or speaking to camera in various ways: *talking heads* as they are called in the business. Only sport, political speeches, and other events deemed important enough to warrant the use of the Outside Broadcast unit, which then broadcasts live into a bulletin, can be said to be seen as they happen. But this is rare. And rare too is the extraordinary film that sticks in people's minds. The Turkish paratroops descending on ITN's Nicholson in July 1974 or the airline owner pulling men into the last plane out of Hué in April 1975 would be two examples. Most of the time, however, we get predictable film. We have noted that within this pattern working people come into the news in a very limited range of circumstances which will be familiar. The factory gate is one essential location for industrial disputes coverage. As a result all those things that enhance a speaker's status and authority are denied to the mass of working people. This means that the quiet of studios, the plain backing, the full use of name and status are often absent. The people who transcribed our material have pointed out to us that the only time they had difficulty making out what was said was in interviews with working people. Not because of 'accent', but because they were often shot in group situations, outside, and thus any individual response was difficult to hear. The danger here is that news coverage is often offering up what amounts to stereotypical images of working people.

It is only film aestheticians who have exhibited any interest in this sort of problem and their work in this country in recent years has been heavily influenced by the French semiologists and the early Soviet art theoreticians: 'Semiology sets an idea of a text as an area of production of meaning, an idea of criticism which is to "follow the rhythm of the text". The emphasis is shifted from what the text means to how it means.'[49] In so far as this is a prime concern of the semiologist, so it matches a major concern of the project. Talking of film, another leading English practitioner remarks: 'Its work cannot be grasped by a simple inventory of codes, it poses analysis new tasks, a new objective.'[50] When faced with the problem of the analysis of the visual tracks in the news bulletins and their relationship to the linguistics of the audio track, and the significances of other sound tracks, we would agree with this. But in the work thus far presented as examples of how these objectives might be met, we have found an unnecessarily complex use of language and a failure to integrate the description of the film text *per se* with the subsequent analysis of that text.[51] In addition to this problem, in this kind of work assumptions are made in an *ad hoc* fashion about the audience's perceptions. But nevertheless, the utilisation of a number of the basic conceptions of semiology is obviously advantageous. It is, after all, the only agreed universe of discourse in the area, however much it might be in its infancy and whatever its problems.

But we have also imported further concepts from the ethnomethodological area outlined above to help create an analysis whereby more systematic assumptions about the audience perceptions can be made. In essence this is to suggest that there are parallel 'viewers' maxims' to the hearers' maxims of Sacks, and that these can be constructed by creating a 'lexicon' of news shots and determining the rules governing their juxtaposition. If such a methodology is to prove effective it must encompass the greatest variety of visual material used on the news, *viz.* newsfilm. In *More Bad News* such a 'lexicon' is attempted.

An examination of the system of news visuals can be used to draw up a list of viewers' maxims. Such an examination reveals visual expression of the underlying pattern of the assumptions of the broadcasters and their ideological base.

There are two essential logics governing the rules for juxtapositioning – for cutting – newsfilm shots. The first of these is a film logic. In the case of the newsrooms this is actually an extremely simple set of rules, coming from the basics of film grammar. In essence the permitted juxtapositioning of any shot is determined by the content of the shot preceding it. Thus, classically, a general shot is followed by a closer shot of something within that general shot or vice versa. If the shots are not related in this way there are two possibilities: first, the second shot is unrelated to the preceding shot because it marks the beginning of a new sequence or, second, the coverage of the material beginning with the second shot will within a few subsequent shots, which relate to it in terms of the main rule, link up with the material for the first shot. Put another way, in the classic narrative film the logic within the frame of each individual shot determines the content of the next shot. It is this logic which is used when film grammar is employed in a pure form by the newsfilm editors. There is nothing sophisticated about the way they use film – they seldom flash back; they never flash forward; they almost never move from shot to shot except by a straight cut. The rules governing how the interior logic should be applied are determined by the routine practices of the film industry around the world.

A trainee film editor will be taught a number of rubrics which govern the limitation of how shot B can relate to shot A when the material of both is the same but viewed from a different angle or at a different distance. First of the rubrics is that the angle of view cannot be too similar. To move from a long shot to a marginally closer shot can give the effect of jumping: it can be a *jump-cut* and destroy the logic of the sequence. The camera must not move from one side of the material to the other, otherwise the action will be reversed on the screen, i.e. a car moving from screen right to screen left will suddenly be seen to be going in the opposite direction if the camera is taken to the other side of the road for the second shot. Action from one shot to another must be matched. If the hand is reaching for the door in the long shot it cannot be seen to be already grasping the handle in the close-up and, similarly, if it has already reached the handle in the long shot it cannot then be still reaching for it in the subsequent close-up. Camera movement (i.e. pans, etc.) must stop before a cut.

These are among the basics of narratives. They are altered subtly by time since they are dynamic. What is permitted – what the film editors assume the audience will not consciously see – changes. Tolerance for jumps has altered in the course of the past decade. Tolerance for the use of wide-angle lens has also grown. Tolerance for time slips, *flash forwards* as opposed to the standard flashback, have become so common that they are often these days used to engage the audience's interest in feature films which would, narrated 'normally', be too boring to watch.

Further, some of the old rules have fallen into disuse altogether. For instance, an instruction to always cut a side view before a view from above is nowadays meaningless. There are many examples of this. But the essence remains. There is a corpus of rules, seen as such within the industry, which governs the way in which the basic rule as to the interior logic of one shot determining the following shot and shots can be applied.

But routinely in newsfilm this logic is not the dominant one. In most newsfilm the shots do not directly relate to one another in the ways we are used to from the feature cinema. Rather they are used to illustrate the audio-text and the rules governing their juxtapositioning come not from the visual but from the audio track – indeed largely from the commentary. Therefore they are filmed and cut according to an alien narrative logic – the journalistic. It is because the journalistic logic dominates the film logic that common professional opinion of television news journalists as film-makers is a low one. 'Wallpaper' is how most of the output of the newsroom camera crews would be described. It is only in situations of danger or raw human emotion that the newsreel cameraperson achieves professional regard. These situations are not however the mainstay of the bulletins.

Of course, the most obvious reason for this dominance is that the facilities necessary on location for achieving the logic of the narrative fiction cinema by definition do not exist for the news camerapersons. For instance, the whole process of moving from long shot to close-up (or the reverse) using only one camera to record the scene obviously requires that any action in the scene be repeated. Equally obviously, the repetition of action is something the news cameraperson cannot and would not go after, since it involves a level of intervention in the action not permitted by the observational role of such technicians.

In the area of current affairs and general documentary filming, the main question at this moment of development in these forms is the extent to which the camera can intervene – and by that is meant exactly how close can a documentary crew come to treating their 'actual' material as a fiction director would treat his/her actors. For the newsreel cameraperson, the routine story does not permit the luxury of this debate, never mind operating on it. The shop stewards' convener will not take the vote again so that the camera crew can get some close-ups. The terrorist will not obligingly appear at the window twice. The march will not restart. The workers will not re-enter the factory.

The structuration of newsfilm is therefore the result of an application of normal journalistic narrative practices as amended by the use of film logic where possible. As a result, the viewers' maxims that can be generated indicate the extreme complexity of the messages and the skill required to decode them on the part of the audience. For the audience must understand not only the simple rules governing the cut on the visual track and the culturally determined visual shorthand that makes up the contents of that track but also how that track is juxtaposed with the commentary.

For instance in classic film grammar, things referred to in the commentary would be seen on the screen. In newsfilm they are often not seen. The journalistic structure might well be referring to absences – to things not happening – to abstractions. The film camera can only shoot objects that are there. As a result these objects are transformed by the process of juxtaposition into symbols. The empty station is not then simply a representation of an empty station but also a symbol of a rail strike. It is seen as such because of the juxtaposition of audio track.

This leads us to an interesting paradox. We would argue that in the bulletins such symbolic use of pictures, *prima facie*, might be least expected, because the bulletins report the world. Yet it is exactly the place in the non-fiction television output where such symbolic use predominates. Indeed, it is impossible to watch a bulletin without understanding the pictures con-tinuously in terms of the symbolic structure created by the dominant logic of the journalistic narrative, even when film logic is simultaneously being used. There are indicators that in terms of comprehension the audience gain little from the visuals – they will understand almost everything from hearing the script alone.[52] However, that the visuals are not an essential carrier of meaning on the deeper level, has not been demonstrated to our satisfaction. The presentational devices in the news, such as the use of supercaptions, give a constant viewer (and that is what viewers are in our culture) important clues for assessing critically the legitimacy of what is heard on the audio track.

Although the rules governing the juxtaposition of shots are therefore on the surface comparatively simple (as say when compared with a modern feature film), the relationship between sound and picture is extremely complex. The symbolic quality, itself a result of the logistics of news filming coupled with the shortness of item duration, is the cause of this.

Analysing news talk and visuals allows us to get at the preferred readings or seeings of a given item. It should be clear of course that the presuppositions of news production can only be revealed by close analysis of talk and visuals, which will not only demonstrate the extent of the vocabulary employed but will show that although a large number of possible visual and verbal descriptions could be generated, only a limited number are consistently presented. The received notions of news selection – the gatekeeping function – are inadequate to the task of this sort of analysis. Selection at the linguistic and visual level is at least as important to an understanding of how the news works as a cultural form as are omissions and inclusions at other levels. Conscious of this, the project was designed to enable analysis on all three levels.

NOTES

1　Sir Charles Curran, 'The impact of TV on the audience for national newspapers, 1945–68' in J. Tunstall, *Media Sociology*, London: Constable, 1970.
2　T. Pateman, unpublished manuscript, 'Television news: contexts and modes of emission and reception'. Cf. also his useful analysis and assessment of 'Television and the February '74 General Election', London: British Film Institute, 1974.
3　C. J. Goodhart, A. S. C. Ehrenberg and M. A. Collins, *The Television Audience*, Farnborough: Saxon House, 1975, p. 50.
4　They developed the 'duplication of viewing law' to explain patterns of viewing for all kinds of programme. This states that 'The proportion of the audience of any television programme who watch another programme on another day of the same week is directly proportional to the rating of the latter programme (i.e. equal to it times a certain constant), ibid., p. 11.
5　Source: *ITV 75: Guide to Independent Television*, London, 1975, p. 111.
6　*Annual Review of BBC Audience Research Findings*, 1, 1973–4, London: BBC, p. 42.
7　BBC Document VR/73/416, London, July 1973.
8　Including Goodhart *et al.*, op. cit.
9　BBC Document, op. cit., p. 16.
10　A. Smith, *Shadow in the Cave*, London: Allen & Unwin, 1973, p. 109.
11　*Ibid.*.
12　ACTT Television Commission, *One Week*, London: ACTT, 1971, p. 11.
13　*Ibid.*
14　Smith, op. cit., p. 110.
15　R. S. Frank, *Message Dimensions of Television News*, Indianapolis: Lexington Books, 1973, p. 11.
16　*Ibid.*, p. 64.
17　*Ibid.*.
18　See J. T. Klapper, *The Effects of Mass Communication*, New York: Free Press, 1960.
19　See S. Cohen and J. Young (eds), *The Manufacture of News*, London: Constable, 1973; and Blumler, McQuail and Brown, 'The television audience', in *Sociology of Mass Communications*, ed. D. McQuail, Harmondsworth: Penguin, 1975.
20　D. W. Smythe, 'Agenda setting: the role of mass media and popular culture in defining development', *Journal of the Centre for Advanced Television Studies*, 3 February 1975, p. 34.

21 Gaye Tuchman, 'Objectivity as strategic ritual: an examination of newsmen's notions of objectivity', *AJS*, vol. 77, no. 4, p. 666.
22 For fuller discussion of the epistemological problems here see A. Gouldner, *For Sociology*, London: Allen Lane, 1973, chs 1 and 2.
23 K. Nordenstreng, 'Policy for news transmission', *Educational Broadcasting Review*, August 1971; reprinted in McQuail, op. cit., p. 390.
24 Erving Goffman, *Frame Analysis*, New York: Harper, 1974, p. 14.
25 Stuart Hall, *The Determinations of News Photographs*. Working Papers in Cultural Studies No. 3, University of Birmingham, Autumn 1973, p. 77.
26 Lazarsfeld and Merton, 'Mass communication, popular taste and organised social action', in N. Schramm (ed.) Mass Communications, Urbana: University of Illinois Press, 1960, p. 505.
27 S. Hood, 'Politics of television', in McQuail, op. cit., p. 418.
28 *Ibid.*
29 T. Burns, 'Commitment and career in the BBC', in Sociological Review Monograph No. 13, ed. P. Halmos, Keele, 1969, p. 37.
30 Asa Briggs, *History of Broadcasting in the U.K.*, vol. 1, London: Oxford University Press, 1961, p. 365.
31 *Ibid.*, p. 366.
32 *Ibid.*, p. 374.
33 N. Garnham, *Structures of Television*, London: British Film Institute, 1973, pp. 25f.
34 A. Piepe, M. Emerson, J. Lannon, *TV and the Working Class*, Farnborough: Saxon House, 1975.
35 H. M. Enzensberger, *The Consciousness Industry*, New York: Seabury Press, 1974.
36 R. Miliband, *State in Modern Society*, London: Weidenfeld & Nicolson, 1969, p. 218.
37 G. Gerbner, 'Mass media and human communication theory', in McQuail, op. cit., p. 51.
38 J. Halloran, P. Elliot, G. Murdock, *Demonstrations and Communication*, Harmondsworth: Penguin, 1970, p. 309.
39 See *BBC Audience Research in the United Kingdom: Methods and Services*, London: BBC, 1970. Robert Silvey, the former head of audience research at the BBC, has given an account of his experiences in *Who's Listening?*, London: Allen & Unwin, 1974. Audience measurement for ITV is provided by an independent research organisation, Audits of Great Britain Ltd. through the Joint Industry Committee for Television Advertising Research which is responsible for the service.
40 S. Hall, 'World at one with itself', in Cohen and Young (eds) *The Manufacture of News*, London: Constable, 1973.
41 J. Galtung and M. Ruge, 'Structuring and selecting news' in Cohen and Young, op. cit.
42 Halloran *et al.*, op. cit., p. 302.
43 Association of Chambers of Commerce Evidence to the Committee on the Future of Broadcasting, reported in *The Times*.
44 See A. Gamble and P. Walton, *Capitalism in Crisis*, London: Macmillan, 1975, ch. 1.
45 See papers in *Directions in Sociolinguistics*, ed. J. J. Gumperz and D. Hymes, New York: Holt, Rinehart & Winston, 1962.
46 See, for example, R. L. Birdwhistell, *Kinesics and Context: Essays on Body Motion Communication*, Philadelphia: University of Pennsylvania Press, 1970.
47 Geoffrey N. Leech, *English in Advertising: A Linguistic Study of Advertising in*

Great Britain, London, 1966, p. 7.
48   J. M. Sinclair and R. M. Coulthard, *Towards an Analysis of Discourse*, London: Oxford University Press, 1975.
49   John Ellis, 'Made in Ealing', *Screen*, Spring 1975, p. 79.
50   Stephen Heath, 'Film and system', *Screen*, Summer 1975, p. 113.
51   Heath's article 'Film and system', *Screen*, Spring 1975 and Summer 1975 *passim* is an example of these failings.
52   R. A. Pride and G. L. Walmsey, 'Symbolic analysis of network coverage of the Laos invasion', *Journalism Quarterly*, vol. 49, Winter 1972, pp. 539–43; K. S. Thompson, A. C. Clark, S. Dinitz, 'Reactions to My-Lai: A visual–verbal comparison', *Sociology and Social Research*, vol. 58, no. 2, January 1974, pp. 122–9.

Chapter 4

Measuring the news

I Measure for measure*

> If Moses came down from Mount Sinai with the Ten Commandments in an era of television, he would certainly be greeted by camera crews.
>
> 'What do you have?' they would ask.
>
> 'I have the Ten Commandments,' replies Moses.
>
> 'Tell us about them but keep it to a minute and a half,' they would say. Moses complies and that night on the news, in still more abbreviated form the story is told. The newscaster begins, 'Today at Mount Sinai, Moses came down with the Ten Commandments, the most important three of which are . . .
>
> (William Small)

A number of observers have noted the 'sameness' of the news from day to day in terms of structure, content and presentation. Newspaper reporting has been criticised by Rock for its ritualised and cyclical nature which conveys an impression of occurrences – and society – as 'eternal recurrence' with no grand design.[1] Frayn has parodied the formal bureaucratic nature of news production as well as the less formal interpretive rules, imagining a computerised system of news production which would break 'its last residual connection with the raw, messy, offendable real world'.[2]

These mosaic patterns of the newspaper have their parallels on the screen. The following analyses can thus be regarded as using similar computer techniques in reverse, a process of unravelling the news bulletins to reveal some of the codes of story classification, placement, duration and presentation which are routinely employed. The results indicate that, given a range of stories from which to choose, they will be contained within a clearly defined structure and will receive predictable treatment. The codes of news

*First published in Glasgow University Media Group, *Bad News*, London, Routledge & Kegan Paul, 1976, pp. 85–101.

production create media packages so obvious as to be instantly available for parody but this does not necessarily mean they are understandable. In this context, familiarity should provoke questions rather than complacency. The indications are that television news producers are relatively unaware of the ways in which they allow their routines of news processing, the effects of time pressures and their need to compete for audiences, to force their output into predictable patterns.

BULLETIN PROFILES

Length

Broadcast news has travelled a long way since the BBC transmitted a single radio news bulletin composed by the wire service and only read after 19.00 (because of the hostility of newspaper proprietors). Today the regularly scheduled news bulletins vary in length from a few minutes to half an hour – or more in certain circumstances. On weekdays both BBC1 and ITN carry bulletins at lunchtime, early evening and at 21.00 and 22.00 respectively. The *Nine O'Clock News* and *News at Ten*, which are regarded by their producers as being competitors, are the main programmes on these two channels, with a well-established format. ITN's *News at Ten*, which began in 1967, is usually 25 minutes in length (excluding titles, openings and closings, which take up to one and a half minutes). The *Nine O'Clock News* is slightly shorter, lasting about 20 minutes. In the early evening, the BBC1 programme (12 minutes) is slightly longer than ITN's (10 minutes). *First Report*, ITN's lunchtime programme, lasts 20 minutes, during which the presenter regularly conducts his own live interviews in addition to the more conventional coverage.

The lunchtime bulletin on BBC1 lasts for less than 3 minutes and has much in common with the summary included in BBC2's *Newsday* programme and the shorter weekend bulletins. *News Extra*, the late news bulletin on BBC2, at the time of the study was more variable in length than other bulletins but normally lasted about 20 minutes. The exception to the generally shorter weekend bulletins is the *News Review* programme on BBC2, which lasts for 40 minutes. This differs from the other programmes in taking stories for the whole week and presenting them with subtitles for the benefit of the deaf. It is transmitted early on Sunday evening.

The length and scheduled time of the news is a product of the historical place of the news in television output as a whole, the daily exigencies of scheduling, and the need to cover extraordinary events. Of these, the first is the most important. Legal restrictions on the hours of broadcast news have long since ended but restriction of the hours of broadcasting still exists. Economic pressures are at least as important. But whatever the hours of broadcasting, the proportion of news and news-magazine programmes within them has remained very stable. The increase in the length of the main evening news programmes has to be seen against the background of an increase in total output. Since 1956, commercial television has included between 6 and 10 per cent of news and news magazines, although the total ITV output has more than doubled in the same period. The BBC carries a similar amount.

It has been argued that the proportion of news in the schedules has less to do with institutional structures of ownership, legal controls or even the policies of broadcasting organisations than with economic pressures and the quest for audiences.[3] However the proportion is to be explained (and the public nature of the BBC confounds a simple economic rationale), a formula has been settled on which seems to have its own justification in terms of scheduling. Any extension of the news is seen by the institution as upsetting this formula and therefore only appropriate to minority times on a minority channel.[4] There are sometimes exceptions to this arising from other scheduling requirements which occasionally encroach on news time. The third set of circumstances – the need to cover extraordinary events – occasionally results in an extended news. This occurs more frequently on ITN than BBC, despite the greater difficulties of liaison with fifteen commercial companies, each with its own programming. Although short extensions are not infrequent, there is actually a greater chance of the bulletin being shorter than the regularly scheduled length. The extended news is a rare occurrence. ITN's coverage of the outcome of the Conservative Party leadership campaign was the longest extension in the first three months of 1975, a three-part programme running for 45 minutes.

The number and duration of items

The number of items in a bulletin does not have a normal distribution, statistically speaking, from day to day. Except in the shortest bulletins, one cannot predict any single number of items as being more likely to occur than another. There are, however, certain regularities between channels and between bulletins. Consider the mean number of items in each weekday news programme and the range and type of variation in this mean (Table 4.1).

In general, the mean number of items, the modal number of items, and the range increase steadily with the length of the bulletins. The longer the news, the more stories are likely to be included, because longer bulletins do not include, as would be possible, fewer longer items. A total of less than four or five items seems to be unacceptable for bulletins of more than 3 minutes in length. However, the bulletins are subject to changes in presentation. In the period of our study, two programmes were moving away from this norm. *First Report* and *News Extra* tended to have fewer items, a smaller range of items, and more editions with a very small number of items. Both have negatively skewed distributions of the number of items in contrast to the positively skewed distributions of the other bulletins. This skewing is the statistical

Table 4.1 Number of items in each bulletin (weekdays)

	Mean no. of items	*Modal value*[1]	*Range*[2]	*Modal length*[3] *mins secs*
BBC1 Lunchtime	5.6	6	5	2.30
First Report	7.1	8	9	21.00
BBC1 Early Bulletin	10.5	9	13	11.30
ITN Early Bulletin	9.3	10	11	10.30
Newsday	6.8	7	9	2.30
Nine O'Clock News	12.2	11	15	23.30
News at Ten	14.1	12	16	25.00
News Extra	5.9	4	9	18.30

Notes:
[1] Most frequently occurring number
[2] Difference between smallest and largest number of items
[3] Most frequently occurring length of bulletins

expression of the fact that these two bulletins were becoming more like current affairs programmes.

In cases of bulletins which are of comparable length and which are scheduled at similar times (the two early bulletins, for example, and the *Nine O'Clock News* and *News at Ten*), there is a close similarity between channels. The slightly greater range and average number of items in the BBC Early Bulletin and *News at Ten* respectively, is connected with their slightly greater average length.[5] Although the BBC1 lunchtime and BBC2 *Newsday* bulletin are normally the same in length, the higher values for the *Newsday* bulletin can be accounted for by a handful of bulletins which were extended beyond this time and had considerably more items. These extensions are because the format of *Newsday* (news bulletin and current affairs interview) facilitates such extension without altering the overall running time. These and other comparisons show that bulletin formats do not vary in random ways but have a similar underlying logic.

This provides some evidence against the argument for an extension of news time as a means of correcting the 'bias against understanding'. In the present situation, all that can be said is that the longer the news, the greater the number of stories covered.[6] It cannot be said that stories are treated at significantly greater length or in a significantly different way. Instead of the longer news bringing a greater element of explanation and commentary to roughly the same number of items – and therefore stories – the effect of lengthening the news is to extend the number of stories. There is one caveat to this conclusion. Despite a greater number of items in longer bulletins, the average duration of items varies from half a minute in the *Newsday* summary to 3 minutes in the longer programme on BBC2 (Table 4.2). Thus, there is a general increase in average item durations with the increase in bulletin

Table 4.2 Mean duration of items in each bulletin

	Mean item duration	
	Weekdays *mins secs*	*Weekends* *mins secs*
BBC1 Lunchtime	0.35	0.50
First Report	2.40	—
ITN Lunchtime	—	2.15
BBC1 Early Bulletin	1.15	0.55
ITN Early Bulletin	1.00	1.00
Newsday	0.30	—
BBC2 *News Review*	—	2.55
Nine O'Clock News	1.40	1.30
News at Ten	1.35	1.30
News Extra	2.50	3.15

lengths. But this increase still leaves the basic number of items deemed necessary for a longer bulletin unaffected. There continues to be a close similarity between the two early bulletins on the one hand and the *Nine O'Clock News* and *News at Ten* on the other. *First Report* and *News Extra* are again exceptions to this, for the reasons outlined above.

How the increasing duration of items is to be reconciled with our finding of a fairly constant number of items in bulletins of different lengths, is shown in Figure 4.1. Essentially the length of items in a bulletin does not keep step with the number of items in the bulletin, although the mean length does increase. Each bulletin has a single peak in Figure 4.1, i.e. a high proportion of the items transmitted during that bulletin will be of one particular length; but this length is different for each bulletin. With *First Report* and *News Extra* this is still true, although the peak is lower: the larger proportion of longer items reflecting the current affairs style of these programmes. The profiles in Figure 4.1 show that in each case the distributions have a single peak in the range of about half a minute. This is even true of the longer bulletins, which thus use the extended time to include a greater range of stories as much as more detailed coverage.

There is a clear indication in the similarity of these profiles that the rules of news production lead to a mix of item durations which does not vary greatly from bulletin to bulletin. Whether the criteria are journalistic (news value or 'covering the waterfront') or aesthetic (the pace of the programme), the mix will include a high proportion of items of less than 1 minute. Half or more of the items in the majority of bulletins are in this category, although ITN has a significantly higher proportion than the BBC bulletins (68 per cent and 56 per cent respectively in the early bulletins and 52 per cent and 46 per cent respectively in the main evening news programmes). BBC bulletins

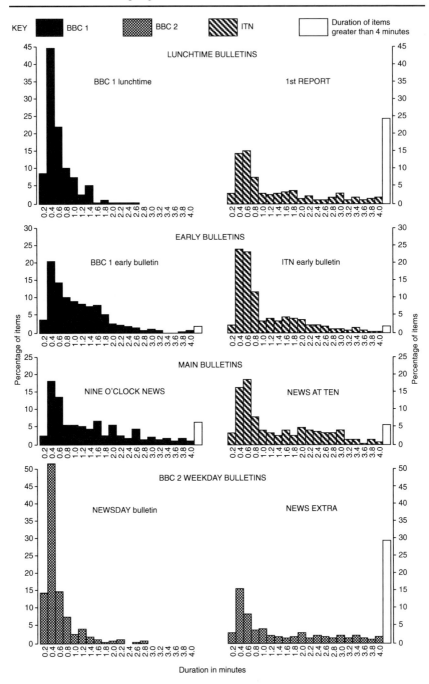

Figure 4.1 Item duration profiles (weekday bulletins)

therefore have a higher percentage of longer items. Further analysis will show that these figures conceal significant variations in the average duration of items in different story categories.

In the case of *First Report* and *News Extra*, whatever the number of items, there is as much chance of an item being 4 or 6 minutes long as there is of its being, say, 1 to 3 minutes long. In other bulletins it can be assumed that, with certain exceptions, the duration of an item is the best indicator of its attributed importance. This is probably true as well of *First Report* and *News Extra*, with the qualifications that both programmes seem to aim to cover a few salient stories at greater length and usually with interviews.

Originally we felt that item durations would be governed by the use of film, graphics or interviews, giving steps in these profiles. The lack of the sharp breaks, therefore, is evidence that item durations are entirely flexible. A lack of film material does not necessarily mean that an item lasts less than half a minute. On the other hand, if film material is used, the item is almost certain to be longer than half a minute. In interpreting the profiles in Figure 4.1, therefore, it can generally be assumed that apart from newscasters, short items (less than 1 minute in length) will contain pictures, maps and other graphic inputs but rarely film; that items between 1 and 4 minutes will usually contain film as well as graphic inputs but not interviews; that longer items will contain a whole range of technical and personnel inputs.[7]

Preliminary cross-national studies of television news indicate that the profiles shown here are not untypical of the majority of European bulletins. Rositi, for example, has demonstrated that news items in Italy, Germany and the UK last little more than a minute and a half on average and that two-thirds or more of the items are below average in length.[8]

French television was the only significant departure from this norm in Rositi's four-nation study. He also encountered greater difficulty at the coding stage in deciding what constituted an item on British television news. A greater proportion of stories were run together by scripting – a clue to the greater propensity to create 'package' items. This does not occur with sufficient frequency, however, to replace the prevailing logic of news as fragments of information with little apparent overall coherence apart from that imposed by the bulletin format, which utilises and expresses the interpretive frameworks of the producers. The average duration of items and the amount of packaging varies according to story category and channel. The variations indicate certain priorities in news gathering and news processing. They also reflect certain organisational arrangements in the newsrooms. Table 4.3 shows the average duration of items in each of the main story categories. The greater overall average in ITN and BBC2 is partly accounted for by extended programmes such as *First Report*, *News Extra* and *News Review*, whose distinctive profiles we have noted. In the case of ITN a greater tendency to run items together in certain categories may be another factor which contributes to the higher figure.

Table 4.3 Average duration of items by story category and channel (all bulletins)

	Average duration of items		
Story category	BBC1 mins secs	BBC2 mins secs	ITN mins secs
10 Politics	1.35	2.00	2.00
20 Industrial	1.10	1.25	1.40
30 Foreign	1.15	2.00	1.35
40 Economics	1.40	1.00	1.15
50 Crime	1.10	0.55	1.30
60 Home Affairs	1.25	2.25	1.35
70 Sport	0.50	1.55	1.10
80 Human Interest	0.55	1.55	1.00
90 Disasters	1.05	1.15	1.10
00 Science	1.15	3.00	1.20
Av. duration (all categories)	1.15	1.45	1.25

A common-sense assumption that some areas, such as economics, require greater time because of their complexity, is not borne out. Even if the relatively short stock and currency market reports are taken into account, only (on BBC1) 50 extra seconds on average are devoted to economics as against, say, sport. On the other channels it is even less and in any case, the duration differences we are here dealing with are quite small. This view must be tempered by the common professional assumption that the compression of information on television means that 50 seconds is a long time. The durations nevertheless reveal that no real presentational differences are possible, since there is a maximum of 50 seconds to play with, as it were.[9] It is also clear that the expected skew in average durations, with longer items being more common in 'serious' categories, does exist – politics for instance, are the longest items on average. All three channels show a similarity at the other end of the scale. Items in the categories of crime, sport, human interest and disasters, all tend to be shorter than average, a feature which is associated with their low priority in terms of placement.

There is one significant difference between channels. The industrial and economic categories do not have the same average item durations across channels. The figure for ITN in the industrial category is significantly above the comparable figure on both BBC channels (Figure 4.2). The picture is reversed in the economic category. BBC1 has the highest average item duration.

ITN carries a significantly higher proportion of lengthier industrial items and the actual number of items is smaller. This is counter to the general tendency for BBC items to be longer. The percentage of industrial items longer than 2 minutes varies from 18 per cent on BBC1 through 25 per cent

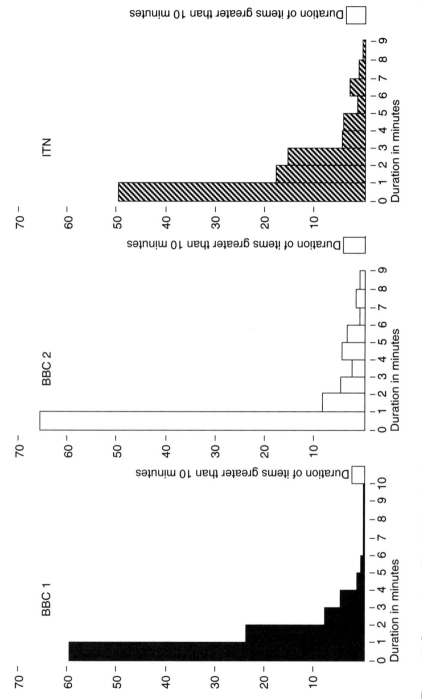

Figure 4.2 Comparison of idustrial item durations

on BBC2 to 32 per cent on ITN. This evidence of a greater amount of 'packaging' by ITN leads us initially to suspect differences between channels in the process of news-gathering and processing itself rather than a simple running together of stories for elegance of style or smoothness of presentation. The organisation of industrial news-gathering includes one major difference between the BBC, who had one specialist industrial correspondent and one economic correspondent and ITN, which had a team of three specialists in industrial, economic and business affairs. This organisational difference directly accounts, we would submit, for ITN's greater tendency to package items in the industrial area, since there is a higher input of specialist reporting. The industrial correspondent appeared to camera in only 30 (7.2 per cent) of BBC1's industrial items, whereas the three ITN specialists appeared in 49 (12.2 per cent) of industrial items on that channel. We are not however suggesting that the greater use of specialists necessarily leads to a parallel increase in cohesion and comprehension. The package is only a presentational device. It can as easily create spurious causal connections as it can lead to an integrated view of the world.

CATEGORY PROFILES

Distribution of items by category

We analysed the content of the news according to categories as described in Appendix 1 at the end of this chapter (pp. 89–92). The number of items in each of these categories is similar from bulletin to bulletin and channel to channel. The relative ranking, as shown in Figure 4.3, remains basically the same for each channel. All three profiles, which indicate the percentage of items in each category, have a distribution which is more like that of the 'quality' than the 'popular' press. A large majority of the items are devoted to political affairs at home and abroad (interpreted as a rule through the activities of political leaders – hence the emphasis in our period on the Conservative Party leadership issue); industrial topics and matters of social and economic management. We shall describe these categories as being at the 'serious' end of the category spectrum. The proportion of time devoted to sport, human interest and other non-public affairs coverage is in the order of 20 per cent – less than even the quality press, in which the corresponding figure is over 30 per cent.[10] This is the opposite end of the spectrum. The relative predominance of the foreign, political and industrial categories is the same for all three channels, industrial items taking third place. Even in the less prominent areas of coverage, the order varies little from channel to channel. For example, there is a similar amount of slightly more economic news (41–44) than home affairs news (61–65) on each channel and (apart from BBC2) this similarity is maintained with the sport, human interest and disaster categories. Figure 4.4 (see p. 80) shows that even within these broad categories, the allocation of items is identical.

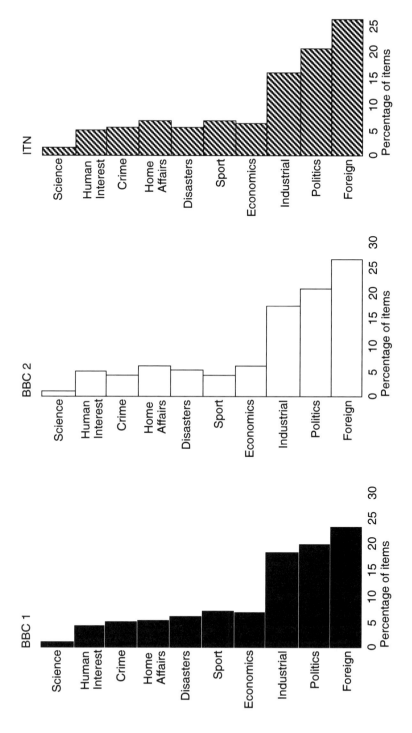

Figure 4.3 Content profiles for each channel (includes all bulletins) showing the percentage of items in each category

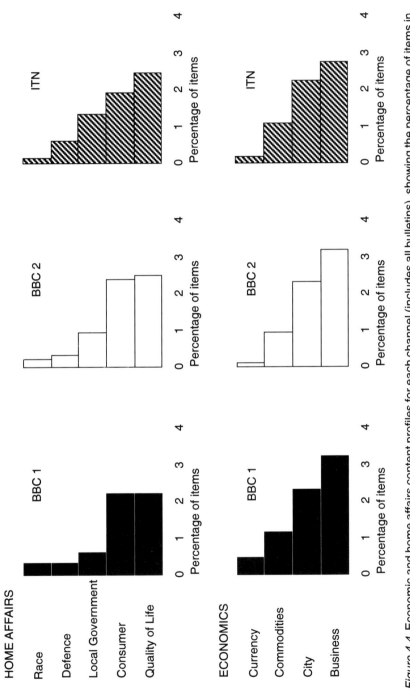

Figure 4.4 Economic and home affairs content profiles for each channel (includes all bulletins), showing the percentage of items in each category

The priorities revealed here are obviously deeply embedded in the practice of making the news. They are rarely if ever debated or justified, whether in terms of audiences or patterns of activity in the world. Yet why, for example, should items on wages, disputes and employment in industry be presented with far greater regularity than items on investment, profits and other aspects of industrial management? Or what is the rationale for the proportion of human interest and 'feature' stories? If, as is most likely, this mix has been inherited from the press – and a minority section of the press – it is interesting to note that the formula is nevertheless used to create a major source of news for the majority of the population.

For most categories, variation between channels is in the order of 1 or 2 per cent of the total number of items. In the larger category of political news (11–19) this variation is still very low. Grouping all the sub-categories, the percentage of political items is 20.6 per cent, 21.8 per cent and 21.1 per cent on BBC1, BBC2 and ITN respectively. The only significant exceptions to this general similarity of profile (see Figure 4.3, p. 79) are, first, the greater predominance of foreign items on both BBC2 and ITN, and second, the relatively low percentage of sports items on BBC2. The explanation for this lies partly in the programme philosophy of *News Extra* discussed above, the early transmission time of *First Report*, and partly in variations of bulletin length between channels.

We did not anticipate such a high degree of similarity. It would not be surprising to find this similarity if the news were manufactured in identical institutions with common resources and aims. But the institutions have slightly different structures and markedly different atmospheres. Their processes of news-gathering are independent and, not least, they are assumed to be in competition and take pride in extremely subtle marks of distinction.

Taking each bulletin separately, such differences as do exist in the mix of categories have chiefly to do with the variation in bulletin length. Thus, instead of a short bulletin having a category profile which corresponds exactly to the average profile for that channel, it tends to have items from a smaller range of categories and more items in the 'serious' categories. The differences remain quite small, however, as Table 4.4 shows.

Catering for different audiences at different times of the day (e.g. women's programmes in the afternoons) is a norm of television scheduling. Table 4.4 illustrates that there appears to be no orientation towards the audiences, which is surprising in view of the fact that much of the internal research of both BBC and IBA has shown significant differences in audience profiles. These are differences of size, social class, age and gender. Only one bulletin is specifically targeted – *News Review*, designed for the deaf.

When examining the exceptional bulletin formats of *First Report* and *News Extra* we find the profiles of categories, although different from the other bulletins, are not seemingly targeted to housewives or, say, tired intellectuals. *First Report* differs from other ITN bulletins in having a higher proportion of

Table 4.4 Distribution of items by bulletin (weekdays), showing percentage of items in each category

	BBC1			BBC2		ITN		
	Lunchtime	Early	Nine O'Clock News	Newsday	News Extra	First Report	Early	News at Ten
10 Political	21.1	22.0	21.6	23.6	25.4	23.6	22.3	21.1
20 Industrial	17.9	16.6	16.6	18.6	15.3	14.3	16.6	13.1
30 Foreign	24.7	21.9	21.1	20.7	25.7	27.3	24.3	25.9
40 Economic	5.2	8.3	9.8	9.7	6.9	7.1	7.7	7.6
50 Crime	4.3	4.8	4.5	5.5	2.8	4.3	5.2	5.1
60 Home Affairs	5.2	6.6	6.9	5.8	6.9	5.6	5.4	7.2
70 Sport	7.1	7.6	7.5	5.0	4.1	6.5	6.0	7.4
80 Human Interest	4.6	5.3	5.4	4.2	5.1	3.2	4.7	6.6
90 Disasters	9.9	6.1	5.1	6.3	5.8	6.7	5.9	4.4
00 Science	—	0.7	1.5	0.5	2.0	1.3	1.8	1.6
Total %	100	99.9	100	99.9	100	99.9	99.9	100
n =	324	685	826	381	393	462	613	942

foreign items (in fact the highest proportion in any bulletin, both ITN and BBC) and a higher proportion of Northern Ireland news. These is also a greater proportion of disasters items. The proportionally smaller categories are human interest, politicians (personal) and science. The lunchtime audience has a high proportion of those housebound through age or family roles but the priorities of *First Report* do not appear to take this into account in any special way. Although Robert Kee's style of presentation may be an adaptation to the lunchtime audience, the high proportion of foreign news, disaster stories and Northern Ireland stories (which frequently deal with terrorist incidents), can be accounted for without reference ot the audience. *First Report* is the first major television news programme of the day and, as such, is likely to concentrate on the major stories which have broken early enough to be included. Many of the important but routine activities of politics, business and industry take place throughout the day and so cannot be fully reported at lunchtime. Untimely events such as disasters or news from different time zones abroad or news which is obtained from the EBU's first news exchange, therefore stands a greater chance of inclusion.[11]

News Extra caters for an audience of a different kind. Does its composition affect the range of story categories used? There is certainly no fundamental re-ordering of these priorities; the overall profile is similar to all other bulletins. As might be expected of a minority channel bulletin with longer than average items, there is a tendency to have somewhat fewer crime, sport and human interest stories and more in the political, foreign and science areas. What is significant for us is that there is no corresponding increase in the industrial news category. With only 15.3 per cent of industrial items, this bulletin has one of the lowest proportions. It would appear that an opportunity for extended coverage of these stories was not taken up in *News Extra*, which concentrated more on political and foreign news.

There is therefore little to suggest that the audience affects the priorities of television newsmen. These are broadly similar regardless of age, sex or class differences among the audience. The mix of news for any of these audience groups is the same as the news for any other group in a way that is quite uncharacteristic of other news media. The variations that do exist can be explained by reference to the time of day and to other factors which we will now consider.

Relative duration of categories

We have already noted that there are significant channel differences in the average length of industrial items. This is true also of categories other than industrial, although the differences are not so great. The distribution of items by category therefore has a profile which differs in certain respects from the profile that represents the allocation of time. Figure 4.5 provides the means for a systematic comparison of these duration profiles with the

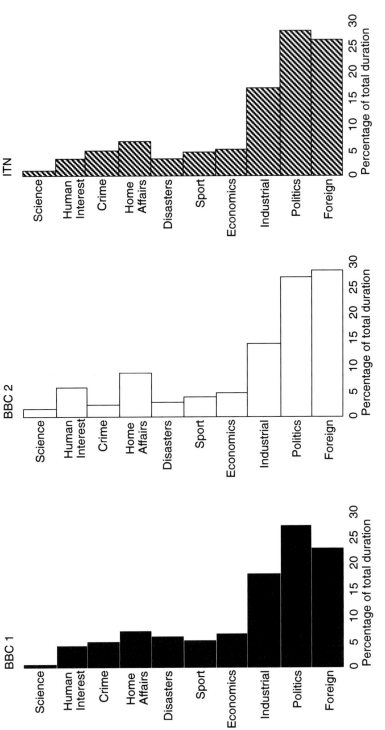

Figure 4.5 Content profiles for each channel (includes all bulletins) showing the size of each category as a percentage of total duration

distribution of items as shown in Figure 4.3.

In certain categories on BBC1 and ITN, the percentage duration is lower than the percentage of items. These are the categories of economic (City), crime, sport, human interest, disasters and science. The majority of political stories, on the other hand, have a significantly higher percentage duration, especially in category 16 (Conservative Party), which attracted a large amount of 'feature' coverage during the leadership election. On ITN, category 19 (politicians, personal) had a smaller percentage duration because these items have much the same function as human interest stories. In the same category on BBC1, the relationship between the number of items and duration is reversed because BBC made much of their exclusive Australian coverage of the Stonehouse story, often running it as a lead. Political news in general also has a higher percentage duration on BBC2 but, in contrast with the other two channels, sport, human interest, disaster and science stories actually received more time than would be anticipated from the count of items.

The most striking between-channel difference is in the relative number of items and the time devoted to them on BBC1 and ITN in the industrial and foreign categories. The differences are expressed in Table 4.5 as percentages of total bulletin items and durations. In each case the number of items allocated to the category is greater than the percentage of time devoted to them, except that ITN industrial items in contrast last longer than a simple item count would suggest. Thus, although individual industrial items are longer on ITN, the gap between the industrial coverage in general on BBC1 and ITN, which is apparent in the item profile, is narrowed considerably in the duration profile. The same is true with the foreign category.

This illustrates the limitations of any content analysis which looks at only one or a limited number of measures of 'content'. For instance, ITN's use of a large proportion of foreign items does reflect a basic journalistic concern to 'cover the waterfront' and aesthetic criteria in providing a contrasting and varied mix of items.

Table 4.5 Comparison of industrial and foreign coverage (all bulletins)

		Percentage of total no. of items		*Percentage of total duration*
Industrial	BBC1	18.5	>	17.4
	ITN	16.1	<	16.6
Foreign	BBC1	15.7	>	15.0
	ITN	19.2	>	16.7

II Who gets on?*

In the period of our study, the news was organised and produced substantially around the views of the dominant political group in our society. We have shown how the views of those who disagree fundamentally with this position, or who offered alternative approaches, were downgraded and under-represented in the news coverage. This is in stark comparison with the careful explanation and heavy emphasis given to the dominant analysis and the political policies flowed from it.

The content of news and the manner in which it was organised embodied a specific way of understanding the social and industrial world. In essence our case is that the numerical repetition of certain themes and explanations, together with the embracing and underlining of them by media personnel, are parts of a general process by which the news is produced from within a limited and partial world view. This is reflected in the choice of material, the themes that are emphasised, the links that are made between these, and the final conclusions that are drawn. At times, as we have shown, fragments of alternative information appear which could be linked, developed and emphasised to produce a quite different body of explanations and policy conclusions. It is a measure of the strength of the dominant social and economic interpretation of the news that this was never done in the whole four-month period covered by our analysis.

At its most basic, the organising principle of this interpretation is that the normal workings of the particular economic system are never treated as if they might themselves generate serious problems. Rather, the causes of economic problems are sought largely in the activities of trade unionists who reject the priorities and purposes of the dominant group. The logic and priorities of the social and economic order thus remain unchallenged. Instead, what we have in the news is a partial diagnosis of what social problems are, and how they may be solved, which is facilitated by a highly selective account of the nature and workings of that economic order.

The importance of this 'world view', which is implicit in journalistic practices, is that it prestructures what the news is to consist of and in a sense what the journalists themselves actually see as existing, or as being significant in the world. Thus information about the decline in investment, which would be a critical part of an alternative world view, is either not treated at all by news journalists, or occurs as a disparate fragment because it has no part in the 'normal' descriptions which they offer of the industrial crisis. The journalists themselves often reply to this with arguments couched in terms of

---

*Source: Glasgow University Media Group, *More Bad News*, London, Routledge & Kegan Paul, 1980, pp. 111–15.

'relevance' or audience-interest – as if investment figures are somehow intrinsically boring while other figures, for example on the amount of car production lost through a dispute, are somehow intrinsically interesting and therefore newsworthy. Yet such appeals to news value are in reality no more than appeals to the validity of their own world view. In the context of a different world view, figures on investment take on a completely different significance and meaning. Suppose, for example, that investment was low in an industry in part because of a management policy of distributing all profits as dividends.[12] Within the framework of *this* explanation of the economic crisis, new and dramatic headlines might suddenly suggest themselves, for example, 'A Million Jobs Threatened by Huge Dividends Payouts'.

The problem with the exclusive appeal to news values which journalists make in their own defence is that it assumes that everyone lives in the same world and sees it in the same way. Therefore newsworthiness is presented as being somehow 'natural' and 'obvious', an intrinsic property which the news journalist recognises instinctively and noses out. Thus a recent BBC pamphlet on the news argues as follows:

> The news value of a story is something immediately recognisable, intuitively sensed by a journalist who has been schooled in the provincial or national newsrooms. . . . The graduates of this school soon learn to spot the significant news point, the relevant detail, the interesting human touch which distinguishes the newsworthy story – the material with news value or news merits – from the candidate for the sub-editors' spike.[13]

This journalistic argument is circular. In fact, the 'significant', the 'relevant', and the merely 'interesting' are all embodied within this view of news values. The same pamphlet comments:

> In a sense the phrase 'news values' is to be used cautiously because it implies that there is an unchanging standard by which news can be measured and that is not true. The news value of a story is what a journalist recognises when he has been brought up in the tradition [editorial] of a particular newsroom or office. The BBC tradition is to tell people accurately and honestly about the most important things going on in the world; then, if there is room, to tell them the things which are very interesting even though they may not be significant, like the winner of the Derby, and in doing so to engage the attention of as many people as possible without lowering standards of judgement.

Of course, significance, relevance and importance can only be judged and are recognisable only by reference to the world view that these news values express. Our argument, then, is that the world view of journalists will prestructure what is taken to be important or significant. It will do this in two ways. First it will affect the character and content of specific inferential frames used in the news, as we showed above in relation to the definition of what industrial problems are. Second, it will set general boundaries on where news is looked for, and on who are the significant individuals, the 'important' people to be interviewed, etc. There are, of course, other news angles (other inferential frames) which are not so closely related to the articulation of the social and political ideologies that we have so far discussed. For example, the fascination with the 'dramatic' aspects of sex or violence.[14] However, it is not enough to characterise the attention to the dramatic, as such, as the prime determinant of what is produced as news. One effect of the political and economic world view of television journalism will be to prestructure the areas in which these dramatic news angles are sought. For example, a news story of an industrial dispute might also feature a commentary on a leading militant getting divorced. There are thus different sources of significance for news angles within the general framework of what is being examined and who is being reported. While some relate to more general social fascination (e.g. sex or violence), others will relate more directly to the social and political explanations which lead journalists initially to focus on an area and specific topics within it. The latter set of frames will take their significance from the explanation of what is wrong with industry: for example, the case of news coverage of production losses 'caused' by strikes. At all times, then, the organisation of news is constrained by the limits of the world view within which it is produced. This applies not only to the specific content of news stories and the generation of frames, but also to the organisation and control of who is allowed access to the media. Such access does not exist as an equal opportunity to express an opinion, put forward a viewpoint, or even to provide information. Even less do the media provide an open chance for all to influence the course of public discussion by affecting the terms of debate or the manner in which issues are structured in reporting. Access is structured and hierarchical to the extent that powerful groups and individuals have privileged and routine entry into the news itself and to the manner and means of its production. Our case study of the Glasgow dustcart drivers (in *Bad News*) indicated the relationship between the way in which an industrial news story is reported – the dominant interpretive framework – and the ability of the actors involved to appear on the news in order to present their case. That relationship, which reinforces the control over explanation in news reporting, is further illustrated in our evidence above.

It is frequently asserted by some journalists that the limitation of such news could be resolved mainly by having more time or space. Selection and interpretation are thus presented as the necessary result of editing, as there is always 'too much' material available. Such arguments, however, are merely quantitative and tell us nothing about the *quality* of what is produced or why it is that the same interpretations are systematically favoured and why alternative frameworks are routinely discarded. The essential argument which we have made is that a journalism which is rooted in a specific set of explanations about the nature of social reality is unable to encompass or explore the rationale of alternative world views. More time or space would really make little difference to this, for, as we have shown, information which could be used as part of an alternative view, even when it appears, is not used to develop in a systematic way alternative themes and explanations. It appears as fragments in a flow of information organised within the dominant framework.

The day-to-day production of news is based on the inherited wisdom of journalistic routines, assumptions about the audience and about the society that is being reported. This is what enables the journalist in the newsroom to 'recognise' the newsworthy truth with apparent certainty. Against this background, the bland assertion of objectivity and impartiality as a regular professional achievement is little more than the unsupported claim to a unique understanding of events. This serves only to obfuscate what is in fact the reproduction of the dominant assumptions about our society – the assumptions of the powerful about what is important, necessary and possible within it.

III Appendices*

APPENDIX 1

Four of the categories were divided into sub-categories. Six were not subdivided. The lighter categories (in press terms) of sport, human interest and disasters, remained as wholes. The only problem was in the disaster area. It was decided to categorise near misses as disasters (e.g. aircraft mishaps), all deaths by accident as disasters even when only one person was involved. But the deaths of the famous, that is where obituary material was broadcast, were categorised as human interest. This area was defined quite strictly, and we sought to place stories perhaps conceived of as human interest into other more concrete categories, e.g. collapsing houses into disaster or home affairs. But we did include royalty in this category; this caused some problems during the second phase since a major political story blew up about the Queen's finances (10) at exactly the moment she was on a state visit to Mexico (80).

Science was largely determined by the presence of the news services' science correspondent. It was not subdivided. It overrode the foreign category since space stories, etc., are normally the province of the science correspondent and not the foreign correspondent in the country concerned. This is not, however, true of crime, therefore the category crime did not override the category foreign. That is to say, crime stories from abroad were categorised as foreign stories.

---

*First published in GUMG, *Bad News*, London, Routledge & Kegan Paul, 1976, pp. 269–87.

The industrial category was not broken up because we knew that a major part of our work would be involved in the detailed analysis of industrial stories and that we would have them to hand on the archive video-cassettes for further breakdown.

Thus politics (10), foreign (30), economics (40), and home affairs (60) were all subdivided.

10–11	Parliamentary politics	16	Conservative party internal
12	Northern Ireland	17	Liberal party internal
13	Terrorist	18	Other parties and pressure
14	Demonstrations		groups
15	Labour party internal	19	Politicians personal

We were less interested in Westminster stories than the newsrooms are. Therefore we tended to reallocate Westminster stories by their subject matter – so that, for instance, government monthly figures would be placed in the appropriate economic category, the doings of the Secretary of State for Northern Ireland in the Northern Ireland category, and so on. We included in Northern Ireland (12) all activities of the IRA in the Republic of Ireland as well as in Britain, all Republican political news if it related to the North. The main problems here were that bomb explosions in the United Kingdom outside the Province were not always attributable to, or indeed attributed to, Irish activists. Therefore, they would be placed in category 13 (terrorist). Rarely would a bomb story remain without a suggested source for the device for more than one bulletin. If it was then attributed to Irish groups all references were placed in 12. Irish Republic stories not relating to the north were categorised as foreign (30). The trials of bombers were categorised as 12 not as crime (50) and this applied also to the trials of other non-Irish 'terrorists'; they were 13 not crime (50).

During this period demonstrations were not generally reported as events in themselves but rather related to the demonstrators' grievances. Thus, protests against imports were placed in the general industrial category (20).

Category 18 relates not only to parties represented in Parliament (SNP, Plaid Cymru) but also to those unrepresented (Communist Party of Great Britain, etc.) and to pressure groups whose activities are directed to Parliament. (These would include the various groups established around the Referendum campaign over Britain's continued membership of the EEC.)

Category 19 relates to those stories which would otherwise be 80, human interest, if the principal figure was not a politician. Mr Heath's yachting was the example in mind. As it happened nearly all stories subsequently categorised as 19 related to John Stonehouse and that, therefore, in this connection, 19 overrode 50, crime.

Categories 15, 16 and 17 are self-explanatory.

30–31 Britain and the World   32   The World

It was thought that this area would be broken down geographically and categories for each area of the world were determined. But after the initial dry-runs we decided to simplify these inputs mainly because it was not an area of primary interest to the project. Only the balance between domestic and foreign was deemed important. Britain and the World (31), included UK foreign policy, all EEC stories, except the Referendum campaign which was nearly always reported as a domestic political story; Britain and the UN and Britons involved in events abroad. Category 32 included all foreign stories except sport, disasters and science. Thus industrial and crime stories from abroad were classified as foreign. Some economic stories were classified as foreign as well – for instance, reports of other countries' balance of payments, unemployment, etc., were foreign but international commodity and currency markets were classified as economic. Foreign-industrial and where appropriate, foreign-economic were kept and transferred to the archive.

40–41 Economics, City   43   Economics, Commodities
42   Economics, Currency   44   Economics, Business

The city category included stock market stories, especially the regular reporting of such indicators as the Financial Times Share Index (FT Index) as well as the government's balance of payments statistics. Category 42 included the performance of the Pound and all stories relating to the international currency market. It overrode the category foreign since it was normally reported by the economics correspondents. Category 43, commodities, included world fuel stories as well as the operation of the international food markets. It did not include gold, which was categorised as 42, nor did it include domestic consumer stories about food prices which were categorised under home affairs. This category too overrode the foreign unless the story was presented as an entirely domestic problem for the country concerned – i.e. third-world food riots would be 32, but such riots related to the operation of the Chicago Grain Market would be 43. Category 44 was concerned with the performance of business, especially as it turned out, with business collapses. It thus overrode category 41 when company shares were suspended; and overrode 50, crime, when companies were accused of fraud. But if such stories included an element of short-time working, layoffs or dismissals, they would be categories as 20, industrial. Pronouncements by the CBI on business performance as well as Parliament's intervention in the affairs of business, would be 44. The general tendency however, was to move such stories towards the industrial category if labour was at all involved in the reporting of the situation.

60–61 Home Affairs, local   63   Home Affairs, the quality of
       government   life
62   Home Affairs, consumer   64   Home Affairs, race

The local government category included all stories relating to charges and services made and provided by local government including primary and secondary education. It also included local government corruption and thus overrode crime (50). Category 62 included public service utilities as well as consumer stories relating to good and services. The environment (63) included pollution stories (but not when they occurred abroad), health (but not in its industrial or scientific aspects), and all stories relating to the preservation of the environment in town and country. Race (64) included all immigration stories as well as reports from the countries from whence immigrants came. It did not include stories of Britons as immigrants which were normally classified as 31, Britain and the World.

APPENDIX 2, INITIAL LOGGING SHEET: EXPLANATION OF TERMS

Basic identification information

Along the top of the Initial Logging Sheet (see Figure 4.6) is the basic identification information. Also across the top are spaces for the names of the television personnel involved in the broadcast and some aide-mémoires to subsidiary classification systems which will be explained below. All information as to date, channel, time and logger (i.e. the person responsible for the log), were standardised to expedite the transference of the information on to computer coding sheets. Thus the date became 263 rather than 26 March 1975 or other variations and the project members were assigned numbers to be used in the logger box.

The time of transmission was normally the advertised time according to the programme journals and the lateness of bulletins relative to such times was not noted. Anyway the BBC1 main bulletins at nine and ITN's *News at Ten* represented fixed scheduling points so that it was only BBC2's *News Extra* during phase two of the project that was regularly broadcast minutes after its advertised time.

Item numbers

The first column on the sheet below these basic identification boxes is for the item number. We did not note the opening titles of bulletins when they did not involve the use of different newsfilm or photographs which changed from bulletin to bulletin. Sometimes, however, a major story would cause a change in the opening which would be noted; e.g. the substitution of Mrs Thatcher for Mr Heath in the standard *First Report* opening title after her election as leader. With the major bulletins, BBC1 at 9 o'clock and ITN's *News at Ten*, the bulletin began with headlines unillustrated on the BBC but illustrated on ITN and punctuated there by a single chime of Big Ben. In ITN these

Figure 4.6 Appendix 2: Initial Logging Sheet

DATE	1–3	PERSONNEL CODE	COR. B	REP. 11	REP. 15
CHANNEL	5	N/C 1	COR. C	REP. 12	REP. 16
T/X	6	N/C 2	COR. D	REP. 13	REP. 17
LOGGER	7		COR. A	REP. 10	REP. 14	REP. 18

INTERVIEWEES:
1. Central Fig
2. Spokesman
3. Opp. Spokesman
4. Vox Pop
5. Witness
6. Conf.
7. Expert

GRAPHICS:
1. Cap Sup
2. Pix
3. Graphics
4. Anim. Gr.
5. Map
6. Wire
7. Cap. Seq.
8. R.C. Cap.

COMMENTS, e.g.:
Non Broadcast Film Source
Amateur Film Source
Promotions
Public Service
Women
Blacks
Length of Item
Multiple Inputs

No.	HEADLINE	SUBHEAD	Overall DUR	PERSONNEL (see Code)			INTERVIEWEES NAME	STATUS	FILM				VTR Live								Lib	RC	GR	T/F	ARCHIVE	COMMENTS
				IN	V/O	INT.			SOF	F/X	BW	Pool		St.	REM	OB	EBU	Sat.	Pool				GR see code	T/F		
10–11	12–13		14	16–18	20–21	22–23	24–25		27	28	29	30	31	32	33	34	35	36	37	38	39	40	41–48	49	

TECHNICS

headlines are known as 'the Bongs'. We noted the contents of the headlines but did not number them as items. Similarly at the end of the first part of *News at Ten* the newscaster reveals the major stories to be seen after the commercial break. Here again we did not number this *hooker* but noted its contents. Some bulletins close with a straightforward and unchanging formula. The main BBC1 news repeated the main points at the end of the bulletin. *First Report* on ITV always concluded with a short item giving the Financial Times Share Index and weather for the day. We did not number these items. Therefore, only the changing items in the bulletin proper excluding openings and closings were numbered.

The tendency of British newsmen to package has been noted (F. Rositi *et al.*, *News and Current Events on TV – An Analysis of Television News on Four European Television Organizations*, Prix Italia Report, Florence, 1975), and above we commented on the difficulties this raised in trying to itemise the bulletins. Indeed, the lengthier the packages, the better the news is seen to be in the eyes of those producing it.

Apart from personnel changes noted above, the guidelines to whether one was dealing with one item, two items, or one item segued out of another, were in the scripts themselves. Thus, a sequence of stories concerned with the parliamentary row about the Queen's finances could be followed by the Queen herself in Mexico and Prince Charles on his way to Kathmandu for the royal wedding. This could be one item if introduced as a Royals package or two items with the royal journeys segueing out of the political story and the Charles element being a payoff to the Mexican story, depending on the form of the script. Statistical stories and general city stories are often used to introduce or pay off and close particular business and economic stories. In such cases these elements would count as one item with the particular story so introduced or paid off.

On occasions there are breakdowns in the presentation and items are abandoned to be picked up later in the bulletin. In such cases the initial item number was re-used. In stories which were breaking as the bulletin was being broadcast, this was not done, and any return to the story for updating was given a fresh item number. In both these circumstances a note was made in the last 'comments' column of the logging sheet.

Headline and subheading column

The headline and subheading column were in no sense designed to make possible systematic content notes. Again they were to reflect journalistic practice to be used as *catch lines*. The headline was a basic indicator of the story while the subheading reflected any developments in the story or some other detail. Thus, the Lesley Whittle kidnapping became 'Lesley' and the subhead would detail developments, e.g. 'Brother offers Ransom'. In packages the subhead column would detail the contents of the package. Thus,

'Car Industry' might yield 'Layoffs at Jaguar', 'Redundancy talks Vauxhall', '25% drop in Car Sales', in the subhead column.

Overall duration column

Overall duration of items did include standardised openings and closings, e.g. 'Good evening'. The only problem encountered was with pick-up lines coming out of the end of one item, e.g. following a film report the newscaster back-announces the name of the reporter. In such cases the back-announcement was timed as part of the follow-item. Items were timed in minutes and seconds, and subsequently were decimalised for computer processing. Hookers (as at the end of the first part of *News at Ten*) and headlines were timed but not, as explained above, given an item number or categorised or included in the total bulletin duration.

TV personnel

The next three columns on the sheet related to television personnel. The project distinguished, as do newsrooms, between newscasters, correspondents and reporters and the numbers entered into these columns were taken from the boxes running across the top of the sheet. Essentially newscasters never leave the studio. If they do they become correspondents or reporters. In ITN during the period of the study, there were three reporter/newscasters and they were entered on to the sheet according to the function they were performing in the particular bulletin. Correspondents were normally introduced as such. If a reporter was introduced as a correspondent, he was noted as a correspondent for that bulletin, not as a reporter. Not all personnel are named. If they were not named, 'un-named' was entered into the reporter box, one entry for every un-named person. Naming could be either by the newscaster or correspondent mentioning the name in script or by the use of a caption giving the name (a supercaption). The reporter/correspondent division does not always reflect the hierarchy within the organisations but does indicate slightly different functions on the screen. Correspondents, especially the Westminster and economic staff, are often reported by the newscaster as explaining the significance of information they do not themselves appear reporting. Reporters, unless eyewitnesses, are never so quoted. In other words the correspondents are partially thus accorded the status of outside experts. At its most extreme they were often interviewed by the newscasters on BBC2's *News Extra*. BBC regional reporters, reporters belonging to other commercial television companies, when named were entered, as were reporters belonging to foreign networks. Residual categories were created for the purposes of computing; un-named foreign reporters for members of other networks; un-named personnel for other ITV reporters; 'sports commentators', for those working for ITV network sports programmes. The newsroom's own sports correspondents were treated like other correspondents.

The three columns 'IN', 'V/O', 'Int' stand for 'in-vision', 'voice-over' and 'interview' respectively. It was decided to note the appearance of personnel in this way because although presentation seeks to establish the personnel as personalities, it was also known that one criterion of effectiveness used by the broadcasters was the extent to which the so-called 'talking heads' 'in vision' could be avoided in the bulletin. 'In vision' means seeing the newscasters, correspondent or reporter talking to camera whether in the studio or outside on film or videotape. 'Voice-over' means cutting away from that talking head while the voice continues over film, videotape, photograph or graphic for however short a time, or indeed never seeing the face at all. 'Interview' means that the personnel concerned conducted an interview whether they were heard or seen during the interview or not. If they were seen asking a question or nodding – the standard device for editing answers to avoid unsightly jumps – this did not count as 'in vision'. In each of these columns the number of the box at the top of the sheet was entered as appropriate.

Interviewees

Interviewees were deemed to include any person not employed by the broadcasting institution who was allowed to speak on camera. This, therefore, included press conferences, speeches, overheard arguments. If no name was given, 'un-named' was entered in the 'name' column. The 'status' column was for indicating why the person was on the news. Thus, if Lord Wigg was being interviewed on the Common Market Campaign, it was his status in that campaign not his connection with the Betting Levy Board that was noted. A short categorisation list was generated for interviewees and it was placed at the top of the sheet as an aide-mémoire.

1   *Central figure* This applied basically to human interest stories or to situations such as the arrival in London of President Makarios following the attempted coup in Cyprus.
2   *Spokesman* This applied to all figures not so directly involved; all officials, police officers, public relations and press officers, politicians. The vast majority of news interviews are therefore with spokesmen.
3   *Opposition spokesman* It was only easy to determine an opposition spokesman in two circumstances; first, where such an interview directly followed a 'spokesman' interview, for example, as when management follow union or vice versa; second, where a member of the parliamentary opposition appeared criticising government policy. This would place him or her in the opposition category whether a government spokesman appeared or not. However, in practice it became difficult to operate the distinction between spokesman and opposition spokesman in any other circumstances.

4   *Vox pop* (*vox populi* – as used by the broadcasting industry). Classically this is a series of short remarks from people in the street on a given topic but we used it to identify all situations where more than one person was interviewed, without being more than generally identified; most typically this would include people in the street but also groups of workers either filmed collectively – any short sequences of separate talking heads where no one is named.

5   *Witness* This category includes witnesses to a situation most usually a crime, disaster or act of terrorism.

6   *Conferences* Normally this is a situation where more than one reporter is present asking questions and therefore it is normally an occasion arranged by the interviewee for the purposes of passing on information. It was also deemed to include situations in which speeches are made but not situations where the camera crew overhears private conversation. Thus, all speeches at party conferences, although these are not designed as press conferences, were included in this category. Under this head all the other categories in this list could also be included. The category 6 never stood by itself.

7   *Expert* Initially it was felt that the expert was more the province of the current affairs programme but occasionally the news turns to experts for information. During the period of our sample, BBC2 *News Extra* frequently treated its own correspondents in this way as has been noted, and *First Report* on ITV also made use of outside experts, normally in the field of science or foreign affairs and normally for the purposes of offering explanations of the events reported on in the bulletin. Experts could normally be distinguished from spokesmen by the way they were introduced, the word 'expert' often being used in the script or implied in the supercaption.

Technics

The remaining columns, headed 'Technics', dealt with a whole range of technical inputs available to the newsrooms. The first four columns dealt with film. Most inputs from locations other than studios will be on film.

Film

During the period of the study the newsrooms were beginning to grapple with a revolution in technique which involved the greater utilisation of videotape from Outside Broadcast units. Until very recently the use of Outside Broadcast units required three lorries, a crew of more than twenty men, and many hours of preparation to bring the unit on line. It therefore represented major utilisation of resources and was typically only used for important breaking stories. Now much smaller and more malleable, Outside Broadcast units are coming into greater use. However, for the period of the study it is true that film was generally still quicker and, with normal two-man units, less demanding of resources than Outside Broadcasts. The great advantage of the Outside Broadcast (OB) is that, when rigged in, it can be used to give instantaneous coverage from an outside source.

Therefore, although this change (to Electronic News Gathering – ENG) was taking place, in filling out this part of the basic logging sheet we assumed film was used unless the story itself revealed that it was either a live input or that it had come in less than one hour before the bulletin. In the latter case it had to be an OB because the process of developing and editing film normally takes longer than one hour.

Even without overt clues, with practice it was felt possible for the research team to distinguish film from electronic sources since the quality of the picture is obviously different. But, there again, during the period of the study this was becoming more difficult since new film stocks had been introduced with the specific purpose of better matching the quality of film to electronic output.

'SOF', 'F/X', 'BW' and 'Pool', mean 'Sound of film', 'Effects', 'Black-and-white' and 'Pool'.

SOF In technical terms almost all film now used on television is SOF; that is to say it is recorded by lightweight silent running cameras ('self blimped') operating in synchronisation with lightweight battery recorders, a system perfected in the early 1960s and now widely used. The newsrooms also use a previously perfected system whereby both sound and picture are recorded in the camera by means of a recording head on to a magnetic stripe running down one side of the film. Whether single system (the magnetic stripe) or double-headed (the separate tape recorder), both systems allow all the sounds of a location to be recorded. The newsrooms still use the single system because, although it only allows for crude editing and can be spotted because of this, it nevertheless gives the possibility of greater speed since with the double-headed system the sound has to be transferred from ordinary $\frac{1}{4}$ inch magnetic tape to special 16 mm magnetic film before editing can begin.

We were not interested in the above distinction and therefore slightly misused the technical expression 'SOF'. By it we indicated speech which the viewer was allowed to hear uninterrupted by other noises. Thus all interviews were 'SOF', as were all reporter or correspondent pieces to camera, speeches, slanging matches, etc. But if at any time commentary drowns out the speech, then the film is not, for our purposes, 'SOF'.

F/X Here again a technical abbreviation was being consciously misused by the project. Before the introduction of the filming systems mentioned above, F/X meant all non-speech noises added to pieces of silent film. We used it to indicate film with commentary spoken over, whether it had noises of its own or not. This included speech when overlaid by commentary.

BW Black-and-white film only appeared when it was taken from the library of newsfilm which both broadcasting institutions maintain or when it came from a source which had not yet colourised. These included the most remote studios in the network (Aberdeen) as well as some foreign sources.

'Pool' We knew there to be an elaborate system of obtaining film from outside sources: primarily the European Broadcasting Union (EBU). Each day newsfilm is passed from the participating European national networks to all other EBU affiliates. Whether the film in question was 'pool' or not could only be determined by comparing BBC with ITN. If the film on all channels was the same, it came from a common source, such as the EBU news exchange. Such film is passed round the EBU network electronically and not physically. It is therefore recorded on to videotape by the accepting network and transmitted in that form. For our purposes, however, we noted it in these columns rather than in the subsequent videotape columns because in its original form it was film and not tape. In the table this is 'Pool A'.

Electronic

The next eight columns refer to possible electronic inputs. This did not include noting the basic mode of the bulletins which were known always to be live and from a central news studio. The eight columns therefore refer to inputs analogous to film inputs. If they are electronic they can themselves be live or stored on tape (VTR). Normally live inserts come from other correspondents and reporters in the same studio. Clues as to whether it is live or VTR can be seen at the beginning and end of an insert – newscaster looking off camera to monitor, obvious reactions to the cue to start talking on the part of the correspondent/reporter are the most evident. If the insert begins with an interviewee, the clue is yet more apparent than this. If the interviewee talks before the interviewer, then it must be VTR since no amateur performer, interviewee, would be trusted to take the cue to begin. The cue must be given to the interviewer and if it is not seen it means that the interview must be recorded so that the front of the interview could be lost and the VTR started on the answer. Other clues as to the use of tape are that if an identical studio interview appears throughout the day, although there may be some ambiguity as to the mode of its initial appearance, thereafter it must be VTR. And this also applies to reports from correspondents and reporters. If the report does not change from bulletin to bulletin then clearly each use subsequent to the first must be VTR.

In the event it was found that this was not as meaningful a distinction as had been anticipated. The assumption was that the use of VTR represented an increased importance in the minds of the newsroom. But our observation study subsequently showed that the use of tape is so well integrated into the routine practices of the studio as to make the assumption unworkable. The problems involved in distinguishing 'live' from 'VTR' were eventually seen as being of minor importance.

The next six columns can be either 'live' or 'VTR' although the tendency is for the last three, 'EBU', 'Sat' and 'Pool', to be on tape.

'St' = Studio This involves noting the use of any other television studio in the United Kingdom. It is normally introduced as being from another studio and often the backing in that studio includes a direct reference to where it is, e.g. 'BBC Leeds' on the flat behind the reporter's head. For the BBC this means all BBC regional studios and for ITN the studios of the fifteen commercial television companies. It also means those studios in Westminster and Broadcasting House which are operated by the BBC remotely from their central news studios at the Television Centre in west London. It also means studios established for particular purposes as at the party conferences each year.

'REM' = Remote' Like SOF and F/X this is a technical term which we use unconventionally. In American television parlance, Remote means the same as Outside Broadcast does in the UK. It is not used in the UK at all. 'Remote' in our usage means a television studio either permanent or temporary in any other company, normally within the EBU or in the USA. It is the foreign equivalent of 'Studio'.

'OB' = Outside Broadcast Unit A mobile television unit carrying with it camera equipment, lights, sound equipment and videotape recorder, requiring some twenty odd men to operate and many hours to bring on line. It can be used either in or out of doors and it sends signals back to the studio by microwave link. Its output can be used live, recorded at the central studio or recorded at the OB. The new generation of OBs mentioned above (ENG) represent a major breakthrough in television technology since the equipment has been made very much lighter and more mobile, requiring a van instead of trucks and five men instead of twenty. During the period of the study this equipment was being experimented with. Normally the Outside Broadcast units use is indicated in the introduction, either by direct reference to it or by the announcement that we are being taken to a remote point for a live report. It represents a major decision as to the importance of a story to commit the OB to it, although as the new generation of equipment is introduced, this will become less true. Eventually, some argue, such Electronic News Gathering (ENG) will replace film in the newsrooms altogether. Apart from direct references of this sort, OBs can be spotted because of the quality of the picture which better matches that of the studio than film and because they have more than one camera at a location, cuts can be made on continuous action; e.g. an interviewer interrupting an interviewee, where we cut to the interviewer as soon as he starts to talk. This cannot be done with a single film camera.

EBU = European Broadcasting Union (or Eurovision) The European television networks exchange news stories on a daily basis. These are usually film in the first instance although they may be transmitted after transference to tape. In receiving countries they are always recorded on to tape since the exchange process involves utilising the cable and microwave linking system of the EBU. Eurovision joins its eastern European equivalent Intervision in Prague. If pictures originate in Eastern Europe, which includes the whole of the USSR to the Pacific, then it was noted in this column and a further note 'Intervision' was made in the 'comments' column. The clues as to the use of the Eurovision news exchange material are, first, that the same footage will be used on BBC and ITN, although often, if there is enough material, two services may transmit it in slightly different ways. Second, there will be a voice-over commentary from the studios, since news change material is passed without commentary. Third, the logistics of the material might well indicate that it could only have arrived via Eurovision; that is to say, film of events in a distant part of Europe which could not have reached London and been processed as film in time for the bulletins. Last, it could well be black-and-white since some EBU services are not yet colourised. If the REM column has been ticked, it is certain that if the reporter or correspondent is in a studio in Europe, the picture must have come via the EBU link. This involved a tick in the EBU column as well, since the factor being highlighted in all these technic columns is expenditure. The news exchange which happens on a 'multilateral' basis is cheaper than a 'unilateral' because the fixed cost of lines, etc. are shared by all participating networks in the former instance but not the latter. This unilateral use of the system is a clear indicator as to the importance of a foreign story in the eyes of the newsroom.

SAT = Satellite Once all pictures arriving by satellite were announced as such. Now with the firm establishment of the system it is only when the picture quality degenerates that the 'via satellite' caption is used. There is no daily exchange of material via the satellite system analogous to the EBU system. It is extremely expensive even when used multilaterally. Opening a satellite for multilateral use or, even more so, for unilateral use, represents considerable expenditure and is therefore used sparingly and this suggests we may regard its presence as an indicator of importance. Even if not announced, its use can be spotted by the same criteria as with EBU above – use of commentary, shared pictures, black-and-white pictures and the impossibility of obtaining pictures from the far corners of the globe quickly by any other means. Most of the world's major sources of stories are within each of satellite stations, sometimes even when there is no really effective parallel print news agency. The cost of the satellites make them prohibitively expensive to use, so that the physical transportation of film back to base, if it is consistent with the importance of the story and the speed deemed to be necessary, will be preferred. Satellite and EBU are modes of communication and can therefore be ticked in conjunction with a number of other columns, most notably film where either system is used to transmit material originated on film as described above.

'Pool' This indicated the use of the EBU or satellite for some joint (multilateral) coverage which itself originated on tape. The most obvious examples being an American televised press conference or rocket launches.

Other pooled material originating as film should be noted in the Film/Pool column. In the tables this is 'Pool B'.

Lower cost inputs

The next three columns represent inputs requiring lower expenditure than the others thus far mentioned in the technics section. They are 'Lib', Library; 'RC', radio circuit; and 'GR', Graphics.

Lib = Library Both institutions maintain extensive archives of film material and in this column the use of such previous filmed material was noted. However, determining whether it came from the library or not required using the following guidelines. Library material was easiest to spot when the film was referred to in the script or by a dated caption as not being current. Occasionally it could be spotted because it was cut into current film but was black-and-white whereas the rest of the story was colour. In oil rig stories from Aberdeen the reverse was true (i.e. the library material was colour). In obituaries, film of the deceased must obviously be library.

More difficult to determine was the use of stock shots. The oil rig is but one example. Stock shots would include general footage of neutral material, i.e. general shots of building sites or car assembly lines and the like. Normally such shots would be used in general stories which did not have other current film in them. Noting the presence of library film in this column also meant noting its form in the film columns; i.e. B/W or SOF, etc.

Although the above concentrates on film library, there is also an archive of videotape which includes important political speeches or interviews that are deemed to have life beyond the immediate. These are a rare input. If used, the appropriate VTR columns were ticked as well as this library column.

RC = Radio circuit This is the cheapest way of using foreign correspondents. It is therefore far commoner than REM. By using the radio circuit or, at a pinch, an ordinary telephone line, the reporter can broadcast voice only into the programme live or on to audio tape. This is normally illustrated by the use of captions. If Radio circuits are used to get the most up-to-the-minute commentary on to film (which can sometimes be spotted because of the quality of voice reproduction involved), that was not noted. It was registered as V/O and F/X in the film columns. Occasionally for a breaking story that happens too late or is not important enough for any use of the OB, the reporter will phone into the programme live from within the UK. This also happens if a story breaks in areas where there are no television facilities. In each of these cases RC was noted.

GR = Graphics This included all non-moving images put onto the screen. Eight categories were distinguished and an aide-mémoire printed at the top of the sheet. The categories are as follows:

1   *Cap. Sup. = Supercaption* The 'nameplate'. It was noted for inter-viewees and personnel. It also includes any superimposed writing placed over another film, tape or live image.

2   *Pix = Photographs* These are of two main sorts: portrait shots of news personalities and general news photographs. The differences between them was not noted after the initial drafts of the logging sheet. There are old news pictures which are used in much the same way as library material. The distinction here was also ignored.

3   *Graphic* Work of the graphics department beyond the 'name-plate'. This includes all graphs, cartoons, logos, and writing that is transmitted without being superimposed onto another image, e.g. football results.

4   *Anim. Gr. = Animated graphic* The greatest amount of effort by the graphic department. It is in essence the same as category 3 except that it moves; normally by pulling away strips of the top layer of the work to reveal further information beneath. This can be used to enliven such matters as the Budget.

5   *Map* This is a self-explanatory category, although it should be noted that if any movement is involved (i.e. to illustrate the progress of a battle) then it was noted as graphics category 4 not 5.

6   *Wire = News photographs received telegraphically* Much of the criteria for spotting these was that used in the case of EBU and Satellite. They are black-and-white, often of poor definition, and their provenance indicates they could not be received by any other means. It is a relatively expensive way of getting photos to the screen. We assumed that unless there were internal clues, most European and all British photographs would be category 2 not 6.

7   *Cap. Seq. = Caption Sequence* This means a set of photographs and graphics used as film (action stills). These often require considerable rehearsal time in the studio. This category does not mean a simple sequence of portrait photographs used one after another to illustrate, say, a political argument. It involves camera movement relative to the graphic material and will normally last for more than 30 seconds. At the outset of the project we expected to find caption sequences entirely limited to illustrating scientific stories.

8   *R.C. Cap. = Radio Circuit Caption* Both ITN and the BBC have a particular sort of graphic to cover voice-only reports sent by telephone or radio circuit. This normally consists of a small photograph of the correspondent or reporter concerned imposed on some iconic photograph of the place he is speaking from with his name and the place written below.

T/F and Archive

The next two columns were for the internal use of the project.

T/F = Transfer A tick in this column indicated that the logger felt the item should be transferred to the archive.

Archive In this column the technicians noted onto which video-cassette the item had been transferred. The video-cassettes were numbered sequentially and each item was separated on transfer by a further number. Thus 263 ITN 2200 item No. 6 (the 6th item in *News at Ten* on 26 March) would become AVC 35 No. 15. The technicians used a simple videcon camera and handwritten cards to put the archive item numbers onto the cassettes.

Comments

The last column was for comments. Many of the suggested areas that might be noted have already been described. In addition we noted here the use of women and black personnel, out of the ordinary caption descriptions of interviewees, material from unusual sources such as amateur film; and we made general comments as to exceptionally lengthy or complex items, poor quality of image, mistakes in presentation and so on.

NOTES

1 P. Rock, 'News as eternal recurrence' in S. Cohen and J. Young (eds) *The Manufacture of News*, London: Constable, 1973.
2 M. Frayn, 'The Tin Men' in ibid.
3 A study of news and current affairs programming in the USA concluded that 'The quantity of news and public affairs programming shown, the types of programming offered, the scheduling factors associated with these programmes, and even the content of the programming were largely explicable in economic terms.... The use to which air time was put was basically a function of the quest for profit and only secondarily a function of other factors.' There is a close relationship between audiences and profits. P. Wolf, *Television Programming for News and Public Affairs*, New York: Praeger, 1972, p. 137.
4 For a 'professional' view see, for example, Paul Fox, 'One hour of television news?', *The Listener*, London: BBC, 20 November 1975.
5 Taking all weekday bulletins there is a correlation of +0.51 (s = 0.001) between the number of items and the length of the bulletin, i.e. length does not account for the whole of the variation in the number of items.
6 John Birt and Peter Jay have claimed that current television journalism contains a 'bias against understanding' which can be attributed to its antecedents in newspapers and documentary film (*The Times*, 28 February, 30 September, 1 October 1975). They imply that one condition for eliminating the bias would be an extension in the length of the news and recommend a daily, one-hour programme containing news headlines and detailed treatment of about six main stories.
7 This does not mean that interviews normally last longer than 4 minutes but that they will be part of items that do. Three out of ten news items contain interviews.
8 Franco Rositi, *The Television News Programme: Fragmentation and Reconstruction of our Image of Society*, Prix Italia Report, 1975; English version, p. 13.
9 With the exception that the average length of items in the home affairs and

science categories on BBC2 arises because many of these items are comparable to feature articles in the press.

10   See for example, Raymond Williams, *Communications*, Harmondsworth: Penguin, 1962, esp. ch. 3.

11   See chapter 6 in which it is shown that unions such as ASTMS aim for *First Report*. Given early coverage, it is possible that the story will reappear in later bulletins.

12   See the British Leyland case study in Glasgow University Media Group, *Bad News*, London: Routledge & Kegan Paul, 1976, Chapter 7, pp. 243–56.

13   *The Task of Broadcasting News*, a study for the BBC General Advisory Council published by the BBC, May 1976, p. 12.

14   This is not to say that ideology and the production of world views operate only at the level of the explicit explanation of the social and economic world, and that what is taken as sensational and dramatic is somehow natural and pre-given. Sex and violence, for example, are dramatic angles in many news stories, but we must ask what kind of a society it is that generates an obsession with these and with property and control as key elements of both. The particular form and content of what is taken as sensational is obviously socially and historically determined, presumably the need to seek out and present the sensational and dramatic is as well.

Chapter 5

Contours of coverage*

No aspect of communication is so impressive as the enormous number of choices and discards which have to be made between the formation of the symbol in the mind of the communicator, and the appearance of a related symbol in the mind of the receiver.

(Wilbur Schramm)

NEWS SELECTION

The notion of 'the gatekeeper function' is one of extreme importance in considering the televising of news. Even more than in print media the editorial process whittles down, from the vast range of events occurring on any given day in the world, an extremely small number of discrete stories which go to make up the bulletins. In answer to the charge of extreme and idiosyncratic selection, the television newsman often responds with what might be called 'the time defence', that is to say the length of the bulletins heavily constrains the number of stories that can be carried and this in turn determines the nature of 'the gate'. We have seen above[1] how the regularities of the bulletin express this production ethic on a day-to-day basis and on what occasions the pattern is disturbed; normally by the process we have called, following Frank, 'swamping'.[2] In the debate about the possibility of extending the news bulletin's time – a demand made in the name of increasing the under-standability of the stories by giving more background information – the professionals concerned indicated that if they were indeed given more space, they would be inclined to increase the discrete number of stories covered rather than the length of the items within the bulletins.[3]

It then becomes reasonable to suggest that 'the time defence' is less an acknowledgement of the technical restrictions of the form involved but rather a legitimation of an editorial function which effectively conceals its character.

---

*First published in Glasgow University Media Group, *Bad News*, London, Routledge & Kegan Paul, 1976, pp. 140–204.

What is hereby offered is therefore not a critique of the practices of the television newsrooms in terms of a theoretical model of journalistic requirements but rather a critique that questions the assumptions underlying selection processes. To do this we shall map the contours of television's coverage of industrial life in the United Kingdom during the first twenty-two weeks of 1975.

A news bulletin is organised as a sequence of items and can vary in terms of its internal complexity. An item may be a simple report.[4] An item may constitute several reports often of only one sentence each. These may be of several different industries and each will be reported.[5] It may constitute a more complex grouping or 'packaging'. For example, an item on the car industry may bring together reports on a strike in one car plant, car production figures, and foreign imports of cars to the UK.[6]

The basic element is therefore the *report*, of which there is generally only one relating to a particular story in a single *bulletin*, but perhaps several reports each relating to different stories within an *item*. A story may run over several days or even weeks and may appear in more than one report. It may be meshed into news items in various ways. The simplest example is the equivalence of one report = one item = one story. In practice this is rare. A story is usually reported more than once. When it is reported, it may take up the whole of an item, or be part of an item. So, for example, the Glasgow dustcart drivers' strike was reported many times, sometimes in items about a number of ongoing Scottish strikes, sometimes in conjunction with the Liverpool dustcart drivers' strike, and sometimes by itself as a whole item. Therefore, identifying and tracing stories involves a good deal of painstaking unravelling because of the variable manner in which news items are constructed. Nevertheless, using transcripts made of the broadcasts it is possible to do this in a systematic way.[7]

We are not importing a notion of the 'news story' as an *a priori* category – it is embedded in journalistic practice.[8] The organising of reporting around certain 'angles' resulting in what we have called the dominant view of an event is not our concern here. The analysis at this point primarily focuses on *which* events are selected for reporting, and how often. To classify these industrial items, we will make use of the Standard Industrial Classification (SIC) (1968). This categorisation is represented in a number of tables throughout the chapter and is routinely used in the Department of Employment Gazette.[9] SIC operates in various ways but there is one major division by industry (industrial order level); another subdivides this industrial order level into sub-categories known as the minimum list headings. For most purposes it has been sufficient to operate at the industrial order level, but we have had occasion to go down to the minimum list headings, notably in the cases of motor vehicles, transport and communication, and public administration. The use of the SIC at once opens up possibilities of using a number of statistical indicators of 'real activity' – which offer publicly available information as to the distribution of events in the industrial world: such as the magnitude of employment, the incidence of industrial disputes, industrial accidents, the agreements on industry-level wage settlements. For some of these purposes we have used the SIC grid with respect to the total five-month period.

By using the SIC, not all industrial stories covered by the bulletins are analysed. A number of industrial stories are reported within bulletin items organised around such overall themes as 'Unemployment' or 'the Social Contract'. The 'packaging' of particular industrial reports in this manner is more common in ITN's *News at Ten* and BBC2's *News Extra*. The industrial story reports have been included in the analysis below while the reporting of the Social Contract, unemployment and the Industry Bill, are assessed as separate stories. Obviously, any total assessment of TV coverage of industrial news must necessarily take these latter into account.

The extent of individual stories and the range and distribution of overall coverage between the three news services, industry by industry, is an important component of the basic contours. What follows briefly is the pattern of story coverage as it relates to each industrial grouping (see also Table 5.1).

Agriculture and fishing

In agriculture there were ten news stories; in fishing there were eight. The only agricultural story to get extensive treatment was the protest by egg producers against imports, sporadically reported throughout February, March, April and May. The remaining nine stories were not extensively covered and, as we shall suggest, this lightness of coverage is reflected in the fact that many of these were exclusives to one channel or another: 4 to BBC1, 2 to BBC2 and 1 to ITN. Of the total of 14 reports on 6 days, 7 were on BBC1 on 5 days, 6 on ITN on 4 days and 1 on BBC2 on 1 day.

Apart from single reports on the agricultural workers' pay claim and the NUF conference, the main theme of the coverage was the anxieties of farmers on the issues of subsidies, prices and imports.

Although fishing had fewer stories (8), it was much more frequently reported; a ratio of stories to reports of 1 to 14 as opposed to a ratio of 1 to 3 in agriculture. Apart from two stories early in the year involving the loss of one trawler and another going aground, the main theme, as in agriculture, related to the economics of the industry. Five other stories were covered by both ITN and BBC1 and four of them were also covered by BBC2: the lost trawler (January); the financial troubles of Associated Fisheries (February); the French fishermen's blockade of the Channel ports (February); and the UK fishermen's blockade of British ports (March and April). It should be noted that the French fishermen's blockade was more extensively covered on the BBC's channels – by no means an automatic result of having more time than ITN.

Table 5.1 Industrial news coverage, January–May 1975

	BBC1			BBC2			ITN			TOTAL		
	Stor.	Reps.	%	Stor.	Reps.	%	Stor.	Reps.	%	Stor.	Reps.	%
Agriculture	7	15	1.8	4	5	1.2	4	10	1.3	10	30	1.5
Fishing	8	50	5.9	6	23	5.4	5	36	4.6	8	109	5.3
Subtotal	15	65	7.7	10	28	6.6	9	46	5.9	18	139	6.8
Mining	7	41	4.8	5	23	5.4	5	33	4.2	7	97	4.7
Food, drink and tobacco	—	—	—	2	2	0.5	3	3	0.4	5	5	0.2
Coal and petroleum prod.	6	19	2.2	6	12	2.8	9	22	2.8	13	53	2.6
Chemicals and allied ind.	3	8	0.9	2	3	0.7	6	14	1.8	6	25	1.2
Metal manufacture	7	35	4.1	8	25	5.9	6	31	3.9	9	91	4.4
Engineering	6	31	3.6	3	14	3.3	7	28	3.6	7	73	3.5
Shipbuilding, etc.	5	7	0.8	2	3	0.7	3	6	0.8	5	16	0.8
Motor vehicles	40	213	25.0	24	93	21.8	38	196	24.9	55	502	24.4
Aerospace	3	4	0.5	1	1	0.2	3	7	0.9	3	12	0.6
Textiles	7	13	1.5	5	7	1.6	3	7	0.9	9	27	1.3
Clothing and footwear	—	—	—	1	1	0.2	1	1	0.1	2	2	0.1
Bricks, pottery, glass and cement	1	1	0.1	—	—	—	—	—	—	1	1	0.05
Paper, printing and publishing	5	28	3.3	6	20	4.7	7	36	4.6	8	84	4.1
Other manufacture	—	—	—	1	1	0.2	—	—	—	1	1	0.05
Construction	9	25	2.9	9	18	4.2	7	21	2.7	13	64	3.1

Table 5.1 continued

Transport and communications												
Railways	5	47	5.5	3	28	6.6	7	67	8.5	7	142	6.9
Roads	5	14	1.6	3	8	1.9	4	8	1.0	6	30	1.5
Sea	8	30	3.5	6	15	3.5	5	19	2.4	9	64	3.1
Docks	4	34	4.0	4	14	3.3	3	41	5.2	7	89	4.3
Air	6	28	3.3	7	15	3.5	5	23	2.9	9	66	3.2
Postal	3	5	0.6	2	4	0.9	2	8	1.0	3	17	0.8
Subtotal	31	158	18.5	25	84	19.7	26	166	21.0	41	408	19.8
Gas, electricity and water	2	18	2.1	2	13	3.0	3	13	1.6	3	44	2.1
Distributive trades	3	8	0.9	2	2	0.5	1	4	0.5	3	14	0.7
Education	8	23	2.7	4	5	1.2	6	10	1.3	12	38	1.8
Medical services	7	30	3.5	5	15	3.5	6	31	3.9	9	76	3.7
Public administration	15	89	10.4	10	35	8.2	17	96	12.0	22	220	10.6
Professional, scientific, business services and public admin. – total	32	142	16.6	19	55	12.9	30	137	17.2	43	334	16.1
Miscellaneous services	6	32	4.3	5	22	5.2	6	19	2.2	9	73	3.2
Total	188	848	99.8	138	427	100.1	173	790	99.9	261	2,065	99.8

ITN carried 4 fishing reports on 2 days, BBC2 carried 5 reports on 4 days and BBC1 carried 9 on 4 days. In addition the BBC had three exclusive stories: the Aberdeen herring men's demand for a 50-mile fishing limit (February BBC1 and 2); the international conference on fishing conservation held in London (May BBC1 and 2) and the action of fishermen from the Irish Republic in support of the blockade of UK ports (April BBC1). The heaviest coverage within this sector was the UK fishermen's blockade in March and April, which was mentioned in a total of 69 bulletins. This was a novel form of protest and the ample opportunities for aerial photography were fully utilised. The importance attached to this story by all three news services is evidenced by the similarity of coverage: BBC1 provided 28 reports in 13 days; ITN, 28 in 12 days; and BBC2 had 13 in 10 days.

Mining

Of the seven mining industry stories, six of them were given light coverage, never more than two bulletin reports per news story. Three stories on questions of production and a new coal mine in Yorkshire were BBC exclusives. All channels reported the deaths of 28 African miners in a riot, the only foreign mining story. Concern was also reported by all channels over the possible prospect of the 'one hundred pounds a week miner' at home. The story which accounts for the greatest number of references is the miners' pay claim (January and February). This was followed through over five weeks to the final settlement on 28 February. The coverage of this story shows the general similarity between BBC1 and ITN, a characteristic of major stories: BBC1 had 32 bulletins on 15 days; ITN, 27 on 12 days; BBC2, 19 on 13 days.

Food, drink and tobacco

The coverage of this sector was not extensive. Five unrelated stories, three exclusive to ITN and two to BBC2, received one report apiece; Tate and Lyle profits; increases in bread prices; short time in the tobacco industry; the dangers to infants of dried milk, and the threat of nationalisation of UK interests in the Portuguese wine industry. This shows that exclusivity in running minor stories is not confined to the BBC because of the greater number of bulletins they have available. Here ITN ran three exclusives while BBC1 ignored these industries.

Coal and petroleum products

The year opened with the financial collapse of the Burmah Oil Company, covered extensively by all three channels in a total of 22 reports in 7 days. There was also a report of falling profits at Shell given by BBC1 Early

Evening Bulletin on 15 May. However, in April all channels brought us the good news, with correspondents all sending film reports from Alaska, of British Petroleum's oil field development.

The dominant concern in reporting this industrial sector was the development of North Sea oil: the prospect of government control, taxation, oil platform building, job prospects and work hazards, and a new oil strike close to the Shetlands. Covering the North Sea, ITN had 5 exclusive stories; BBC2 had 2; and BBC1 had 1. It also shared one other story with its sister channel. Most of these stories appeared in only one or two bulletins.

Chemicals

News from the chemical industry mainly concerned explosions – both of profits and plants. ITN reported the high profits of Unilever (May), and LaRoche (March), and also carried the story of an explosion of a chemical factory in Kent. Both BBC1 and ITN reported an explosion in a Belgian chemical plant in Antwerp (February) and all bulletins except *News Extra* reported the poisoning of workers at the Cyanamid factory in Gosport on 4 February. The Flixborough accident inquiry was reported by all channels. Amidst the generally light coverage of chemicals, Flixborough still dominated.[10]

Metal manufacture

Nine stories are reported in this category but coverage of the British Steel Corporation's manning proposals and their implications for closures and redundancies dominated the news. There were a number of elements to the story but the conflict between Sir Monty Finniston, the Chairman of BSC, and Mr Tony Benn, the then Minister of State for Industry, was most widely reported – 24 reports in 11 days on BBC1; 21 on 9 days on ITN; and 13 on 11 days on BBC2. The even coverage between BBC1 and ITN, for what is seen as an important story, is again evident. The remaining lightly covered stories related to closures and layoffs with some attention being given to pay claims. There were 8 of these, and, as happens with less important stories, there were more exclusives: 2 to BBC and 1 to ITN – a foreign story on the Swedish steel industry and the EEC. The only non-steel metals story was a report on *News Extra* on 14 March, of a fire which had been burning for eight years in a waste tip at the Rio Tinto Zinc plant in Bristol.

Engineering

Seven stories were reported from the engineering industry. One was exclusive to ITN, a progress report on the Fisher–Bendix co-operative. In addition to stories on the engineering workers' pay claim and Ferranti's request for government financial aid, there were two further stories which received extended treatment. One was the sit-in at the Imperial Typewriters factory in Hull following its closure by the multinational Litton Industries. The other was a strike at the Dunlop engineering plant in Birmingham. Here 700 clerical workers struck on 18 April in pursuit of pay claims. The strike continued into May and led to the layoff of 12,000 workers in the motor industry, principally at BLMC. BBC1 ran 8 reports on Imperial Typewriters on 5 days in January and February, and updated on 30 May in the *Nine O'Clock News*; BBC2 ran 3 reports on 3 days; and ITN 6 on 3 days. For the Dunlop strike (April and May) BBC1 ran 16 reports on 7 days; BBC2, 9 reports on 8 days; and ITN, 16 on 10 days.

Aerospace

Three stories were covered. A strike at Herne Airport British Aircraft Corporation plant in February was carried by BBC1 and ITN in two bulletins each. The effects of defence cuts on the future production of the Harrier jets and possible redundancies was run in all ITN bulletins on 21 February and one bulletin each on ITN, BBC1 and BBC2 in May. The government nationalisation plans for the aircraft industry were also reported on the main evening news by ITN and BBC1 on 15 January.

Motor vehicle manufacture

This industry was more extensively covered than any other – 55 stories and 502 reports: a ratio of stories to reports of 1 to 9. The coverage dominated industrial news in every month except March. In February, it shared its dominant position with the coverage of the miners' pay claim. Eleven strikes were covered. Twenty-three news stories dealt with various aspects of new orders, sales and new models in the industry, including foreign competitors. Two stories dealt with pay claims (not involving strikes) at particular plants. Five stories dealt with short time in various firms, and 10 stories with questions relating to government financial aid. Eighteen of the stories were exclusive to BBC and 13 to ITN. But, again the exclusives were not repeatedly referenced and often were included in only one bulletin. Three stories in particular received extensive coverage: the Cowley engine tuners' strike; the Chrysler pay claim strike in Coventry and the Ryder inquiry into BLMC. A comparison between the coverage on the three channels can be seen in Table 5.2.

The close similarity between news services illustrated in the more prominent stories is reflected in overall coverage. Table 5.1 shows that reporting of the motor vehicle industry constituted 25 per cent of all industrial reporting on BBC1; 24.9 per cent on ITN and 21.8 per cent on BBC2.

Table 5.2 Comparison of coverage of three motor vehicle industry stories

Cowley engine tuners' dispute (Jan./Feb.)	ITN 41 reports on 19 days BBC1 35 reports on 16 days BBC2 18 reports on 9 days
Chrysler plant pay claim strike (May)	ITN 31 reports on 14 days BBC1 37 reports on 16 days BBC2 24 reports on 15 days
Ryder and BLMC	ITN 42 reports on 19 days BBC1 32 reports on 17 days BBC2 11 reports on 10 days

Textiles

In essence, news stories here concentrated on foreign imports, layoffs and unemployment, together with requests for government financial aid. None of the stories received particularly extended coverage. BBC covered more than ITN – 6 exclusives as against 1 ITN exclusive. One story was covered both by BBC and ITN. This was concerned with government aid to the industry and its import restriction plans. ITN made reference to this on 15 March and it was taken up by all channels in May. BBC2's *News Extra* exclusively reported a fire at a textile factory, treating this as a further aggravation of the unemployment problem. The Hosiery Workers' conference was reported on BBC1 early evening news on the same day. There were nine stories altogether.

Clothing and footwear

Here there were only two stories in one bulletin apiece. Both were concerned with the problem of foreign imports relating to shoes and shirts respectively. The first was reported on BBC2 and the second on ITN.

Bricks, pottery, glass and cement

Here just one reference reported on BBC1 *Nine O'Clock News*, on 25 February, the announcement of redundancy plans by Pilkington's glass company.

Paper, printing and publishing

The eight stories reported in this sector all related to newspaper publishing. Two were exclusive to ITN, both in April. There was a report on the closed-shop issue discussed at the NUJ conference (*News at Ten*, 24 April) and a report of a pay claim by SOGAT members working on provincial newspapers (early evening news, 10 April). BBC2 exclusively covered an NGA dispute with the *Peterborough Standard* over the introduction of new machinery, on 29 May. The remaining four stories were covered on all channels. One involved NATSOPA and the *Mirror* group, reported through 17–20 January (BBC1, 8 reports on 4 days; ITN, 9 reports on 4 days; and BBC2, 5 on 3 days). The other major Fleet Street dispute in January concerned the NGA and the NPA. Over the period 14–22 January BBC1 gave 9 reports on this on 5 days; ITN, 16 reports on 8 days; and BBC2, 9 reports on 6 days. The unofficial strike of warehousemen at the *Daily Mirror* (March–April) and the ongoing struggles of the *Scottish Daily News* co-operative (March–April–May) were also reported.

Other manufacture

One report on BBC2 (*News Extra*, 3 January) is subsumed here – the announcement that Goodyear and Dunlop were going on to short-time working. This was linked with the recession in the car industry, but unlike the Dunlop story referred to above, which was concerned with the company's vehicle component manufacturing, this story was exclusively about rubber – in SIC terms, 'other manufacture'.

Construction

Thirteen stories were reported. Five of them ran on all channels: a report of official figures showing a slump in private house-building (early January), the serious danger of high alumina cement beams in local authority buildings (May) and UCATT members '20 per cent pay deal' on 21 January. The two stories, however, which received heaviest coverage were the axing of the Channel Tunnel project in January (BBC1 carried 4 reports on 2 days; BBC2, 5 reports on 3 days; and ITN, 7 reports on 3 days) and the continuing controversy surrounding the jailing of two Shrewsbury pickets. On this last it should be noted that the timing and number of references was different between channels. Only BBC1 followed the story throughout our period: BBC1 ran 8 reports on 5 days (January, February, March and May); BBC2 ran 5 reports on 3 days (January and February); ITN, 3 reports on 1 day (January).

BBC's coverage in this sector was generally more extensive than ITN's. BBC1 reported two accidents, one involving the death of a worker on a Portsmouth motorway site (28 April) and another a fatality in Liverpool (8 May). BBC1 and 2 reported the complaint of British construction workers in Canada that they had been beaten up by Canadian construction workers and forced to leave (22 February). BBC2's *News Extra* had three exclusives: an early report on the alumina cement scandal in January, a statement on unemployment in the industry by David Basnett, General Secretary of the

TGWU on the same day (7 January) and the Skelmersdale council building site on which sabotage by workers was alleged to have taken place (21 February). ITN's one exclusive story reported on a race to build a brick house in record time (23 January). ITN carried an early report (11 January) on the strike-bound Montreal Olympic site, devoting further reports to it in May, when BBC1 also referred to it (21 May).

Gas, electricity and water

ITN ran a brief item on nuclear health hazards at de-radiation stations (30 January, *News at Ten*). There was a more extended reporting of electricity price rises on all channels in February and March. The only heavily covered story, however, related to the power workers' pay claim. BBC1 was the only channel to raise the matter as early as January. All three channels took it up in March, April and May. BBC1 ran 16 reports on 9 days; BBC2 ran 11 reports on 9 days; and ITN, 9 reports on 6 days.

Transport and communication

In this sector, as Table 5.1 shows, there were 41 stories and 408 reports. We have found it necessary to make use of the various minimum list headings which the detailed Standard Industrial Classification subsumes. Seven rail stories gave rise to the largest number of reports within the transport category – 142. Apart from a reference to a rail strike in Japan on ITN, the stories all concerned British Rail's financial problems and the ongoing wage negotiations. We can see from Table 5.3 that three stories received relatively heavy coverage: the signalmen's strike over pay in February and March, the NUR/ASLEF pay claim from February to May, and the work to rule of British Rail maintenance workers in support of a pay claim during March and April.

The similarity of coverage between ITN and BBC1 is very marked in the first two of the above stories, but in the case of the maintenance men's work to rule, ITN's coverage is more extensive.

Table 5.3 Comparison of coverage of three rail industry stories

Signalmen's strike	ITN 20 reports on 11 days
	BBC1 18 reports on 11 days
	BBC2 8 reports on 8 days
NUR/ASLEF pay claims	ITN 23 reports on 12 days
	BBC1 20 reports on 12 days
	BBC2 16 reports on 14 days
British rail maintenance men's work to rule	ITN 14 reports on 7 days
	BBC1 6 reports on 6 days
	BBC2 4 reports on 4 days

Road transport

This received less coverage. The main story was the protest and sympathy strike following the death of a London bus conductor who had been assaulted whilst on duty in January. BBC1 carried 7 reports on 4 days; BBC2, 5 reports on 5 days; ITN, 4 reports on 3 days. Of the remaining five stories, one related to a strike response to football hooliganism on London Transport in May. This was not covered by ITN as it was off the air as a result of the ACTT dispute with the commercial television companies. The only ITN exclusive was a report on the financial troubles of the National Bus Company in *News at Ten*, 15 January. The story of the death by poisoning of a lorry driver working at a waste tip in Essex received moderate coverage. BBC1 reported the redundancies pending in the National Freight Company in two bulletins on 7 May. There was one foreign story – a report of the petrol delivery drivers' strike in the Irish Republic, on BBC1 and ITN in April.

Sea transport

News from the sea began with reports on the loss of the MV *Lovat*, a prominent story covered in 6 bulletins on BBC1, 4 on BBC2, and 6 bulletins on ITN during 25, 26 and 27 January. Another ship lost was the *Compass Rose*, an oil survey vessel, reported by ITN in 3 bulletins in April and May and on BBC1 in 3 bulletins on 16 April. Two other accidents in February were reported; a collision of foreign ships in the Channel (BBC2's *Newsday* bulletin, 4 February) and the fatal fire on board the *Pegas* off Guernsey (lunchtime news, BBC1, 27 February). One story exclusive to BBC1, on 8 February, concerned allegations of theft by the crew of a cargo ship. All channels reported the *QE2* luxury cruise in January and again in April; the seamen's pay claim also in April; and the strike in March against proposed cuts in Sealink ferry services. Whilst ITN was off the air during the lockout of ACTT members in the commercial TV companies, BBC1 and 2 reported a seamen's strike arising from the introduction of a new channel ferry (BBC1, 7 bulletins; BBC2, 4 bulletins on 27, 28 and 29 May).

Port and inland water

The 'container dispute' was clearly the most prominent story, running in 72 bulletins during February, March and April (BBC1, 27 reports on 13 days; BBC2, 10 reports on 9 days; ITN (giving it closer attention) 35 reports on 17 days). Three other disputes were reported: ITN covered stoppages in Hull and Manchester docks in April, and BBC1 and 2 reported a stoppage in Southampton docks in May. Exclusive coverage was given to two further stories by the BBC: a report on the profits of the nationalised ports (May, BBC1 and 2), and a fatal accident in Port Talbot docks in January (BBC2).

The pay deal for London dockers, agreed in April, was reported by BBC1 and ITN in 2 bulletins each on the 29 April.

Air transport

Only in March did air passenger transport fail to make significant news, with BBC2's *News Extra* alone reporting that British Airways planned to cut its staff by some 1,300. In the other four months, four strikes of airport ground staff received attention. Two were covered by all three news services – a strike at Manchester airport over pay in April (BBC1, 5 reports; ITN, 3 reports; and BBC2, 1 report), and a strike by APEX members over the organisation of the introduction of the Glasgow–London 'shuttle' service in February (BBC1, 8 reports; ITN, 24 reports; BBC2, 6 reports). The opening of this service in January was also covered by the three channels. The attempts of Laker Airway's 'walk on–walk off' flight service to get off the ground were reported exclusively by the early evening bulletin on ITN (7 February). ITN also reported the British Airways' engineering maintenance staff pay claim at Heathrow airport, in three bulletins on 30 and 31 January. The three other stories were shared by BBC1 and 2: the criticisms from BALPA over the handling of the hijack at Heathrow (*News Extra* and *Nine O'Clock News*, 8 January), and two strikes, one of ground staff at Manchester airport in February (BBC1, 2 bulletins; BBC2, 1 bulletin) and the strike of maintenance engineers at Heathrow airport in May (BBC1, 8 bulletins; BBC2, 4 bulletins on 29, 30 and 31 May). (This latter story appeared during the ITN off-air period.) Other airport services stories concerned local authority staffs and are dealt with below.

Postal services

The Post Office Workers' Union appeared first during March, in reports of the Department of Employment's criticism of certain clauses in the union's new pay award (BBC1, 2 reports; ITN, 3; and BBC2, 3), and second during the union's conference in May where an important decision on mechanisation and manning levels was taken (total of 5 bulletins, 16 May). ITN carried two further reports concerning the conference discussions of the Social Contract on 19 May. The announcement of increased postal charges was reported exclusively by BBC1 *Nine O'Clock News* on 21 February.

Distributive trades

A strike by Co-operative Society workers was exclusively reported on *Nine O'Clock News* on 9 March. Two other issues which focused on the attitudes of USDAW members to the Social Contract were covered on all channels. These were a speech by Lord Allen, the union's General Secretary, reported by *News Extra*, and the early evening bulletins of ITN and BBC1 on 27 February; and the union's conference in April covered in 5 bulletins on BBC1, 4 on ITN and 1 on BBC2's *News Extra*.

Education

Reflecting the general interest in union conferences displayed by television news in 1975 (not least because of the importance attached to monitoring the performance of the Social Contract), the conference of the NUT at the end of May was the biggest education story covered. It was reported on 6 BBC1 bulletins and 2 bulletins on BBC2.

Other news items received light coverage, rarely being included in more than one bulletin on any channel. There were four strikes reported; the Buckinghamshire teachers' one-day strike and demonstration against education cuts appeared exclusively on ITN's *News at Ten* on 14 February; a return to work after a two-year strike by teachers in Redcar and the Scottish teachers' strike both covered by ITN and BBC1 in January; and the strike of university teaching staff in May covered by all three channels.

Another demonstration against education cuts, this by teachers in Richmond, was reported exclusively on ITN *News at Ten* on 22 February, whilst BBC1 and BBC2 together reported the teachers' pay claim on 30 April and the NUS grants campaign on 23 May. ITN and BBC1 both covered the elections to the NUS executive (8 April), the acceptance by Scottish teachers of a £6 pay offer (12 May) and reported on the planned government reductions in teacher training programmes.

Medical

During January, February, March and April the hospital consultants' work-to-rule in their dispute over their NHS contracts and subsequently over pay-beds, was followed on all channels. BBC1, 17 reports on 11 days: ITN, 17 reports on 13 days; and BBC2, 8 reports on 7 days. This was the dominant story. BBC's *News Extra* (19 March) informed us of a US doctors' strike, cross-referencing our own consultants' work-to-rule.

The pay negotiations of the junior hospital doctors and GPs were reported on all three channels in January, with ITN including an update in February. Other pay deals within the NHS were also reported: the radiographers' on all three channels and on ITN a mention of the dentists' pay agreement, both in January. All channels reported a 30 per cent pay increase for such doctors as agreed to it in April.

On 21 February BBC1 *Nine O'Clock News* reported that GPs could now prescribe the contraceptive pill on the NHS; all BBC1 bulletins on 23 May told of the protest made by some doctors to the BMA against amendments to the Abortion Act. All ITN bulletins and BBC1's *Nine O'Clock News* on 22

May reported the General Medical Council's ruling on foreign doctors' qualifications to practise in the UK. Other hospital services stories, concerning non-medical employees, are dealt with below.

Public administration

Exactly half of the large number of stories in this sector relate to industrial stoppages. The 11 disputes included 2 with particularly heavy coverage. The Glasgow dustcart drivers' strike January to April had 36 reports on 19 days on BBC1; 43 reports on 22 days on ITN; and 17 reports on 13 days on BBC2. And the Scottish ambulance controllers' strike had 11 reports on 5 days on BBC1; 9 reports on 5 days on ITN; and 5 reports on 4 days on BBC2, through the period 12–19 January.

The strike of Glasgow Corporation electricians, which affected Glasgow airport amongst other places, during the same period as the dustcart drivers' dispute, received much lighter coverage. BBC1 carried 6 reports on 5 days; ITN, 3 reports on 3 days; and BBC2, 1 report only. The three news services also reported during March the successful strike of dustcart drivers in Liverpool, ITN giving coverage in 8 bulletins and BBC1 and 2 making 3 reports each. A strike by bin-men at Southwark was reporting only on BBC1's early evening news on 10 May. The other BBC exclusive was a strike by NUPE members at Christie Hospital, Manchester, given on the *Nine O'Clock News* on 6 March. In February there was an NUPE strike at Morriston Hospital, Swansea, which BBC1 reported 3 times on 3 days; ITN, 8 times on 4 days; while BBC2 carried one report.

ITN had 2 exclusive dispute stories. *News at Ten* on 3 February told of a strike by Avon Council workers in protest against computer miscalculation of their wages. On the early evening bulletin of 13 May, the national firemen's pay-claim dispute was reported.

In March there was an unofficial strike of civil servants at Westminster and Whitehall and this received even coverage as between BBC1 and ITN, in a total of 14 bulletins. ITN and BBC1 both covered the unofficial strike of prison officers during April.

The Civil Service pay deal was noted on the main evening bulletins of both BBC1 and ITN on 14 April. Three further stories received moderate coverage in May: BBC1 ran 4 reports on 2 days; ITN ran 4 reports on 2 days; and there was one mention on BBC2 of the controversy between NALGO and the Secretary of State for the Environment over proposed cuts in government expenditure on local authorities. BBC1 and BBC2 ran 3 reports each and ITN 2 reports on the armed forces' pay rise. The NUPE conference, where, as with other union conferences reported, the important news angle was the Social Contract, was covered by BBC1 in 6 reports on 2 days; ITN ran 4 reports on 2 days; and BBC2 ran 3 reports on 3 days.

Of the remaining seven stories, ITN exclusively reported the MPs' pay rise on *First Report* on 7 March, an NUPE study of local authority child minders on *First Report* on 10 March and the same union's action over the private patients issue in Oxfordshire and Berkshire on *First Report* and *News at Ten* on 14 April. On 20 May *News at Ten* reported the acceptance of wage cuts by council workers in Bournemouth. BBC1's exclusive coverage was a report on the prospect of redundancies facing civilian workers as a result of defence cuts (19 March, *Nine O'Clock News*) and the police pay claim noted on three bulletins at the end of May. BBC2's *News Extra* alone informed us of a Civil Service Report on Jobs and Conditions (19 February).

Miscellaneous services

The actual coverage in this sector is not as diverse as the catch-all title might suggest. There were five stories in sport and recreation and four in entertainment. These groupings are minimum list headings within the category.

The biggest story by far in sport and recreation was the stable lads' strike in April/May at Newmarket: BBC1, 11 reports on 6 days; ITN, 9 reports on 4 days; and BBC2, 6 reports on 5 days. As with the fishermen's blockade, this dispute was in some respects a novel form of action. Strikes in sport are rare and picketing of race courses hitherto unheard of. Other stories in this group received very light coverage. The lifting of the women professional tennis players' boycott threat to Wimbledon on a pay question was noted on all three channels on 26 February in one bulletin each. The remaining three stories were: the Racing Board's Financial Report (ITN, 29 January); the Aintree owners/Jockey Club/Betting Levy Board dispute which put the Grand National at risk (BBC1, 4 March); and the financial difficulties of the National Trust which threatened employees with redundancy (BBC2, 5 April).

In the entertainment category there was one dispute which both made news and cancelled it. This was the ACTT members' dispute in May with the commercial television companies over pay. ITN in three bulletins reported the impending action which left only BBC on the air to report the ensuing strike and lock-out, which they did – BBC1, 15 times on 7 days, and BBC2, 12 times on 8 days.

Finally, all channels reported the increase in the TV licence fee on 29 January; the main evening news on ITN and BBC1 informed us of projected IBA cutbacks in expenditure. ITN, with understandable loyalty, reported ITCA's evidence to the Annan Commission on the Future of Broadcasting in its two evening bulletins on April.

Table 5.4 draws together a number of salient findings on the distribution of coverage. Taking the three SIC categories that have the largest amount of news coverage (motor vehicles, transport and communication, and public administration), we see that 54.8 per cent of all reports are concentrated there. This large proportion is reflected by all three channels, 53.9 per cent on BBC1, 58 per cent on ITN, 48.8 per cent on BBC2.

Table 5.4 Areas of major industrial coverage expressed as a percentage of total (industry-specific) coverage, by channel (Jan.–May 1975)

Industry category	BBC1 % reports	BBC2 % reports	ITN % reports	Total % reports
Motor vehicles	25.0	21.9	25.0	24.4
Transport and communication	18.5	19.7	21.0	19.8
Public administration	10.4	8.2	12.0	10.6
Total	53.9	49.8	58.0	54.8
Engineering	3.6	3.3	3.6	3.5
	n = 848	n = 427	n = 790	n = 2,065

Table 5.5 Great Britain: estimated number of employees in employment, June 1975

Industry (SIC 1968)	No. of employees (000s)	% of total employed population
Agriculture, forestry and fishing	388.0	1.8
Coal mining	303.8	1.4
Other mining and quarrying	47.2	0.2
Food, drink and tobacco	714.0	3.2
Coal and petroleum products	39.8	0.2
Chemicals and allied industries	425.3	1.9
Metal manufacture	500.3	2.3
Engineering	1,871.5	8.5
Shipbuilding and marine engineering	176.6	0.8
Motor vehicles	456.7	2.1
Aerospace	205.2	0.9
All other vehicles	88.6	0.4
Metal goods not elsewhere specified	542.3	2.4
Textiles	503.8	2.3
Leather, leather goods and fur	41.1	0.2
Clothing and footwear	389.4	1.8
Bricks, pottery, glass, cement, etc.	277.8	1.3
Timber, furniture, etc.	261.5	1.2
Paper, printing and publishing	561.9	2.5
Other manufacturing industries	322.3	1.5
Construction	1,241.9	5.6
Gas, electricity and water	345.9	1.6
Transport and communication	1,499.2	6.8
Distributive	2,641.8	11.9
Professional and scientific, finance and business services	4,548.0	20.5
Miscellaneous	2,119.5	7.6
Public administration	1,623.8	7.3
Total, all industries and services	22,137.2	100

Source: *Dept of Employment Gazette*, January 1976.

For comparative purposes, we have indicated in Table 5.4 the amount of coverage given to the engineering industry. We have chosen this as it is the category in the manufacturing sector with the greatest number of employees (Table 5.5). The amount of coverage measured by reports is uniformly low in all three channels. This immediately demonstrates that there is no direct relation between the size of an industry as measured by employment magnitudes and the amount of coverage given to it in television reporting. This can be further shown by reference to Tables 5.5 and 5.4. In the case of engineering, we have an industry involving 8.5 per cent of the employed population which makes only 3.5 per cent of industrial news coverage. If we now compare this with motor vehicles, we observe that 2.1 per cent of the employed population are represented by 24.4 per cent of industrial news reporting. In the same way, the point applies to transport and communications, where 6.8 per cent of the employed received 19.8 per cent of industrial news reporting.

The reverse side of the case is further illustrated if we look at the overwhelmingly un-newsworthy distributive trades category. Although representing 11.9 per cent of all workers (over 2.5 million people) only 0.7 per cent of total industrial news is related to them.

Figure 5.1 shows the extent to which each sector of industry appeared in the news bulletins during the analysis period, January to May 1975. The industries are grouped in accordance with the SIC but only those areas which are covered by news reports are shown. Thus two broad groupings received no coverage – the timber industry, including the manufacture of furniture, etc., and 'metal goods not elsewhere specified'.

Considering those areas that received significant coverage (i.e. average of approximately 10 or more reports per channel), we find at least broad general similarities between ITN and BBC1, in many cases amounting to very close agreement over the industrial areas from which news is drawn. With the single exception of the textile industry, the proportional distribution of BBC2's coverage, despite the untypical structure of its main bulletin, closely follows that of ITN and BBC1.

BBC2 has no reports in one sector – bricks, pottery, glass and cement. BBC1 has no reports in three sectors: bricks, pottery, glass and cement; clothing and footwear; and other manufacture. ITN has no reports on two sectors: bricks, pottery, glass and cement; and other manufacture.

Both the channel absences and exclusives are found within the areas of light coverage. What is covered extensively tends to be covered by all.

The major areas of industrial news in the period were transport and communications, public administration (being mainly concerned with hospital staffs and other local authority service workers) and the car industry.

The distribution of the coverage month by month is shown in Figures 5.2–5.6 (pp. 125–9). The channels show greater variety in the overall amounts and proportions within different industrial areas on a monthly basis. However, the same sectors of industry predominate throughout the period.

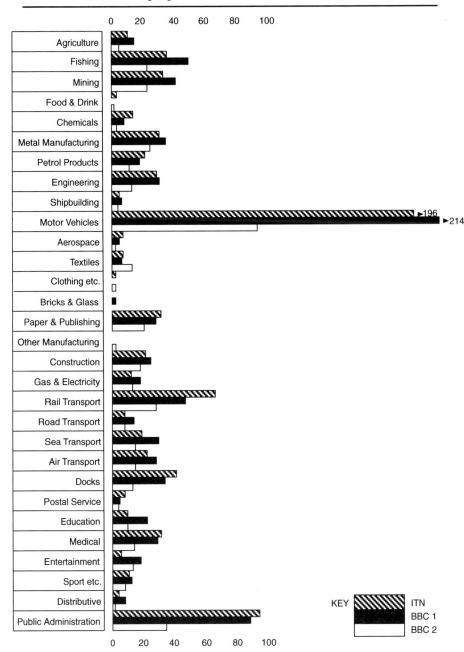

Figure 5.1 Industrial coverage, Jan.–May 1975. Showing distribution of news reports by channel and industry sector
Source: Department of Employment, SIC 1968

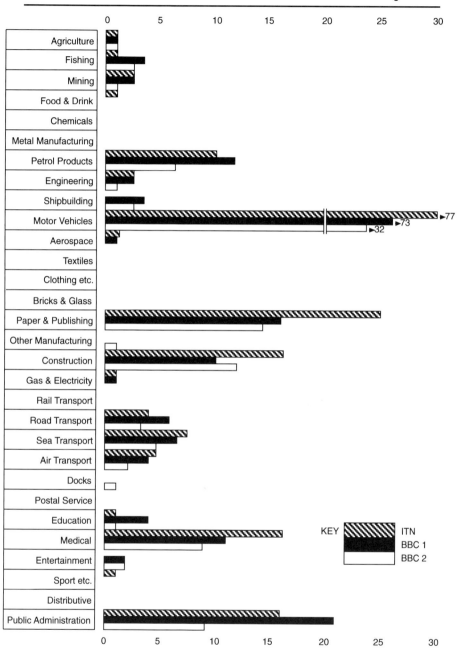

Figure 5.2 Industrial coverage, January. Showing distribution of news reports by channel and industry sector
Source: Department of Employment, SIC 1968

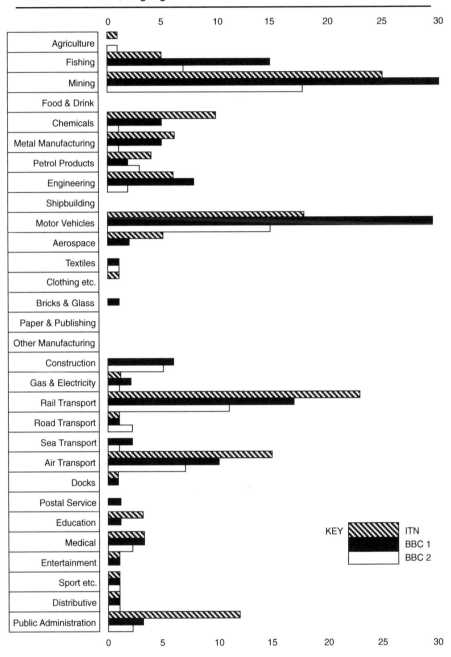

Figure 5.3 Industrial coverage, February. Showing distribution of news reports by channel and industry sector
Source: Department of Employment, SIC 1968

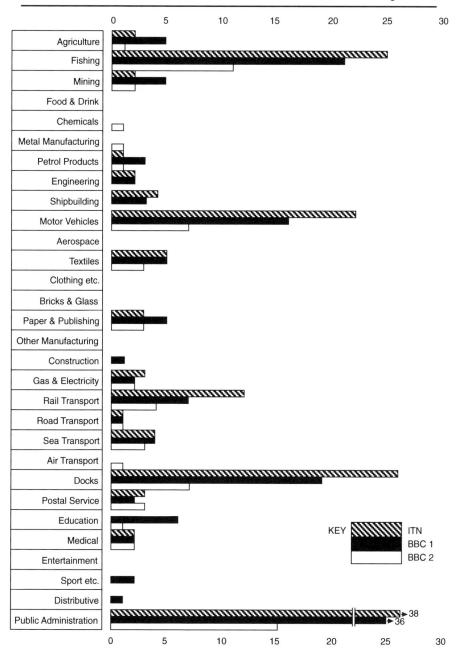

Figure 5.4 Industrial coverage, March. Showing distribution of news reports by channel and industry sector
Source: Department of Employment, SIC 1968

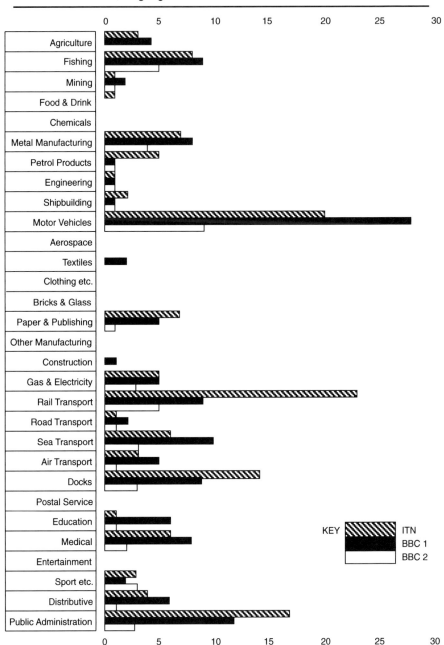

Figure 5.5 Industrial coverage, April. Showing distribution of news reports by channel and industry sector
Source: Department of Employment, SIC 1968

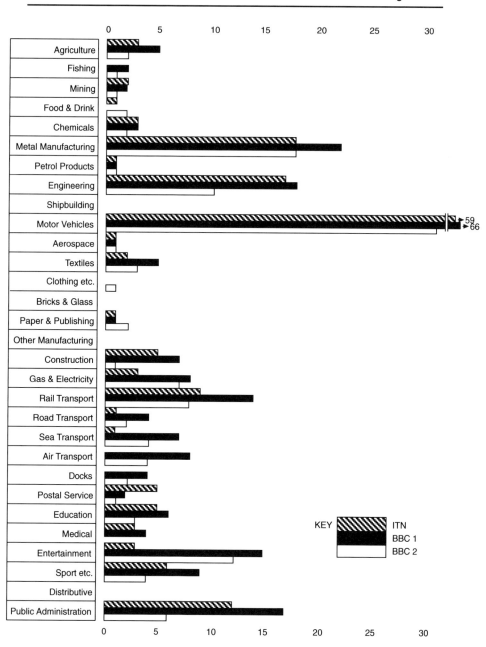

Figure 5.6 Industrial coverage, May. Showing distribution of news reports by channel and industry sector
Source: Department of Employment, SIC 1968

Table 5.6 UK industrial stoppages, strikes, lock-outs. TV coverage Jan.–May 1975

SIC	BBC1			BBC2			ITN			Total		
	Stor.	Reps.	%	Stor.	Reps.	%	Stor.	Reps.	%	Stor.	Reps.	%
Metal manufacture	1	2	0.6	1	1	0.6	1	3	0.96	1	6	0.7
Engineering	2	18	5.3	1	9	5.3	1	16	5.1	2	43	5.3
Motor vehicles	8	95	28.0	5	47	27.8	8	83	26.6	11	225	28.0
Aerospace	1	2	0.6	–	–	–	1	2	0.6	1	4	0.5
	9	97	28.6	5	47	27.8	9	85	27.2	12	229	28.4
Shipbuilding and marine engineering	1	1	0.3	–	–	–	–	–	–	1	1	0.1
Textiles	3	5	1.5	1	2	1.2	–	–	–	3	7	0.9
Paper, printing and publishing	3	22	6.5	4	16	9.5	3	29	9.7	4	67	8.3
Transport and communications												
Rail	1	18	5.3	1	8	4.7	1	20	6.4	1	46	5.7
Road	2	8	2.4	2	7	4.1	1	4	1.3	2	19	2.4
Sea	2	11	3.2	2	7	4.1	1	4	1.3	2	22	2.7
Docks	2	28	8.3	2	11	6.5	3	39	12.5	4	78	9.7
Air	4	23	6.8	4	12	7.1	2	17	5.4	4	52	6.5
			26.0			26.6			26.8			27.0
Distribution	1	1	0.3	–	–	–	–	–	–	1	1	0.1
Public administration and education	3	9	2.7	1	2	1.2	3	5	1.6	4	16	2.0
Local/national government	9	70	20.6	6	29	17.2	9	79	25.2	11	163	20.2
	11	88	23.3	11	45	18.4	8	84	26.8	13	217	22.2
Miscellaneous	2	26	7.7	2	18	10.7	2	12	3.8	2	55	6.8
Total	45	339	339	32	169	169	36	313	313	54	805	805

INDUSTRIAL DISPUTES

There is no consistent relationship between the stoppages recorded during the first five months of 1975 (see Table 5.8, p. 132) and those reported by television news (see Tables 5.6 and 5.7). There are no news stories of the stoppages occurring in seven of the industrial sectors: mining; the manufacture of food, drink and tobacco; coal and petroleum products; chemicals; other manufacturing industries; gas, electricity and water; and the construction industry.[11] However, there were stoppages in these sectors according to the Department of Employment disputes statistics and they accounted for a total of 17 per cent of all the recorded working days lost and 37 per cent of all stoppages in the period.

Further, when disputes are reported, there is no direct relation between the amount of coverage they receive and their severity. For example, whilst the significance of the labour relations problems in the car industry would seem to be reflected in the proportion of coverage devoted to it (reports in 225 bulletins, 28 per cent of all strike reporting), shipbuilding disputes are represented by a single report in only one bulletin on BBC1. This industry recorded 38 major stoppages and 6.7 per cent of the total working days lost. The engineering industry recorded 24.9 per cent of the total days lost in 260 stoppages (of a total of 1,086 stoppages for all industries). Yet engineering stoppages disputes were covered in only two news stories spread over 43 bulletins on all channels. This constitutes only 5.3 per cent of total dispute reporting.

Working days lost due to disputes is not the only possible indicator of the severity of a strike. However, attention to other indices or strike activity – the numbers of workers involved, and the incidence rates of days lost and number of stoppages per worker – also reveals the non-representative nature of reporting in this area of industrial news.

The coverage of the car industry could be justified by the extent of the stoppages in the area, as revealed in Table 5.8. On all indicators there is no doubt that, coupled with the importance of the industry, the period in question was by no means peaceful and television coverage therefore appropriate.

Table 5.7 Major areas of industrial dispute coverage on TV, expressed as a percentage of total *dispute* coverage (Jan.–May 1975)

Industry category	BBC1 % reports	BBC2 % reports	ITN % reports	Total % reports
Motor vehicles	28.0	27.8	26.6	28.0
Transport	26.0	26.6	26.8	27.0
Public administration	23.3	18.4	26.8	22.2
Total	77.3	72.8	80.2	77.2
Engineering	5.3	5.3	5.1	5.3
n =	339	169	313	805

Table 5.8 Number of stoppages (Jan.–May 1975)

Standard Industrial Classification	Stoppages beginning in period	Stoppages in progress Workers involved	Stoppages in progress Working days lost	Stoppages per worker*	Working days lost per worker†
Agriculture, forestry, fishing	—	—	—	—	—
Coal mining	95	12,900	25,000	31.3	82.3
All other mining and quarrying	1	100	1,000	2.1	21.2
Food, drink and tobacco	40	7,200	46,000	5.6	64.4
Coal and petroleum products	1	600	7,000	2.5	175.8
Chemicals and allied industries	34	16,300	73,000	8	171.6
Metal manufacture	65	24,700	102,000	13	203.8
Engineering	260	84,600	733,000	13.9	391.6
Shipbuilding and marine engineering	38	20,400	202,000	21.5	1,143.8
Motor vehicles	72	88,900	522,000	15.76	1,142.9
Aerospace equipment	21	8,800	65,000	10.23	316.7
All other vehicles	12	9,200	132,000	13.54	1,489.8
Metal goods not elsewhere specified	60	12,100	101,000	11.1	186.2
Textiles	25	8,200	44,000	4.9	87.3
Clothing and footwear	17	3,700	23,000	4.36	59.1
Bricks, pottery, glass, cement, etc.	20	3,700	16,000	7.19	57.6
Timber, furniture, etc.	13	2,300	15,000	4.97	57.4
Paper, printing and publishing	19	5,900	36,000	3.4	64.1
All other manufacturing industries	25	9,900	99,000	7.7	307.2
Construction	88	12,000	92,000	7.1	74.1
Gas, electricity and water	9	3,600	8,000	2.6	23.1
Port and inland water	32	21,900	271,000 ⎫		
Other transport and communication	45	29,400	51,000 ⎭	5.13	214.7
Distributive trades	30	4,300	53,000	1.1	20.1
Administrative, financial and professional services	48	14,200	199,000	0.77	32.2
Miscellaneous services	16	4,200	27,000	0.75	12.7
Total	1,086	409,000	2,944,000		

Notes:
* Expressed as stoppages per 100,000 employees
† Expressed as days lost per 1,000 employees
Sources: Figures calculated on June 1975 employment figures (Department of Employment Gazette, January 1976, pp. 20–3) and 'Evidence of Industrial stoppages in the UK' (Gazette, February 1976, pp. 115–26).

However, we are here concerned not with what was present in the bulletins but what was absent. In terms of stoppages and days lost in relation to levels of employment in the industry, shipbuilding demonstrates a more serious position, not reflected in the bulletins. Also largely absent were three sectors where the frequency of stoppages per worker was very prominent: other sections of the vehicle industry not reported (re. SIC 'all other vehicles'), engineering, and, above all, coal mining.

Thus, these aspects are not conveyed by the relative absence of strike reports from these important areas of industry. However appropriate the coverage of certain sectors might be, the lack of coverage of other sectors results in an overall skewing of the picture given of disputes in industry. The 'time defence' which justifies the selection process means that those sectors covered are thrown into sharp relief – less time more evenly distributed would better reflect the actual incidence of these events overall. Add to this the fact that reporting of strikes and disputes involving stoppages of work accounts for 39.1 per cent of all industrial coverage, but only 20 per cent of the total number of industrial stories. Table 5.9a shows the close similarity between the three news services in this respect.

And there is a further point. In the nature of the case, the relative duration of disputes as against many other stories, means they are reported more often. This is indicated by the fact that they receive coverage in a greater than average number of bulletins than other kinds of industrial news story (Table 5.9b). The skewed nature of reporting of strikes is correspondingly amplified by the repetition of reports that the nature of disputes demands.

Table 5.9a Percentage strike reports and stories of total industrial coverage

Channel	Bulletin reports %	Stories %
ITN	39.7	20.8
BBC1	39.7	23.9
BBC2	39.5	23.2
All channels	39.1	20.7

Table 5.9b Average number of bulletin reports per industrial news story

Channel	Bulletin reports per story	
ITN	3.6	Industrial non-dispute stories
BBC1	3.6	
BBC2	2.4	
ITN	8.7	Dispute stories
BBC1	7.5	
BBC2	5.3	

The greater figure for strike coverage on ITN shown in Table 5.9b arises from the fact that ITN covered a smaller total number of strike stories, 36 compared with 45 different strike stories covered by BBC1.[12] At the same time, the total number of ITN bulletins that report these stories is relatively high and is comparable with the total for 45 strike stories on BBC1 (ITN total bulletin reports 313; BBC1 total 339: see Table 5.6, p. 130).

Whilst BBC1 covered stoppages in 11 different sectors, ITN covered 8 sectors, none of which is not also covered by BBC1. BBC1 reported strikes exclusively in shipbuilding, textiles and distributive trades. In addition, ITN reported fewer strikes in 4 sectors (engineering, road transport, sea transport and air transport) but reported more disputes on the docks than did BBC1.

BBC2 bulletins, within the five-month period, covered strikes in 8 different sectors with similar absences to ITN in shipbuilding, and distributive trades. BBC2 did however report a strike in the textile industry but did not cover the dispute in the aerospace industry at the British Aircraft Corporation factory, Herne airport, which was reported by both ITN and BBC1.

It can be argued that television news gives much the same picture of the industrial scene, and indeed the world at large, with respect to the tendency to report the same aspects of a particular story from one news service to another and in choosing those stories from the same restricted areas of possible choice. The case studies demonstrate the close similarity of content and treatment found in the reportage of particular stories by the news bulletins on the three channels. There is close agreement between ITN and the BBC as to which parts of the industrial world shall be allowed through the selection 'gate'. Even if different stories are chosen, they tend to be drawn from the same sectors and tend to relate to the same sort of events. For example, both ITN and BBC1 cover 8 strikes each in the motor vehicle industry. ITN bulletins carry reports of three disputes not covered by BBC1, whilst BBC1 reports a further two strikes exclusively, and shares coverage of one other with BBC2.

The result of this is not significantly to alter the overall amount of car industry coverage on either channel. And anyway, such exclusives tend to be reported in just one or two bulletins.

The selection of news stories between channels is as follows: of a total of 36 strike stories chosen by ITN, 8 are exclusive to that news service. These are three strikes in the car industry, at Vauxhall Ellesmere Port (January), the BLMC Cowley plant (against short time) and Fords, Dagenham (April); two strikes on the docks, at Manchester (April) and in Hull (April); a one-day strike by teachers in Buckinghamshire (February); a strike involving Avon County Council workers (February), and the firemen's dispute in May. Only two of these stories appear in as many as three bulletins per channel. The remainder are reported in one bulletin each.

BBC2 has only one story which does not appear on the other channels, a dispute involving NGA members at the *Peterborough Standard* newspaper (*News Extra*, 29 May).

The BBC news bulletins covered some 17 strikes that ITN did not report. All of them appeared on BBC1, whilst 7 of these were covered on BBC2 as well, indicating a significant level of co-operation and sharing of resources between the two news services. (In many cases the scripted studio report and the film reports used in BBC1 and BBC2 bulletins, covering the same story, are identical.)

The ten stories exclusive to BBC1 were strikes at Fords, Swansea (April) and at Fords, Halewood (February); two strikes by textile workers in Lancashire (5 March) and in Manchester (11 April); a strike by Co-operative Society workers (9 March); the ending of a two-year strike by teachers in Redcar; a dustmen's strike in Southwark; the strike action taken by NUPE members in the private beds dispute at Christie Hospital in Manchester; a strike at the Plessey telecommunications factory in Liverpool (25 February), and at Swan Hunters Shipyard (14 January).

The seven stories covered by both BBC1 and BBC2 (but not ITN) were a strike at Jaguar, Coventry (8 and 9 May); the strike and demonstration of Lancashire textile workers (25 March); a London Transport strike in protest against football hooliganism (May); a Southampton dockers' strike (May); the strike of seamen caused by the introduction of a new ferry (May); a strike by Manchester airport ground staff (February), and the strike by maintenance engineers at Heathrow airport in May. As with the ITN exclusives, these stories received only 'light' coverage. In only 2 cases out of the 15 is there a story included in more than 2 or 3 bulletins. Exclusive stories tend to be treated 'lightly' and not run in many bulletins, and exclusive strike stories are no different from other industrial stories in this respect.

There are 28 news stories (of a total of 54) which are shared by both BBC1 and ITN. BBC2 reported 24 of these, omitting the strikes at BAC Herne airport (February); at Vauxhall, Ellesmere Port (4 April); the Scottish teachers' strike (January); and the unofficial strike of London prison officers (1 April).

The individual differences between news channels do however occur within an overall pattern of similarity and are minor variations on a common theme.

In 10 cases ITN carries more reports on a story common to all channels and BBC1 has more than ITN on 10 other shared stories. As would be expected, BBC2 has less reports per news story. Its stories are included in less bulletins than either BBC1 or ITN. The only exception to this occurred during the ACTT strike and lockout during the last weeks of May, where BBC2 carried reports in 12 bulletins between 22 and 30 May, of the strike itself, as against 15 on BBC1 and 3 on ITN.

The stories covered by all three news services are those, not surprisingly in the light of the other evidence on close similarity, which are deemed of greater significance. In only three cases for ITN and in one case for BBC1 is the story coverage run in less than three bulletins. In only one further case for

Table 5.9c Extent of coverage, strike stories covered by all channels

Channel news service	Av. no. of bulletin reports	Av. days of story coverage
ITN	12.3	6.3
BBC1	11.9	6.2
BBC2	6.4	4.8

ITN does the story receive less than two days' coverage. The number of reports per story amongst this group of shared stories, is above the average for strike stories (Table 5.9c).

'PROMINENT STOPPAGES OF WORK'

A useful review of the performance of television news covering the 'big story' amongst industrial disputes is provided by the Department of Employment survey of 'prominent stoppages' in 1975. The Department of Employment analysis selects those disputes that resulted in the most serious stoppages of work, recording a high number of working days lost, causing noteworthy disruption of production.

We have listed all those prominent stoppages as published by the Department of Employment, which took place during our recording period, and examined the extent and nature of the coverage they received in the news bulletins. The details of this analysis are contained in Table 5.10 and prompt the following observations.

Of 20 strikes selected by the Department of Employment analysis as 'prominent stoppages', television news covered 11. Ten strikes in this group are covered by all three news services (these 10 being amongst the 24 stories common to ITN, BBC1 and BBC2 dealt with above). An additional story, the strike against the imposition of short-time working at the Cowley car plant, is the only exclusive and was reported by ITN.

There is a significant level of agreement between news services. However, there is an interesting tendency in reporting prominent stoppages for ITN to report over a longer period of time and in a greater number of bulletins. ITN's journalistic criteria for an important dispute story thus correspond more closely to the DE's notions of prominent stoppages than do the BBC's. Only in the case of the London Transport strike in January and the Birmingham toolmakers' strike in February, does BBC1 give comparatively more coverage in terms of number of bulletins and days run.

Table 5.11 (p. 142) compares the incidence of stoppages recorded by the industry sector with the strike coverage selected by the TV news. The television news bulletins did not cover the major strike in the shipbuilding industry or in the other manufacturing sectors. The fact that 5 of the 11 strikes

Table 5.10 Prominent stoppages: extent and nature of coverage

Prominent stoppages*	Month	SIC order	BBC1		BBC2		ITN		Total	
			Days reported	No. of reports	Days reported	No. of reports	Days reported	No. of reports	Days reported	No. of reports
Sanctions in support of a pay claim imposed on certain jobs by workers at a Coventry manchine tool factory led to the suspension of an employee for refusing to carry out his normal duties. Some 1,600 production workers then withdrew their labour on 2 January in protest. Work was resumed from the nightshift of 15 January following acceptance of an improved pay offer made by the company.	Jan.	7	—	—	—	—	—	—	—	—
At an Oxford car assembly plant, 250 engine tuners involved in a grading dispute withdrew their labour, initially on 6 January, and continuously from 9 January, after unsuccessful interim talks. At present classed as production workers, the tuners were demanding skilled status which could benefit them in forthcoming pay negotiations in which higher differentials for skilled workers would be an issue. About 12,000 body-plant workers who were laid off on 6 January worked normally thereafter and were able to maintain production at a high level. The tuners returned to work on 4 February, on union direction pending the outcome of an investigation into the status question initiated by the Advisory Conciliation and Arbitration Service (ACAS).	Jan./Feb.	11	16	35	9	18	19	41	20	94
In support of a demand for better protective measures against assaults by members of the public, and in token of sympathy, on the day of the funeral of a conductor who died as a result of such an incident, London Transport and Home counties bus crews, depot staff, and sections of London Underground Railway Staff, stopped work for 24 hours on 29 January. Nearly 18,000 people were involved.	Jan.	22	4	7	5	5	3	4	6	16

Table 5.10 continued

Prominent stoppages*	Month	SIC order	BBC1		BBC2		ITN		Total	
			Days reported	No. of reports	Days reported	No. of reports	Days reported	No. of reports	Days reported	No. of reports
Objection to the grading within the pay structure of a new automatic plating process introduced by a Coventry telecommunications equipment company led to a stoppage by 27 platers on 10 January; as a result over 1,700 production workers were laid off progressively during January and February. Following a meeting chaired by ACAS, Midland Region, work was resumed on 5 March to allow further negotiations on the details of a proposed settlement.	Jan./Feb.	9	—	—	—	—	—	—	—	—
Electricians employed by local authorities in various areas of Scotland withdrew their labour in support of a claim for wage parity with contracting electricians in the private sector. The stoppage, which began on 10 January, was still in progress at the end of February, when nearly 900 workers were involved, principally in the Glasgow area.	Jan./Feb.	27	5	6	1	1	3	3	7	10
A six-week stoppage by 70 crane drivers at a Birkenhead shipbuilding yard, in support of a claim for wage parity with boiler-making trades, caused the progressive layoff during this period of 1,200 other workers. The claim was not conceded, but acceptance of a lump sum advance payment in respect of oiling and greasing time was followed by a return to work on 24 February.	Jan./Feb.	10	—	—	—	—	—	—	—	—
At a Birmingham car plant about 600 toolmakers stopped work on 10 February after rejecting a pay offer by the company in annual negotiations. Their action in support of a demand for an increase which would restore their traditional pay differential with production workers, resulted in the progressive layoff of over 4,000 other workers at the same establishment. The dispute was unresolved at the end of the month. At the same company's Oxford plant more than 800 warehouse workers withdrew their labour on 18 February in protest against security measures which led to allegations that an employee was followed home by a works policeman. The stoppage ended on 27 February.	Feb./Mar.	11	4	6	3	3	2	2	7	11

In a dispute with the management of a Stafford firm of electrical engineers over pay differentials between testers and other skilled workers, an offer based on a pay and grading exercise was rejected and 118 testers stopped work on 26 February in support of an across-the-board increase. As a result 1,200 production workers were laid off from 8 March. A resumption of work took place on 26 March after the testers had accepted a marginal graded increase.	Mar.	9	—	—	—	—	—	—	—	—
At a Bathgate, Scotland, truck and tractor assembly plant, 96 electricians and pipefitters withdrew their labour from 6 March in support of their union's refusal to accept a new joint wage and conditions agreement operative from 3 January, recently accepted by unions representing hourly paid workers. The issue was related to pay differentials between skilled technical staff and semi-skilled operatives. Work was restarted on 24 March after minor modifications had been made to the agreement. The stoppage had meanwhile caused the progressive layoff of 3,800 other workers.	Mar.	11	—	—	—	—	—	—	—	—
A stoppage of work by 9,000 dockers in the Port of London which began on 27 February continued throughout March. The dockers' objective was to secure more of the container handling work at inland depots retained by road haulage contractors. Intensive picketing by dockers involved counter-action by road haulage workers. A panel of investigation was set up by ACAS. The dockers voted overwhelmingly for a return to work on 7 April.	Feb./April	22	13	27	9	10	17	35	23	7

Table 5.10 continued

Prominent stoppages*	Month	SIC order	BBC1		BBC2		ITN		Total	
			Days reported	No. of reports	Days reported	No. of reports	Days reported	No. of reports	Days reported	No. of reports
Drivers employed by Glasgow Corporation cleansing department returned to work on 14 April after a thirteen-week stoppage during which troops were used to start clearing the tons of refuse building up throughout the city. The drivers, holders of HGV licences, claimed parity with rates paid by private hauliers, and their stoppage was supported, progressively by drivers from other corporation services.	Jan./April	27	19	36	13	17	21	42	27	94
A seven-week stoppage by 160 male employees at an East Kilbride telephone and cable factory caused 1,000 women production workers to be laid off. The men were in dispute over a pay offer which the women, who had been awarded an additional increase towards equal pay, had accepted. Following a meeting with ACAS, Scotland, agreement was reached under a new offer and work was resumed on 14 April.	Feb./April	9	—	—	—	—	—	—	—	—
At a Coventry engineering firm which supplies the motor industry, 700 clerical workers withdrew their labour on 18 April in support of a claim for more pay to close part of the gap between their earnings and those of the manual workers. This led to the progressive layoff of about 2,000 production workers at the same plant and caused over 12,000 workers to be laid off in the motor industry elsewhere due to lack of essential components. The stoppage was still in progress at the end of the month.	April/May	7	7	16	8	9	10	16	11	41
In protest against 150 of their colleagues being put on short time, 2,000 indirect workers at a Ford car plant withdrew their labour on 18 and 21 April in the first of a planned series of absences to coincide with the pattern of short-time working. As a result 1,300 production workers who were not on short time were laid off. The dispute had not been solved at the end of the month and the stoppage was repeated on 2 and 5 May.	April/May	11	—	—	—	—	2	3	2	3

Description	Date									
Six hundred maintenance engineers at a Wolverhampton tyre and rubber plant returned to work on 14 April after a four-week stoppage which caused 3,900 production workers to be laid off. Settlement of the dispute, which was over weekend working and the maintenance of pay rates, followed acceptances of the company's offer to increase the basic rate of pay.	Mar./April	19	—	—	—	—	—	—	—	—
Most independent television companies resumed broadcasting on 30 May after being off the air for seven days. A three-day withdrawal of labour by about 2,000 technical staff in support of a claim for pay allegedly lost during the period of wage restraint in 1973 was followed by a lockout. The claim remained unresolved at the end of the month.	May	26	7	15	8	12	2	3	9	30
A stoppage by 70 doorhangers and welders which began on 23 April caused about 5,000 workers to be laid off at a Dagenham car plant. The manning dispute, which arose over management's proposal to reduce the number of doorhangers on each shift in the body plant, was still in progress at the end of the month.	April/May	11	4	5	1	1	2	2	5	8
At a Coventry engine plant 4,000 production workers withdrew their labour on 9 May in support of a pay claim for an increase in basic rates of £15 a week. As a result of their action 3,700 workers at the Company's Ryton factory were laid off during the second week of the stoppage. Work was resumed on 5 June, following acceptance of an interim offer of £8 a week which shop stewards intimated they would seek to improve.	May/June	11	16	37	15	24	14	31	19	92
About 4,600 workers employed by a Coventry agricultural machinery manufacturer stopped work on 1 May having failed to reach agreement over annual pay negotiations. During the stoppage, picketing and occupation prevented administrative staff from entering the main factory. An improved pay offer led to the decision, by a narrow majority of workers, to end the stoppage. Work was resumed on 16 June.	May/June	7	—	—	—	—	—	—	—	—

*Source for this column: *Department of Employment Gazette*, February–June 1975

Table 5.11 Prominent stoppages compared to TV reports

Industry	No. of stoppages recorded by Dept of Employment	No. of strikes reported by TV bulletins
Engineering	6	1
Shipbuilding	1	—
Motor vehicles	7	5
Other manufacturing	1	—
Transport and communication	2	2
Miscellaneous	1	1
Public administration	2	2
Total	20	11

selected for reporting are in the car industry, out of the 7 deemed important by the Department of Employment, again speaks for television's attraction to this area of the economy in 1975.

The importance of the engineering industry, as reflected in the incidence of major stoppages, is clear – 6 prominent stoppages in the first 5 months of 1975. Only one of these was reported on television. Two of the engineering stoppages, which were not reported, occurred in Coventry where disputes in the car industry were routinely covered. The absence of coverage is not then a result of geographical distance or inaccessibility or the special nature of the subject. In fact, engineering is reported only with respect to its implications for the motor industry. The one stoppage selected by television news was the strike by clerical workers in April at the Dunlop components factory in Coventry. In this case there was a clear link with the car industry since it led to progressive layoffs of workers at BLMC. This aspect of the strike was predominant in reporting and was the news angle that lifted the story out of the obscurity of the engineering industry onto the TV screen. The remainder of the television reporting shows a selection that mirrors the Department of Employment's selection of significant industrial disputes.

A TWO-MONTH COMPARISON

It is possible to mount a critique of television news journalism in terms that question the basic assumptions of all current journalistic practice, whether broadcast or print. Much of the above is on this level. The absences noted, the angles used and the tendencies exhibited, are not specific to television. They also apply to the press.

Yet it is possible that a further sense of the assumptions used by television newsmen could be gained by comparing their output with that of their print colleagues. A second level of critique specific to television, but leaving aside basic questions as to the nature of news, could thus be created.

To attempt this, we have taken a two-month period, January and February of 1975, and effected a comparison by counting the number of disputes as registered by the Department of Employment and the number of times they were reported in the media, broadcasting and press. The sample for this research was all the nationally networked television news bulletins on all three channels for this period, five national newspapers (the *Daily Mirror*, the *Daily Express*, the *Daily Telegraph*, the *Guardian* and *The Times*), and the general wire service abstract of the Press Association.

The Press Association was founded by a group of provincial newspaper editors in February 1870 to break the monopoly of the private telegraph companies – an action which led directly to the GPO taking over the telegraphic service.[13]

Today, in line with its initial *raison d'être*, the Press Association services local newspapers and broadcasting organisations, but also provides a full news service to the national press. It was the abstract of this full Press Association service, described as the 'General Wire Service', that was used as the basis of comparison with the television bulletins.

The Press Association General Service is limited by the amount of teleprinting it can generate in any one day. It operates between the hours of seven and midnight and in addition to its reporting, it carries hourly news headline summaries. It runs four minutes behind the main service of the Press Association. There are no other constraints. That is to say, in print terms, it does not have to balance copy against space or, in broadcasting terms, copy against time. The considerable fluctuations from day to day in the number of Press Association stories, therefore, were a reflection of the 'gatekeeping' of their reporters and editorial staff which is, as it were, more purely limited by base notions of what constitutes news than any of the takers of the service can afford themselves.

The sample of national newspapers was drawn up to account for a large sector of the readership and spanned the range of readerships by social class.[14] However, in order to highlight any possible contrast between the range of press and television reportage, the sample was skewed towards the 'quality' dailies, as such papers aim for both range and depth in their reporting. In addition, as described in Chapter 4, there exists a similarity between the profile of the television bulletins and that of the quality dailies by story category. But despite this tendency for the television news to favour the 'quality end' of the spectrum, we wished to examine whether its news values in the industrial area were actually closer to those of the popular press. For this sample, a count was made of dispute reports receiving bold type headline or any mention in excess of $\frac{1}{2}$ column inch. Hence, single sentence mentions of disputes 'packaged' with other items were not included in this newspaper count.

The PA tape, in contrast to the newspapers who normally print only one

Table 5.12 Press Association dispute reporting, January and February 1975

	January		February		Total*	
SIC	Disputes	Reports	Disputes	Reports	Disputes	Reports
Mining	—	—	1	1	1	1
Coal and petroleum products	1	1	—	—	1	1
Metal manufacture	—	—	1	1	1	1
Engineering	1	4	1	1	2	5
Shipbuilding	2	2	—	—	2	2
Vehicles	5	27	6	13	10	40
Textiles	1	1	—	—	1	1
Paper, printing and publishing	2	19	—	—	2	19
Construction	1	1	—	—	1	1
Transport and communications	5	11	8	30	12	41
Distributive trades	—	—	1	1	1	1
Administrative, financial, business and professional services	4	29	7	28	11	57
Miscellaneous	2	5	—	—	2	5
Total	24	100	25	75	47	175

Note: *Several of the disputes are reported in both January and February, thus total disputes over the two-month period in some sectors are not simply additions of the monthly dispute columns.

report per edition and the television news which presents one report per bulletin, appears continuously over some 17 hours, often carrying reports, reminders and updates of the same story several times in one day. Thus in the PA analysis only the presence of reports, regardless of the repetitions, was recorded.[15]

Reports of 'threatened' strike action, that subsequently materialised, ongoing developments and settlements of disputes, were also counted. But reports of work-to-rule, overtime bans and work-ins were not included in the count, as these are not recorded by the Department of Employment statistics as industrial disputes under the stoppages of work heading. The Department of Employment record of strike activity could then be 'read' against the media record.

During January and February of 1975, the PA reported disputes in 13 out of the 22 sectors in which disputes were recorded, covering 10 sectors in January, 7 in February (Table 5.12). The press sample showed a broader range of 16 sectors over two months: 13 in January and 12 in February (Tables 5.13

Table 5.13 Press coverage of disputes, January 1975

SIC sector	Daily Express		Daily Mirror		Daily Telegraph		Guardian		Times	
	Disputes	Reports	Disputes	Reports	Disputes	Reports	Disputes	Reports	Disputes	Reports
Food, drink and tobacco					1	1				
Chemicals					1	1	1	1	1	2
Engineering					1	1	2	2	1	1
Shipbuilding										
Vehicles	2	13	2	18	2	20	1	17	2	22
Textiles	1	1					1	1	1	1
Paper, printing and publishing	2	7	2	3	2	15	2	15	2	12
Transport	4	11	3	6	5	14	5	12	4	13
Distributive									1	1
Administrative, financial and professional	3	6	2	2	6	11	10	16	7	12
Miscellaneous	1	1	1	1	1	1	1	1	1	4
Total	13	39	10	30	19	64	23	65	20	68

Table 5.14 Press coverage of disputes, February 1975

SIC sector	Daily Express		Daily Mirror		Daily Telegraph		Guardian		Times	
	Disputes	Reports	Disputes	Reports	Disputes	Reports	Disputes	Reports	Disputes	Reports
Coal mining					1	1				
Metal manufacturing	1	2	1	1	1	2	1	3	1	3
Engineering							1	1	1	1
Shipbuilding										
Vehicles	3	7	2	4	3	3	3	10	4	14
Paper, printing and publishing	1	1			2	7	3	4	3	4
Construction					3	5	1	1		
Gas, Electricity and Water					1	1	1	1		
Transport	3	20	5	17	6	31	8	35	6	26
Distributive					1	1	2	2	1	1
Administrative, financial and professional	3	6	1	1	4	10	8	17	9	11
Total	11	36	9	23	22	61	28	74	25	60

Table 5.15 TV coverage of disputes, January and February 1975

SIC sector	Dispute story	January				February				Total Two months
		ITN	BBC1	BBC2	Total Jan.	ITN	BBC1	BBC2	Total Feb.	
Metal Manufacture	Ebbw Vale Steel Plant	—	—	—		3	2	1	6	6
Engineering	Plessey, Liverpool	—	1	—		2	2	—	2	2
Shipbuilding	Swan Hunter, Shipbuilders	—	—	—	1	—	—	—	—	1
Aerospace	British Aircraft Corporation	—	—	—	—	2	3	—	5	5
Motor vehicles	BMLC, Cowley	38	33	16	87	2	3	—	8	95
Vehicles Motor vehicles	Vauxhall, Ellesmere Port	1	—	—	1	—	—	—	—	1
Motor vehicles	Ford, Halewood	—	—	—	—	—	—	2	2	2
Motor vehicles	BLMC, Castle Bromwich	—	—	—	—	2	4	3	9	9
Paper, printing and publishing	National Graphical Ass./Newspaper Proprietors Ass.	16	9	9	34	—	—	—	—	34
	NATSOP/*Mirror* Newspapers	9	8	5	22	—	—	—	—	22
Other transport and communication and	London Transport, Bus Crew	3	6	3	12	1	1	2	4	16
	British Airways, 'Shuttle' service clerks	—	—	—	—	14	8	6	28	28
	British Rail signalmen	—	—	—	—	17	15	7	39	39
Port and inland water	Docks (mainly London) containerisation dispute	—	—	—	—	—	1	—	2	2
	Manchester airport 'Service Air'	—	—	—	—	1	2	—	3	3
Education, Administrative, financial and professional services	Teachers, Redcar	—	1	—	1	—	—	—	—	1
	Buckinghamshire teachers	—	—	—	—	1	—	—	1	1
	Scottish teachers	1	3	—	4	—	—	—	—	4
Public Administration	Glasgow Corporation Dustcart drivers	6	6	3	15	3	—	—	3	18
	Glasgow Corporation Maintenance Electricians	1	4	1	6	—	—	—	—	6
financial and professional services	Scottish Ambulance Officers	9	11	5	25	—	—	—	—	25
	S. Wales Hospital staffs (mainly Swansea)	—	—	—	—	8	3	1	12	12
	Avon County Council workers	—	—	—	—	1	—	—	1	1
Total		84	82	42	208	56	45	23	125	333

and 5.14). The television, however, shows a much reduced range, covering disputes in 8 different sectors overall: 6 in January and 6 in February (Table 5.15).

Within the press sample, there were marked variations between the coverage of individual newspapers. The *Daily Mirror* reported disputes in 6 sectors, the *Daily Express* in 8. In contrast, the *Guardian* reported over 15 sectors, the *Daily Telegraph* 13, and *The Times* 12. Although the television news shows a similar profile by story category with the quality press, the range of industrial dispute reporting is more akin to the popular dailies.

The quality papers report disputes over a wide range of the economy, covering many other areas of industry eschewed by the popular press. The television coverage shared the 6 sectors reported in the *Daily Mirror*, only the BBC differing its inclusion of one report on shipbuilding (BBC1, 21.00, 14 January) and two reports on engineering (BBC1, 17.45 and 21.00, 25 February). In contrast, the *Guardian* covered 7 additional sectors and the *Daily Telegraph* 5 sectors, which received no coverage in the television bulletins.

The number of working days lost through disputes, although an indicator of strike severity, does not necessarily have any effect on 'newsworthiness' for television, as we have shown above. This seems to be equally true of the other media (Table 5.16). In the case of the construction industry, where the Department of Employment recorded 8 major stoppages involving a total of 900 workers and 5,000 days lost in January, there was no coverage in either the national press or TV.[16]

In the distributive trades, 5 major disputes began in January involving 2,000 workers, resulting in 29,000 working days lost. Whilst *The Times* and *Guardian* covered only one such dispute on one day, neither the PA nor the television carried any reports. Disputes in this sector accounted for 9.5 per cent of the total working days lost in January.

There are other examples where only light coverage was given to many sectors where a large number of working days were lost through disputes. For example, in the engineering industry, 77 disputes involving 30,500 workers lost 140,000 days during January and February – the highest recorded figure of any sector in the two-month period. The PA reported 2 of these disputes on 5 days. In the press sample there were only 3 reports concerning 2 disputes (2 in the *Guardian*, 1 in the *Daily Telegraph*). On the television 1 dispute was covered in 2 bulletins.[17]

The shipbuilding industry is similarly neglected by the news media. Here the Department of Employment recorded 17 major disputes involving 15,400 workers, resulting in 109,000 working days lost in January and February. The Press Association covered 2 disputes on one day each. Of the press sample, only the 'qualities' included reports, 6 in all covering 5 different disputes. The television bulletins reported none of these disputes, but the BBC included a brief mention of the settlement of a previous strike in its *Nine O'Clock News*,

Table 5.16 Number of stoppages, January and February 1975

SIC	January 1975			February 1975		
	No. of stoppages beginning in period	Stoppages in progress		No. of stoppages beginning in period	Stoppages in progress	
		Workers involved	Working days lost		Workers involved	Working days lost
Agriculture, forestry, fishing	—	—	—	—	—	—
Coal mining	18	3,100	4,000	16	2,600	5,000
All other mining and quarrying	—	—	—	—	—	—
Food, drink and tobacco	5	300	2,000	12	1,100	8,000
Coal and petroleum products	—	500	6,000	—	—	—
Chemicals and allied industries	6	1,200	4,000	10	4,800	13,000
Metal manufacture	1	400	3,000	12	8,100	14,000
Engineering	29	12,700	70,000	48	17,800	70,000
Shipbuilding and marine engineering	8	9,000	68,000	9	6,400	41,000
Motor vehicles	5	13,900	29,000	15	21,100	67,000
Aerospace equipment	2	300	1,000	5	500	4,000
All other vehicles	1	—	1,000	—	—	—
Metal goods not elsewhere specified	10	3,300	16,000	12	1,400	24,000
Textiles	4	2,300	8,000	7	2,500	5,000
Clothing and footwear	—	200	1,000	5	1,000	7,000
Bricks, pottery, glass, cement, etc.	3	200	—	4	900	—
Timber, furniture, etc.	1	200	—	4	900	—
Paper, printing and publishing	3	1,800	3,000	4	200	1,000
All other manufacturing industries	2	2,000	10,000	2	100	4,000
Construction	8	900	5,000	21	2,620	26,000
Gas, electricity and water	2	300	1,000	1	100	1,000
Port and inland water	2	700	3,000	7	10,400	17,000
Other transport and communication	4	18,000	21,000	12	4,400	10,000
Distributive trades	5	2,000	29,000	8	400	4,000
Administrative, financial and professional services	8	2,300	20,000	13	5,300	58,000
Miscellaneous services	—	—	—	6	1,300	5,000
Total	127	75,600	305,000	233	93,920	384,000

on 14 January. Shipbuilding accounted for 15.7 per cent of working days lost over the first 2 months of the year and received 1 per cent of dispute reports in both press sample and PA.

A consideration of those disputes that featured extensively in news coverage again indicates the absence of any direct relationship between the number of working days lost and the amount of coverage that disputes in any area of the ecomomy will receive. A high proportion of working days lost in any dispute or any industry does not in itself appear to constitute news.

In paper, printing and publishing there was extensive coverage of disputes in all three media. In the Press Association tapes the sector ranked fourth highest in terms of dispute coverage (19 items covering 2 disputes), representing 10.8 per cent of the total dispute coverage over 2 months, and 19 per cent in January. In the press sample this sector ranked fourth (67 reports covering 4 disputes) with 12.8 per cent of total dispute coverage for 2 months, 20 per cent in January.[18] In terms of the Department of Employment record of working days lost, this sector in fact ranked eighteenth with 1 per cent of the total in January, and 0.6 per cent over the two-month period.

Despite the rather arbitrary relationship between strike severity and news coverage, it remains that the three sectors given most prominence in the media all had a significant dispute record. But a careful consideration of the overall pattern of coverage reveals its highly mediated character.

It can be seen in Table 5.17 that the press and television concentrated heavily on one particular sector of the economy in each of the two months. In January 'vehicle construction' was the top dispute sector; in February, transport. As we have said, disputes in these sectors did rank high in terms of both working days lost and workers involved, but not so high as to justify, of itself, their dominant position in the coverage.

Having given a particular priority to disputes in a sector, this priority does not appear to rise or fall in a simple relation to the working days lost or the number of workers involved in disputes in these sectors.

As working days lost is obviously a retrospective indicator, journalists might more readily make judgements about newsworthiness in terms of the number of workers involved in a dispute. However, the amount of coverage does not appear to be affected by either factor. In the case of transport, there was a small increase in working days lost and a fall in the number of workers involved in disputes, from January to February. Television coverage of disputes in this sector, however, increased from 7.5 per cent of all dispute coverage in January to 60.5 per cent in February.

Converse, television coverage of disputes in the vehicle construction industry, fell from 41.5 per cent of all dispute items in January to 19.3 per cent in February. During the period, working days lost through disputes increased from 10.1 per cent in January to 18.4 per cent in February, as did the number of workers involved, increasing from 18.7 per cent to 23.1 per cent. A similar

Table 5.17 Press and TV coverage of particular economic sectors

	DE		DE		PA		Press		TV	
	Working days lost		Workers involved		Dispute items		Dispute items		Dispute items	
Sector	Rank	%	Rank	%	Rank	%	Rank	%	Rank	%
Jan.										
Vehicles	3	10.1	2	18.76	2	27	1	33.4	1	41.5
Transport	5	7.8	1	24.7	3	11	3	21.5	3	7.5
Public admin.	6	6.5	7	3.0	1	29	2	17.0	2	24.1
Feb.										
Vehicles	1	18.4	1	23.1	3	17.3	3	16.4	2	19.3
Public admin.	3	15.1	7	5.7	2	37.3	2	17.6	3	13.4
Transport	5	7.0	3	11.5	1	4.0	1	51.0	1	60.5

inverse relationship exists for strike activity recorded by the Department of Employment and coverage within the press and Press Association.

This erratic shift in emphasis is the result of the highly specific focus upon chosen disputes within some sectors. This practice routinely occurs across both press and television, but it is particularly evident in the popular dailies and the television news bulletins because of their narrower total range of stories. 'Heavy' coverage becomes proportionately 'heavier'. There is a tendency to overstate contextually the significance of disputes isolated in this way.

The high proportion of television coverage in the motor vehicle industry is accounted for by one dispute – that of the engine tuners at the BLMC Cowley plant. In fact, one other motor vehicle dispute was reported that month, a strike at the Vauxhall plant at Ellesmere Port. This appeared exclusively on ITN (17.50, 13 January 1975). Coverage of the Cowley dispute thus accounted for 96.6 per cent of the total dispute coverage of the motor vehicle industry in January and 41 per cent of the total disputes covered in all industries in that month. As can be seen in Table 5.18 the heavy coverage given to this story is evidenced equally by all three channels, all bulletins. Emphasis on the Cowley dispute is also evident in the press. Cowley coverage accounted for 94.5 per cent of all dispute reports of the motor vehicle industry in January, and 31.8 per cent of the total of all dispute coverage.

In the Press Association tapes, Cowley reports accounted for 77.7 per cent of the coverage of disputes in the motor vehicle industry in January and 27 per cent of the total dispute coverage. As was indicated above, the wider range of coverage over all news categories in the PA is evidenced within the industrial category reports. Thus Cowley accounts for a smaller percentage of all such items in January although it receives comparable emphasis in terms of total dispute reports.

The 'quality' press shows a similar range to that of the Press Association whereas the range of the popular dailies is much narrower. Thus Cowley reports represent a greater proportion of the dispute coverage in the popular press as other stories are not so much in evidence. The *Daily Mirror*, for example, gave 56.6 per cent of its dispute coverage to Cowley.

This heavy emphasis is further influenced by the tendency to run only one or two items on most of those disputes covered. The popular press rarely carries updates on disputes, most of which, as stated, appear only once.

The range of television coverage was narrow. Eleven dispute stories appear in January, the overall result being again a high proportion of Cowley reports. In the remainder of its coverage, the television news, generally for all channels, displays the tendency noted in the popular dailies, running only 1 or 2 items per dispute story before dropping it for another.

The heavy coverage given to one dispute in the car industry must be seen partly as a consequence of a journalism which describes the world via particular cases which are effectively set before us as a general model. News

Table 5.18 January 1975: coverage of Cowley disputes

Medium	Total of disputes recorded No. of disputes	No. of reports	No. of Cowley reports	% of all dispute reports
PA	27	100	21	21
Press				
Daily Express	13	39	11	28.2
Daily Mirror	10	30	17	56.6
Daily Telegraph	19	64	19	29.6
Guardian	23	65	17	27.4
The Times	20	68	21	30.8
TV bulletins				
BBC1 Lunchtime	6	16	10	62.5
BBC1 Early Evening	9	30	10	33.3
Nine O'Clock News	9	36	12(1)*	33.3
Newsday	7	17	8	47.0
News Extra	6	19	7	36.8
News Review	6	6	1	16.6
First Report	7	22	9	40.9
ITN Early Evening	8	27	13	48.1
News at Ten	5	35	16	45.7

Note:
*(1) indicates a further bulletin (not normal transmission time) on BBC1.

is produced as a set of discrete stories whose taken for granted 'newsworthiness' is the criterion of their 'natural' selection. Selected news events are often presented as implying significance for whole areas of industry not otherwise reported, and are more likely to receive prominence as news if they can be characterised or defined in a given frame of reference.

The strike by engine tuners at the BLMC Cowley plant, in January 1975, was newsworthy because it was 'a manifestly avoidable stoppage of production'; because of the role of BLMC in the economy not least as an exporter; and because of the general 'crisis' in the car industry. Such recognisable news angles could account for the dispute's extensive coverage in January.

Given that all these factors remained of great importance throughout 1975, the dramatic change in the amount of coverage of disputes in the motor vehicle industry in February, points to a peculiar inconsistency in the application of news values. It is almost as if the newsmen themselves were becoming bored with their own coverage, assuming a similar boredom in their audience and readership and in consequence cutting back.

The viewer of the television news might well have believed that in February strikes in the car industry ceased to appear as a major problem. Disputes in the car industry simply did not figure prominently in February. The television news covered 3 disputes; a strike at the Ford body plant, Halewood (28 February 1975: BBC1, 21.00 and BBC2, 12.55), a strike at the BLMC Castle Bromwich plant (21, 23, 24, 26 and 27 February in 4 bulletins on BBC1; 3 on BBC2; and 2 ITN bulletins); and on 3 February some reports of the Cowley tuners' strike which began in January (in 3 BBC1 bulletins, 2 BBC2 and 3 ITN bulletins).

Of the three disputes reported in the television news, the Castle Bromwich strike featured most prominently in all the media sampled. 'The strike has made 14,300 idle at three plants.... Production of the Mini and Jaguar lines has been halted.... The strike has cost British Leyland nearly £9 million in lost production at the rate of 400 Jaguars a week and 2,800 minis' (*Financial Times*, 28 February 1975 p. 12). Six hundred toolmakers were on strike for over three weeks.

The coverage this dispute received in no way reflected its similarity to the Cowley strike of the previous month. The Press Association devoted 21 per cent of its dispute coverage in January to Cowley and 6.8 per cent to Castle Bromwich in February. The quality papers devoted 28.9 per cent to Cowley in January and 14.8 per cent to Castle Bromwich in February. The popular papers devoted 40.5 per cent to Cowley in January and 11.8 per cent to Castle Bromwich in February. The television bulletins devoted 41.8 per cent to Cowley in January and 7.3 per cent to Castle Bromwich in February (Table 5.19).

Table 5.19 Media coverage of Castle Bromwich strike

Medium	Dispute reports Number	% of all disputes
PA Teletape	5	6.8
Press sample		
Daily Express	4	13.3
Daily Mirror	3	12.5
Daily Telegraph	4	6.5
Guardian	7	9.8
The Times	9	16.0
TV		
BBC1 Lunchtime	—	—
BBC1 Early Evening	2	12.5
Nine O'Clock News	2	9.5
Newsday	2	14.3
News Extra	—	—
News Review	1	20.0
First Report	—	—
ITN Lunchtime	—	—
ITN Early Evening	1	4.5
News at Ten	1	4.5

A comparison of the potential news angles reveals one significant difference – the Prime Minister's speech on strikes in the car industry by then nearly two months old. The 'crisis' in the car industry had not disappeared in February and British Leyland's significance for the economy was presumably unchanged. It would seem that the labelling of the Cowley tuners' dispute by the Prime Minister was crucial for that event to emerge so prominently as news. As the case of the study of the Cowley strike demonstrates,[19] the Prime Minister's statement provided the media with a dominant view on which to hang the tuners' story.

In February, the focus changed, as we have suggested, not simply because the pattern of events changed. The disputes that received the most extensive coverage that month were mainly in transport: railway signalmen, London bus drivers and the British Airways' 'shuttle' strike.

THE COVERAGE OF INDUSTRIAL ACCIDENTS ON TV NEWS

Although one cannot know when or where industrial accidents are going to occur, it is possible to establish a base line in which the incidence of accidents may be ascertained across a range of industries. Here we may have a good working idea of which industries are relatively high risk so far as serious and/ or fatal accidents are concerned. In HM Chief Inspector of Factories Annual Report 1974, Appendix 5 provides information reported to SIC order 3–20 (including minimum list headings) which covers manufacturing and construction. The information brought together there gives, for 1974, total and fatal reported accidents and the incidence rates of reported accidents per 1,000 for that year. In addition, for the period 1971–4, averages of fatal and Group 1 (i.e. the most serious for the person) accidents, are given per 100,000 employees at risk. A summary version of this table is reproduced here at SIC industrial order level (Table 5.20). Since this is the report of the factory inspectorate, some industrial areas such as sea transport are not covered. The television news ran some stories in these areas as noted above.

For 1974, the three industries having the most fatal accidents were construction (166), metal manufacture (53), and chemical and allied industries (46). The industries with the highest incidence rates of reported accidents for the year 1974 were metal manufacture (70.4), shipbuilding (61.5), and coal and petroleum products (55.6). For the period 1971–4 the industries with the highest fatality rates were construction (18.6), metal manufacture (14.2), and shipbuilding (13.0). For the same period, the industries with the highest Group 1 accident rates were metal manufacture (1,050), shipbuilding and marine engineering (840), and bricks, pottery, glass, cement, etc. (790). On all criteria therefore, metal manufacture and shipbuilding are the most dangerous industries to work in.

Table 5.21 (p. 157) shows TV coverage of accidents as they relate to manufacturing and construction. In the manufacturing and construction section of

Table 5.20 Reported accidents 1974 by industry (SIC 1968)

		Total reported accidents		(1) Incidence rates of rep. accid. per 1,000	(2) Av. of incidence rates per 100,000	
SIC		Total	Fatal		Fatal	Group 1
3	Food, drink and tobacco	24,992	24	39.0	3.3	650
4	Coal and petroleum products	1,718	3	55.6	10.0	610
5	Chemical and allied industries	9,825	46	34.6	9.0	590
6	Metal manufacture	26,685	53	70.4	14.2	1,050
7	Mechanical engineering	25,772	20	36.4	3.3	650
8	Instrument engineering	1,473	1	15.0	0.8*	250
9	Electrical engineering	12,547	3	20.6	0.8	320
10	Shipbuilding and marine engineering	8,939	15	61.5	13.0	840
11	Vehicles	17,371	10	30.9	2.2	460
12	Metal goods not elsewhere spec.	16,949	16	35.8	3.1	670
13	Textiles	12,447	9	26.4	2.7	500
14	Leather, leather goods and fur	745	1	19.0	3.1	400
15	Clothing and footwear	2,699	2	7.0	0.4	110
16	Bricks, pottery, glass, cement, etc.	11,474	16	45.5	7.2	790
17	Timber, furniture, etc.	6,946	14	30.1	4.2	780
18	Paper, printing and publishing	10,064	8	24.2	2.1	500
19	Other manufacturing industries	8,444	3	30.6	2.6	510
20	Construction	—	—	—	—	—

Notes:
(1) Annual all accidents incidence rates, 1974 (per 1,000 employees at risk).
(2) Averages of fatal and group 1 incidence rates 1971–4 (per 100,000 employees at risk).
*This is a correction to the published figure following consultation with the relevant department of employment–statistician.

industry, 9 accident stories were reported: 6 on BBC1, 6 on ITN, and 2 on BBC2. BBC1 and ITN reported industrial accidents on seven days. The difference in the number of mentions between BBC1 and ITN is accounted for by two more mentions of the Flixborough explosion inquiry by ITN and the reference to diving accidents in the oil industry which BBC did not cover.

The nine stories straddle three SIC categories and half of them are

Table 5.21 Industrial accident coverage on TV, Jan.–May 1975, for manufacturing and construction

SIC order	Event		Coverage		
			BBC1	BBC2	ITN
Oil and Petroleum	Fire on oil rig.	No. of days	1		1
	Oil industry	No. of mentions	1		1
	accident.	No. of days			1
	Cousteau	No. of mentions			1
	criticism on	No. of days			1
	diving deaths.	No. of mentions			1
Total stories	3	No. of days	1		3
		No. of mentions	1		3
Chemical and	Flixborough				
allied	Inquiry into	No. of days	2		2
industries	explosion.	No. of mentions	3	1	5
	Kent chemical			2	
	factory				
	explosion.	No. of days			1
		No. of mentions			1
	Gosport				
	Cyanamid				
	factory				
	workers				
	poisoned by	No. of days	1		1
	gas leakage.	No. of mentions	3	1	3
	Antwerp,			1	
	Belgium, plant				
	explosion	No. of days	1		1
	fatalities.	No. of mentions	2		3
Total stories	4	No. of days	4	2	5
		No. of mentions	8	3	12
Construction	Portsmouth				
	Motorway				
	bridge	No. of days	1		
	1 killed.	No. of mentions	1		
	Liverpool site	No. of days	1		
	1 killed.	No. of mentions	1		
Total stories	2	No. of days	2		
		No. of mentions	2		
Grand total	9	No. of days	7	2	7
		No. of mentions	11	3	14

located in chemical and allied industries. As it happens, the four accident stories constitute almost the total profile of the chemical industry so far as TV coverage is concerned. One of the stories is a foreign one relating to a plant explosion in Antwerp when six people were killed. Another explosion occurred in a Kent chemical plant when one person was killed and a case of workers being poisoned in the Gosport Cyanamid factory was reported. The Flixborough explosion took place in 1974 and is reflected in Table 5.21. The reports here relate to the findings of the Court of Inquiry.

It is of course entirely appropriate that the Flixborough story, which was by any definition an industrial accident of great magnitude, should be updated to include the Court of Inquiry findings. The 1974 Annual Report records that 'a total of 28 people working on the site at the time (i.e. 1 June 1974), were killed and 36 others were injured. Outside the works injuries and dangers were widespread but no one was killed. However, 53 people were recorded as casualties by the casualty bureau and hundreds more suffered relatively minor injuries. Some 1,821 houses and 167 shops in the surrounding area suffered damage' (Annual Report, p. 15). However, it is perhaps necessary to point out that the chemical industry is by no means the one with the highest incidence rates, as can be seen from Table 5.20.

The construction industry and the coal and petroleum products grouping, are both examples of industries with high accident rates, especially the first as Table 5.20 makes plain. These two industries account for the remaining four stories, two a piece. At the same time it can be seen that shipbuilding and marine engineering, metal manufacture and bricks, pottery, glass and cement, which have high accident rates on several of the criteria noted, are not reported at all. Given that the area of industrial accidents is a significant aspect of industrial life and work experience, the TV coverage is somewhat limited. With the particular exception of Flixborough, there is no clear rationale as to why some events are covered and others not. It appears, as it were, to be a hit and miss affair with no clear evidence of systematic coverage in this area. In so far as any rationale does appear to operate, it is linked with the coverage of disaster stories rather than with any routine concern with accidents in industry as a general social issue.

The general case for a more pronounced concern with accidents at work is detailed in *Safety and Health at Work* – the report of the Robens Committee 1970–2 (Cmnd 5034, HMSO, 1972).

And a further point can be made. General industrial health is particularly significant in the light of the high health hazards run in certain industries such as mining. Needless to say, the more general issue of industrial health receives little or no coverage on the television news.

Table 5.22 Principal wage settlements reported in 1975 (January–31 May 1975) and extent of TV coverage

Wage settlements				Extent of coverage									
					BBC1		BBC2		ITN		Total		
Date of agreement	Operative date	Industry or undertaking and district	Brief details of change	SIC order	Reports	Days	Reports	Days	Reports	Days	Reports	Days	
8 January	12 January	Gas supply – GB	Increase of 21p an hour (inclusive of consolidation of threshold payments of 11p an hour) to all adult workers, with proportional amounts for young workers.	21	—	—	—	—	—	—	—	—	
27 January	3 February	Building – GB	Increases (inclusive of consolidation of £4.10 a week threshold payments) in standard rates of £5 for craftsmen, of £4.40 for labourers, with proportional amounts for young workers together with increases of 40p or 20p a week in guaranteed bonus and the introduction of a Joint Board Supplement of £2.60 a week for craftsmen and £2.20 for labourers.	20	2	1	2	1	2	1	6	1	
	30 June	Building – GB	Weekly increases: standard rates: craft operatives, male £3, female £8.20. Labourers, male £2.40, female £3.40 to £6.80. Joint Board Supplement increased by £2.40 for craft operatives and £2 for labourers. Guaranteed minimum bonus increased as follows: craft operatives 60p; labourers 80p.										
27 January	3 February	Civil engineering construction – GB	Increase (inclusive of consolidation of £4.40 a week threshold payments) in standard rates of 12.5p an hour for craftsmen, of 11p for general operatives, together with increases of 40p or 20p a week in guaranteed bonus and the introduction of a Joint Board Supplement of £2.60 or £2.20 a week respectively, with proportional amounts for trainees and young workers.										
	30 June	Civil engineering construction – GB	Increases for craftsmen of 7.5p an hour in standard rates, of £2.40 a week in Joint Board Supplement and £0.60 a week in guaranteed bonus. General operatives' increases – 6p, £2 and 80p.										
30 January	20 February	Laundering (Wages Council) – GB	Increases (inclusive of threshold payments of 6p an hour) in general minimum time rates of 13.87p an hour for adult male and female workers 19 and over with varying amounts for young workers.	26	—	—	—	—	—	—	—	—	
20 February	First full pay week commencing on or after 31 March	Cast stone and cst concrete products – England and Wales	Increase of 8.375p an hour in minimum bsic rates.	16	—	—	—	—	—	—	—	—	

Table 5.22 continued

Wage settlements				Extent of coverage								
Date of agreement	Operative date	Industry or undertaking and district	Brief details of change	SIC order	BBC1 Reports	Days	BBC2 Reports	Days	ITN Reports	Days	Total Reports	Days
24 February	24 February	Retail meat trade – England and Wales	Increases (inclusive of consolidation of £4.40 a week threshold payments) of varying amounts according to occupation and area for workers 21 and over with proportional amounts for young workers.	23	—	—	—	—	—	—	—	—
1 March	First pay day in March	Footwear manufacture – UK (except East Lancs and the Fylde Coast)	Increases in minimum day wage rates of £1.375 a week for men 19 and over, of £1.875 for women 19 and over with proportional amounts for young workers.	12	—	—	—	—	—	—	—	—
3 March	1 March	Coalmining – GB	National standard weekly rates increased (inclusive of consolidation of £4.40 threshold payments) by amounts ranging from £9 to £16 according to occupation for adult workers, with proportional amounts for young workers, together with the introduction of a national production bonus scheme.	2	32	15	19	13	27	12	78	17
	First pay week in July	Coalmining – GB	No national production bonus was payable during the third quarter of 1975; this involved reductions in minimum entitlement of £2.90 a week for adults and £1.95 for juveniles.									
5 March	26 March	Dressmaking and women's light clothing (Wages Council – England and Wales)	Increases in general minimum time rates of 9p an hour for men 21 and over, of 11.25p for women 18 and over with varying amounts for late entrants, learners and young workers.	15	—	—	—	—	—	—	—	—
	31 March		Increases in general minimum time rates of 3p an hour for all workers with proportional amounts for learners and young workers.									
12 March	10 March	Retail distribution, Co-op societies – GB	Increase of £2.50 a week for male and female workers 21 and over, with proportional amounts for young workers.	23	—	—	—	—	—	—	—	—
12 March	14 April	Seed crushing, compound and provender manufacture – UK	Increase in basic rates of £6.11 a week for men and £6.61 for women 18 and over inclusive of consolidation of £3 from existing payments.	3	—	—	—	—	—	—	—	—
19 March	14 April	Clothing manufacture – GB	Increases in general minimum time rates and yield levels of 6p an hour for all workers.	15	—	—	—	—	—	—	—	—
25 March	1 January	Post Office – UK	Increases of varying amounts following revision of pay scales for manipulative grades (postmen, postmen higher grade, telegraphists, telephonists and postal officers).	22	2	1	3	2	3	2	8	2

Table 5.22 continued

Wage settlements				Extent of coverage								
					BBC1		BBC2		ITN		Total	
Date of agreement	Operative date	Industry or undertaking and district	Brief details of change	SIC order	Reports	Days	Reports	Days	Reports	Days	Reports	Days
10 April	First full pay period commencing on or after 1 March	Rubber manufacture – GB	Increases in minimum earnings levels (inclusive of threshold payments of £4.40 a week) of £7.50 a week for men, of £8.25 for women, with proportional amounts for young workers.	19	—	—	—	—	—	—	—	—
5 May	1 April	Vehicle building – UK	Increase in minimum wage rates of 8.75p an hour for adult workers with proportional amounts for young workers.	11	—	—	—	—	—	—	—	—
8 May	5 May	Retail distribution: Co-op societies – GB	Increases (inclusive of consolidation of threshold payments of £4.40 a week) of varying amounts, according to occupation, for general distributive workers.	23	—	—	—	—	—	—	—	—
14 May	26 May	Engineering – UK	Increases in national minimum time rates of £4 a week for skilled men, of £3.20 for unskilled men and £3.25 for women, with proportional amounts for young workers.	71,819	2	1	—	—	2	1	4	1
	24 November	Engineering – UK	Increases in national minimum rates of £4 a week for skilled men, of £3.25 for unskilled men and of £4.25 for women (thus giving parity with unskilled male rates).									
16 May	5 May	Cotton spinning and weaving – Lancashire, Cheshire, Yorkshire and Derbyshire	Increase in current wage rates of 12.5 per cent.	13	—	—	—	—	—	—	—	—
20 May	26 May	Shipbuilding and ship repairing – UK	Increases in national minimum time rates of £4 for skilled workers, £3.62 for semi-skilled workers and £3.25 for unskilled workers, with proportional amounts for young workers.	10	1	1	1	1	2	1	4	1
	Beginning of pay week containing 24 November	Shipbuilding and ship reaping – UK	Increases in national minimum time rates of £4 a week for adult skilled workers, of £3.63 for semi-skilled and £3.25 for unskilled workers, with proportional amounts for young workers.									
22 May	12 March	Electricity supply – GB	Increases in salaries ranging from £375.50 to £507.50 a year for adult workers, with proportional amounts for young workers.	21	16	9	11	9	9	6	36	13
23 May	Beginning of first full pay week in June	Motor vehicle retail and repair – UK	Increases in minimum rates ranging from 4.5p to 10.25p an hour according to occupation for adult workers, with proportional amounts for young workers and apprentices together with a restructuring of grades.	23	—	—	—	—	—	—	—	—

Table 5.22 continued

Wage settlements				Extent of coverage								
Date of agreement	Operative date	Industry or undertaking and district	Brief details of change	SIC order	BBC1 Reports	BBC1 Days	BBC2 Reports	BBC2 Days	ITN Reports	ITN Days	Total Reports	Total Days
27 May	14 June	Post Office – UK	Cost of living supplement of 5 per cent on basic rates for manipulative grades.									
	18 July	Post Office – UK	Further non-enhanceable cost of living supplement of 2 per cent on basic rates for manipulative grades.									
	First full pay week following 15 August	Post Office – UK	Further non-enhanceable cost of living supplement of 1 per cent of national basic rates for manipulative grades.									
	First full pay week following 12 September	Post Office – UK	Further non-enhanceable cost of living supplement of 1 per cent of 22 national basic rates for manipulative grades.		See ref. above	25 March	See ref. above	25 March	See ref. above	25 March	See ref. above	25 March
	First full pay week following 17 October	Post Office – UK	Further non-enhanceable cost of living supplement of 1 per cent of national basic rates for manipulative grades.									
	First full pay week following 14 November	Post Office – UK	Further non-enhanceable supplement of 1 per cent of national basic rates for manipulative grades.									
27 May	First full pay week following 12 December	Post Office – UK	Further non-enhanceable cost of living supplement of 2 per cent of national basic rates for manipulative grades.	3	—	—	—	—	—	—	—	—
30 May	2 June	Cocoa, chocolate and sugar confectionery manufacture – GB	Increases of £4.35 a week for full-time men and women.									

Source: Department of Employment Gazette, Feb.–June 1975

PAY CLAIMS AND WAGE SETTLEMENTS

Table 5.22 lists the principal wage settlements concluded between 1 January and 31 May 1975 and records the extent to which these settlements (and in some cases the negotiations preceding them) were covered on the three television channels. The six industrial sectors reported were mining, engineering, shipbuilding, the construction industry, electricity supply and the postal services. Reports were carried by all news services in each case, with the one exception that BBC2 did not mention the engineering pay deal. Although there were some twelve settlements in Table 5.22 that were not reported at all, it can be seen that these included a number of groups that, as far as the economy on the whole is concerned, are somewhat peripheral. It would have been surprising to have had a report on the seed crushing, compound and provender manufacture pay settlement for instance. But enough of the major industry wide agreements are reported to make this an area of routine news coverage.

In four of the cases, the focus was on the settlement itself, referred to on one or at the most two days. These are clearly quite different in emphasis to the mining industry and electricity supply industry claims, which were followed over an extended period. The recent history of the mining industry in connection with its pay claim and strike that brought down the last Conservative government, is well known. The 1975 pay claim was defined as critical in relation to the future of the Social Contract and the eventual settlement provided the occasion for inquests and speculation on the likely efficacy of government pay policy. The power workers' claim was also seen, by the television correspondents, as a potential challenge to the government's policy, particularly because of the union's concern with the erosion of differentials brought about by flat rate wage increases. Both mining and electricity supply are examples of industries which can have a direct effect on the rest of the productive system in the event of industrial action and we believe the closer monitoring of these industries reflected that awareness and gave something of a dramatic character to reporting on the subject.

Our argument that pay claims and settlements are routinely reported is strengthened by further evidence of two kinds. First, a number of pay settlements not listed by the Department of Employment's analysis (see Table 5.23) were also reported. These related to teachers, radiographers, dentists, the armed forces and members of parliament. Second, a number of claims which were actually settled after the period of our study were reported (see Table 5.23). These concerned agricultural workers, steel workers, railwaymen, university teachers, doctors, policemen, seamen and civil servants. In the case of the railwaymen, the coverage was extensive and included the signalmen's strike. Apart from national wage settlements, with which we have dealt here, there were other more localised claims (related to particular firms or geographical localities) that were reported, as in the case of London docks and the Chrysler plant in Coventry.

Table 5.23 Additional coverage of wage claims and settlements (Jan.–May 1975)

SIC		BBC1 Rep.	Days	BBC2 Rep.	Days	ITN Rep.	Days	Total Rep.	Days
01	NUAAW claim	—	—	—	—	1	1	1	1
06	Steelworkers' claim	1	1	4	3	2	1	7	3
22	Seamen's claim	5	3	2	2	3	2	10	4
25	Teachers' EIS claim and settlement Scotland	4	3	—	—	2	2	6	3
25	University teachers' claim	3	2	2	1	3	1	8	2
25	Teachers' claim	1	1	1	1	—	—	2	1
25	NHS doctors' pay rise	2	1	1	1	2	2	5	2
25	Junior doctors' and GPs' claim	4	3	4	3	6	5	14	5
25	NHS Radiographers' pay deal	2	1	1	1	1	1	4	1
25	Dentists' pay deal	—	—	—	—	1	1	1	1
27	Armed forces' pay rise	3	2	3	2	2	1	8	3
27	Police pay claim	3	2	—	—	—	—	3	2
27	Civil Service pay	1	1	—	—	1	1	2	1
27	MPs' pay rise	—	—	—	—	1	1	1	1

All of this leads to the conclusion that pay deals and claims were indeed subject to regular scrutiny. The relationship of pay to the government's management of the economy and the health of their Social Contract may be seen as an important organising device for handling industrial and economic news; in fact for the majority of these stories the dominant view was often simply whether they were settlements within the Social Contract. The rival industrial correspondents did not always agree on this, as our case study in Chapter 8, Section II shows.

JOURNALISTIC CRITERIA

The question may be put: If there is no clear relationship between indicators of real activity and industrial news coverage, what light does this throw on news values? At once the caveat should be entered that in the case of wage claims and settlements, the Social Contract was used as the basis of reasonably systematic coverage. In relation to the other indicators, however – employment magnitudes, strike statistics and accident rates – there is no consistent matching between them and the events reported on television industrial news. The information given by television on these events is, in a statistical sense at least, unrepresentative. This itself is an important conclusion about the skewed nature of industrial reporting in relation to specified criteria.

The response may be made: news is about the extraordinary not the ordinary, about the 'significant' events not the mundane ones. This response has been partially considered in our discussion of prominent stoppages. To this we would add a further comment. It is not difficult for this response to operate as a circular argument. The significant is what is covered. The insignificant is what is not covered. It is quite a good protective device from a debating point of view since the concept of significant absences is ruled out by definition. It is also possible for this response to serve as an underpinning for a view of journalistic criteria which treats them as an arcane mystery known only to the practitioners of the craft. At the intuitive level it is all about having a 'nose' for a good story.

As an information service, there is something to be said for covering routine matters systematically and that this itself could constitute a journalistic criterion if policy governing news was so disposed. Moreover, as a matter of empirical analysis, the appeal to the value of significance does not result in a random collection of stories: the anarchic product, as it were, of competing journalists and news services. What emerges is a pattern of coverage which in terms of the industries, the stories covered and the number of reports, reveals great similarities between BBC and ITN. It is like looking at the synoptic gospels, and facing the almost irresistible question: What is their common source?

Are there then principles of selection which may be detected and at least by implication, suggest something about prevailing journalistic practices? Recall the dominant coverage allocated to the car industry, transport and communications, and public administration. The first of these is the pre-eminent example of mass-production industry. It may be used to summarise what are held to be the problems of production in an advanced industrial society: strike-prone workers who, despite high wages, are not content; the cycle of prosperity and depression always more dramatic with a consumer product in a mass market; the competitiveness of the international market and the relevance of this for the balance of payments; the relation of government to industry as it pertains to financial aid, control structure and the promotion of industrial efficiency. In a phrase, the car industry may be said to embody a concern with the principle of industrial (even social) survival in a society exposed to the stiff winds of competition and inflation.

The emphasis on transport and communications and on public administration, reveals, we suggest, another criterion. It is a concern for the inconvenienced consumer of goods and services. A strike that grounds aircraft is highly inconvenient to the holidaymakers and businessmen; a railway strike is very troublesome to the commuter; a doctors' work-to-rule or hospital workers' boycotting of private patients is distressing to the consumer of health services; and a strike of dustcart drivers is a growing difficulty for the consumer wishing to dispose of unconsumed leftovers.

These are two of the essential journalistic criteria in the industrial area, which are embedded into, and structure, the news on television. They have to do with unscheduled interruptions to production processes and consumption patterns. Given this emphasis, it is difficult to structure news in a way that does not, implicitly at least, blame those groups or individuals who precipitate action that, in one way or another, is defined as 'disruptive'. This structuring often demands a search for the 'disruptive' element, which is exacerbated by the lack of historical perspective – an element of news presentation that often results in a somewhat arbitrary allocation of blame for the disruption. The other side of the coin, the concern with a particular kind of social order, is revealed in the preoccupation with the 'social contract' in its many ramifications. Thus we would deny that the constraints of bulletin duration, technical limitations, human resources, programme budgets, geographical and other access difficulties, result in a haphazard picture of industrial life. The journalistic criteria outlined above and other elements not mentioned, result in a coherent frame for the reporting of industry. The contours of coverage never deviate from this frame.

Given these working assumptions about industrial news values, we would be hard put to demonstrate any 'bias' at all.

NOTES

1 Chapter 4.
2 R. S. Frank, *Message Dimensions of Television News*, IndianapolisL: Lexington Books, 1973, pp. 21–2.
3 *Inside the News* discussion programme transmitted on BBC2; this point was made by both the Editor BBC News and the Editor ITN.
4 For example, 'The strike at the Chrysler Engine Works at Coventry is to go on. Shop stewards today told the 4,000 workers on strike to go on with their demands for an immediate eight pounds a week rise.' Fourth item in *Newsday* bulletin, BBC2, 14 May 1975.
5 For example, 'News at home included Chancellor Denis Healey's warning of the lunacy of inflationary wage increases. Unemployment figures were up by 10,000 and there was an even bigger increase in short-time working. Still no end to the big London dock strike but a new container work offer has been suggested by the government. The rejection by both rail and power workers of pay offers from their boards which are within the Social Contract. Each union is quoting the miners' 30 or more per cent increase as the basis of a claim for similar treatment and with dustcart drivers back in work at Liverpool, but still on strike in Glasgow, the City Corporation called in the professionals.' (There followed a short report with film and interviews on the situation in Glasgow.) *News Review*, BBC2, 23 March 1975.
6 For example, *Newscaster*: On the day that it has been announced by the government that new car sales last year were down by 25 per cent on 1973, the Director of British Leyland's Cowley Plant has warned of a calamity if the strike situation there gets worse. Figures out today show that private car and van registrations dropped from 1,688,000 in 1973 to 1,273,000 last year and all vehicle registrations were down nearly as much by 20 per cent. The warning came in a letter from the Plant Director, Mr John Symons, to Leyland employees as the Company and the Engineering Union agreed to talks tomorrow at the Conciliation and Arbitration Service to try to solve the strike

of engine tuners at Cowley. Mr Symons said that the strike had meant that Cowley was failing to meet what he called its survival budget. He also gave a warning that a further deterioration would be calamitous with the strongest likelihood of a major reduction in manufacturing and employment at Cowley. Here is our Industrial Correspondent, Giles Smith:

Smith: Mr Symons' warning to Cowley's 12,000 workforce is easily the strongest since this dispute started a month ago. In using words like 'calamity' and a 'major reduction in manufacturing and in employment' he has got the full authority of Lord Stokes and the Board. The message is simple: if this dispute isn't sorted out very quickly indeed, the government may well choose not to help the company in this difficult time. Meanwhile the problems of the industry as a whole have been highlighted by today's figures [. . .] in sales last year down 25 per cent. This has seen tens of thousands of the industry's half a million workforce going onto short time and unsold cars piling up in the car parks. All this in the year when Aston Martin went broke, British Leyland went to the government for help, and the three Americans, Ford, Vauxhall and Chrysler warning they might have to transfer operations to the Continent. Chrysler is probably the worst hit with their Ryton plant near Coventry being the main casualty. Between Ryton and their Scottish plant at Linwood, Chrysler have 10,000 men on a 2-day week. Linwood, in fact, closes next week. One thousand have lost their jobs altogether, there is short-time working at the Stoke engine plant and they've got 28,000 unsold cars waiting to go to the dealers. Vauxhall, the General Motors subsidiary which should be getting 15 per cent of the market but isn't, is not much better off. At their plants at Luton, Dunstable and Ellesmere Port 6,000 of their workers will be going on 3-day working by the end of this week. Of the Americans, Ford is the least affected, at Halewood and their other big plant at Dagenham, the company sales of Capris and Cortinas continue to go well. There is no short-time working yet though not much overtime either. Even they, however, have laid off 12,000 white-collar workers. The company's main bright spot is the launch tomorrow of their brand new version of the Escort. A car, they hope, will help them weather the energy crisis. The problems of our biggest and only British-owned company, Leyland, are well known, particularly at Cowley. Here the jobs of 12,000 are tonight in the balance, and Leyland are not just talking about temporary layoffs until the tuners go back to work.

Elsewhere the company's 20,000 employees at Longbridge haven't worked any overtime for months and Jaguar the export leader have put 7,000 workers on a 4-day week.

All this, the most depressing scenario for an industry whose exports last year totalled nearly £2,000m, nearly one-fifth of the country's total overseas sales.

If Britain is to make any sort of attempt at clearing the present staggering Balance of Payments problem, it can certainly not do without a healthy motor industry for the investment, the manpower and the will to defy the energy crisis and step up sales.

(First item, ITN, *News at Ten*, 22 January 1975)

7   We should make clear that in this context we are not measuring the amount of time allocated to these stories. Time allocation of news items has, however, been discussed above. The base for all the counting in this chapter is the complete television news output for the 22-week period. There are two possible sources of distortion which are taken into account. First, there is the nine-day period at the end of May during which ITN was off the air because of an industrial dispute. Second, a small number of the bulletins were not recorded. These accounted for only 5.7 per cent of the total output in the first three months and the number

lost in April and May was even fewer.

8   See P. Hartmann, *Industrial Relations Journal*, vol. 6, no. 4, Winter 1975, pp. 4ff. for an alternative view based on his own identification of 'major themes'.

9   Official statistics, like the news itself, are 'products' which pose their own problems of interpretation. For a discussion of the epistemological arguments surrounding their use, see B. Hindess, *The Use of Official Statistics in Sociology: a Critique of Positivism and Ethnomethodology*, London: Macmillan, 1973. Our use of the Department of Employment's statistics in this chapter has one main purpose: to demonstrate the existence of an independently derived and publicly available alternative description to that of the news. The conceptual model and technical apparatus used in the production of these statistics, though not beyond criticism, does not pose any major theoretical problem.

10   See Accidents, pp. 155–8 above.

11   'The official series of statistics of stoppages of work due to industrial disputes in the United Kingdom relates to disputes connected with terms and conditions of employment. Stoppages involving fewer than 10 workers or lasting less than one day are excluded except where the aggregate of working days lost exceeded 100. Workers involved are those directly involved and indirectly involved (thrown out of work although not parties to the disputes) *at the establishment where the disputes occurred*. The number of working days lost is the aggregate of days lost by workers both directly and indirectly involved (as defined). It follows that the statistics do not reflect repercussions elsewhere, that is, *at establishments other than those at which the disputes occurred*. For example, the statistics exclude persons laid off and working days lost at such establishments through shortages of material caused by the stoppages included in the statistics.'

Notes on the compilation of dispute figures from the Department of Employment statistics

(1) The monthly index of 'stoppages', 'working days lost', and 'workers involved', published in the *Department of Employment Gazette* (HMSO) is cumulative. Thus figures published in February 1975 show disputes for January 1975; those published in March 1975 show total dispute figures for January and February; and those published in April show totals for January, February and March, etc. The separate monthly indices were thus established by simple subtraction.

(2) The only available figures recording stoppages, days lost, etc., was a classification by industrial sector which contains certain sectors otherwise considered separate. For example, mechanical, instruments, and electrical engineering (sectors 07, 08, 09), are treated as simply 'Engineering' in the dispute index. Similarly, leather goods (14), and clothing and footwear (15), are combined while insurance, banking, finance, business services (24), professional and other services (25) are combined with public administration (27).

12   N.B. ITN was off the air for one week during the period in the study.

13   Francis Williams, *Dangerous Estate*, London: Arrow, 1959, p. 107.

14

| | Circulation 1974 | | Readership by social grade* | | |
	m.	AB	C²	C¹	DE
Daily Mirror	4.6	6	21	42	32
Daily Express	3.2	15	28	31	27
Daily Telegraph	1.4	42	35	14	10
Guardian	0.4	40	36	16	9
The Times	0.4	5	28	13	9

Note: *By Registrar General Class Studies
Source: JICTARS National Readership Survey, July 1973–June 1974.

15 Thus a possible indication of a further dimension of news value in frequency of Press Association tape items was not utilised.

16 The Press Association carried *one* dispute report in this area in January – no reports in February.

17 Plessey, Liverpool – strike in protest of Post Office contract given to a Swedish firm (BBC1, 17.45 and 21.00, 25 February 1975).

18 There was no television coverage of dispute in this sector in February.

19 The press sample shows coverage of these three disputes in February and two others. The PA also covered those three with an additional three strikes.

Chapter 6

News talk

I Assembling the news text*

> Each sentence, each word, must be made to count. We must learn to handle words as if they were gold.
>
> (BBC *News Guide*)[1]

We now turn to the properties of news talk at the level of the text as a series of more or less meaningfully *related* sentences, since we have previously argued that syntactic and lexical analyses are of themselves insufficient for our purposes. We shall attempt to uncover some of the rules of composition which represent a form of 'competence' (in the linguistic sense described above) in the language of news and also a professional, journalistic competence or expertise.

The codes and rules involved are not necessarily intentional. The features that set the news text apart from other forms of discourse are only partly related to conscious practices and procedures. Those rules that do get articulated are picked up in the course of professional socialisation and are embodied in rules-of-thumb or conventions which journalists adopt when they edit texts for transmission. A crude indication of these professional skills may be found in house style books or in journalistic primers, the rules of which are exemplified in the following extract from ITN's house style book:[2]

> A well-written ITN programme sounds clear, intelligent, friendly and authoritative all at once. Though space is limited, good writing is tremendously important. Don't be frightened to be dramatic in your writing, if the story merits it. But try to secure your dramas by facts, not by adjectives. The *fact* that Mrs Kennedy cried out 'No, no!' when Kennedy was shot is of more value than a dozen adjectives. But adjectives can be useful too, provided they are appropriate, and the kind you would

---

*First published in Glasgow University Media Group, *More Bad News*, London and Boston, Routledge & Kegan Paul, 1980, pp. 138–64.

use in spoken speech. Sentences should be kept short and simple, and must be completely comprehensible at first hearing. The viewer, unlike the reader, cannot pause to refer back or digest a point. The simple pattern of subject, verb, object usually fits television speech best. Not every sentence needs to be complete, and the verb can be omitted surprisingly often.

Our evidence from observation of newsrooms indicates that style books are used no more than as glossaries of terms which pose difficulties (e.g. the ambiguities surrounding the use of 'freedom fighter', 'terrorist' and 'guerrilla'). They are not normally used as a text on how to write news items. This set of journalistic imperatives begs several questions, the most basic being whether or not journalists regularly follow such advice. In practice it is difficult to conceive of a set of rules which would allow them to achieve the desired effects in terms of clarity, intelligibility and authority. This latter competence is a product of 'experience' rather than instruction.

The majority of the rules of composition remain unarticulated, just as the rules of story classification, placement, duration and presentation remain implicit in the structuring of news bulletins. This structure was described in *Bad News*, and we demonstrated how the content of the news is arranged in predictable ways which vary within narrow limits. The language of the news functions both to uphold the divisions described there and at the same time binds the fragments of 'news' into a coherent whole. Building on Halliday's work on language function, which in turn draws upon the work of the Prague School of Linguists, we analyse news talk in terms of language *usage* in an attempt to explain why the text is structured in one way rather than another.[3] One of Halliday's main academic contributions has been to demonstrate that the structure of the clause involves at least three functions. He terms these the 'ideational' function, which expresses the content and refers to extralinguistic reality; the 'interpersonal' function which expresses and maintains social relationships between speakers; and finally the 'textual' function, which concerns the structuring of the text itself, the delineation of message units and distribution of message units within texts. Any clause may embody one or all of these functions or 'options'. So, for example, to analyse the opening sentence of a news item about a strike by maintenance workers at the Houses of Parliament would involve identifying the multiple functions of the sentence. In this example (BBC1, 21.00, 10 April 1975) the sentence is as follows:

Strike pickets have been out at the Houses of Parliament.

Here, the content (the ideational function) of the sentence is embodied in three elements which correspond to the classes of noun, verb and adverb or adverbial group. These are the participants, the process and the circumstance respectively. The interpersonal function which defines the roles of participants in the speech situation is expressed in the 'mood', which is declarative; i.e.

it is a statement and not a question, response, command or exclamation. The modal subject, in our example 'strike pickets', is the same as the subject of the ideational functional. This is generally the case except in the imperative mood. If, for instance, this sentence were cast in the imperative (which is rare in present news talk in part because it supposedly trades on the past and present not the future), then the subject would be the speaker, '[We say] strike pickets out at the Houses of Parliament'. This frequent absence of the newsreader as subject helps of course to reinforce the supposed neutrality and objectivity of news.

The third function, that of structuring the text, can best be illustrated by rearranging the sentence as follows:

At the Houses of Parliament strike pickets have been out.

This cannot be done without altering the emphasis and therefore the meaning of the sentence. In English the theme of a clause is the element which is placed first. The textual function of the original sentence is therefore expressed in 'strike pickets'. Halliday describes this as the peg on which the message is hung. He points out that the actor (the ideational subject), the subject in the interpersonal function and the theme are often identical. Where they are different, as in the passive form, there may be practical or linguistic reasons. In this example, as in others, if the report were passive the three subjects would be different. Putting the example into the passive we might get: 'The Houses of Parliament have been hit by strike pickets'. Put this way, 'who are the strikers?' and related questions immediately arise, but with 'strike pickets' as the modal subject, such questions are not necessarily on the agenda because the subjects are all functionally related. None of this detracts from the approach which indicates that the grammarian's notion of 'subject' combines at least three distinct functional elements which can be independent of one another and which are glossed over in a purely grammatical account of sentences. Our own analysis (unlike Halliday's) does not take the clause as the basic unit, but uses that understanding of the ordering and function of elements at this level to apply to discourse units larger than the sentence. It alerts attention to the fact that discourse is not necessarily unitary but may serve more than one function. The news text is not simply a set of discrete sentences. Its assembly and structure carry an ideological meaning of their own which is directly related to its conditions of production and its claim to objectivity.

The sample on which the analysis is based consists of one week's complete news broadcasts between 11 and 17 May 1975. The analytic units are not simply to be regarded as higher levels of grammar but should be seen to lie between the level of grammar and non-linguistic organisation. A unit may consist of a word, a clause or more than one sentence and at the same time it may coincide with a short item, an interview or some other element of extra-linguistic organisation.

HEADLINES

Trade figures – some cheering news.

(ITN, 22.00, 14 May 1975)

And there may be some good news for the motor industry . . .

(ITN, 13.00, 16 May 1975)

Headlines are seen as having crucial importance in the language of newspaper reporting.[4] They are one of the most important devices for summarising and drawing attention to a story and, so far as the press is concerned, are also one of the strongest visual indicators of style. In television news they have no exact equivalent because the audience's hearing of the bulletin follows a logic which is predetermined by news producers and over which the viewers can exercise no discretion (say, over running order) except to switch off – mentally or physically.[5] They cannot turn or jump pages.

The graphological distinctions of the newspaper can have no precise corresponding variation in loudness, stress, pace, or the kinesics involved in the reading of the news. Instead, the significance of items has to be weighted by the amount of time allocated to them, their placing in the bulletin, and the status of those who appear as interviewees. In certain bulletins the most salient stories are underlined, as it were, by repetition – by summaries of the 'main points' at the beginning or end of the bulletins. On ITN's *News at Ten* these points are actually compressed into verbal headlines between the 'bongs', the chimes of Big Ben. In the case of commercial television's *News at Ten*, because of the so-called 'natural break', an item may be underlined by as many as four repetitions.[6] For it could be mentioned in the opening, again as part of the hookers to hold people over the ads (the natural break), until the second half where it could appear as an item; and finally it could be mentioned in the summing-up at the end of the programme, when that is done.

Most television newspersons would agree that the placing of an item in the running order is an indicator of its importance. However, analysis of the headlines reveals that they do not follow the convention slavishly with a direct correspondence between the headline and the running order. See, for instance, the headlines and running order in *News at Ten* on 16 May in Table 6.1. To omit a headline for Item 2 and to include a headline for Item 14 serves as a 'hooking' device. The audience are given some broad notion of attractive stories from the whole bulletin. In effect they are invited to stay tuned and, as in the above example, it is often a key human interest or sports story from the second half of the bulletin that occupies the last 'bong' position. But it is rare that any headline will be taken out of order, as it were. The ranking of the headlines matches the ranking of the stories in the bulletin whatever the omissions in the headline list. One example of this was *News at Ten* on 13 May 1975, which began with the headlines shown in Table 6.2. The normal hierarchically related headlines here deviate in that headlines 3 and 4 refer to

Table 6.1 Headline order: ITN, 22.00, 16 May 1975

Headline order	Actual running order
1 Britain's inflation rate a record figure – far worse than expected	1
2 The Dunlop strike is over – 18,000 go back to work	3
3 But Chrysler throw 8,000 out of a job tonight	4
4 The armed forces get a 29 per cent pay rise	5
5 Tennis – Nastase and Taylor in trouble at Bournemouth	14

Table 6.2 Headline order: ITN, 22.00, 13 May 1975

Headline order	Actual running order
1 Captured cargo boat – US warships and marines stand by	1
2 Work has stopped on printing Britain's banknotes	5
3 Mr Foot tells the Chrysler strikers to go back to work	8
4 CBI forecast a deep recession and rising unemployment	7
5 The once-a-year soccer match fit for a Queen	15

items 8 and 7 respectively. There is at least a suspicion of a causal connotation in the headline sequence, as they are presented together; the foreign and human interest stories having no obvious connection in terms of subject matter. The reversing of the actual running order of the economic and industrial items into a new headline order unintentionally or otherwise creates the possibility of the audience causally associating strikes with recession. Sometimes there may be some pragmatic reason for this, for instance it may be necessary to separate two pieces of film or tape by a still photograph or graphic to facilitate cueing the different types of material into the sequence. However, these technical considerations did not seem to apply in the bulletin in question. Instead, what may be illustrated here is the general tendency to associate 'economic' and 'industrial' affairs in preferred ways. In these examples, the selection as well as the ordering of items in the headline sequence is closely consistent with the inferential framework which we found was used in the coverage of inflation and the Social Contract.[7] The examples tend to reflect the structure and the packaging of the bulletins as a whole by bringing together the subject matter of inflation, recession, strikes and pay. The use of headlines in this way is important in establishing, through repetition, the priorities expressed in the bulletin proper. Here the headlines serve as a signifier of the tone of the bulletin.

We are not only being given the most salient 'facts' of the day's news; we are being invited to take an interest, follow a lead, and ultimately and subtly join in a stance – a stance revealing the basic inferential frameworks used by the broadcasters. In the absence of any imperative form which would immediately reveal the involvement of the newsman with the audience and hence undermine the impression of objectivity, we are asked indirectly to take note of something important, to be intrigued, entertained and informed. Amending Halliday, we can apply that analytic to highlight the 'textual' function of the headlines, which are the initial structuring acts of news discourse.[8]

BOUNDARY MARKERS

More bad news from the car industry
                                         (BBC1, 21.00, 24 February 1975)

Good news today for one of Britain's major shipbuilders
                                         (BBC1, 21.00, 14 February 1975)

In many bulletins there are no headlines as such and the bulletin has to 'speak for itself' – via the running order of items, the ways in which they are treated, and the time allotted. There are a number of linguistic indicators as well as paralinguistic indicators (pauses, head movements, etc.) which demarcate one item from another. These literally mark a boundary in discourse.

In essence boundary markers are phrases that do not contain propositions which are part of the news item's message; rather they serve to specify that a news item is beginning and often they indicate the nature of the item. They refer most frequently to time and places. Often they consist of no more than the simple conjunction and adverb 'And . . .' or 'And now . . .'.

The most common boundary markers separate foreign from domestic news; for example: 'At home . . .', 'Here at home . . .', 'In Britain . . .', or 'In this country . . .'.[9] Details of place are often used to signal a shift from one item to the next. Although the phrases 'In Glasgow . . .', 'On Merseyside . . .' and 'At London's Heathrow airport . . .' have a content with an 'ideational' function, their position at the very beginning of an item indicates that their function lies in marking the boundary rather than introducing the theme or in giving an important detail.[10] Sometimes the boundary between items is marked but not specified, as in 'And now some other news . . .'.[11] Less frequently, the boundary markers provide the linguistic context for editorial comment in which the news is defined as 'good' or 'bad' or is otherwise evaluated; as for instance in the above quotations 'More bad news from the car industry', 'Good news today for [shipbuilders]', and 'It's been a critical day for the Health Service' or even 'Very much less glamorously in Glasgow . . .'.[12] These are some of the occasions on which the inferential framework of those who produce the news most obviously comes to the surface. This framework is always there but is usually implicit rather than explicit. We have previously described the inferential framework of industrial reporting. These instances indicate that the framework trades on and assumes a consensus of values. There is no way in which 'good' and 'bad' news can be readily understood if the question 'Good or bad for whom?' is admitted.

Boundary markers not only set one item apart from another; they sometimes take the form of subheads which label as well as delineate the item. This type of specific boundary marker is called a 'catchline' by professional broadcasters. Schlesinger states:

> Thus: 'Industrial News', 'The Commons', 'The Watergate Affair' are all phrases intended to swiftly cue in the audience to the content of the next story, while making the assumption that people are sufficiently familiar with its past developments to comprehend present ones. Catchlines contribute to a news style which both looks and sounds economical.[13]

Industrial stories, once they have become running stories, acquire tags (specific catchlines) such as 'The London dock strike', and 'The railway signalmen's dispute' which are used simply as labels, without being formed into sentences. 'Now rubbish' – a label for the Glasgow dustcart drivers' dispute – is one of the more idiosyncratic examples.[14] Like the paging conventions, headlines and subheadings in a newspaper, these tags (including 'Now some industrial news') give the audience clues to what is to follow. Stories which may have wider implications, or events that occur in industry but which are not reported as 'industrial' news, are usually not included in what follows such catchlines.

One major exception to this is news of pay and pay claims, which is often linked to news of prices. Thus 'After today's pay and prices news, one further item about the economy' and 'Now to news of rising prices and rising pay'.[15] Given the basic inferential framework – that is that wages were primarily responsible for inflation in this period – these boundary markers are only to be expected. 'Industrial' is in fact generally applied to the employment and industrial relations aspects of industry and not to the financial, administrative, production or consumer aspects.

The process of 'labelling', or in Goffman's terminology 'framing', is well understood in sociology and social psychology and it can be shown that circumstances may be altered, behaviour reinforced and conditioned, attitudes affected and perceptions changed by the consistent application of labels.[16] The use of apparently neutral names to describe stories is therefore not as straightforward as it seems. Indeed, Dengler has argued that a study of something as detailed as film labels or titles provides a basis for tracing the pattern of cultural themes in the history of movie-making. Using the *General Inquirer* and the *Psycho-Sociological Dictionary*, he claims that his work lends

precision to generalisation gained from a mere perusal of titles and lends support to historians of film who have pointed to the role Hollywood played in reflecting American Society and culture and exploiting it at the box office. The domestic preoccupations of the first decade, its latent work ethic set in a communal tone with highly moral undercurrent, gives way to the blatant enticements and fantasies of the 1920's and 1930's, the incisive and personalised propaganda of the 1940's, and the suggestions of nihilism and degradation in recent times. Movies have shifted their focus from what is publicly most cherished and best reputed in the good life to what is most personal and perverse. In the process of change movies have moved from light entertainment to the convulsive.[17]

Thus a close retrospective analysis of film titles can reveal their connection with broader cultural themes. The simple label 'industrial news' demarcates an area in like fashion. Indeed, the labels for industrial disputes, for instance, contain a single act or group of actors – this 'actor' being the labour side of the dispute, as we shall demonstrate in the section on vocabulary (see p. 191 below). The omission of one party in the dispute must give a preferred reading that the labour side is the active, responsible party and, by implication, the one that precipitates the action.

Boundary markers are not always labels. The use of the adverb 'Meanwhile' is a case of a boundary marker whose function is almost purely 'textual'.[18] In natural conversation and narrative, 'meanwhile' is generally used to link temporally concurrent activity which is separated by location – classically. 'Meanwhile, back at the ranch ...'. The nature of the news frequently renders the use of 'Meanwhile' redundant, as one can assume that the news is the news of the day and is *ipso facto* temporally connected. More crucially perhaps, the word 'Meanwhile' is conventionally used in narrative to refer to a connection between events if this connection is implied or hidden. If 'Meanwhile' is used to mark a boundary in television news, its function is chiefly 'textual', but because it carries overtones of sequentiality and ordering it can function to contribute to the internal coherence of the news; i.e. give it the quality of narrative even though discrete news items are not in fact elements in a single plot.

Boundary markers are crucial to the audience's decoding process. The news, we have argued, presents a surface confusion in that disparate events are reported with little or no surface thematic connections. We have shown that when such connections are made, they carry semantically significant implications for decoding. But in general the deeper structuring of the bulletins presents a coherent world picture. Basically, the predictability of what sort of events will be covered, at what length, in what order, and with what presentational devices, all work towards this coherence. Boundary markers therefore serve to sequence the surface disorder of the message and relate that disorder back to the basic inferential frames governing the production of the bulletins. They thus offer the audience crucial clues to aid the decoding process.

THE STRUCTURING OF INFORMATION WITHIN ITEMS

In general the structure of news stories in television is linear: there is a single theme established at the outset which is elaborated in a single direction by additional information, illustration, quotation and discussion, even if these inputs appear to contradict one another. The logic of this has to do partly with notions of balance, partly with presentation, and partly with the requirement of editing both film and news scripts. The formulas of the bulletins allow little or no time for scene-setting; the first few phrases – the first few seconds – have to attract and hold the interest of the viewer and at the same time give the most important information. To create interest by giving priority to the bizarre, unusual or humorous would be to abandon 'objectivity'. To give salient facts without regard to their presentation would be to ignore the demands of the audience. In theory, each succeeding section after the opening should contain information of decreasing importance. Regardless of the overall length of an item and whether or not it contains a piece of film, the opening phrases delivered by the newscaster in vision are unlikely to vary in any significant way. This is because the opening phrases establish the theme by presenting 'the main facts of the story in an arresting and lucid fashion'.[19] How this works in practice and how the choice of the lead paragraph situates the report and establishes its basic framework is demonstrated in the television's coverage of the Chrysler strike in May 1975 (see Tables 6.3 and 6.4), which was featured in the week chosen for visual and linguistic analysis.

The Chrysler strike story

The pay claim by Chrysler workers and the strike that ensued was a major running story which was reported thirty-one times on ITN and thirty-seven times on BBC1. At a Coventry engine plant 4,000 production workers withdrew their labour on 9 May in support of a pay claim for an increase in basic rates of £15 a week. Work was eventually resumed on 5 June, following acceptance of an interim offer of £8 a week. Interpretations of the dispute were complicated by the fact that Chrysler had simultaneously published proposals for worker participation. Whilst the workers insisted that this was a separate issue, some reports (for example, those in Table 6.4) were quick to imply that the workers' initial response to the proposals showed evidence of their unreasonable attitude. However, it is not our purpose here to provide a detailed case study of the Chrysler strike story but rather to show, with examples, some of the general principles whereby themes are established and elaborated.

In each BBC bulletin on Thursday 15 May the theme of the opening paragraph was the same – the vote to continue the strike. The two-sentence item in the short BBC lunchtime bulletin contained little more than this except

Table 6.3 The Chrysler strike: reported by the BBC on Thursday, 15 May 1975

Lunchtime bulletin	Early evening bulletin	*Nine O'Clock News*
		At home the two big disputes in the car industry.
		A peace formula has been worked out in the Dunlop dispute but the Chrysler strikers have voted to stay out. (Report on Dunlop dispute.)
The 4,000 strikers at Chrysler's engine factory in Coventry voted overwhelmingly to continue their stoppage which began on Monday. They want a firm offer of £8 a week more as part of their claim for a £15 a week rise.	But the 4,000 workers at Chrysler's engine factory in Coventry have noted overwhelmingly to continue their strike. They want a pay rise of £8 a week now and another £7 later. Peter Colbourne's been covering this story too: *PC*: The strikers were told that Chrysler should get out of Britain if they can't pay a living wage. The workers were being used as cheap labour and have become the poor relations of the car industry.	The 4,000 workers at Chrysler's engine factory in Coventry voted overwhelmingly to stay out on strike. They want a firm offer of £8 a week more from July. Peter Colbourne reports on the mass meeting: *PC*: The strikers were told that Chrysler should get out of Britain if they can't pay a living wage. The workers were being used as cheap labour and have become the poor relations of the car industry.
	Morris (shop steward): And I ask you to vote unanimously for this recommendation. The manipulation of the press, the mass media in vision, and the unprecedented intervention of the First Minister of the Land – who spoke about something when we weren't even on strike – Mr Wilson, your platitudes and your attitudes and your political inspiration – you horrify me. (Applause.) *Second speaker*: All in favour of that recommendation please show . . . (cheers) . . . those against . . . (cheers).	*Morris (shop steward)*: And I ask you to vote unanimously for this recommendation. The manipulation of the press, the mass media in vision, and the unprecedented intervention of the First Minister of the Land – who spoke about something when we weren't even on strike – Mr Wilson, your platitudes and your attitudes and your political inspiration – you horrify me. (Applause.) *Second speaker*: All in favour of that recommendation please show . . . (cheers) . . . those against . . . (cheers).
	PC: An overwhelming vote to stay out. So tomorrow night all Chrysler car production will have to stop. There's no hope of a speedy end to the strike and the men aren't to meet again for a week. But earlier at the meeting the workers voted in favour of the principle of worker participation at Chrysler's.	*PC*: An overwhelming vote to stay out. So tomorrow night all Chrysler car production will have to stop. There's no hope of a speedy end to the strike and the men aren't to meet again for a week.

Table 6.4 The Chrysler strike: reported by ITN on Monday, 12 May 1975

First Report	Early evening bulletin	*News at Ten*
Well, to add to the general gloom the Chrysler car workers (recently offered, you will remember, part ownership in the company) decided this morning to continue their strike – a strike which Mr Wilson in that TV interview yesterday described as 'deplorable'.	The Prime Minister also said yesterday that he utterly deplored the prospect of a strike by Chrysler workers. He said he was horrified to feel that the company's proposals for participation had ben rejected without full examination.	In spite of the Prime Minister's warning yesterday that he deplored the stoppage at Chrysler, shop stewards in the engine factory at Coventry have voted to strike.
Talks over the weekend between the men and the American-owned company management have led to some hopes that the strike might be averted. It's being staged by 4,000 men at the engine-building plant at Stoke in Coventry and it's meant the layoff of 6,000 more workers at other Chrysler factories throughout Britain. But this morning 140 shop stewards having got a report on the weekend-long discussions ended any hopes of an early return to work and from Coventry now Trevor MacDonald sends us this report:	But today Chrysler's shop stewards at the company's engine factory in Coventry voted to go ahead with their strike for higher pay. This could put 10,000 men out of work at three Chrysler factories by the weekend. And more than 12,000 British Leyland workers will have to stay off work because strikers at a Dunlop components factory in Coventry are continuing their strike.	It could put 10,000 men out of work at three Chrysler factories by the weekend. And more than 14,000 British Leyland workers will have to stay off work because 700 clerks at a Dunlop factory in Coventry are continuing their strike.
	Trevor MacDonald reports:	Trevor MacDonald reports:
TM: When the meeting ended a short while ago the mood of the men was in no doubt. The shop stewards remain as firmly as ever on their demand for £8 a week now as part of an eventual £15 a week pay.claim to be achieved by July 1st. Paradoxically, if any single factor could be held to have hardened attitudes here about the strike, it's perhaps the Prime Minister's statements on television yesterday, which have been widely interpreted by the men as a condemnation of their dispute. Bob Morris, senior transport workers' union's shop steward at Chrysler's engine plant, who last night said he was 'absolutely stunned by Mr Wilson's outrageous interview', said after this morning's meeting	*TM*: There was never any doubt about the mood of the men at Chrysler's, even before today's crucial meeting began. And when it ended the shop stewards' tough line was confirmed. Their spokesman, Bob Morris, was critical not only of the Chrysler management, but also of what some shop stewards saw as the Prime Minister's unhelpful intervention in interviews he gave yesterday. *BM*: What they should do – they should sack Harold Wilson. Yes. *TM*: But don't you think that his call for some sort of national stand on the question of wages and prices deserves some . . . attention?	*TM*: There was never any doubt about the mood of the men at Chrysler's, even before today's crucial meeting began. And when it ended the shop stewards' tough line was confirmed. Their spokesman, Bob Morris, was critical not only of the Chrysler management, but also of what some shop stewards saw as the Prime Minister's unhelpful intervention in interviews he gave yesterday. *BM*: What they should do – they should sack Harold Wilson. Yes. *TM*: But don't you think that his call for some sort of national stand on the question of wages and prices deserves some . . . attention?

Table 6.4 continued

First Report	Early evening bulletin	News at Ten
at the Stoke Plant Social Club that the men will not go back to work unless they get the money they're demanding now. He scornfully dismissed Chrysler's plans for greater worker participation and profit sharing, saying that the unions had not yet fully studied the plan. And when I asked him whether the men should not go back to work until the union's had an opportunity to study the company's proposals, he said there was no chance of that. And as though to reinforce the tough line the unions are taking on this whole question, the shop stewards have decided against bringing forward Thurday's mass meeting. Given the mood of today's ninety-minute session, there is no question now about the sort of recommendation the men will be asked to ratify on Thursday. Trevor MacDonald, *First Report*, Coventry. (Report on Dunlop dispute)	*BM*: Certainly. But Mr Wilson yesterday – his comments and so on – we haven't refused worker participation. We want the details so we can examine the position of worker participation. We haven't refused to do anything. *TM*: But aren't there any good points at all about the plans for industrial democracy – for more worker participation? *BM*: When we find out the details it may be a wonderful thing, but we know no details and it's not the basis to call off a strike. *TM*: But shouldn't you go back to work, until you know the details, and perhaps then consider strike action? *BM*: No, no. Our strike is on the basic. We are on strike for a living wage, full stop. *TM*: Will you call forward the meeting which you planned for later this week to try to get this thing settled a little earlier? *BM*: No, no. Wednesday the stewards meet again – we meet all our massed workers on Thursday at 12 o'clock and that's it and the strike will continue. *TM*: (Report on Dunlop dispute) Trevor MacDonald, ITN, Coventry.	*BM*: Certainly. But Mr Wilson yesterday – his comments and so on – we haven't refused worker participation. We want the details so we can examine the position of worker participation. We haven't refused to do anything. *TM*: But aren't there any good points at all about the plans for industrial democracy, for more worker participation? *BM*: When we find out the details it may be a wonderful thing, but we know no details and it's not the basis to call off a strike. *TM*: But shouldn't you go back to work, until you know the details, and perhaps then consider strike action? *BM*: No, no. Our strike is on the basic. We are on strike for a living wage, full stop. *TM*: Will you call forward the meeting which you planned for later this week to try to get this thing settled a little earlier? *BM*: No, no. Wednesday the stewards meet again – we meet all our massed workers on Thursday at 12 o'clock and that's it and the strike will continue. *TM*: (Report on Dunlop dispute) Trevor MacDonald, *News at Ten*, Coventry.

for a statement of the workers' demands (not the company's refusal to make an offer, it may be noted). The BBC's early bulletin was prefaced by the boundary marker, 'But', which separated it from a report of the dispute at Dunlop. There were two additional sections in this report: a piece of film of the vote, together with a commentary by an industrial correspondent; and a statement about a previous vote on the issue of worker participation. Appearing as it did at the end of only one of the three items, this report of an earlier vote was clearly the most dispensable piece of information as far as the newsroom was concerned. As such it illustrated the propensity of television news to cover events rather than issues; cases rather than their connections. The item as it appeared in the *Nine O'Clock News* was deliberately 'packaged' with the Dunlop story, so there was a joint headline and boundary marker, 'At home the two big disputes in the car industry' and a subheading '... but the Chrysler workers have voted to stay out'. Repetition helped to establish the theme. The first paragraph remained virtually unchanged from the early bulletin except for details of the wage demand (again no details of the company's response and the possible use of the participation offer as a ploy) and the film report of the vote was identical. The theme of the story was the vote and its elaboration through film and commentary. In the two longer items the information was sequenced in such a way as to give space to the 'conflicting possibility' of the labour view.[20] This was presented in the indirect form 'strikers were told ...' spoken over film indicating speakers at a mass meeting. But viewers were left in the dark as to who the speaker might be.

In even longer industrial stories other points of view (management, government, CBI, etc.) are likely to be presented but even this example shows that alternative possibilities are introduced by virtue of the theme and not in opposition to it. The correspondent's reporting of the speech at the mass meeting introduces a new possibility – the 'living wage', 'cheap labour', and comparative rates in the car industry – but the return to the film report of the vote reasserts the 'strike vote' theme, excluding any development of the alternative view. It actually reinforces the impression that the strike is about a wage demand of £8 a week and a further £7, a 'fact' which was established at the outset. But analysis of the internal evidence of these reports (i.e. the words spoken by the Convenor of Shop Stewards in *sync.*) reveals that the meeting was also concerned with the wider issues of media manipulation, intervention by politicians, the power of multinational corporations, and with the worker participation offer. The 'factuality' of the (selective) reporting of the vote is undoubtedly enhanced by the piece of film, which is the key piece of supporting evidence for the theme as presented.

A comparison of the lunchtime bulletin with the corresponding sections of the other two reports illustrates some of the stylistic changes which may occur in the process of editing and updating. These have to do with presentation rather than content but they are not insignificant, as our analysis of vocabulary will show (see next section). The reference back in the lunchtime bulletin in the phrase '... which began on Monday' was omitted in the subsequent reports. This detail is of some importance since the gravity of a strike is a function of the length of the strike and the numbers directly involved. Reference back – even of this rudimentary kind – is not a regular feature of television news, so it is unsurprising that it was edited out of the later bulletins, possibly in order to make the key opening sentence shorter and simpler. The change of the two nouns 'strikers' and 'stoppage' in the lunchtime bulletin to 'workers' and 'strike' in the later bulletins was especially significant. 'Stoppage' is one of the most frequent nominal forms used to describe industrial action (see Table 6.5 p. 204) and one, we argue, whose agent is consistently assumed to be labour. In this case we see that 'stoppage' and 'strike' were used interchangeably, although 'stoppages of production' have a variety of causes.[21] The change between these reports in a single day may involve recognition of the ambiguity of this use of 'stoppage' but it is more likely to have been prompted by the substitution of 'worker' in place of 'striker'.

ITN's three daily bulletins differed in certain ways from those of the BBC. As we showed in *Bad News*, ITN has a greater propensity to report several stories in a single 'package' in the industrial area and there are obvious stylistic differences, particularly in *First Report*. Table 6.4 contains the reporting of the Chrysler story on ITN on the Monday (12 May) before the Thursday (15 May) which was used in Table 6.3. ITN reported the Chrysler vote story on the Thursday but with less variation between bulletins. Table 6.4 has a number of additional features which show how items are assembled and adjusted in the course of a day's reporting.

The length of the first sentence in the item on *First Report* is the key to the style of this bulletin. The sentence is complex, with a parenthesis and several subsidiary clauses. The essential information is contained in the words 'the Chrysler car workers ... decided this morning to continue their strike'; the remainder is a gloss on 'workers', 'strike' and the item as a whole. This practice of identifying a piece of news as 'good', 'bad', 'unusual', 'troubling' or even 'big news', together with an informality and flexibility of presentation (compare the 'you will remember ...' in the first sentence), enhances the presenter's role as an individual personality. It does not, however, affect the framework of the story even though the style is more discursive than in the other bulletins. The gloss on 'strike' in the first sentence legitimated by the phrase – 'described as "deplorable"' by Mr Wilson – is a contextual feature used in the two later bulletins. Its importance in establishing a preferred and 'dominant view' is clear. In *Bad News* we showed that a similar strike by engine tuners at British Leyland was consistently reported by situating the strike as an instance of Mr Wilson's criticism of 'manifestly avoidable stoppages'. As we showed there, such a method is dubious in character, for in the later bulletins the view ascribed changed from stoppages involving both management and labour to stoppages caused solely by workers' action. The Prime Minister's view of the dispute is undeniably newsworthy but the function of the ascribed quote in this item is more ideological than informative. The use of the conjunction 'But' in the third sentence of the early evening bulletin and 'In spite of' to open the *News at Ten* report, shows how, at the same time, the information is structured to give a preferred hearing of the strike as an act of obstinacy and against the national interest. The same kind of structuring occurs in an even more open way in the interview with the shop steward, which is an elaboration of this 'dominant view'. Trevor MacDonald uses the union reservations about the Chrysler participation plan to reinforce the 'tough line' view, despite Morris's attempts to redefine the strike as separate from the worker participation issue. The news interpretation was shown to be unjustified because the workers later voted to accept in principle the participation proposals while voting at the same time to stay out on strike.

One effect of the frequent 'packaging' of discrete stories on the content of the bulletin is the association of unconnected events in a manner that suggests more than simple juxtapositioning. The inclusion of the Dunlop story between two parts of the Chrysler story in the evening bulletins, linked by the conjunction 'And', effectively places it in the same ideological category as the main Chrysler story. Thus even a simple conjunctive can function ideologically to connect disparate stories, regardless of differences of cause or consequence. The similarity of geographical location is itself merely a function of where the main elements of the motor industry reside. Packaging helps to create artificial coherence by placing 'industrial' stories together and by cementing them linguistically with the use of superficial conjunctions. Table 6.4 provides examples of both artificial coherence and linguistic cementing, additional industrial news being reported at the end of the two evening bulletins.

As the production of *First Report* is basically a separate operation from the production of the early bulletin and *News at Ten*, little can be inferred about the editing process of this bulletin from later bulletins. In the two evening bulletins there is hardly any change, since the interview remains the same. The introduction is slightly shorter in *News at Ten* and this does reflect a priority. In the shorter *News of Ten* version two significant elements have been omitted. In the course of simplifying the Prime Minister's reported statement, the reference to Chrysler's proposals for worker participation is dropped and the phrase 'for higher pay' which gives the one piece of information regarding 'strike' is omitted. Since these pieces of information emerge later in the interview situation, they could possibly be counted as 'dispensable'. But without them both the news item and the action of the Chrysler workers are barely intelligible. The omission of details of the claim and the unelaborated references to the worker participation proposals lead to an image of an action without cause – an explanatory vacuum rapidly filled by the broadcaster's inferential framework which in this area matches popular misconceptions and stereotypes of industrial action; i.e. the 'unreasonable worker' ideology.

If there is a theory which specifies the ways in which the parts function, news items could be said to be bound by a deep structure. We have shown that even within a single sentence, language may function in several ways, and that information is likely to be arranged in order of declining importance (according to the value priorities of journalists). Combining these two levels – the functions of language in use and the journalistic value process respectively – we can consider establishing a number of *sequencing rules* which govern the relation of item elements (e.g. boundary markers, interviews, closings) to one another. The term 'sequencing rules' has been employed by Schegloff to describe the pattern of interaction in telephone conversations and to explain their orderliness.[22] In the study of folk tales, myths and narratives, structural analysis identifies the parts in a sequence and shows how they function to create unity, continuity and resolution.[23] With news talk, as in the above studies, words cannot be considered in isolation but have to be regarded as serving functions in a larger whole, so the elements of a news item are not isolated bits of information whose arrangement is unimportant. There is a structure, not necessarily explicit, but deeply embedded, which can be revealed by comparing the relative position of key elements in the narrative. According to its practitioners, television news journalism:

> seeks above all to answer the questions WHO, WHAT, WHERE, WHEN and HOW. It is primarily concerned with new facts and the factual background to them. Its interest in the question WHY is confined to the audience's urgent interest in understanding what has just happened within the bounds of immediately available information.[24]

These could be taken as the elements whose regular ordering in certain ways constitutes a structure of thinking and interpretation. But this is a view of news as 'bits' of information – hard 'facts' – supplied through a neutral channel. It pays little but lip-service to the framework which renders any fact or set of facts intelligible. This context includes the whole range of expectations about 'news' and 'television' to be found among viewers of television news. It also includes the context of the text itself, the other pieces of information which are available.

The second sample, January–April 1975

The regularities which can be observed in the text of industrial action stories – reports of the beginning of a strike for example – show that the WHO, WHAT, HOW and WHY elements follow one of several possible sequences according to the story type. Details of time and place are more flexible since their function in the news is to express immediacy and precision and they are, as it were, dependent rather than independent variables. There is a basic sequence of key information corresponding to the WHO, WHAT and WHY questions, in that order. The following item illustrates this, in its most commonly occurring form:

Two thousand dockers at Hull have begun an overtime ban and a series of weekly one-day token strikes over a pay dispute. A docker's spokesman said that they'll continue their action until the employers honour an agreement to offer a pay rise based on the retail price index. And tonight 900 Manchester dockers also stopped work over a pay dispute.

(ITN, 22.00, 9 April 1975)

Two-thirds of the reports of industrial action by both ITN and BBC in the four-month sample period (January–April 1975) had this form, the subject of the opening sentence being the labour disputants. Most frequently the subject was placed at the beginning of the sentence, as in this example. The elaboration of the report through indirect speech which occurred in this and other items will be discussed below. Where the subject of the opening sentence is not the labour disputants, a different kind of introduction will be sought. Occasionally, reported statements also contained basic information and could be used to open an item, but only when the framework of the story had been established in earlier bulletins. In the following example, which is part of a running story, the subject of the first sentence is the 'strike'. This opening, which assumes that viewers have prior knowledge of the strike, is only possible in the later stages of a running story:

Here at home the strike of 250 engine tuners at British Leyland's Cowley works will not be called off when the men meet on Monday, according to Mr Reg Birch of the engineering union. Mr Birch, who attended arbitration talks in London today, said any return to work would have to be a union decision, but he said he was prepared to attend further peace talks next week.

(ITN, 22.00, 24 January 1975)

Moving from the WHO, WHAT, WHERE and WHEN questions, the WHY question in the dockers' example is answered in the phrase 'over a pay dispute', even though the information given is very rudimentary. In many items consequences are reported but not the cause, giving a different emphasis as 'strike' becomes the subject of the first sentence and 'production' (rather than the firm, managements or the dispute) its predicate. For example:

A strike by 700 clerical workers at the Dunlop factory in Coventry has brought nearly half British Leyland's car production to a standstill. Dunlop supplies suspension parts for British Leyland and the stoppage, which has made about 8,000 car workers idle, is costing the company £1.5 million a day.

(ITN, 22.00, 30 April 1975)

The vocabulary of this item is revealing. Once again 'stoppage' is used synonymously with 'strike', and the term 'idle' is applied to non-striking workers who have had to stop work. Raymond Williams has traced the usage of this word and its associations both past and the present, showing that there has been a steady 'ideological resistance' to the distinction between unemployment or being laid off (a social situation) and idleness (a personal characteristic).

> The resistance is still active, and in relation to the words is especially evident in the use of *idle*, in news reporting, to describe workers laid off, locked out or on strike. With its strong moral implications, *idle* in this context must have ideological intentions or effects.[25]

Unfortunately, the highly dubious practice of emphasising effects rather than causes and other aspects occurs in as much as 40 per cent of reports of industrial action; that is, in two out of every five reports in our sample. Moreover, as often as not this constitutes the professional defence: these are usually stories which involve large numbers of 'consumers', more or less indirectly. Disputes in transport (railways, ferries and buses) and essential services (the ambulance service, refuse collection) were treated in this way. It was the rail passengers, for example, who were cast in the role of innocent victims – and by implication, they were victims of the 'militant signalmen' rather than victims of the breakdown of 'normal' relations between British Rail management and workers:

> Rail passengers today suffered the worst disruption yet in the series of one-day unofficial strikes by militant signalmen. South and east of London many commuter services did not run and important main line services to the west and north were also affected. But the disruption was patchy depending on where signalmen joined in the stoppage. There were trains from London to Devon but not to South Wales; to Scotland but not to Manchester. Peter Stewart reports.
>
> (BBC1, 21.00, 13 February 1975)

In certain areas, especially, when direct inconvenience to the public looms large in the reporting, the consequences of industrial action are emphasised, thus serving, ideologically or unwittingly, to avoid the question WHY? This has been documented by other observers.[26] There is only one case in the sample period of a cause providing the main signification of a strike report. It is the exception that proves the rule, since the item occupies the final place in the running order of the bulletin – the space usually reserved for 'joke' or human interest stories. These sequencing rules which operate to structure the information have little to do with the 'demands' of the subject matter. They are not merely some routine way of arriving at an objective account which faithfully expresses the 'facts'. They represent choices, made more or less deliberately, and are based in the first instance on journalistic values and conventions about what is interesting or important. In favouring events rather than processes, effects rather than causes, management rather than labour, the structuring and sequencing of news talk, in spite of its apparent flexibility, is one of the main props which upholds the rigid definitions and dominant views of strike activity which, as we have already shown, operate in the categorisation and selection of industrial news. Thus journalistic values work to buttress the basic inferential framework of the broadcasters, which has broader ideological components.

REPORTED SPEECH

On first hearing, the language of the news seems to be in a form that would allow fairly simple tests of its truth or falsity. It has the appearance of being entirely constative (propositional and capable of being shown either true or false) and not performative. These terms are Austin's. He distinguishes between constative and performative utterances, indicating that when a speaker engages in a performative utterance, the speaker is not simply delivering a proposition but is performing an act in the process of speaking. The classic example is the utterance 'I promise ... ' but other examples include commands and greetings. The usual greeting 'Hello' or 'Good evening' is about the only example in the news of an Austinian performative utterance – a statement in which the speaker accomplishes an act in producing the speech.[27] But it has been pointed out that this distinction breaks down on close scrutiny, since the production of any language involves the production of meaning, and meaning is not simply representational. As Halliday describes, every use of language is 'meaningful, contextualised and in the broadest sense social'.[28] We have therefore been describing news language as a form of social behaviour. But a significant proportion of the language of the news is the reporting of someone else's speech; so it is equally a form of social behaviour in a more restricted sense. It follows that although the language appears to be reporting facts, propositions and descriptions, the reworking of these elements into stories involves the creation of ambiguities, contradictions and meanings which may well be absent from some 'ideal' account. A question therefore arises concerning the forms of conventional journalism for handling other people's accounts. A corollary of this is whether the routine violence done to other's accounts occurs systematically along the plane of one ideological viewpoint rather than another. In short, does the transformation from speech to reported speech to news talk simply mediate or does it transform or mediate in a particular direction?

Traditionally there have been two ways of representing speech and they have been labelled direct and indirect. In writing, the former is signalled by quotation marks and is frequently preceded by a verb of saying. A comma or colon may also be used to mark the boundary. Indirect speech is a 'transformation' of direct speech according to grammatical rules which convert the present tense in direct speech to the past tense and which change possessive adjectives from the first and second person in direct speech to the third person in indirect speech. There are in fact other ways in which a writer can represent speech and thought – by using a 'stream of consciousness' technique or by omitting the introductory verb of saying, for example, 'She said' may be dropped in some forms of writing.

For the speaker, especially the television journalist, the problem of representation is rather more difficult since the verbal signal of 'commence quote – end quote' is so cumbersome. The alternative is to modulate voice tones and use pauses to mark the beginning and end of reported speech. There is also greater reliance in written-spoken news talk on the verb of saying than in the written word. In fact, this is a possible source of ambiguity because what is ostensibly the reproduction of meaning can become via transformation the production of new meaning.

In the four-month sample period, the written-spoken parts of the bulletins on BBC and ITN contained 16 per cent and 19 per cent reported speech (both direct and indirect) respectively. The rather higher proportion on ITN is to be expected in the light of that channel's smaller proportion of items with interviews (noted in chapter 4 of *Bad News*), since reported speech can be seen as a substitute for interviews. On both channels, however, reported speech occupies a significant proportion of the bulletins. Content analysis of this sample shows that the profile of people quoted has similar characteristics to the profile of the people interviewed: they are selected almost exclusively from high-ranking politicians, trade-union officials and senior management. Our analysis of interviewee input in *Bad News* showed that in the industrial category (but not in the economic and business categories) there were more interviewees speaking for labour. Analysis of attributed speech in this sample shows that 26.5 per cent of quotations were from management and 31.5 per cent from labour. Formally there is the appearance of balance between these and other 'points of view', but many of the remaining 42 per cent of quotations were from government, judiciary and police sources, with a number from professional associations. Yet, as we noted in *Bad News*, quotations from labour are more likely to include extreme differences of opinion than are quotations from management; as for instance when, in a dispute story, anti-strike workers and officials are used. As with the pattern of interviewees, the lack of expert comment, the absence of unofficial labour spokesmen and the relative prominence of political figures is noteworthy. The evidence continues to support our claim that, despite the appearance of balance, the 'hierarchy of access' operates to exclude the systematic representation and quotation of subordinate groups.

News items rarely begin with a quotation. Reported speech is located within a frame that embodies the dominant view of a story, so that reported statements are rarely used as 'facts' in themselves. The occasions on which this does happen are statements and speeches by those of very high status, including the Prime Minister. 'Mr Wilson has said in the Commons that ...' is newsworthy in itself and may be the opening sentence of an item.[29] Conversely, significant absences are spokesmen for the poorly paid, low

status, badly organised or relatively inarticulate groups such as the ambulancemen, the engine tuners and the Glasgow dustcart drivers. Quotations
from hospital consultants and from National Graphical Association
representatives in the Fleet Street dispute are relatively abundant. These
regularities may be formulated as a rule: that the higher the status of the
subject, the less the mediation. This is not to deny that journalists mediate
what is reported, even by those of high status. The editing of a speech for
reporting directly or indirectly is a creative process; new sentences may be
formed by cutting and new functions may be imported. The use made by
television news of a speech by the then Prime Minister to establish the
dominant view was described in the case study of the Cowley dispute
included in *Bad News*. In the following extracts from two bulletins on the
same channel in the same evening, the use of what might be called 'free
indirect speech' (i.e. the omission of a verb of saying) is part of the process
of reduction which operates in favour of the dominant view. The key opening
sentences of each item were:

> The Prime Minister in a major speech tonight on the economy appealed to
> management and unions in the car industry to cut down on what he called
> manifestly avoidable stoppages.
>
> (BBC1, 21.00, 3 January 1975)

> The Prime Minister has appealed to workers in the car industry to cut down
> on avoidable stoppages.
>
> (BBC1, 22.45, 3 January 1975)

The obvious difference between the first extract and the second is the
ideological reduction of 'management and unions' to 'workers' and the
omission of 'what he called'. The verb of saying is one of the first casualties
in the editing process in this instance, as one would expect from the inverse
relationship between status and mediation. The higher level of mediation
involved in using 'He said' may be carried to the opposite extreme of
effectively degrading a statement, such as Leslie Huckfield's comment on Mr
Wilson's car industry speech: '*He said* the Prime Minister clearly knew very
little about the car industry. The real cause of the trouble was the chronic
failure of management to invest, *he said*' (ITN, 22.00, 3 January 1975; our
italics).

In terms of the constative/performative distinction, many quoted statements
– 'threats', 'appeals', 'calls' – can be regarded as performative. The Prime
Minister's appeal is one such. But in free indirect reported speech the
distinction is frequently blurred as there is no reliable way to tell whose words
are being spoken. Compare these two reports of the miners' pay claim which
are equivalent in most respects:

> The miners are to use every clause and avenue within the Social Contract

to win substantial pay rises, but they still haven't said how much they want.

(BBC1, 21.00, 9 January 1975)

The mineworkers' leader, Mr Joe Gormley, has said his union will use every clause and avenue within the Social Contract to win substantial pay rises for Britain's 260,000 miners.

(ITN, 22.00, 9 January 1975)

In the first example the phrase 'every clause and avenue' is broadcast in a constative form; in the second it is clearly attributed as a quotation. The effects of this work in contrary directions: the indirect, unattributed quotation creates a more detached, neutral and factual impression while the attributed quotation gives an impression of immediacy, actuality and possibly direct-ness. These stylistic features and the question of whether they represent consistent styles of presentation on each channel are less important than the fact that reported speech can be used in a variety of intentional or simply functional ways for impression management. Despite the apparent objectivity of 'quoting a point of view', journalists never succeed in removing their presence from the story. The evidence is overwhelming that, in the use of reported speech, the current forms, routines and conventions of television news work unwittingly or otherwise to produce a bias against the under-standing of trade union and labour viewpoints.

II Vocabulary and industrial action*

We also say of some people that they are transparent to us. It is, however, important as regards this observation that one human being can be a complete enigma to another. We learn this when we come into a strange country with entirely strange traditions; and, what is more, even given the mastery of a country's language. We do not *understand* the people. (And not because of not knowing what they are saying to themselves.) we cannot find our feet with them.

(L. Wittgenstein)[30]

One of the ways in which we are able to identify a person's class, status or beliefs is through their vocabulary – the stock of words which they use to categorise the world. We instinctively recognise the vocabularies of political and cultural discourse used in different institutional settings. The ranges of words, phrases or descriptions applied to sets of activities are heavy carriers of social meaning. They provide the attuned hearer with ways of locating the

*First published in Glasgow University Media Group, *More Bad News*, London and Boston, Routledge & Kegan Paul, 1980, pp. 165–90.

proferred descriptions in relation to the larger belief systems of society. As C. Wright Mills observed:

> a vocabulary is not merely a string of words; immanent within it are societal textures – institutional and political co-ordinates. ... in studying vocabularies, we detect implicit evaluations and the collective patterns behind them – 'cues' for social behaviour. A thinker's social and political 'rationale' is exhibited in his choice and use of words. Vocabularies socially canalise thought.[31]

This generalisation applies to all vocabularies, including the vocabulary of news. Even specialised vocabularies, including those of science and technology, embody ways of looking at the world and have value preferences and judgements built into them.

It may be claimed that the vocabulary of the news is not the outcome of deliberate choice by the news personnel from among a number of alternatives but merely reproduces the vocabulary of the wider society: in the case in hand, the currently available vocabulary of industrial relations. If this were true, there would be inconsistencies, ambiguities and instances of the same terms being applied in a number of different ways. However, our research reveals that this is not the case. For, as we will show, there are significant absences in the vocabulary of industrial news reporting which, along with the vocabulary which is used, reveal selectivity and value preference for a particular view of the causes and nature of industrial conflict. It is not that this vocabulary is incomprehensible or even unacceptable. Rather, it is simply not what it claims to be. It is not impartial, it is not balanced, and it is not merely telling people 'accurately and honestly about the most important things going on in the world.[32] Nor is it that editorial values and editorial judgements have accidently intruded, for such intrusions would be random or variable.

In fact, the language of industrial reporting contains what C. Wright Mills called a 'vocabulary of motive', by which he meant linguistic behaviour which functions socially to co-ordinate and control systems of action. Motives in this phrase are the acceptable grounds for social action rather than private states within individuals. In this view, 'the research task is the locating of particular types of action within typal frames of normative actions and socially situated clusters of motive'.[33] Our analysis of the particular case of news vocabulary therefore involves a description of the lexical system not simply as a list of denotative and connotative terms, but as the verbalisation in a specific situation of a 'vocabulary of motive'.

As such, the problem of news vocabulary does not concern newsproducers' intentions but reflects a collective value system and choices – a 'strange tradition' of a kind Wittgenstein was referring to in the quotation at the start of this section. It centres on those conventions in use which, whether articulated or not, circumscribe and delineate the vocabulary. In our examination of the vocabulary of industrial disputes, we will show that it amounts to a preferred view of industrial disputes which corresponds all too easily with a particular (albeit sophisticated) version of managerial ideology.

THE SAMPLE

The sample of words used here is the same four-month sample as used in our description of the textual characteristics of news items. We are mainly analysing one mode of news discourse: the written-spoken mode used by the newscaster, whether spoken to camera or voiced over film or stills. Initially, this excludes both commentary by correspondents and reporters and interview situations (which are dealt with later). This element is the most concise and formal type of news discourse. It regularly takes up about one-third of the news bulletins. For this analysis we define a lexical item or unit of vocabulary to be either a single word or an idiom like 'industrial action' or 'work to rule'.

The sample size is designed to cover a wide range of industrial reporting and to allow for comparisons between channels. It consists of all industrial dispute, wage claim and wage settlement stories in the main evening bulletins, namely the *Nine O'Clock News* and *News at Ten* for the period 1 January–30 April 1975. A number of other areas of industrial and economic reporting are excluded – industrial accidents, conferences, lobbies and demonstrations (outside the scope of collective wage bargaining) do not appear in this sample. Reports of short-time working, layoffs and redundancies are not included unless they are involved as part of the collective bargaining process; neither are protests by producers against foreign competition (for example the fishermen's blockade and the textile workers' demonstrations). The initial newscaster sample consists of approximately 30,000 words. (The remainder, some 60,000 words, consists of reports and commentaries by broadcasting personnel and accompanying interviews.) The detailed study of the lexicon is based on a third, smaller sample covering the whole of one month's scripted news talk in the area defined above, a total of about 7,000 words (January 1975). The subjects dealt with in the sample are those classically focused upon by industrial reporting, typically those occasions on which 'normal' management and labour relationships break down. In *Bad News*, we showed how this area of coverage is thrown into sharp relief, so that, for example, reporting of strikes and disputes involving stoppages of work accounts for 20 per cent of the total number of industrial stories but for 39 per cent of all industrial coverage by item.[34] Industrial disputes provide topics which in our view best test the application of the norms of impartiality and accuracy in a particularly sensitive area. The choice of bulletins (the main BBC and ITN bulletins) and the four-month span of the coverage in the second sample maximise the possible variations while keeping the data within manageable proportions.

The language used by the news to refer to industrial relations trades on a set of fairly familiar industrial terms and descriptions. For a description to be recognisable, as Sacks has argued, a hearer has to be familiar with the social categories referred to by it, and the cultural associations the category has.[35] In fact, a vast number of descriptions are available in this cultural domain although the siting of their meaning is not without ambiguity. Most terms and descriptions carry a plurality of meanings and therefore the consistent realisation of one set of meanings or connotations is often the result of the routinisation of cultural preferences and practices. For example: 'And now some industrial news' (ITN, 22.00, 21 March 1975) cuts down on the uncertainty of what sort of news is to follow. But only the routine use of the word 'industrial' to describe a very specific set of stories would allow culturally attuned viewers to predict with a high degree of certainty that they are likely to be getting stories about strikes, disputes and disruption. Indeed, industrial accident stories are unlikely to follow such an introduction for they are usually treated as a species of disaster story.[36] Descriptions such as 'industrial', 'economic' or 'business' could denote a multitude of story types. In television practice these categories are restricted by the conventions of use and these conventions work over time to prelocate their meanings. These predefined working conventions seem to orchestrate the particular and preferred meanings of the terms, such that any attentive viewer should be able to make the predictions given above. The categories are also enshrined in the division of labour among correspondents. In short, the conventions and practices of television journalism give specific meaning to general descriptions as a result of the cultural labour of journalists.

The choice of linguistic forms and the practices governing their usage can therefore be seen as a realisation of social meanings and categories. They are, however, realised within a broadcasting and news system which is monologic in character, highly stratified in structure, and elitist in its recruitment. These factors combine to produce a vocabulary for industrial news stories which has a bias towards a particular understanding.

News talk has special linguistic and social features which define it as a form of communication. One reason why it should be important for us to reveal some of the rules of news talk is to assess these rules against a notion of 'normal' talk or more 'authentic' talk, to use Blum's term.[37] In the phrase 'the strikers are demanding a pay rise of £10 a week', the strikers are alien to mankind in general – strikers are not you or me, they are somebody else. Thus when it is our strike, we are cut out of the message. It follows from this division, which is a regular feature of industrial news, that the royal, all-inclusive *we* or *us* will be minimised. Other news may stress a notion of communal interest such as the *nation*. In general, we would expect less use of first-person plurals in industrial news talk than in other areas of coverage. Where first-person plurals are used or implied, they will appeal to common-sense understandings and problems 'about which we would all agree' – for example, 'the cost of just one day's layoff was 1,200 cars, worth 1.75 million pounds'.[38] 'The cost' is not specified as a cost to anyone in particular. The implication is that it is a cost to *us*, to the community, to Britain. But here the cost is in fact an estimated cost to the firm. Costs to the workers are not counted, neither are market conditions.

Where there is an appeal to communality of interests, such appeals can often be revealed as partisan. As often as not they are concerned with 'production', and this production or accumulation remains sacrosanct. Social relationships are normally treated as matters of secondary importance. Indeed, while almost any breakdown in production is possible in industrial news, changes that do not affect production are unlikely to receive coverage.

The social organisation of values in our present society as interpreted by the broadcasters requires that problems of the social organisation of production take precedence over all other social problems. For example, in the period of our study the report of the Flixborough plant explosion was run mainly as a disaster aftermath story and not as a social issue. The story was presented in terms of the accident and interrupted production. Even the cost to lives was played down. The historical antecedents which raised larger questions were buried or by-passed.

Thus the problems of capital accumulation are presented in such a manner as to assume that they are everybody's problems, while the problems of the workforce are presented as 'failure' – failure to communicate, to resolve, to understand, to wait, or as moral failure by a greedy minority. For capitalism, success is constant and expanding production and all else is failure; so much so, that it can even, on occasion, make a strike look a good thing. Reporting on the April 1975 trade figures, Dominic Harrod said:

> I think tomorrow's trade figures will come as a bit of a disappointment after the figures published a month ago for March because those figures, because of a dock strike in London which held up more imports than exports going out of the country, were exceptionally good. In fact for the first time in about three years we had a plus in the total balance of payments for the month of March.
>
> (BBC2, 23.05, 13 May 1975)

These examples begin to show the directions which a study of 'authenticity' in news talk might take. Sacks's work on conversational data already sensitises us to the fact that the social organisation of talk is law-like – and that such laws are, as Wittgenstein would say, part of a form of life. It is clear, of course, that the discovery of these laws and the purposes and presuppositions of industrial news talk will depend on a close analysis of the output. Our analysis not only demonstrates a restricted vocabulary but will show that, of the very wide range of possible descriptions which could be generated by this vocabulary, only a limited number are consistently presented.

The analysis of language and the analysis of social phenomena converge on the same material. Language analysis must, however, go beyond the simple correlation of linguistic forms with social features. Sociolinguistics has encountered numerous problems arising from the oversimplified notions of language and society which this implies. Instead, linguistic forms must themselves be subjected to close analysis of their construction at the social as well as the grammatical and semantic levels. Here, of course, defined knowledge of the lexical system is a prerequisite for proper work. Speakers' choices cannot be evaluated without an understanding of the range of terms available and how their meanings are presented and actualised by the conventions in use.

Meaning in this view is not purely referential or semantic. Usually it is defined in terms of the relations between linguistic signs, objects or configurations which are non-linguistic and the response which these provoke in a hearer. We would maintain that a sign can only rarely be tied unambiguously to a referent and that a lexicographical approach involving the collection of a number of representative contexts in which a word appears does not exhaust its meaning. This meaning cannot be equated with the 'thing' denoted nor with its range of uses in a variety of contexts. The organisation and use of a given vocabulary or linguistic field forms a *Gestalt* which in itself expresses the structure of social relationships. It was one of the earlier insights of scholars of language, including de Saussure and Sapir, that the vocabularies of different languages may divide up particular fields of description in different ways; that semantic distinctions are made in one language which are not made in another.[39] Although comparative work of this kind is beyond our present study, we know that language can be used in more than one way to impose order on the complex subject-matter of industrial relations. Having shown that news language is highly limited, convention-bound, restricted and formal, we will demonstrate the manner in which a preferred sense and order are 'constructed' in the sphere of industrial news.

THE LEXICAL SYSTEM: COMPONENTS OF INDUSTRIAL ACTION

The description of vocabulary is bound to take account of the frequency with which words are used. However, a narrowly statistical approach would only show the triviality of many of the differences. 'The' is usually the most frequent word in the written-spoken material but its use will rarely yield important clues to style and meaning; neither will uncontextualised statistics of more significant items. In the present sample of news language the context is clearly and unambiguously defined, yet even here differences of frequency are often quite predictable. News stories about a rail strike will include items such as train, railwaymen, station and commuters, simply because news items centrally refer to the subject being reported. Our study therefore makes a selection from the widest possible range of lexical items, on the grounds (embedded in news ideology and practice) that: (a) people are central to the ordering of industrial affairs and that certain groups of people are clearly definable; (b) action takes place according to predictable patterns characterised by the people who act; and (c) explanatory concepts are called into play only when the complexity of the description demands it.

Consider the following brief report – some lexical items are more significant than others for our present purposes:

> Signalmen are expected to go on strike for twenty-four hours on Thursday in their pay dispute with British Rail. Disruption is likely to affect the biggest area since the signalmen first started their stoppages three months ago. The main areas likely to be hit include Manchester, Liverpool, Stoke, Crewe, Stafford, Doncaster and Cambridge. The National Union of Railwaymen's executive meet tomorrow to consider British Rail's offer of £3 a week.
>
> (ITN, 22.00, 10 February 1975)

According to the above criteria, the most significant words are those that refer to the people and organisations involved (signalmen, British Rail, NUR executive) together with any modifiers, if present, and terms which refer to types of action (strike, dispute, stoppage, offer) and their associations (disruption). Other categories (locations, time, etc.) have an important function in the item to the extent that they construct the events described within a temporal and geographical frame. However, they do not explain social relationships and to this extent they have a subordinate role in the construction of social reality in the news – a fact reflected in their placing in the text. Consistent with the false and received notion that news mediates reality with the minimum possible intervention, the use of explanatory devices is limited, indeed absent, from the above example. But this absence itself is significant. As we will show, the consistent lack of qualification – even the use of 'pay' to qualify 'dispute' is uncommon – can only leave room for the kind of interpretation that suggests that industrial action is unnecessary, non-rational activity, or for the factually incorrect assumption that disputes are always about pay.

Of the industrial relations news read by newsreaders in the course of the smaller sample, there were 40 items on BBC and 46 items on ITN. The majority of the 20 stories in this sample were covered on both channels but 3 were exclusive to BBC and 4 were exclusive to ITN. This does not mean that these 'exclusive' stories were never covered by the other channel; only that the stories did not appear in the main evening bulletins. The presence of exclusive stories is of course likely to entail greater linguistic variety than if the range of topics were identical. But the stories appearing on only one channel, such as the farm workers' pay settlement (ITN) and the dispute involving electricians in Glasgow (BBC), were almost invariably single reports. The main areas of reporting in January were the National Health Service (including consultants, junior hospital doctors, general practitioners and dentists as well as the paramedical professions); the dispute between British Leyland and engine tuners at Cowley; two disputes in Fleet Street; strikes by dustcart drivers and ambulance officers; and wage negotiations involving miners, building workers and teachers. The range of stories included the full cycle of collective bargaining from claims through disputes to settlements and the full range of occupations from unskilled manual workers to the professions.

The close similarities of category content profile on all channels reported in *Bad News* led us to expect further similarities of language between channels. The number of words transmitted in the January sample by ITN was slightly more than for BBC: 3,630 compared with 3,460.[40] This can be accounted for by the larger number of items on ITN. The average speech rate on each channel is about three words per second. From the average for the month of January it appears that ITN regularly has a smaller number of words per item (an average of 79 compared with BBC's 86). In view of ITN's greater propensity to 'package' items, this implies that complex industrial stories and packages are introduced more briefly and crisply than on BBC, although industrial news items as a whole tend to be longer. This is consistent with other stylistic features noted in chapter 4 of *Bad News*. However, the differences are not big enough to allow great linguistic variety between channels.

In fact, the vocabulary is limited in the ways that would be anticipated from the structural properties discussed above. The clear finding emerges that the vocabulary is a tightly closed system in that it constitutes a peculiar and restricted use of even its own limited range of words, which does not convey the openendedness of the situation to which it refers. Of course there is a constant inflow of 'new' words, but these are nearly all context-specific. However, there is a basic core of categories and concepts which are not context-bound, which *constantly* recur and which guarantee the system's closure. Longer items do not necessarily alter this picture: they contain more information, more names and words but they do not modify the key concepts and key words. Our definitions of 'keying' here follows Goffman. We 'refer here to the set of conventions by which a given activity, one already meaningful in terms of some primary framework, is transformed into something patterned on this activity but seen by the participants to be something quite else.'[41] Indeed, our argument would be that, although the key words of the industrial vocabulary are comprehensible in terms of the primary framework of any English-language culture, their manner of orchestration and restricted usage creates a situation where many workers would not recognise the accounts of their own disputes as in any way adequate.

Although it is hazardous to define vocabulary size, since the criteria for what constitutes a 'word' may be refined to a greater or a lesser degree, there are certain general features of the stock of lexical items used in the industrial news which can be stated without encountering these difficulties. The figures used below are approximations to the nearest 5 per cent, as greater precision would be fruitless with a sample of this size. The 7,000 lexical items in the sample (names, titles and numerals are included in this count) are drawn from a range of just over 1,000 discrete items. This is a highly restricted use of the vocabulary involving little use of most words and frequent use of a few ideologically key words.

The Type–Token Ratio (the relation between the total number of items in a text and the number of separate items from which this total is made up), which is one clear measure of linguistic diversity, is therefore 0.14. As would be expected of a formal, even stereo-typed mode of discourse, this is low compared with the TTR measured for several other varieties of discourse. The Type–Token Ratio is a measure of diversification which:

> is the ratio of the number of different words (types) to the total number of words (tokens) in the passage. In the count of newspaper English, for example, there were 44,000 tokens and 6,000 types, and so the TTR is 6/44 or 0.136. One difficulty with the type–token ratio is that it gets smaller as the size of the sample gets bigger. If the passage contains only one word, this one word is one type and one token and so the TTR must equal 1.00. If the passage consists of two word tokens, these two tokens will probably be different types. We must take a passage of about 10 tokens before one type occurs more than once. As the length of the passage is increased it becomes more likely that words will be repeated and less likely that new, unused words will occur.[42]

If we compare the size of our sample with the number of tokens in the newspaper sample, it is clear that for a sample of 7,000 words, the TTR for newspaper English would be considerably higher. That is, according to this rather rudimentary measure of diversification, television news is a highly restricted form compared with another major branch of journalism.

Restrictedness need not necessarily make for greater clarity of expression or understanding of news messages. In fact we will show that it tends towards obscurity. It might be argued that use of a constant basic vocabulary which avoids specialised terms is a requirement imposed by the mass audience. But according to the rule-of-thumb known as the Clarity Index, industrial news on television is not particularly clear.[43] The Clarity Index, like the Type–Token Ratio, is an arbitrary measure, useful only for comparisons. It is based on the assumption that longer sentences and words are generally more difficult to read and understand than shorter sentences and words. It is calculated by adding the average number of words per sentence to the percentage of words with more than two syllables. Thus the higher the index number, the more 'complex' the text. The tabloid newspapers write to an index number of about 30, which is assumed to be within the reading skills of the average sixteen-year-old school leaver. As one would expect, the number for *The Times* is considerably higher, in the order of 50 or more. The Clarity Index for the sample of industrial reporting both on BBC and ITN varies between 35 and 40. It is therefore unlikely that the restrictedness of the vocabulary can be explained simply as a result of deliberate efforts to achieve clarity and reduce complexity. But these measures are at best only rough indicators. Other measures can show the way in which the vocabulary is restricted in its application as well as in its range.

One perhaps more familiar method of assessing the vocabulary is to analyse the distribution of the well-known elements of the text such as nouns, verbs or prepositions.

Nouns in use: industrial action

In our sample the 'structural' words – adverbs, articles, auxiliary verbs, conjunctions, prepositions and pronouns – accounted for about 15 per cent of the basic stock of 7,000 words. Semantically speaking, we would expect these to have little importance; they modify and relate and tend not to carry the central meaning of the text. For instance, in the following sentence the structural words can be omitted without total loss of meaning: 'The engine tuners on strike at British Leyland's plant at Cowley, Oxford, are seeking official union backing' (BBC1, 22.00, 11 January 1975). In fact, newspaper headlines consistently omit such words. If this were to happen in ordinary news talk we would get the following string of words, which still carries meaning but with less precision and more ambiguity – rather like a telegram: '——— engine tuners ——— strike ——— British Leyland's plant ——— Cowley, Oxford ——— seeking official union backing'. In short, the 'structural' words are not the heaviest carriers of denotive or connotative meaning.

Names, place-names and titles account for, on average, another 10 per cent of the stock of words. Obviously the more very long items there are, the lower this proportion tends to be. Names, place-names and titles situate and concretely designate events, people and actions. From many points of view this may be the least important part of a news message. After all, cause and consequence rather than people and place are the key elements to be examined when analysing the neutrality of reporting, since cause and consequence, involving who and what, depend upon explanations. A Swedish study has revealed that most viewers' recall of news items is such that where recall occurs, it concerns place more than persons or things involved, and these more than causes and consequences.[44] The point is made in this study that broadcasters are perhaps paying too little attention to this 'unbalanced recall' factor. However, it is upon the crucial explanatory elements of the text that we have decided to concentrate. Excluding the structural words, names, place-names and titles which together involve 25 per cent of the stock of words, the remaining 75 per cent includes both words that are exclusive to one channel and words that are used in common. There are about 1,750 words that are used on both channels. They can be said to constitute the basic fund of categories which are used by both newsrooms to organise the reporting of industrial relations. This basic vocabulary is structured consistently around a few key terms. Many linguists are agreed that nouns and their modifiers are particularly significant. Recent research has argued that in terms of opening up the range of linguistic options, the role of nouns is central. For instance, Hawkins demonstrates that 'in system-structure terms, the category *noun* is the entry condition to a greater number of systems than the category *pronoun*'.[45] Noun and pronoun usage has in fact proved to be a good predictor of class differences – the middle class using a greater variety of nouns and showing a relatively greater flexibility of linguistic choice than the working class.

The group of nouns that refers to the 'industrial action' domain provides the central element of the coding of the remainder of the coverage. Unfortunately the processes of collective bargaining are rarely deemed newsworthy in their own right. At present for an item to be newsworthy industrial action must be 'threatened', occurring or have recently ended.

Our research reveals that the noun group consists of half a dozen 'key words' used with great frequency. In the one-month sample period the six terms most commonly used to denote industrial action were, in order of frequency: strike; action (usually qualified by the word 'industrial' or 'disruptive'); dispute; disruption, work to contract and stoppage.

Theoretically this list could be arranged other than by frequency. For instance, in Standard English usage 'dispute' need not necessarily imply any form of 'action'. In fact, in news talk it is applied almost exclusively to situations in which action is promised or ensuing. So although this vocabulary could in theory have a variety of associations and connotations, in practice this is not so. Moving from the general to the specific in news talk the following order seems to hold: dispute, action, stoppage, strike and work to contract. Although 'disruption' is one of the key words in this list, it would have to come at the end since in this month it was applied exclusively to the dispute of the members of the National Graphical Association with their employers, the Newspaper Publishers Association, which was described in the bulletin as a 'campaign' of 'disruptive practices'.

If these nouns were not key ideological terms but were merely neutral dictionary definitions, then theoretically they could be applied to a range of groups involved in a dispute: unions, management, men, women, workers, etc. In practice, both the terms that are clearly specific to action by labour (strike, work to contract) and those that could theoretically embrace all groups (dispute, disruption) are applied solely to labour. Therefore it should be clear that, far from being neutral descriptions, industrial stories are constructed in practice so that the labels and imagery constantly imply causal action by labour rather than any of the other elements involved. Consider the following examples:

> Dustcart drivers start another pay strike. The dustmen's strike follows
> another last autumn.
>
> (BBC1, 21.00, 13 January 1975)

> In Scotland, where ambulance control officers have begun their strike,
> Glasgow and the heavily populated Central Belt have been worst affected.
>
> (BBC1, 21.00, 13 January 1975)

Even when the range of groups and organisations involved is mentioned, the
causal denotation is made in the same way:

> In an attempt to resolve the Cowley engine tuners' dispute, British Leyland
> and the Amalgamated Union of Engineering Workers will tomorrow meet
> the government's Advisory, Conciliation and Arbitration Service.
>
> (BBC1, 21.00, 22 January 1975)

> In the Cowley engine tuners' strike, the unions and British Leyland have
> agreed tonight that there should be an independent enquiry into the
> dispute.
>
> (ITN, 22.00, 27 January 1975)

The ideological reduction involved in designating a story in terms of a
single protagonist when the activity by nature involves at minimum two
groups systematically structures the reporting. It diverts the audience's
attention from the causes and the material circumstances of the dispute and
implies that the breakdown in social relationships is the responsibility of
labour. The effect of this is to shift the balance of the story away from the
actions and role of the employer (firm, corporation, government) and to
minimise circumstantial and causal detail. Thus the labour force is often
painted in a manner that gives it the appearance of being a group of people
with apparently suspect motives precipitating unnecessary action against
organisations whose legitimacy is taken for granted.

These points are not unimportant in terms of the likely effect of such
messages on the audience. It is not simply that they routinely reinforce a
predominantly managerial view of cause. We know from retention studies that
audiences find it easier to recall the where, who and what of an event and have
greater difficulty in recalling causes and consequences.[46] British television
news is produced in such a manner that the who, where and what of an
industrial story are usually given primacy (as are consequences), while the
causes – if mentioned at all – are visually ascribed to labour or merely implied
by the nature of the language. Lord Annan's Committee, reporting on *The
Future of Broadcasting*, noted that television news coverage of industrial
affairs was 'inadequate and unsatisfactory', precisely because of this kind of
significant absence:

> The causes why people come out on strike are often extraordinarily
> complex. No reporter does his job adequately if he interviews only the

leading shop steward or union official. The fact that a strike is not backed by the union does not exonerate broadcasters from discovering why the workforce is out.[47]

In short, the structure of news talk often serves to obscure managerial responsibility for the antagonisms in social relationships which at times explode into the disputes reported.

In order to give greater depth to this analysis of nouns and categories, we extended the sample to cover the whole four-month period, January–April 1975. We discovered that the general pattern remained unchanged although the number of new words obviously increased with the length of the sample. Table 6.5 shows the frequency by channel of the nouns denoting 'industrial action'. The terms already mentioned remained the most prominent, with similar frequencies on both channels. Despite the larger total of items in the ITN sample, the BBC had slightly more 'exclusive' words, i.e. words that were not used by the other channel in the same period. The number of these items was rather small but it tends to negate the idea that the vocabulary of the commercial company is more emotive or sensational than that of BBC. If anything, the BBC's use of 'row' and 'clash' suggests the opposite. More important, however, was the very high degree of overlap between the categorisation devices on both channels over an extended period.

For example, the term 'disruption' was used with identical frequency by BBC and ITN during the four months. Occasionally the novelty of a particular dispute and the action taken led to slight divergence. This happened in the case of the hospital consultants' action in reducing their hours to those stipulated in their contracts. Assuming that this followed the precedent of 'working to rule' set in other industries, ITN initially used this phrase. BBC, perhaps taking note of the consultants' rather peculiar insistence that they were not taking 'industrial action', adopted the phrase 'work to contract' from the start. This usage was eventually taken up by ITN as well, 'work to rule' being reserved for railway workshop supervisors and other non-professional groups. Thus, the consultants' dispute, which had all the marks of industrial action taken against an employer, was labelled in such a way as to set it apart from corresponding types of action in other spheres.

This list of noun usage in television news talk revealed that the category 'strike', as we would expect, was by far the most important both in terms of frequency, and unfortunately, as we have shown, in defining the organisation of industrial stories. 'Action', 'dispute' and 'stoppage' were used in a very similar way to 'strike'. The exception was the word 'disruption', which is clearly not in the same lexical class since in conventional usage it contains the meaning of forceful separation or breaking apart. It carries more connotations and is not a simple denotative term.

'Dispute' is the one other important term which does not denote, by definition, a practice limited to industrial situations. Normally it implies

Table 6.5 Frequency of terms denoting industrial action: main evening news
bulletins, Jan.–April 1975

	BBC1	ITN	Total	% of total
Strike	103	138	241	45
Dispute	39	52	91	17
(Industrial) action	29	43	72	13
(Strike) action	4	—	4	1
(Disruptive) action	1	1	2	*
Disruption	15	15	30	6
Stoppage	9	12	21	4
Work to contract	14	5	19	4
Work to rule	5	13	18	3
Campaign	5	1	6	1
Overtime ban	2	4	6	1
Protest	3	3	6	1
Occupation	2	1	3	1
Walkout	1	1	2	*
Sit-in	5	—	5	1
Sanctions	2	—	2	*
Row	2	—	2	*
Tactics	1	—	1	*
Boycott	1	—	1	*
Clash	1	—	1	*
Withdrawal of labour	—	1	1	*
Practices	—	1	1	*
Demonstration	—	1	1	*
Total	244	292	536	100

Note:
*Denotes < 0.5 per cent

disagreement or controversy. The word 'disruption' could of course be
applied to the rupture of the normal relationships between employers and
employees in dispute but this in practice does not happen. The list includes
'disruption' because it is regularly applied in the same way as any other term
to describe industrial action. In news talk the way in which the term
'disruption' is used to describe employer–employee relationships seems to
entail the preferred view that a break-up is caused by organised labour. For
disruption is ascribed — implicitly or explicitly — solely to workers and
unions. To return to a procedure previously used, the simple process of
substituting terms confirms that there is an equivalence of meaning between
'strike', 'disruption' and 'stoppage' in the language of industrial news talk.
Consider this news item:

> Signalmen are expected to go on strike for twenty-four hours on Thursday
> in their pay dispute with British Rail. Disruption is likely to affect the
> biggest area since the signalmen first started their stoppages three months

ago. The main areas likely to be hit include Manchester, Liverpool, Stoke, Crewe, Stafford, Doncaster and Cambridge. The National Union of Railwaymen's executive meet tomorrow to consider British Rail's offer of £3 a week.

(ITN, 22.00, 10 February 1975)

Here, each of the terms used in the first two sentences could replace any other without significantly altering the nature of the report. This example illustrates well the problems of neutrally reporting a story under the current limitations of time and space.

This story contains a sequence of actions with at least three elements: the bargaining process with its demands and offers; the decision to stop work for one day (the strike); and the consequences of this action for rail users (disruption of the usual service). Part of the first element occurs at the end of the item in a sentence about the union executive meeting to consider British Rail's offer. But the background and sequential ordering which would make the event intelligible are telescoped so that effectively the semantic content is reduced to a neat ideological formula which runs as follows:

Signalmen's action: – causes stoppage = strike = disruption

A normal professional defence of this kind of report is that the importance of the story turns upon the 'consumer' angle, since the number of people who may be affected is far greater than the number of people likely to be involved in the strike. While this defence might be a case for ordering the sequence in such a way as to give the consequences of the strike priority (although we noted the dubiousness of this earlier), it provides no grounds whatsoever for equating concepts or categories in the above fashion.

In some stories, the *causes* rather than the consequences of the strike may be emphasised. This is very rare, however, and only occurred in two stories during the four-month sample period – the London bus strike and demonstration following the death of a conductor in an assault, and the strike by workers of Avon County Council.[48] Such special treatment tends to square the ideological circle which we have noted in the news coding that strikes are normally about pay. The strike by busmen is an instance which so obviously contradicts this assumption that its cause had to be elaborated. In general, however, industrial action and the breakdown of 'normal' relationships in industry are not seen as needing causal elaboration. The concentration normally tends to be on the consequence, effects and inconvenience of any dispute. Cultural rules and coding are breakable if broadcasters are prepared to challenge the prevailing assumptions and dig deep. The second clear departure from the norm of implicit causes occurred in the reporting of a strike by Avon County Council workers. It provides the exceptional case which 'proves the rule'. Although it was clearly a strike story it was given a special place in the structure of the bulletin as a final, human interest item.

This in itself is highly untypical and alerts attention to other features, including the attribution of cause and the use of metaphor. The item, which included a filmed report of a picket, was introduced by the newscaster as follows:

> Finally, a computer in Bristol has gone off the rails and has caused hundreds of people to go on strike. It belongs to Avon County Council and works out wages for council employees. Recently it has been giving thousands of pounds too much into some pay packets and in others nothing at all.
>
> (ITN, 22.00, 3 February 1975)

It is noteworthy that even in this example the cause is assigned to the computer itself rather than, as could easily have been done, to the responsible and accountable authorities. Thus it is written within the referential framework of autonomous technology getting out of hand or 'going off the rails'. This treatment of the story in human interest terms provides not so much a counter-example as confirmation of our general conclusion that the language of industrial reporting as structured at present cannot cope with multicausality and, whether by ignorance or default, almost invariably lays responsibility at labour's door.

The interchangeability of the terms 'strike' and 'disruption' is less likely if the news item is long rather than short. In longer items explanations, however culturally unbalanced, are more likely to be spelt out. The causal relationship is made clear in the following sentence from a longer item: 'another unofficial 24-hour strike by signalmen tomorrow will cause widespread disruption to commuter and inter-city services' (ITN, 22.00, 19 February 1975). The frequent, close association of two essentially different terms, even if it does not always amount to the equivalence noted above, can only tend towards ideological glossing or obscurity. The use of 'disruption' is not limited to the suspension or breakdown of services. It is also applied to the production process. Thus Mr Harold Wilson's January speech which referred to car manufacturing was later reported to be 'a warning about avoidable disruption in the car industry' (ITN, 22.00, 6 January 1975) and 'disruption today cost the *Daily Telegraph* and the *Sun* 360,000 and 170,000 copies respectively' (ITN, 22.00, 15 January 1975). The BBC's usage is almost identical: 'last night the group lost 1.5 million copies of the *Daily Mirror* because of disruption by members of the union SOGAT' (BBC1, 21.00, 25 March 1975). Although there may be some variation in the ways in which these statements are understood by different social groups and classes, the linguistic evidence strongly suggests that they have to be heard or read in terms of a single preferred conceptual category: strike disruption caused by labour.

Nouns in use: collective bargaining

The group of nouns that refers to the collective bargaining domain shares certain structural properties with the 'industrial action' list. There are fewer key words and a larger number of words which occur much less frequently – many of which were 'exclusive' to one channel during the sample period. As in Table 6.5, there are more of these 'exclusives' on BBC than on ITN, suggesting that the BBC uses a slightly larger though structurally similar vocabulary to that of ITN. In some cases the differences can be accounted for in one channel's use of the nominal form and the other's preference for the corresponding verb. ITN, for example, used the form 'to give a warning' on several occasions when BBC used the verb 'to warn'. However, the way in which some of the most frequent items are applied is more important.

Not surprisingly, the most frequently occurring nouns are 'talks', 'meeting' and 'mass meeting'. These are the events around which the shifting social relationships between employers and employees are structured.[49] Unfortunately they are merely the devices which allow other, more newsworthy, statements to be made about the protagonists. Since the mythology of industrial relations in capitalist society is that of the marketplace, it might be expected that the language of 'free' collective bargaining would embody the idea of equal exchange. In reality this is far from the case: the unequal exchange between labour and capital is heavily one-sided and involves the language of rights and coercion rather than the language of free exchange. The most commonly occurring words are 'claim', 'threat', 'offer', 'proposal', 'appeal' and 'demand' and they are used with about the same frequency on each channel. Although our discussion is restricted to the use of the noun forms, each term is also used in the verb form and a list of these would have a similar pattern of distribution. The list which is drawn from the January sample may be arranged as follows, showing how the terms are applied in practice to organised labour, to management or to both (Table 6.6). It illustrates the fundamental lack of reciprocity in a vocabulary in which the terms could apply reciprocally to both labour and management.

The language of the news is inhibited from using forms like 'labour offer to work harder' or 'management demand higher output', which are perfectly possible. A. J. Liebling, the American journalist and critic of the press, made

Table 6.6 Frequency of terms denoting collective bargaining: BBC1 and ITN main evening bulletins, January 1975

	Appeal	Claim	Demand	Offer	Proposal	Threat
As applied to:						
Labour	2	16	6	—	3	3
Management	2	—	—	6	5	6

a similar observation about the press reporting of strikes:

> The employer, in strike stories, always 'offers', and the union 'demands'.
> A publisher, for example, never 'demands' that the union men agree to
> work for a four-bit raise; the union never 'offers' to accept more.

Liebling also points out that 'demand' in English is an arrogant word; 'offer',
a large, generous one.[50]

The language thus conforms to a logic that is not simply a reflection of the
reported events or relationships *per se* but one that pertains to a more general
cultural 'code'. The absurdity of applying concepts like 'offer' and 'demand'
to the 'wrong' side shows how this code woks to legitimate the side that
responds and makes concessions rather than the side that makes requests as
though of right. The state has somewhat altered the appearance of the
'bargain' by introducing the limits of the Social Contract, but the vocabulary
is still serviceable within these limits.

The vocabulary of conflict resolution is small compared with the vocabulary of industrial action and the bargaining process. It is simply an extension
of the latter, with the expected terms 'award', 'agreement' and 'settlement'
occurring most frequently. The small number of news stories in this category
does not provide a good basis for generalisation but the group of words
contains the same ambiguity which is found in the other two groups. There
is a set of terms which can refer to a bargain struck in a free market situation
('agreement', 'settlement', 'deal') and another set which implies a different
relationship – that of contest, winning 'concessions', getting 'awards'. Like
many items in the 'industrial action' vocabulary, this second group is only
applied to labour. The use of imagery as such is very limited and
circumscribed. The image which does occur with some regularity is that of
competition, with overtones of warlike hostilities. Industry is conceived as
two 'sides' engaged in a 'conflict' in which labour may win something from
management. The progress of the 'fight' is portrayed in war terms – 'tactics',
'truce', 'peace move'. The persistence of these images (which are of course
used by the protagonists themselves as well as by newsmen) is significant
because they oversimplify generally complex relationships which involve not
just two but three or more 'sides'.[51] There is an example of this reduction in
the following report of British Leyland's decision to reopen the Cowley
works in the hope that the strike by engine tuners would be called off:

> The decision follows talks between *men and management and union
> officials*. Afterwards, the union agreed to recommend the 250 engine
> tuners, whose strike led to the shutdown, to go back to work and await
> further talks. Leyland management are optimistic that the strike will be
> called off. *Neither side* would say tonight whether there had been any
> political pressure for a quick settlement after Mr Wilson's warning.
>
> (ITN, 22.00, 6 January 1975; our italics)

Here a trinity is reduced to the normal ideological duo. The absence of alternative images of industrial life in its normal aspect (including the routine workings of collective bargaining) contributes further to the lack of causal and functional concepts in the vocabulary of industrial news.

These deficiencies, absences and distortions may best be illustrated via a diagrammatic representation of the conceptual organisation of industrial news (Figure 6.1, p. 210). The 'tree' or diagram is made up of the most frequently occurring terms in the bargaining, breakdown and resolution stages of the industrial relations process. It is arranged vertically since it represents a temporal as well as a logical sequence. The categories allow only the most simple distinctions to be made. The noun vocabulary does not provide a balanced set of descriptions of the so-called 'free collective bargaining' approach to industrial relations. If such a pluralistic approach were to operate, there are a number of key terms which are absent which would have to be present. For example, labour would offer and make concessions and management would make claims and demands. Even less do they allow room for the expression of fundamental differences of values based on class opposition. The language implies a unitary frame of reference skewed towards management, who exercise control as of 'right'. The dominant value assumptions which are entailed by this view limit and qualify the use of causal and interpretive concepts (e.g. concepts which would explain behaviour in terms of 'class' or 'radical opposition' instead of 'militant', with its ambiguous, aggressive connotations). This deficiency is all the more serious because recent work by Moorhouse on political consciousness and beliefs about class in Britain reveals that in fact the mass perception of the class system is dichotomous.[52] It is very close to the 'us' versus 'them' view. When asked in a political context whether there is a 'class struggle' in Britain, most people seem to believe that there is. Gallup showed that in May 1974, 60 per cent of the respondents believed that there was class struggle, while 62 per cent of the *Daily Telegraph* poll in the same year also believed that there was a class struggle.[53] But as the language of news reporting clearly reveals, this does not appear on our screens. It is lost in the process of mediation.

From the point of view of information theory, the usage of the noun vocabulary has a high degree of predictability and redundancy. In short, what is present in the vocabulary is used in a constrained fashion, while the significant absences which we have highlighted above mean that industrial news noun vocabulary presents the viewer with a seriously deficient 'vocabulary of motive'. As Hyman and Brough have suggested, this deficiency may exert a real influence upon industrial behaviour – an influence for which the broadcasters are at least partly if not intentionally responsible:

The manifest absence of socially available justifications for uncompromisingly oppositional behaviour by workers – which would be dismissed as 'sheer bloody-mindedness' and hence irrational – is clearly an inhibiting

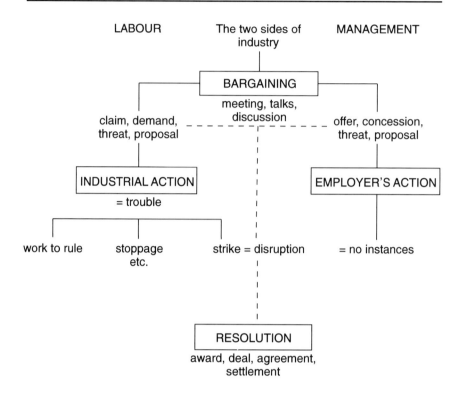

Figure 6.1 The conceptual organisation of industrial news

factor against uncompromising resistance to managerial priorities in the course of the negotiation of order at workplace level. And similarly, the general modesty of wage aspirations is in part attributable to the absence of any vocabulary of motives which would provide a manual worker, for example, with a plausible rationale for demanding a level of income or the associated material advantages conventionally regarded as the prerogative of higher-status groups.[54]

Of critical importance here, as our study reveals, is the dearth of terms on the management 'side' to denote the activities which might be said to constitute 'industrial action' by management. Terms such as 'lockout' are theoretically available. Even the use of 'strike' and 'go slow' in referring to underinvestment is now not uncommon in trade-union circles. These, however, were never used in the sample period.[55]

Moreover, as far as television news is concerned, industrial 'trouble' is basically trouble with (labour) strikes and not the difficulties arising from mismanagement or the economic situation as a whole: 'British Leyland's Austin Morris plant at Cowley in Oxford has shut down for the weekend because of industrial trouble' (ITN, 22.00, 4 January 1975); 'Disruption looks like continuing in the national newspapers ... the trouble is over pay differentials' (BBC1, 21.00, 17 January 1975); 'The industrial troubles that have been affecting Fleet Street papers are temporarily suspended in the dispute which cost the *Daily Mirror* group more than £1 million since Wednesday' (ITN, 22.00, 20 January 1975).

The idea of industry as 'troubled' can only be understood within the value consensus framework. Trouble must mean trouble for someone and in this case it is the 'industry' (the 'two sides' are temporarily forgotten). It is those not on strike or in dispute, who are troubled. There is no equivalent expression for the 'trouble' of those in the subordinate situation. The long-term effect of such underlying values is continually to reinforce a managerially skewed view of industrial relations. The causes ascribed or inferred are rarely given in a balanced manner, so that the workers involved in any dispute may come to be regarded by many viewers as essentially the trouble-makers.

CONCLUSION

The language of news is highly organised and structured in a number of ways which we have attempted to describe. Some of this description has a common-sense ring about it, but the formality and predictability of news talk is something that can be accounted for only in part by the professionals' own understanding of their activities. Many organised features of news talk which appear to be natural or inevitable cannot be neatly described as a system of journalists' lore or rules-of-thumb. However, unspoken assumptions, practices and perspectives are no less important than those which are made explicit, for they help constitute the 'primary framework', in Goffman's phrase, which renders the news talk meaningful. Industrial relations news relies heavily on a few key ideological propositions which inform everything that falls into the industrial category. They include the identification and labelling of industrial disputes in terms of labour, the attribution of cause to labour, and the routine reduction of workers' aspirations to cash 'demands'.

The reporting of industrial news in its encoding effectively conceals the primary assumptions beneath apparent neutrality and naturalistic presentation. We examined the lexical code and found it to be statistically highly predictable over an extended period of time not because of an inherent lack of descriptive terms, but because certain key terms were consistently preferred. In a similar way, we found that industrial news items were structured (by headlines, boundary markers and the use of reported speech) to close off the possibility of multicausality in industrial disputes. Also, there were indications that headlines referring to industrial and other topics were run according to certain preferred connections. This received further strong support in our study of the Social Contract coverage, which showed that the primary framework of industrial news meshed with a larger framework which informed the reporting of economic and political relationships on the large scale.

Ultimately, the present coding of industrial news talk presents its claim to authenticity via its 'neutral' form, which patterns all the information that comes within its orbit. When analysed, this 'neutral' form is resolved into an array of routine codes and practices which effectively rest upon a cultural imperative to hear the causes of disputes in one way rather than another.

NOTES

1 BBC Radio News, *News Guide*, mimeo, London: BBC, May 1972.
2 Quoted in R. Tyrell, *The Work of the Television Journalist*, London: Focal Press, 1972, pp. 40–1.
3 See M. A. K. Halliday, 'Language structure and language function' in J. Lyons, *New Horizons in Linguistics*, Harmondsworth: Penguin, 1970, and *Explorations in the Function of Language*, London: Arnold, 1973.
4 See D. Crystal and D. Davy, *Investigating English Style*, London: Longman, 1969, especially chapter 7, 'The language of newspaper reporting'.
5 With CEEFAX, ORACLE and VIEWDATA this circumstance will change. However, during the period of our study this involved a minute fraction (less than 1 per cent of the 17.7 million licensed sets in 1975–6). Market research indicated that by the end of 1977 the total of teletext receivers and adaptors may have reached 50,000 (see *Sunday Times*, 27 February 1977).
6 See Television Act, 1974, Rules Concerning Advertisements, paragraph 4: 'Advertisements shall not be inserted otherwise than at the beginning or the end of programmes or in natural breaks therein.' Leaving aside the nicety of the fit between the professional ideology of television journalism and the notion of naturalness, there remains the unanswered question of whether the news has a 'natural break' at all. Our findings in *Bad News*, London: Routledge & Kegan Paul, 1976, chapter 4, would indicate that it does not.
7 There was an exception. The interpretation of the armed forces' pay rise was as follows: 'The Government Review Body said that pay rates for the armed forces had fallen behind civilian levels and, while they took the social contract into account, servicemen should not be treated less favourably than the rest of the community.' (ITN, 22.00, 16 May 1975).
8 See Chapter 7, Section I of this book for a detailed discussion of visual inputs to titles and openings.
9 For example, ITN, 20.20, 1 January 1975; BBC1, 21.00, 16 January 1975; BBC1, 21.00, 21 March 1975; ITN, 22.00, 17 April 1976.
10 For example, BBC1, 21.00, 24 January 1975; BBC1, 21.00, 28 February 1975; ITN, 22.30, 1 February 1975.
11 For example, BBC1, 21.00, 28 February 1975.
12 See BBC1, 21.00, 24 February 1975; BBC1, 21.00, 14 January 1975; BBC1, 21.00; 2 February 1975; ITN, 22.00, 24 February 1975.
13 P. Schlesinger, 'Newsmen and their time machine', in *British Journal of Sociology*, vol. 28, no. 3, September 1977.
14 See BBC1, 21.55, 30 March 1975; ITN, 22.00, 27 February 1975; ITN, 22.00, 21 March 1975.

15 See BBC1, 21.00, 18 April 1975; BBC1, 21.10, 29 April 1975.
16 For systematic discussion of labelling theory and its use and limitations, see I. Taylor, P. Walton, J. Young, *The New Criminology*, London: Routledge & Kegan Paul, 1973, chapter 5. For a discussion of the limitations of social psychology and the labelling approach with special reference to the mass media, see N. Armistead (ed.), *Reconstructing Social Psychology*, Harmondsworth: Penguin, 1974, especially the articles by G. Murdock, H. Resler and P. Walton.
17 Ralph Dengler, S. J., 'The language of film titles', *Journal of Communications*, Summer 1975, pp. 51–60.
18 For example, ITN, 22.00, 3 April 1975, Between Items 3 and 4.
19 R. Tyrell, *The Work of the Television Journalist*, London: Focal Press, 1972, p. 37.
20 Gaye Tuchman describes the 'presentation of conflicting possibilities' as one of the strategic procedures used by newsmen to claim objectivity; see 'Objectivity as strategic ritual', *American Journal of Sociology*, vol. 77, no. 4, pp. 665 ff.
21 There is a further illustration of this usage in Table 6.4 in the opening sentence of the *News at Ten* report.
22 E. A. Schegloff, 'Sequencing in conversational openings', *American Anthropologist*, vol. 70, no. 6, 1968.
23 See for example V. Propp, *Morphology of the Folktale*, Bloomington: Indiana Research Center in Anthropology, 1958.
24 *The Task of Broadcasting News*, London: BBC, 1976, pp. 9–10.
25 R. Williams, *Keywords*, London: Fontana, 1976, p. 275.
26 Including D. Morley in his discussion of the 'event orientation' of the media in 'Industrial conflict and the mass media', *Sociological Review*, May 1976.
27 J. L. Austin, 'Performative–Constative' in C. Caton (ed.), *Philosophy and Ordinary Language*, Urbana: University of Illinois, 1963.
28 M. A. K. Halliday, *Explorations in the Function of Language*, London: Arnold, 1973, p. 20.
29 BBC1, 21.00, 25 February 1975.
30 L. Wittgenstein, *Philosophical Investigations*, Oxford: Blackwell, 1973, p. 223e.
31 I. L. Horowitz (ed.), *Power, Politics and People*, The Collected Essays of C. Wright Mills, New York: Oxford University Press, 1967, pp. 433–4.
32 *The Task of Broadcasting News*, a study for the BBC General Advisory Council published by the BBC, May 1976, pp. 9, 12.
33 *Ibid.*, p. 452.
34 *Bad News*, London: Routledge & Kegan Paul, 1976, p. 169.
35 H. Sacks, 'On the analysability of stories by children', in R. turner (ed.), *Ethnomethodology*, Harmondsworth: Penguin, 1975, pp. 216–32.
36 See *Bad News*, pp. 193–200.
37 A. Blum, *Theorising*, London: Heinemann, 1974.
38 ITN, 22.30, 7 January 1975.
39 For example, frequently quoted differences in colour terms. See J. Lyons, *Introduction to Theoretical Linguistics*, Cambridge: Cambridge University Press, 1971, pp. 56–8 for discussion of this point.
40 Figures for the word counts are rounded to the nearest ten words.
41 E. Goffman, *Frame Analysis*, London: Penguin, 1975, p. 44.
42 G. A. Miller, 'Statistical indicators of style', chapter 10 in N. N. Markel (ed.), *Psycholinguistics*, Homewood, Ill.: Dorsey Press, 1969.
43 See *Sunday Times* Business News, 20 March 1977.
44 O. Findahl and B. Hoijer, *Fragments of Reality: An Experiment with TV News and Visuals*, Audience and Programme Research Dept, Swedish Broadcasting Corporation, 1976, pp. 14–15.

45 P. R. Hawkins, *Social Class, the Nominal Group and Verbal Strategies*, London: Routledge & Kegan Paul, 1977, p. 45. See also D. Henderson, 'Contextual specificity, discretion and cognitive socialization', *Sociology* vol. 4, no. 3, 1970.

46 O. Findahl and B. Hoijer, 'Effect of additional verbal information on retention of a radio news program', *Journalism Quarterly*, vol. 52, no. 3, Autumn 1975.

47 *Report of the Committee on the Future of Broadcasting* (Annan Committee), Cmnd 6753, London: HMSO 1977, p. 272.

48 See for example BBC1, 21.00, 22 January 1975 and ITN, 22.00, 3 February 1975.

49 This is in keeping with the 'events' orientation of industrial news which we noted in *Bad News*, p. 19.

50 A. J. Liebling, *The Press*, New York: Ballantine, 1975, pp. 92, 240.

51 See A. Gouldner, 'Reciprocity and autonomy in functional theory', in L. Gross (ed.), *Symposium on Sociological Theory*, New York: Harper & Row, 1959, p. 270.

52 H. F. Moorhouse, 'Attitudes to class and class relationships in Britain', *Sociology*, vol. 10, no. 3, September 1976.

53 Moorhouse, op. cit., pp. 477–8.

54 H. Gerth and C. W. Mills, *Character and Social Structure*, London: Routledge & Kegan Paul, 1954, pp. 116–18; referred to in R. Hyman and I. Brough, *Social Values and Industrial Relations*, Oxford: Oxford University Press, 1975, pp. 206–7.

55 This usage has occurred more recently, in quotation at least, in the quality press. See, for example, *The Times*, 4 August 1976. At the time of writing it does not appear to have been used in television news reporting.

Chapter 7

News visuals*

I Halting the flow

> Analysis of a distribution of interest or categories in a broadcasting programme, while in its own terms significant, is necessarily abstract and static. In all developed broadcasting systems the characteristic organisation, and therefore the characteristic experience, is one of sequence and flow. This phenomenon, of planned flow, is then perhaps the defining characteristic of broadcasting, simultaneously as a technology and as a cultural form.
>
> (Raymond Williams, *Television: Technology and Cultural Form*)

OPENINGS

Raymond Williams draws attention to the essential difference in the experience of the television viewer from, say, that of an audience at a play or a football match. The television audience is invited to watch a sequence of miscellaneous 'items' (programmes), often interspersed with plugs for programmes to be shown later, channel announcements, and on commercial television, commercial breaks. The continuousness of this sequence has grown over the years. No more is the programmatic format punctuated by channel continuity icons like the potter's wheel. The sequence now is more of a planned flow designed to keep the viewer 'hooked'. This has little to do with the technical requirements of the medium, but is rather the product of the competition for ratings and channel loyalty.

The viewer does not by and large watch individual programmes but chooses channels. Inheritance of audience from one programme to another is a crucial factor in determining any single programme's audience. The programmes are obviously perceived as separate but the experience of

---

*The two sections that comprise this chapter were first published in *More Bad News*, London, Routledge & Kegan Paul, 1980, pp. 241–81.

television relies rather on their sequentiality.

In this situation the opening and closing of each programme is important. The different genres of programming – a difference institutionalised by the existence of different departments within the broadcasting organisations – all adopt styles of opening titles offering instant clues as to the type of programme that follows. With news and current affairs there are clear differences governing the styles of titles. Current affairs programmes, at the time of the study, offered as a dominant mode a tapestry of faces, sometimes concentrating on the presenters involved in the programme as well as other newsworthy people. The news bulletins eschew the possibility of using the reporters, correspondents and newscasters in this way. All new titles refer either to the events of the day (which mean that the opening image changes although the superimposed name of the bulletin and the opening music remains the same), or they have standard openings ranging from a simple animated caption (*News Extra*) to a complex film title lasting around fifteen seconds or more as in the case of *First Report*. The images of these standardised openings are all drawn from a narrow range. In the *First Report* title the faces shown are those of the three major political leaders and President Ford. During our period the Heath photograph was substituted by a photograph of Thatcher following her election as leader (Figure 7.1). *News at Ten* uses the parliament building, panning from black (the dark Thames waterfront) on to the House of Commons and then zooming in to the clock face (Figure 7.4, p. 219). Delayed bulletins feature the correct time (although, as Richard Collins points out without theoretic explanation, the weather is unchanging). The pan and zoom last around 15 seconds in each edition.

During our period the main BBC bulletin featured the newsroom itself via a permanently installed camera (Figure 7.2, p. 218). This gave a general view of the room which could be matted-in to other pictures generated in the news studio some floors below. Thus the opening sequence involved shots of the newsroom with an animated title over, followed by shots of the news studio showing both newscasters and on occasion other correspondents, as in Example 7.1. The system of shots worked except that the relative distances of the newsroom camera from the scene it was photographing and the news studio camera from its scene were different, with the result that on occasion some person in the newsroom could loom giant-like behind the newscaster in the news studio. An example of this can be seen in Figure 7.5 (p. 219). The shape behind Kenneth Kendall (who is paying off the bulletin of Wednesday, 15 May) is that of a newsroom worker crossing too close to the newsroom camera. Commenting on the implications of these opening images, Collins suggests that the use of parliament by *News at Ten*, 'invests the news programme with the authority of parliament and, reciprocally, constitutes the British parliament as the centre and source of news'[1] (Figure 7.4). Of the ten still photographs that make up the surround in the *First Report* opening title, Collins says, 'the newsworthy world is constructed as bounded by British

Example 7.1 BBC1, 21.00, 13 May 1975

1 GV newsroom: empty desks, etc. 0.2 1a *Super Nine O'Clock News* cap. (Photo 7.2) 0.5 CUT	*VOICE-OVER* This is the *Nine O'Clock News* Music
	Music cont.
2 3 shot Baker F/G MS profile Biddulph B/G MS profile (SCR RHT) Whitmore B/G MS 7/8 to CAM (SCR LEFT) + BLINDS (Photo 2c) 0.4 CUT	
3 MS Baker (newsroom GV *Chromokey* + *Nine O'Clock Super* upper SCR LEFT) desk (inc. mike and nameplate)	(Fade music) *BAKER (Newscaster) TO CAM* Good evening . . .

Figure 7.1 Mrs Thatcher on *First Report*

Figure 7.2 Nine O'Clock News: newsroom and super

Figure 7.3 Nine O'Clock News: news studio three – shot

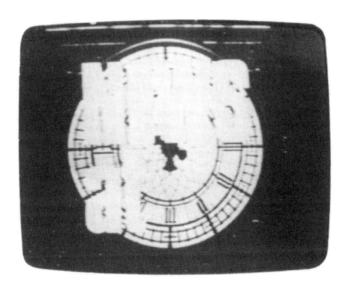

Figure 7.4 *News at Ten*: zoom in clock face, animate super

Figure 7.5 A 'giant' in the newsroom

parliamentary politics defined in leaders; the world outside Britain, as represented by the US President Ford and the EEC; economic activity by images connoting energy, consumption and exchange'.[2] We would support these subjective observations of what he calls 'the "ideal" content of British television news' by noting that his interpretation of this list of images accurately squares with the percentage pattern of story inputs that we have found. There is no image of sport, disaster, science or crime, these being of less importance generally in the running order of the bulletins.

The *Nine O'Clock News* suggested that the news came not from parliament but from the newsroom, which is perhaps a closer reflection of the reality of mediation. It was nevertheless an odd choice of image (since dropped in favour of a satellite view of the world) because the newsroom during the transmission of the day's final bulletin is not a busy and thriving place. One could compare the nightly levels of inactivity with the early Saturday bulletin inserted at a couple of minutes' length from the newsroom via the same camera. Here, on this 'thin' day, the newscaster sat on the edge of the desk and read a short piece directly to the camera with more activity going on round him than was usual on the *Nine O'Clock News*.

World leaders, centres of political power, newsrooms and the world itself limit the range of changes on which the opening images in this sort of sequence are rung. Apart from the absence of newscasters themselves (a conscious reflection of the British avoidance of making the news personnel stars as they are in the United States)[3], there is now little emphasis on technology – on images of the control room (or gallery as it is called in the BBC), cameras, lights and the rest of television's paraphernalia. The earliest titles (*Roving Report* or *Television Newsreel*) often involved transmitting masts. Perhaps the audience is now presumed to have had its fill of what might be called electronic wonders. In the titles discussed here, titles which reveal a clear social agenda, there is less overt reference to the technology of mediation.

The other standard openings are much simpler, involving plain typographic devices simply announcing the bulletin with music over. And these caption cards are also used to close bulletins. In the use of typography both to open and close bulletins, the relationship of the new electronic journalism with the older traditions of print journalism can be seen. The main characteristic of all the typography on the news is that of sans serif typefaces, modern and uncluttered. The '2' in the *News Extra* (Figure 7.6) is a bastard face specially designed and reflecting the way in which the television picture is constructed line by line. In the *First Report* title the ground on which the inserted images are placed is an abstracted 'degraded' image of hands at a typewriter (Figure 7.7), a clear reference back to print. The music, too, often reflects the twin sources of television news practice – journalism and show business. Typewriter rhythms meld into show business trumpet calls.

Figure 7.6 News Extra: the straight typographics

Figure 7.7 First Report: the inheritance of print journalism

'NATURAL FRUIT JUICE'

News music is unique in television in that those who commission it require it to be *empty* of myth content. We could paraphrase Barthes and suggest that myth is a kind of music defined by its intention. The clearest use of music-as-myth is that of commercial jingles. It is not for nothing that they have been called 'the folksongs of a consumer society'. For example, the folksiness of the breakfast cereal jingle:

> There are two men in my life
> To one I am a mother
> To the other I'm a wife
> And I give them both the best
> With Natural Shredded Wheat.

is an appeal to the powerful mother-provider requirement of our culture, the rustic sun-filled kitchen being a fantasy for millions of city dwellers.

Advertisers go about the business of myth-manipulating with seriousness, and in recent years 'jingle factories' (studios specialising in providing accurate jingles or utility music for advertisers, radio stations, etc.) have proliferated along with specialist independent composers and musicians. That it is a successful and therefore lucrative business is witnessed by the high rates paid to session musicians for jingle recording sessions.

The skills developed by advertising companies in the creation of culturally loaded music themes have been used by television programme producers who look to the specialist to provide themes for new programmes. Retrospectively, since signature tunes pay handsomely in the form of repeat fees, there is always fierce competition for such plums as a series offer.

Looking at specific examples, what precisely is the siren call of the theme of *Coronation Street* (Granada TV) to its particular audience? The theme features a horn melody on a blues scale, seemingly inappropriate to signify the location of the series, a working-class back street in a large northern industrial town. It is inappropriate until we recall a popular hit of 1965, *Strangers on the Shore* by Acker Bilk, whose traditional jazz band had been one of the most popular bands of the British traditional jazz revival for years before that. Acker Bilk represents a manifestation of what was most popular with the British working-class youth of the 1950s who became the middle-aged and still working-class audience that form the faithful viewers of *Coronation Street*.

The theme tune for *Match of the Day* (BBC1) is rich in associations. It is a predominantly brass orchestration over a strong two-beat march rhythm: a martial sound in celebratory mood. It encapsulates the football experience on television – machismo in a fun mood. The Latin-American figure is a reminder of the apogee of football skill and entertainment: the Brazilian national team. There is, too, the possibility that the appeal is to that vast audience who go or hope to go on package tours to the Costa Brava, dancing to the latest cod-Spanish song, 'Viva Espana' or the like: experiencing, as in the World Cup, a vague sense of internationalism.

The use of modern jazz themes to introduce current affairs or interview programmes is interesting since again it would appear, after years of snips from the classical repertoire, to be an inappropriate style. Mozart, Bach *et al.* always registered serious purposes. The switch to modern jazz was probably at first a mimicry of American chat-shows, initially a David Frost innovation. Since then, this kind of music has acquired a cultural familiarity and has become a musical sign that the programme is metropolitan, sophisticated as well as intelligent. The older use of classical borrowings became too sober for programme planners trying to widen their audiences without lowering their emphasis. (Its use is also an indication that jazz has finally been relegated to the cultural elite.)

News music, however, is unique in that those who commission it overtly require that none of the above applies. In that sense it is supposed to be 'empty'. When interviewing some of the composers of news themes, we asked what brief they were given for the commission. The replies suggested that the requirement was that the theme should be emotionally neutral; it should signal the news programme without drawing attention to itself.

The 17.50 ITN news music, 'Non Stop', was written by Malcolm Batt (a television screenwriter and lawyer). It was not in fact custom-written but sent by his music publisher in answer to a general request by the ITN for suitable themes. The selection was adjudicated by Sir John Barbirolli. Malcolm Batt claims that its merits as a news theme are that it is 'tuneful, recognisable, difficult to hum. Since musically it is in a circular form it speaks of continuity, constant business, without any further programmatic content. It is without diminuendo or crescendo.' He goes on to describe it as comfortable and predictable.

BBC2's news theme was written by Peter Hope as a response to a general enquiry from the BBC to various music publishers. The idea of the teleprinter and typewriter sound was suggested by them, with the instruction that the piece should indicate immediacy without being over-dramatic and it should have no musical programmatic theme. It should also be serious but not foreboding. Peter Hope describes it as 'neutral fruit juice'.

First Report's search for a theme prefigures the new reliance on specialists. It was commissioned by ITN directly from a company called Emison, with much the same brief as previously outlined. Emison provided the music for French ORTF news programmes, as well as six identification packages for local radio stations in this country, and many more throughout Europe.

It is easy to forget that there are very strong precedents for more emotive musical introductions to the news. The stirring signature tune of Pathé Gazette film news, the chimes of Big Ben on BBC radio, and the use of Wagner and Beethoven on early television are forceful reminders that de-mythologised music was not always deemed necessary.

The change in news musical style demonstrates the discomfort with which the news programme itself fits into the flow of television. It is potentially intrusive and contentious. These are qualities that can be of great value in programmes that appear irregularly, but the news is always with us. The music emphasises the image the television companies wish to sustain: that the news is balanced and impartial; that in no way are the news personnel personally involved. The news occupies a neutral space in the sequence into which events and facts project themselves almost mechanically. The clackety-clack of the teleprinters and the electronic bleeps that have become the predominant themes of news music draw attention to the *processes* of news collection and presentation; they reflect the typographical origins of 'news'. The news comes, the music suggests, through neutral air waves on to neutral type-writers, a balanced mix of electronic show business and print.

CHANGING IMAGES

The weekend and the two early evening bulletins use music as the unifying factor for their opening because they change their opening image from bulletin to bulletin. The major story of the day is therefore introduced as an image before it is revealed in spoken text. There is a view of television journalism which says that the newsroom's ability to deliver a full report on the day's events is hampered by the need to provide vivid images.[4] We have

Figure 7.8 ITN, 18.05, 11 May 1975

Figure 7.9 BBC1, 12.55, 13 May 1975

Figure 7.10 BBC1, 17.45, 15 May 1975

gone some way to denying this premise by pointing out that never less than 25 per cent or so of any bulletin is newscaster reading to camera, and that the total amount of time spent by newscaster and correspondents reading to camera is far greater. Add to this interviews, speeches and press conferences and our contention that the news largely consists of 'talking heads' must be sustained. In other words, these factors coupled with our analysis, which reveals the predominance of parliamentary, economic and industrial news, means that the newsrooms are not primarily motivated in their daily agenda-setting tasks by what is most visual. Further discussion of this will be found below. But for the moment it is interesting to note that in those bulletins with a changing-image title, where visual considerations might be expected to be greatest, nevertheless it is still the major story (irrespective of its visual quality) that is placed in the prime lead position.

Thus the opening images of these bulletins are often file photographs, library film or graphics. The opening images of these bulletins are listed in Table 7.1. All have the bulletin title (e.g. 'BBC News', 'ITN News') superimposed (*supered*) over them. The most crucial point about Table 7.1 (in view of the arguments about the existence of what might be called a 'visual imperative') is how few of the images directly and indisputably relate to the day on which they are transmitted. Only the black-and-white news picture of the American marines on the Thursday and the shots of the *Mayaguez* docked at Singapore on Saturday are in this sense 'news pictures'. The rest range from maps, library film (or film if specially shot that could just as well be from the

Figure 7.11 BBC1, 12.55, 16 May 1975

Table 7.1 Index of opening images (Index 2): week 11–17 May 1975

Date	Channel	T/X time	Description: visual track	Description: sound track
11/5	BBC1	18.05	*Still portrait*: Wilson	Mus. + V/O
		21.30	Ditto	Mus.
	ITN	18.05	*Composite still*: Portrait Wilson + Ryton factory sign (Fig. 7.8)	Mus.
		22.00	*Still portrait*: Wilson	Mus.
12/5	BBC1	12.55	*Graphic*: '£'	Mus. + V/O
		17.45	Flixborough *Library Film* of fire	2 shot Mus. + 1 shot V/O
	ITN	17.50	*Graphic*: '£' declines	Mus. animate V/O
13/5	BBC1	12.55	B&W *Photograph*: *Mayaguez* (Fig. 7.9)	Mus. + V/O
		17.45	Ditto	Mus. + V/O
	ITN	17.50	Ditto	
14/5	BBC1	12.55	*Photograph*: Chrysler HQ colour	Mus.
		17.45	*Map*: Cambodia, Gulf of Thailand	Mus. + V/O
	ITN	17.50	*Map*: Utapao, Cambodia, Ko Tang Kompong Som Phnom Penh Gulf of Thailand *Mayaguez*	Mus. + V/O
15/5	BBC	12.55	*Map*: Ko Tang Cambodia Thailand	Mus. + V/O
		17.45	*Graphic*: Dunlop and British Leyland logos (Fig. 7.10)	Mus. + V/O
	ITN	17.50	*News picture*: B&W: US marines alighting under fire from helicopter GV	Mus. + V/O
16/5	BBC1	12.55	*Film*: British soldiers marching LS/MS	1st shot Mus. (Fig. 7.11) 2nd shot V/O (Fig. 7.12)
		17.45	*Colour photograph*: Shopping precinct (Fig. 7.13)	Mus. animate (Fig. 7.14) V/O
	ITN	17.50	*Film*: (Library?) Track MS down supermarket shelves	Mus. + V/O + super (Fig. 7.15)
17/5	BBC1	17.20	*News picture*: B&W: *Mayaguez* aerial on tow	Mus. + V/O
		21.35	*Film*: *Mayaguez* docked at Singapore GV bows zoom in CU name	Mus. + V/O
	ITN	13.10	*News picture*: B&W *Mayaguez* at sea + *Film*: Docked at Singapore 4 LS crew + name of ship	Mus. + V/O
		17.10	*Film*: *Mayaguez* docked: GV bows pull back, pan RHT.	Mus. + V/O
		22.30	*Film*: *Mayaguez* docked: 3 LS men on deck, pull back	Mus. + V/O
	BBC2	19.30	*Film*: *Mayaguez* docked: flag + GV bridge	Mus. + V/O
		22.30	*Still portrait*: Jack Jones	Mus. + V/O

Figure 7.12 BBC1, 12.55, 16 May 1975

library, as in the BBC2 lunchtime soldiers footage), still portraits which are on file or graphic designs of various sorts – the most extreme being the Dunlop/British Leyland logos used by the BBC on the same day the ITN used the marines.

There seems to be a general tendency, as exhibited in Table 7.1, for the newsproducers not to worry overmuch about the visual quality of the opening icon. In other words, even if the stories of major importance were more accessible, criteria other than the visual would still be used to determine the lead item, and in consequence the lead image. The news, at least in its opening moments, is not the prisoner of sensation-seeking producers thrusting instantaneous, dramatic, but unimportant images at their audience.

The sense of urgency and immediacy that the bulletins have is here conveyed as much by the music and by the typography of the title as by the image. In this way the changing image titles match the unchanging ones. The types of title impose via music and typography a sense of urgency independent of the news images of the day. This enables the titles to function as attention-getters but also allows the producers to put visually dull political, economic and industrial affairs in the lead position.

It follows that the majority of the above images are not used iconically. Take for instance the composite still image ITN used for the 18.05 bulletin on Saturday 11 May 1975. Neither element of the composite – the Wilson portrait or the Ryton factory gate (Figure 7.8) – was necessarily taken on the day in question. The composite assumes that the audience will read a visual headline

Figure 7.13 BBC1, 17.45, 16 May 1975

– Prime Minister comments or acts on industrial situation at Chrysler. Similarly, when faced with the economy, always difficult to visualise, images of supermarkets or shopping precincts are used so as to give clues to the type of story involved. Here, because supermarkets and shopping precincts are an all-pervasive locale for the inflation story in all its aspects, screen writing is required to make the visual headline clear (e.g. BBC1, 17.45, 16 May 1975; (Figures 7.13 and 7.14).

There are thus two extremes in these images. On the one hand there is the image that does express the story iconically. Marines landing on Ko Tang Island are photographed doing so and reported as doing so. The *Mayaguez* at the dock in Singapore is filmed there and is reported as being there. At the other extreme there is a photograph of the Prime Minister, taken at an undetermined time, and a photograph of a factory gate, also taken at an undetermined time, together signifying in some detail an industrial situation. Or there are the two company logos standing symbolically for the companies, as indeed they were designed to do (Figure 7.10). In between there are images which are undetermined as to the time they were collected but stand in a midway indexical relationship to the event they represent. The portrait stills of Mr Wilson not composited with other images (ITN, 22.00, 11 May 1975), the picture of Mr Jones (BBC2, 23.20, 17 May 1975), and above all the only available picture of the *Mayaguez* (until its release) are examples of this. The image of the *Mayaguez* (Figure 7.9) is indubitably an icon of the ship; but it is being used to represent the ship in a particular place – Ko Tang. There is no available image of the ship in that place and therefore the iconic image is used indexically. Most of the images in the news, whether stills, film or tape, are indexical in this sense. Only when incorporeal and intangible subjects, such as the economy, are being dealt with does the material become symbolic; and only when events take place in front of the camera, as in the case of sport, does the image become iconic. These last two are rarer.

We have further commented on the overall similarity of the bulletins channel to channel. In Table 7.1 we can see that similar responses are called out for similar stories. In other words, after allowing for the fact that the notion of what is important is common to both services, the visual response (as it were) is also common. It would be unfair to cite the *Mayaguez* story under this heading since clearly only one picture of the ship was available for a good part of the week. But the response to the inflation story on the Friday (BBC colour photograph of shopping precinct with information *supered* and ITN film of supermarket, Figures 7.14 and 7.15), or the use of the Cambodian map on the Tuesday, are examples of this tendency to find the same solution. Against this has to be placed the failure of the BBC's early bulletin to use the news picture of the marines, one of the only icons to emerge from the *Mayaguez* affair, as the lead on the following day. But the point can nevertheless be maintained. Competition between these two early evening bulletins does not extend, in practice, into the selection of the opening images.

Figure 7.14 BBC1, 17.45, 16 May 1975

Table 7.1 reveals the range of possibilities available for this sort of changing-image opening. All the openings we have described have a standard piece of music and a standard superimposed bulletin identification. The images come from an almost full range of the inputs generally available in the bulletins: film, news pictures, file portrait stills, graphics, general ('other') photographs, maps. News personnel, whether live, on film or tape, or in the radio circuit caption mode, did not appear. Neither, in this particular week, did live, filmed or taped interview shots.

If the image was a still of any kind then there would be just one used. Animating further written information (that is, other than the bulletin identification) on that still was possible. If there was more than one shot in the opening sequence then the input was always film. In other words, only one still image was used per bulletin. The music always covered the opening image and the identification *super*. Then either the newscaster appeared to camera or he (Angela Rippon not being involved in any of the bulletins using this repertoire of openings) would speak over. If he voiced-over the image, a cut would occur as he began to speak on those occasions when film was used. But on one occasion in the week in question, the voice-over began four words before the cut. The music never exceeded 10 seconds, running usually between 7 and 8.5 seconds. On the BBC the voice-over sections never exceeded 6 seconds if only one image was involved or, in the case of multiple film shots, the total for the two shots was 6.5 seconds. The lunchtime bulletin

Figure 7.15 ITN, 17.50, 16 May 1975

voiced-over every day except Wednesday; the BBC1 early evening bulletin voiced-over every day.[5] ITN did it every day except Tuesday but did not use the technique on the two Sunday bulletins, when BBC did; nor on one of the Saturday bulletins, when both BBC1 and BBC2 did. This is an area of directors' (or general production) choice and the significance is to be found not in the range of differences, but in the similarities involved.

A difference nevertheless is that when ITN does use voice-over, rather than cutting to newscaster-to-camera, it does so for longer than the BBC does: 9 seconds on the Monday, 23 seconds on the Wednesday (which involved a slow zoom into the Cambodian map), 11.5 seconds on Thursday and 17 seconds (over the tracking shot, on film, of the supermarket shelves) on Friday. Matching this are the BBC2 bulletins on Sunday, the earlier of which went for three shots of the *Mayaguez* lasting 3.5, 5 and 18 seconds following the opening music. In fact the film of the *Mayaguez* at the Singapore dockside was broken by a map and then continued, so it was not until 2 minutes 25 seconds into the bulletin that the newscaster appeared. The later BBC2 bulletin took 55 seconds of voice-over before showing the newscaster.

One difference between changing and unchanging image titles is that in the former case, whether voice-over is used or the newscaster appears immediately, there is no greeting – 'Good afternoon', etc. In the unchanging image title there is always a newscaster greeting – Kee's 'Hello' and everybody else's 'Good evening'. This is true even of *News at Ten* which, as we shall see, combines in the opening 'bongs' sequence a changing image follow-up to one unchanging image opening. Normally, then, with these changing-image openings moving talking heads do not appear, although still portraits do. Images such as maps with writing on them can be used. Only one still image per opening is preferred, but if film is used, up to three shots can appear. The commentary voice-over normally starts after the first cut and follows the shot, over which identification of the bulletin is *supered*. Normally, the music does not last for more than 10 seconds. If one image is being used there is a tendency to move the camera relative to it after ten static seconds.

It is our contention that these routine practices work with other cultural conventions and codes to establish a set of hidden 'viewers' maxims', by which the audience understands the bulletins. If any of the above is happening on the screen, a bulletin is beginning. With the standard unchanging opening titles, the process in terms of viewers' maxims is easier, but we should again note that the longest of these (*First Report*) did not run for more than 17 seconds, *News at Ten* for about 15 seconds, and the three shots at the start of the *Nine O'Clock News* for about 12 seconds. The maxims attached to these are therefore simpler. Since the images never change (except in major revisions from time to time) they can be deemed to be more recognisable than the changing-image openings. The BBC *News Extra* was the most iconic and the simplest of all: a straightforward caption. All the other bulletins were short inserts into other programmes, verbally introduced by other non-newsroom performers. Unchanging-image openings do respond to the events of the day. In such bulletins there is always a summary of upcoming stories. These are anyway the longer bulletins and repetitions are therefore deemed more possible. In the case of *First Report* and the *Nine O'Clock News* this summary or list of headlines was simply read to camera by the newscaster or presenter; in the case of *News Extra* they were read by the newscaster but with changing images on the *Chromokey* screen behind him or her; and, most elaborately, in *News at Ten* they were voiced-over images, punctuated each time by a single chime of Big Ben (the 'bongs').

During the week the *Nine O'Clock News* took on average 33 seconds to read its headlines; *First Report* took 50 seconds. These differences again reflected the more current affairs style pacing of the earlier bulletin. *News Extra* also took 33 seconds on average to read its headlines but the range was greater than the *Nine O'Clock News*'s, where 9.5 seconds separated the shortest and the longest headline text; in *News Extra* there was a 23-second spread from the shortest (at 26.5 seconds) to the longest (at 49.5 seconds).

The use of the *Chromokey* for *News Extra*'s headlines was among the more complex uses of this device during our recording period. We will leave detailed discussion of these five opening newscaster shots in *News Extra* until *Chromokey* in general is discussed below. However, it can be here noted that during our period the possibility that *Chromokey* has to allow film, tape or any input to be matted in behind the newscaster's head is eschewed in favour of stills alone. Thus the iconic quality of the images in these headlines is much reduced. For instance, with Aubrey Jones in the studio for an interview, the image on the headline was a file still photograph of him. A still colour photograph of a hospital bed indexed a story on private medicine. A general view (colour photograph) of a steel mill at work denoted redundancy in the steel town of Irlam, where the mill had closed. Both of these last were film features and therefore film was available. Similarly Flixborough appeared as a colour photograph in the *News Extra* headline shot and the 'Chrysler Wives' as a black-and-white news picture when footage of these events was available and was later used in the bulletin. Thus stills seem to be preferred.

The same is not true of ITN's 'bongs' sequences in the main bulletin. These lasted about 24 seconds and involved the greatest rate of image change. Their spread was from a shortest of 17.5 seconds to a longest of 37 seconds, but the shots within the sequence varied only from 3.5 seconds to 5 seconds, the vast majority lasting a regular 4 or 4.5 seconds. Here every type of input was utilised, involving the most complex regular directing operation in any bulletin on any channel during the time of our sample (see Examples 7.2a–7.2e). The director's discretion in this area can be seen in such matters as whether the 'bong' – the single chime of Big Ben – comes before or after or (as on the Friday) over the cut. Otherwise the regularity of the time is again noticeable: 3.5 to 5 seconds for stills images and a total of up to 5 seconds for film or tape (which never exceeds to shots). The stills are sometimes subjected to camera movement.

Example 7.2a News at Ten, opening headlines 'The bongs', Monday 12 May 1975

Opening title: pan GV Parliament Sq: zoom in Big Ben *super News at Ten* CUT 0.15		0.15	Music F/X 'Bong'
GV *Mayaguez* at sea *B&W photograph* CUT 0.5		0.20	*BOSANQUET (Newscaster) VOICE-OVER* The Cambodian navy seizes an American merchant ship. F/X 'Bong'
President Ford MCU *Portrait still* ease-in (slight) CUT 0.4		0.24	*BOSANQUET VOICE-OVER* President Ford says piracy and demands its immediate release F/X 'Bong'
£ in crystal ball *Graphic* CUT 0.4½		0.28½	*BOSANQUET VOICE-OVER* The pound slides again but not by much. F/X 'Bong'
GV new fertilizer plant under construction CUT 0.2½	*Film*	0.31	*BOSANQUET VOICE-OVER* Flixborough explosion – it was caused by a faulty repair.
CUT GV 2 stacks – pull back Aftermath CUT 0.2½	*Film*	0.33½	F/X 'Bong'
MLS Orantes serves CUT 0.2½	*Tape*	0.36	*BOSANQUET VOICE-OVER* Tennis – Spain have beaten us in the Davis Cup.
LS GV down court – balls delivered CUT 0.1½	*Tape*	0.37½	*BOSANQUET TO CAM*
Bosanquet MS + CSO insert			Good evening . . .

Example 7.2b News at Ten, Tuesday 13 May 1975

Opening title: pan GV Parliament Sq: zoom in Big Ben *super News at Ten* CUT 0.14		0.14	Music F/X 'Bong'
GV *Mayaguez* at dock *B&W photograph* CUT 0.4½		0.18½	*GARDNER (Newscaster) VOICE-OVER* Captured cargo boat; American warships and marines stand by. F/X 'Bong'

Example 7.2b continued

			GARDNER VOICE-OVER
Display of £ notes	*Graphic*		Work has stopped on printing Britain's banknotes.
CUT 0.4½	0.23	/	F/X 'Bong'

			GARDNER VOICE-OVER
CU Foot	*Portrait*	*Still*	Mr Foot tells the Chrysler strikers to go back to work.
CUT 0.4	0.27	/	F/X 'Bong'

			GARDNER VOICE-OVER
CU Cover CBI report			CBI forecast a deep recession and
	Graphic		rising unemployment.
CUT 0.4½	0.31½	/	F/X 'Bong'

			GARDNER VOICE-OVER
GS 6 Japanese (ceremonial robes) players	*Film*		The once-a-year soccer match fit for a Queen.
CUT 0.4	0.35½	/	*GARDNER TO CAM*
Gardner MS + CSO insert RHT			Good evening . . .

Example 7.2c News at Ten, Wednesday 14 May 1975

Opening title: pan GV Parliament Sq: zoom in Big Ben *super News at Ten*	Music	
CUT 0.15	/	F/X 'Bong'

			GARDNER (Newscaster) VOICE-OVER
Map: Thailand Cambodia Utapao Gulf of Thailand Phnom Penh Kompong Som Ko Tang *Mayaguez*			The captured cargo boat; America sinks Cambodian warships.
CUT 0.4½		/	F/X 'Bong'

			GARDNER VOICE-OVER
GV *Mayaguez* at dock *B&W photograph*			No one knows what's happened to the crew of thirty-nine.
CUT 0.4		/	F/X 'Bong'

			GARDNER VOICE-OVER
GV Cranes/Ship dock scene *Colour photograph*			Trade figures – some cheering news.
CUT 0.4½		/	F/X 'Bong'

Example 7.2c continued

CU Ballot box, hand dropping in vote *Colour photograph* CUT 0.4	GARDNER VOICE-OVER The referendum: we'll know the result by teatime on 6 June. F/X 'Bong'
CU Rapist – identikit picture B&W *Portrait Still** CUT 0.4½ Gardner MCU plain B/G	GARDNER VOICE-OVER The Cambridge rapist – a report from the nervous city. GARDNER TO CAM Good evening . . .

*So classified.

Example 7.2d News at Ten, Thursday 15 May 1975

Opening title etc. CUT 0.15	Music F/X 'Bong'
GV *Mayaguez* at dock *B&W Photograph* CUT 0.4½	GARDNER (Newscaster) VOICE-OVER After the rescue the *Mayaguez* is heading for Singapore. F/X 'Bong'
MLS 4 shot marines out of helicopter zoom in CU *B&W News picture* CUT 0.4½	GARDNER VOICE-OVER 16 marines are dead or missing. F/X 'Bong'
GV pan strike crowd *Tape? Film?* CUT 0.4½	GARDNER VOICE-OVER Chrysler strikers vote to stay out. F/X 'Bong'
CU Dunlop company logo *Graphic* CUT0.4 Gardner MS + CSO insert RHT	GARDNER VOICE-OVER Settlement is on the cards for Dunlop. GARDNER TO CAM Good evening . . .

Example 7.2e News at Ten, Friday 16 May 1975

Opening title etc. CUT 0.15	Music F/X 'Bong'
Shrinking £ effect: *super* graphic £ zoom back over GV top shot shop *colour photograph + Graphic* CUT 0.4½	BOSANQUET (Newscaster) VOICE-OVER Britain's inflation rate a record figure, far worse than expected. F/X 'Bong'

Example 7.2e continued

CU Dunlop company logo – zoom in *Graphic* CUT 0.3½	*BOSANQUET VOICE-OVER* The Dunlop strike is over, 18,000 go back to work . . . F/X 'Bong'
Chrysler Ryton plant, Stoke: GV gate zoom back and pan *Colour photograph* CUT 0.3½	*BOSANQUET VOICE-OVER* . . . but Chrysler throw 8,000 out of a job tonight. F/X 'Bong'
2 MS armed soldiers *Colour photograph* CUT 0.5	*BOSANQUET VOICE-OVER* The armed forces get a 29 per cent pay rise. F/X 'Bong'
Nastase/Taylor montage 2 CU (in whites) *Portrait stills* CUT 0.4½	*BOSANQUET VOICE-OVER* Tennis, Nastase and Taylor in trouble at Bournemouth. *BOSANQUET TO CAM*
Bosanquet MCU plain B/G	Good evening . . .

Beyond this one can again see that the range of images is not dictated by the visual quality of the stories. The stories are determined by journalistic criteria, not by a purely visual one. It is however possible to see, as in the case of the Japanese footballers on Tuesday and the Cambridge rapist on Wednesday, a tendency to also headline (as a 'hooker') stories from the second half of the bulletin which follows the commercial break. These two examples were both exclusive but the tendency is not limited to such features. For instance, the sports story which closed the 'bongs' on the Friday was shared by the BBC. It is fair to hypothesise that in this last spot in the headlines choice is determined more by the visual excitement of the image than by a journalistic sense of the importance of the story.

The tendency to subordinate the visual to the journalistic must again be pointed out. For instance, on the Thursday the most dramatic and iconic image of the week – the news picture of the marines landing on Ko Tang – was second to the indexical image of the *Mayaguez*, which had already figured three times as the opening image of the changing-title bulletins as well as having been used every previous night of the week on the 'bongs', as well as on eighteen other occasions in the body of the bulletins for voicing-over and on three occasions in *Chromokey*. Freshness of image is often adduced by critics to be a major newsroom concern and is coupled with the suggestion that it involves trivialisation. But it is not very apparent here. The serious business of agenda-setting is too important, as far as we can tell, for the visual imperative to be a major consideration.

The need to visualise the headlines leads to symbolic imagery, especially, as we have previously noted, in the areas of economic and industrial reporting. The '£ in crystal ball' graphic used in Monday's 'bongs' involved a distorted Union Jack which took us a number of viewings to decode.[6] Locked-out banknote printers were signified by a display of pound notes which also served as a backing for the economic correspondent on another occasion; a general picture of the dockside signified trade figures; an industrial settlement was symbolised by the company logo (not, by the way, joined by the union badge). Inflation became a visual pun with a visibly shrinking pound sign, achieved by zooming out from a '£' symbol on the caption. Of the 26 images involved in the week's 'bongs' only 4 were iconic (Orantes serving – 2 shots; the marines on Ko Tang – 1 shot; the Chrysler strike vote – 1 shot) and happened on (or in the case of the marines nearly on) the day they were transmitted. To this must be added the shot of the cover of the CBI economic trends report. And one must also add the iconic image of the Japanese footballers, although that did not happen on the day of transmission but some days earlier. Of the rest 11 are indexical and 9 symbolic.

Just as the above title sequences indicate to the audience particular nature of the broadcast, namely a news bulletin, so the final images indicate its end and the start of other genres of programming. All the final images, with one exception, were straightforward typographic captions naming only the newscasters. The exception was the late Saturday bulletin on BBC2, where a changing image was used (in the week of the sample it was Princess Anne on horseback). It was the one bulletin that had neither a mention of later bulletins nor a 'Good night' before the final image began. The most significant thing about these final captions was that they routinely mentioned only the newscasters. The news bulletins, together with the weather, commercials and presentation, were the only genres of programmes which detailed neither producers nor technical staff, as far as public on-screen announcements (credits) were concerned.

It is true that live transmission often means that the closing credits are lost, but even in those current affairs magazines where the credits are not automatically played, there is normally one edition a week in which they appear. The only programme emanating from the newsrooms in our period for which this was true was the Sunday news for the deaf. This general lack is significant. We would argue the bulletins must hereby be assumed not to be produced in the sense that other programmes are produced. This is an important expression of the neutrality that is supposed to underpin the bulletins. We might see newsroom personnel in the background of the *Nine O'Clock News*'s presentation but basically it is the faces on screen that are responsible for the bulletins.

Since some bulletins, as we have shown above, use appreciable amounts of time at the outset with repetitive and unchanging opening routines, the argument that time alone is responsible for this lacuna in naming producers is not entirely sustainable. Each day *First Report* gave no information about the events of the day for upwards of 20 seconds; the *Nine O'Clock News* did the same for upwards of 12 seconds and *News at Ten* for 15 seconds. Such an allocation of time at the other end could at least be used to add to the names of the newscasters those of the producer and director responsible for the bulletin, as has now happened with ITN. Or is anonymity the BBC's final guarantee of neutrality?

II 'Good Evening'

Whom but a dusk misfeatured messenger
No other than the angel of this life
Whose care is lest men see too much at once

(Browning)

Television from its beginnings has followed the dominant naturalistic traditions of the early-twentieth-century stage in its settings; a tradition which has also dominated film design. Thus, rather than utilise, except for special purposes, alternative non-naturalistic symbolic or expressionist styles, television has followed the Theatre of the Fourth Wall and the cinema in making, as it were, a constant assumption of reality. All situation comedies and most dramas are set, like outside broadcasts, in environments that are to be perceived by the viewer as real. For those programme forms that are more particular to television (current affairs, 'chat' shows and the news bulletins), there is no real equivalent of this 'normalcy' upon which to call.

The various responses to this lack are not entirely satisfactory. Tynan, in describing an appearance by Sir Ralph Richardson on *The Russell Harty Show*, draws attention to this:

> The setting was the usual mock-up, in this case a semi-circular arrange-ment of window draperies with nothing behind it, and a low window seat and a pair of tulip-shaped chairs (one of them occupied by Harty) in front of it.... Sir Ralph enters around one side of the draperies.... Sir Ralph; 'You've got a very nice place here, haven't you.... You've got a lot more cameras in your place than I've got in mine.'[7]

The problem of setting can be formulated as a paradox. In those programmes in which television most directly comments on the world, the most obviously non-naturalistic settings are employed. The 'chat' show ranges from Harty's sub-naturalistic drawing room to variants of the airport departure lounge. The most characteristic element in the setting of the 'chat' show is the armchair – the 'easy chair', normally of an extremely expensive modern type.

Studio-based current affairs programmes, although often having an arm-chair area in the set, create their own even less naturalistic setting. This vision of 'current affairs land', as it were, is characterised not by these expensive leather chairs but by the desk behind which the presenters sit. Desks are authoritative, we would argue, since in our culture for centuries authority has been found behind desks – with its knees covered. The pulpit, the judge's bench, the schoolmaster's table are prime examples of this. Of these three, in current affairs programmes the schoolmaster's is the one most called to mind. This is because, in most settings over the past decade, various devices (back projection, *Chromokey*) have been used to project images on to the wall (i.e. flat) behind the desk. The desk is therefore matched by the blackboard. Since the easy chair element is lacking in the settings for the news bulletins, the schoolroom feel is thereby increased. A naturalistic setting would be the open studio (as used in *That Was the Week That Was*), but this is eschewed, partially because camera crew appearing in vision require, under union agreement, payment for so doing. Further, it would call attention to the electronic making of the news which, as we have argued in the matter of fixed-image main titles, is apparently to be avoided. Thus the main characteristic of the news studio is the desk, accompanied in some bulletins with the inlaid 'blackboard' screen.

Without the *Chromokey* screen, in our period there were three possibilities for backing the newscaster. First there was the plain flat behind the newscaster's head (Figure 7.16). This was used by ITN on the Saturday and the Sunday. It is also the effect achieved on *News at Ten* when the *Chromokey* was not being used; that is to say, when we had a medium close-up (MCU). This basic shot could be framed most widely by placing the top of the presenter's pocket at the bottom of the screen and most tightly by placing his buttonhole there, rather than a midshot (MS). Midshots are characterised by either being at the start or end of bulletins or to allow *Chromokey* inserts (Figure 7.17) or live interviews. The plain background was also used by the BBC2 bulletins (with the same *caveat* as to the possibility of a *Chromokey* [CSO] screen to be noted in connection with *News Extra*).

The second variant used by the BBC1 lunchtime bulletin, and the competing early evening bulletins on BBC1 and ITN, was to texture the flat behind the newscaster with some form of simple pattern. Both BBC and ITN used a similar pattern in our period. The BBC's (which was also used at the weekends) consisted of rows of extruded parallelograms (Figure 7.18, p. 242). ITN used extruded rectangles of the same general size. At the extremes of subtle viewing the rectangles might be considered marginally less 'urgent' than the parallelograms but both illustrate the general point about the non-assumption of reality in this area of programme-setting. For where can such wall textures otherwise be seen? ITN's *First Report* also used squares, larger than those in the early evening and lunchtime bulletins, arranged on flats behind the shallow semi-circular desk. These flats gave *First Report* an

Figure 7.16 Studio settings: the plain background. Buttonhole close-up

Figure 7.17 Midshot for *Chromokey* screen (CSO)

Figure 7.18 Studio settings: patterned background

identification not just in terms of its news presenter, but also in terms of those interviewed in the set. Indeed, ITN have on file portrait stills of news personalities clearly taken in this setting. The *First Report* set also had within it a 'screen' on which *Chromokey* could be used in much the same way as *News Extra* for presenter-conducted interviews.

The BBC1 main bulletin, when the newsroom was not matted-in (as happens during the title sequence), backed the newsreaders with a plain venetian blind. But there was also the possibility of suggesting an office with filing cabinets. This was used infrequently (Figure 7.19), in fact only once during the week under study (see Example 7.9a, shot 100, p. 254).

The keynote of these settings is an attempt to achieve a certain neutrality. They are restrained in that they either have no pattern or minimal patterns. They are further restrained as to colour, being for the most part shades of beige or grey. They give no information except that by their unique neutrality they are the material embodiment of those practices that signify the news. Only station announcers are so plainly presented. Within the news settings the *Chromokey* inserts contain information. Otherwise the settings allow the newscaster an absolute dominance of the image. The one exception to this is perhaps the midday Saturday BBC1 bulletin broadcast from the edge of a desk in the newsroom. Here the reality of the setting (it is more iconic than the use of the newsroom via *Chromokey* in the weekday main bulletins) is emphasised by the wide midshot pose which can serve to stress the setting's 'weekend' informality. The informality of this bulletin, inserted into the

Figure 7.19 Studio settings: the 'office' background

Figure 7.20 A studio two-shot interview using *Chromokey*

week's main sports transmission, via the newsroom camera, also allows some of the news studio technical crew to be absent and to come on duty later in the day.

The restraint of the setting is in general pointed up in a number of other ways. First, the range of shots taken in these settings is limited. They are overwhelmingly single shots. In fact in the main BBC and ITN bulletins two or three shots are used only at the start and the finish. Further, only in the BBC main bulletin, in *News Extra* and in *First Report* is there any deviance from the straight-on, eye-level camera position. In the main BBC1 bulletin angled three shots (Figure 7.3, p. 218) are used only at beginnings and at the end. In the current affairs type bulletins such angled shots are used in interview contexts (shot 36 in Example 7.3; shots 9 and 10 in Example 7.4) (Figure 7.20).

Example 7.3 ITN, 13.00, 13 May 1975

33 Kee: CU (bottom of pocket) *First Report* set		*KEE (News presenter) TO CAM* Anti-marketeers, however, say categorically, that if the vote is 'Yes' your food must cost more. Well, with m (leans
CUT 1.48	7.48	back) e in the stud /
34 Rippon: CU (top of pocket) *First Report* set (eyeline SCR, RHT)		*KEE VOICE-OVER* io now is Mr Geoffrey Rippon, who as the Conservative Minister with special responsibility for the Common Market negotiated our entry under Mr Heath, two
CUT 0.9	7.57	years ago and Mr (scratches chin) /
35 Buchan: CU (top of pocket) *First Report* set (eyeline SCR, LEFT)		Norman Buchan who until he resigned last October was Minister of State for Agriculture Fisheries and Food and who is against our continued membership of the
CUT 0.12	8.9	EEC. Mr Buchan, why do you /
36 3 SHOT: Kee (mike-in) + Rippon MS over Buchan's shoulder MCU		*KEE TO CAM* say that a Yes in the referendum will mean dearer food? *BUCHAN*
CUT 0.5	8.14	Well, for/
37 as 35 *super*		*BUCHAN sync.* two reasons principally, and you partly /
37a supercaption: *First Report*, Norman Buchan, MP: Anti-Market losse *super*		explain it in your initial introduction. When, you say any cheaper food coming in automatically has a levy placed upon it in order to make the food dear /
		and the truth is that the common agricultural policy is a high price policy.

Example 7.4 BBC2, 23.05, 14 May 1975

Videotape

8   Humphrys MS *Colour*   HUMPHRYS *(Correspondent) TO CAM*
    photo: day ext White
    House GV on *CSO* as B/G
    Full screen (via unilateral
    satellite ex Washington)   ... There will be divisions of opinion and
                                      they will continue because there are those
                                      people who fear that he is starting on a
                                      dangerous trail here but overall he will
                                      have the support that he wants.
                                      RIPPON VOICE-OVER
    CUT 0.49   4.11½   Well, I think /

9   Rippon MCU (Top of   *RIPPON sync.*
    pocket) ¾ profile Plain B/G   we have a picture in this country tonight of
                                      the might of the United States navy lined
                                      up with guns pointing at the Cambodi /

---

10 WIDE 2 SHOT: MS Rippon   an Coast. Now what are the chances of
    over shoulder (inc. desk   those guns being used again?/
    foreground) B/G screen
    with Humphrys MS & B/G
    White House (as 8) CSO
    (Figure 7.20)
    CUT 0.4   4.21½

11 Humphrys MS as 8   **HUMPHRYS TO CAM**
                                    I think we have got to consider them fairly
                                    strong, diplomatic action hasn't been
                                    totally exhausted, that is to say
                                    Washington is suggesting it hasn't been
                                    totally exhausted.

None of this, however, involves camera movement. The camera in the news studios is virtually always static. The only exception to this across the whole range of bulletins is in the headlines to a medium close-up. By doing so it loses the *Chromokey* screen and gives the MCU with a plain background (Example 7.5). But even here there is an alternative to camera movement. After the *Chromokey* headlines a close-up with plain background can be achieved (Example 7.6) with a straight cut. This involves the newscaster turning to look at a second camera. Again this is the only presentation where this is necessary. *News at Ten*, the only other bulletin to use *Chromokey*, as a general rule moves from midshot with 'screen' to close-ups not on camera but during voice-overs.

Example 7.5 BBC2, 22.20, 12 May 1975

CUT		RIPPON (Newscaster) TO CAM
1	Rippon MS (½ arm on desk) SCR RHT *Colour portrait still* Ford Cu (US flag out of focus as B/G) on CSO screen left	Good evening /
	1a *Super* 'Angela Rippon'	President Ford warns the Cambodians of dire consequences and describes their seizure of an American merchant ship as an act of piracy.
	Change CSO	A report on American reaction in a moment. /
	1b *Graphic* banknotes montage Change CSO	With the pound in your pocket now worth 75 pence, that's since it was floated, I've been talking to Mr Prices and Incomes /
	1c *Colour portrait still* Aubrey Jones CU (collar) (Plain B/G) 1a lose *super*	about our econom /
	Change CSO	ic crisis. The Flixbor /
	1d *Colour photo* aerial CU plant day ext. with smoke 0.30	ough explosion. The official report blames the management and we ask the management if they accept it (moves papers) /
	Lose CSO screen: tighten ... Hold MCU Rippon (head and shoulders) plain B/G	An American merchant ship, the *Mayaguez* and its crew of 39, all of them American nationals, has been seized /
CUT 0.49½	0.49½	by a Cambodian warship in the Gulf of Siam. It's not known what the *Mayaguez*'s cargo is but she's described in the records as a container ship owned by the Sea Land Corporation. She was en route from /
2	*Map*: Thailand Cambodia South Vietnam Kompong Som Gulf of Thailand	RIPPON VOICE-OVER Hong Kong to Thailand when, say United States officials, she was fired on and boarded some 60 /
	2a *Animate* 'X' CUT 0.12 1.01½	miles off the Cambodian mainland. The *Mayaguez* has been taken to the Port of Kompong Som. /
3	Rippon CU plain B/G	RIPPON TO CAM President Ford, who was told about the ship's capture at an Intelligence briefing today, called it an act of piracy.

Example 7.6 BBC2, 23.05, 13 May 1975

CUT		*RIPPON (Newscaster) TO CAM*
1	Rippon MS SCR RHT + *Graphic* CBI survey cover on CSO screen. SCR LEFT Change CSO (0.12)	Good evening from *News Extra*. Another voice joins the gloomy chorus. The CBI says we're heading for a deep recession and we ask, as the clouds gather, is there no silver lining anywhere? From the/
	1a *Colour photo* GV steelworks day ext. Change CSO (0.04)	steel town of Irlam we've got a report on what redundancy can mean. We hear what/
	1b *Colour photo* GV hospital bed day ext. Change CSO (0.06)	private medicine is doing to fill the gap as it's expelled from the Health Service and then how/
	1c *Colour photo* pack shot Babycham bottle & glass CUT 0.28 0.28	champagne protected its name against the interlopers. (Looks off) /
2	Rippon MCU (top of pocket) plain B/G	There'll be a Commons debate on the economy next week, probably Thursday. The Prime Minister announced this soon after the CBI's gloomy forecast of deep industrial depression and more people out of jobs.

MOVING THE CAMERA

The limitations on the number of persons seen in a single shot and the normal immobility of the camera is further reflected in the movements made by the newscasters themselves.

The range of movement is extremely limited. They never leave their desks. They seldom look anywhere but at the lens. We have already discussed the limited circumstances in which *two shots* or *three shots* occur. It is obviously only possible for glances between personnel to occur in these circumstances. In fact the glance to the other newscaster in the main bulletin is a final kinesic full stop to the bulletin since it never occurs until the last words have been exchanged or spoken. It covers the moments of *supering* closing titles and music. Thus to look at the other caster is to signify the end of the newsreader character – in fact to come out of character, to be seen as human in a more ordinary sense. It is at this point that sometimes the scripts of the bulletin are shuffled – an action which, as Professor Stuart Hood has often pointed out, signifies in our culture a tidying up, the imposition of order on the chaos of information given in the bulletin.

Otherwise, body movement is almost non-existent. There is no turning (the cut to shot 2 in Example 7.6 being the only regular exception to this); the monitors on which the newscaster can see leader material (i.e. film leaders or video-tape clocks, which are put on the front of film and tape inserts to enable the machines – Telecine and videotape recorder (VTR) – to run up to speed and enable the performer to read down to the start of the insert) are placed in the studio to minimise eye movement away from the camera lens. In other words, the settings are organised to allow the newscaster to maintain maximum eye contact with the lens and thereby with the audience. All scripts, except for later emendations and additions (which are the exception not the rule), are typed on to an autocue system which enables them to be projected directly in front of the lens so that the performer appears to be speaking rather than reading. Glances down are a form of punctuation, normally serving to paragraph the bulletin. For instance, in the 12.55 bulletin on 12 May Richard Whitmore clearly looked off camera at the end of the first item about the exchange rate. He looked down during the second item being the report of the Chrysler and Leyland strikes and the report of the resignation of the Managing Director of Jaguar. He looked off camera to a monitor when cueing-in the Peart pro-EEC speech on film. But he also glanced down in the middle of the introductory sentence of the Jenkins defence of Benn story (an unusually short shot for this bulletin – see Example 7.8b, p. 254).

Robert Kee as a news presenter in the more current affairs format of *First Report* had a greater range of movement than the other performers. He was more often reading from script than autocue. He looked down rather more often and even on occasion, as for instance when introducing interviewees sitting with him, he leaned back. But even he tended to use the glances down as paragraphing. On the morning of 12 May he looked down after his headline on the exchange rate and after the Chrysler strike headline, for instance.

Within this limited repertoire of movement a number of viewers' maxims can be adduced. Although the possibility of late additions to the script, autocue breakdowns and personal predilections render them somewhat tentative, basically it can be said that glances down paragraph reports within a story distinguish between one story and the next; that looks off camera most often indicate cueing of film or tape inserts; that looks to other newscasters, in the two-presenter shows, are a final punctuation to the bulletin and that their place (as signifiers of the end of 'newscaster' role) is taken by the smile in the single presenter bulletin.

Mention has been made of the framing of these shots. The single shot (with the exception of the BBC Saturday bulletin) is never below waist and never tighter than head and shoulders, cut off at buttonhole level. It should be noted that in portrait stills and in interviews it is possible to frame at the tie-knot and in certain circumstances even tighter – i.e. at the line of the chin. Tighter than that (just below the mouth) has only regularly been used in some current affairs shows, and is seen professionally as a deviant frame.

Gaye Tuchman has pointed out how these tighter shots reflect a closeness to the subject which would only be possible in our society among intimates. It is therefore no surprise that shoulders are normally seen in all news shots. Framing closer is to frame more intimately. The shoulder shots (from MS to MCU in our designation) therefore reflect a cultural norm. They are in fact at the limits of close social space, and the shots do not go over those limits either into the area of far social space or closer intimate space. They are therefore the most appropriate for the newscasters; for the personnel are neither familiars nor strangers.

Thus the dominant image here is of a person at a close social distance, the median point in our culture in the social structuring of interpersonal distances. It is therefore arguable that this again reflects the search on the visual level for a cultural neutrality. The neutral size of the person with the frame (neither intimately close nor distant) matches the neutrality of the bland set colours, the eye-level camera and the lack of camera movement.

All of this is without prejudice to the basic fact that between a quarter, in the case of the main bulletins, and over a half, in the short bulletins, of the duration is taken up with the newscaster addressing the lens directly.

NEWSCASTER TO CAMERA

But for how long does the newscaster talk in any one shot? The rates of image change in this category run from *News Extra* (1.35 changes per minute) to *News at Ten* (3.37 changes per minute). Thus, since these two bulletins use *Chromokey*, it can be said that *Chromokey* does not, *of itself*, affect the length of time the newscasters speak per shot. Basically the distinction remains between current-affairs style bulletins and other types.

The current-affairs style bulletin allows the performer 44.4 seconds (*News Extra*) and 31.6 seconds (*First Report*) on average per shot (rates of 1.35 and 1.89 respectively). The short bulletin allows 20.4 seconds (*Newsday*) and 18.5 seconds (lunchtime bulletin) (rates of 2.94 and 3.24 respectively). The main bulletins allow 18.2 seconds (BBC *Nine O'Clock News*) and 17.8 seconds (ITN *News at Ten*) (rates of 3.31 and 3.37 respectively). It should be noted that the first part of *News at Ten* allows a longer average shot than the second part, 19.2 seconds as against 16.7 seconds. The early evening bulletins allow 21.2 (BBC) and 18.6 seconds (ITN) – rates of 2.83 and 3.22.

Thus ITN allows the newscaster to speak uninterruptedly for shorter periods than the BBC. This is also true of *First Report* as against *News Extra*, although *News Extra* does use *Chromokey* to increase visual variety.

News at Ten spends 24.5 per cent of its time with the newscasters but they talk 0.3 of a second less per shot than the BBC *Nine O'Clock News* casters who have 26 per cent of the total duration of their bulletin. (Again the increased visual interest of the *Chromokey* which is used in *News at Ten* should be borne in mind.) In the early evening ITN's total percentage duration with newscasters is, at 32.9 per cent, less than BBC's at 34.8 per cent. And again ITN allows the newscasters a rather more significant 2.5 seconds or so less per shot on average than does the BBC.

The overall length of the bulletin does not seem to affect the average shot durations. Neither of the two shortest bulletins, BBC1's lunchtime one and BBC2's *Newsday*, allows the newscaster appreciably more or less time than the other main and early evening bulletins. Thus presentational style rather than overall length determines the time newscasters address the screen without interruption. The use of film and tape in the lunchtime bulletin and stills in *Newsday* does not affect the figures either. It is the more expansive current-affairs style which conditions the major significant difference in average 'newscaster-to-camera' shot duration.

The lengths here are longer than most other inputs except for correspondents, whether they appear to camera or on radio circuit. Film and all graphic inputs are appreciably more quickly cut on the screen. 'Newscaster-to-camera' are in the upper range of shot lengths. We have argued that this implies an assumption on the part of the newsproducers that the audience will watch these talking heads for these uninterrupted lengths of time. This we feel contributes to the authority with which they speak. As will be shown below, there is a relationship between social status and this time factor.

The charge of visual sensationalism is again not supported by this willingness to allow the newscasters these shots at these lengths. The newscaster can be used to read a report of an otherwise unillustrated story to camera. These yield the longest shots. In the short bulletins in the week in question, the maximum shot was on the Monday lunchtime bulletin, when the newscaster spoke for 62.5 seconds. On *Newsday* that same day 54.5 seconds was the longest shot. For the rest of the week, however, in these two bulletins the longest newscaster shot was under 45 seconds and on four occasions under 30 seconds. For the early evening bulletins the longest was 85 seconds on the BBC on Monday and 75 seconds on ITN on Wednesday. Otherwise the BBC was under 1 minute on every other night of the week and ITN was under on two nights. The longest newscaster shot, however, was never under 30 seconds. The main bulletins offer a contrast. Only once (ITN, Thursday) was the longest shot over 1 minute. Indeed the BBC *Nine O'Clock News* only exceeded 50 seconds once during the week, and (aside from Thursday) ITN exceeded 50 seconds only twice – but it should be noted in their case that of these four long speeches to camera, three were backed with *Chromokey* and, further, they each occurred in the first half of the bulletin. For the second part of *News at Ten*, only once during the week was 40 seconds exceeded.

As would be expected in the current affairs style bulletins, all the longest shots are over 1 minute, except for *First Report* on the Monday. The longest newscaster speech of the week was in *News Extra* on the Monday at 2 minutes and 5 seconds. (But again in *News Extra* every one of these shots was backed by *Chromokey*; see Example 7.7.)

Example 7.7 BBC2, 22.20, 12 May 1975, the longest newscaster-to-camera piece

CUT	10.15½ /	
28	Rippon MS + *portrait still* Howe CU (down shot) (blinds B/G) on CSO SCR LFT	RIPPON *(Newscaster) TO CAM* The Conservative Shadow Chancellor, Sir Geoffrey Howe, tonight called for a coalition of understanding between politicians and different parties to fight inflation. Speaking on BBC2's *Newsday* programme, he said there was broad agreement between the Conservatives and a large chunk of the Labour Party that there should be big cuts in public spending and strict cash limits for wage
	Change CSO (0.26)	settlements. /
	28a *Colour photo* 'Avenger' line GV, nearest car MCU, day, int.	And now some industrial news. The strike at Chryslers in Coventry is to go on. In the absence of any immediate cash offer from the company, shop stewards decided the strike should continue and they made no move to bring forward a mass meeting scheduled for Thursday. 4,000 men could be laid off before
	Change CSO (0.18)	then. /
	28b *Colour photo*: Dunlop factory GV day, ext.	And the strike at Dunlops in Coventry is also to continue. After 700 clerical workers turned down a new pay offer. It fell short of their demand for an extra £10 a week. Dunlops themselves have already laid off 2,000 workers and tonight British Leyland laid off another 1,700 men, that makes over 14,000 British Leyland workers laid off because of the Dunlop
	Change CSO (0.24)	strike. /
	28c *Colour photo*: 2 shot MS/MCU + Post Office tent over manhole, day, ext.	But Post Office engineers are to get the 25 per cent pay rise in July, a deal which will cost the Post Office about £83 million. It's made up of a flat raise of 18 per cent plus the consolidation of thresholds. A Post Office spokesman said the offer accords fully with the guidelines of the
	(0.19)	Social Contract /
	Lose CSO screen: tighten (200m)	. The head of the railways' white-collar union, Mr Tom Bradley, /
	Hold Rippon MCU + plain B/G	has criticised some unions for not honouring their side of the Social Contract. Mr Bradley, who's a Labour MP on the party's national executive, told his union's annual conference that he found the remarks of some union leaders frightening in their implications for

Example 7.7 continued

		society as a whole. The three rail unions together recently rejected what British Rail say is a 21 per cent offer, claiming around 30 per cent. Mr Bradley argues that in real terms the rises are not as high as that and he told John
CUT 2.05	12.20½	Burns of his belief in the Social Contract /
29 *Film* Bradley MS, day, ext., arm on rail: seaside cliffs B/G		*BRADLEY (sync.)* I am interested in honouring the Social Contract. My union together with other unions put their hands up in favour of the Social Contract at a special TUC meeting in January 1974 and at the TUC Congress in September 1974.

The newscaster can also be used for shots inserted into stories normally involving a variety of other visual inputs. These yield the shortest values of 'newscaster-to-camera' shots. In other words, in a sequence which uses film, graphics, etc., the newscaster might appear fleetingly to punctuate items or bridge a visual gap (Example 7.8a, shots 102, 109). Thus in the early evening bulletins and the main bulletins the lowest values are in the 2–3 second range. Since the lowest values are attached to the sophistication of inputs, it is not surprising that low values of 3–4 seconds also appear in *First Report* and *News Extra*. And conversely the shortest bulletins might be expected to have, as indeed they do, longer minima – 5 seconds for *Newsday* for instance. The lunchtime bulletin on Monday does have a 2-second shot but it is sandwiched between film and a portrait still and can therefore be accounted for in terms of sophistication of input (Example 7.8b). Also, since Whitmore looks down throughout, it could be an error. In other words, the cut should have been from film to still, and he should not have been seen.

The average length previously noted in the range of 17–20 seconds can be said to reflect a third newscaster function occupying in duration a median position between the two classes of shot just described. It reflects the newscaster's other main task which is, in addition to reading unillustrated, or comparatively unillustrated, stories (Example 7.9a), also to introduce correspondents, films and tapes. In the latter case it should be noted that the Telecine and VTRs require a run-up time (Example 7.9b). Cueing-in these inserts is therefore simplified if the newscaster is reading straight down (as it were) to them. This means an optimum of 10 seconds.

It should further be noted that this requirement does not apply to non-synchronous film since that can be started on the first frame as the sound does not have to get up to speed.

The fact that newscasters can take up such a large percentage of the overall

Example 7.8a ITN, 22.00, 15 May 1975, bridging the visual gap – shot 102, shot 109

Film	*CHANCELLOR VOICE-OVER*
	They don't mind lending the Europeans our Westminster stewards but that's as far as it goes. Alexander Chancellor, *News at Ten*,
CUT 5.43½	Luxembourg.
102 Gardner MCU plain B/G	*GARDNER (Newscaster) TO CAM*
	In the commons, the Northern Ireland
CUT 0.3 5.46½	Secretary, Mr Rees,
103 Rees CU (bottom of tie) plain B/G *portrait still*	*GARDNER VOICE-OVER* said the murder of a policeman in Londonderry last weekend could only slow down progress
CUT 0.7 5.53½	towards peace and security in the province.
104 Gardner MCU plain B/G	*GARDNER TO CAM*
	A girl of nineteen had her right foot amputated after being injured in a pub explosion on the outskirts of Belfast last night. Six other people
CUT 0.9½ 6.03	were hurt. Ma
105 GV pub day ext. *Film*	*GARDNER VOICE-OVER* ny more customers in the Catholic-owned Hill tavern, probably escaped injury because of
CUT 0.5 6.08	quick thinking
106 MS oildrum + rubble day ext. *Film*	by a security guard. Moments after two armed youths placed the cylinder bomb inside the pub, the guard kicked it back through the door
zoom in	and it exploded while it was rolling
CU rubble	on to the footpath. Shortly after the explosion a newspaper received a phone call claiming that
CUT 0.15 6.23	the bomb was the work
107 CU wall + stain (blood) day ext.	of the Protestant Action force.
CUT 0.2½ *Film* 6.25½	
108 GV 2 cars + pub B/G	
CUT 0.1 *Film* 6.26½	
109 Bosanquet MCU plain B/G	*BOSANQUET (Newscaster) TO CAM*
	Five hundred policemen moved on to the
CUT 0.2½ 6.29	
110 GV building: LS students leaving	*BOSANQUET VOICE-OVER* Warwick University campus at Coventry th
CUT 0.3 *Film* 6.32	
111 LS police: administration building: B/G	is morning to clear a sit-in by
Film	

Example 7.8b BBC1, 12.55, 12 May 1975, bridging the visual gap – shot 6: an error

	Film		*PEART (sync.)* . . . and of the relationship that now exists between the developed and developing
CUT		2.03	countries of the world./

6	Whitmore MCU (above breast pocket) + EEB backing – looking down		*WHITMORE (Newscaster) TO CAM* The union leader Mr Clive Jenkins has /
CUT 0.2		2.05	

7	Jenkins CU (out of focus blinds B/G) *Colour portrait* *still*	*WHITMORE VOICE-OVER* sharply criticised the press for its alleged character assassination of the industry Secretary, Mr Wedgwood Benn.

Example 7.9a BBC1, 21.00, 15 May 1975: the comparatively unillustrated story

CUT	19.51½ /	

97 Baker MCU + blinds B/G		*BAKER (Newscaster) TO CAM* An Old Bailey judge claimed today that parts of South London, once peaceful, had been transformed by immigrants settling there. In sentencing five West Indian teenagers to five years' detention or jail for robberies on
CUT 0.15	20.06½	unaccompanied women/

98 Morris J. in wig (bottom of pocket) black B/G night ext. *Colour portrait still*		*BAKER VOICE-OVER* Judge Gwynn Morris said that these attacks were a monotonous feature in Brixton and Clapham, areas which within living memory had been peaceful, safe and agreeable to live in, but immigrant resettlement over the past twenty-five years had radically transformed
CUT 0.15	20.21½	that environment. /

99 Baker MCD + blinds B/G	*BAKER TO CAM* Later Judge Morris said he wanted to emphasise that he was not attacking the great majority of immigrants, who proved themselves to be law-abiding citizens. Tonight the Runnymede Trust said it was high time judges stopped making crudely reactionary statements disguised as objective comments on cases before them. And the Chairman of the Community Relations Commission, Mr Mark Bonham-Carter, said the comments of a highly placed judge would do more to foster racial tension than the offences of five under-privileged youngsters./

Example 7.9a continued

CUT 0.30 20.51½	

100 Kendall MCU (top of pocket) + filing cabinets B/G (Figure 7.19)	*KENDALL (Newscaster) TO CAM* A major British shoe manufacturer has announced that it's to pay off 750 . . .

Example 7.9b ITN, 13.00, 15 May 1975, cueing-in

37 Kee MCU (top pocket)	*KEE (Newscaster) TO CAM* However, the continuing violence, it seems, is being evenly applied too, and last night yet another pub on the outskirts of Belfast was
CUT 0.12	12.59 bombed. Ian Sanderson of Ulster Television. /
38 GV: ext. pub	*Film SANDERSON (Reporter) VOICE-OVER* It would appear that this was a /
38a *Super: First Report,* Ian Sanderson reporting from Belfast	sectarian . . .

Example 7.10 BBC1, 21.00, 12 May 1975 (Table 7.2, Item 6)

CUT 10.4½ /	

46 Harrod SCR RHT mid pocket MCU B/G = 5 shot exchange dealers, GV room int *colour photo* 'BBC Nes Economics' *supered*	*HARROD (Correspondent) TO CAM* Indeed one reason for the present nerves in dealing is doubt about just when the British government will take firm steps to stop the slide. The government view, as the Chancellor of the Exchequer said on May 1st, is that while inflation in Britain is higher than in our major trading partners the pound is likely to sink against other currencies. And today there was more evidence about inflation in this country. In the past three months the prices charged by industry are up more than 5 per cent. Much of that comes from higher wage costs but something like a ½ per cent in the last month has come from the fall in the pound and
CUT 0.36	10.40½ consequent rise in import costs. /

durations of the bulletin, and take it up, first, in shots of such lengths, is a prime factor in resisting any visual imperative arguments and defences. It also has the effect of confirming the newscasters' high status, by visually

Example 7.11a BBC1, 17.45, 14 May 1975 (Table 7.2, Item 20)

5.6½ /	
14 Ross SCR LEFT (top of pocket) MCU B/G = Congress House, medium GV ext. day, *Colour photo*	*ROSS (Correspondent) TO CAM* This is not the first time that the backroom economists of the TUC, including Mr Murray, have tried to stiffen up the unions' commitment to pay-restraint and had their fingers rapped by individual union leaders …

Example 7.11b BBC1, 21.00, 14 May 1975 (Table 7.2, Item 23)

14.12 /	
53 Ross SCR LEFT (top of pocket) MCU B/G = Congress House, medium GV ext. day, *Colour photo* 'BBC News Industry' *supered*	*ROSS (Correspondent) TO CAM* No one at Congress House would dispute the view that gaping holes have been punched in the Social Contract.

connecting them with those few who are regularly framed in the way illustrated above and who are allowed such durations of uninterrupted speech.

Second, flexibility in shot lengths which allows the newscasters to appear almost fleetingly at times, have further significance. They enable the bulletins to be hung along the line of the newscasters' appearances. The newscasters are the visual final fall-back if other inputs fail. These two modes mean that the image of the newscaster looking neither up nor down, neither right nor left, framed at pocket-top at an impersonal distance, is the typical basic image of the news bulletin.

HERE'S OUR CORRESPONDENT

Correspondents are allowed to address the camera directly for greater lengths of time than newscasters. Correspondents tend to talk for longer uninterruptedly than any other class of speaker on the news, even if one includes interviewees (who anyway address not the lens but the interviewers); only one interviewee, on film, was allowed to give an answer lasting more than 1 minute; otherwise all interview shots lasting more than 1 minute were interrupted by questions. The uninterrupted interviewee was Dr Hans Mast, a Swiss banking economist. As regards filmed speeches, only President Ford and Enoch Powell spoke for more than 70 seconds without shot change. In studio/VTR interviews Mr Wilson and Maurice Edelman gave answers, uninterrupted by questions, of more than 1 minute in length. What characterised all these interviewees and speechmakers was their high status. Correspondents, it can therefore be argued, have the slowest rate of shot change and most closely match the highest status of interviewees and other speakers on the news.

The category of correspondent used here does not refer to the internal status of the news employee but to how he (or she)[8] is presented on the screen. Essentially we have placed every news employee who talks directly to the lens in a studio within this category. In other words, it also includes reporters in studio, and editors, but does not include correspondents, editors or reporters to camera on film or outside broadcasts (live or taped). The correspondent category for our purposes here depends on the studio, on the person being so introduced, or in the utilisation of a standard repertoire of presentational forms; not on the persons' actual status in the newsroom's hierarchy.

Correspondents, thus defined, do not appear in the shorter bulletins nor are they much seen in the current-affairs style bulletins. *First Report* tended not to use them and *News Extra* treated them often as interviewees (in which capacity they are not counted here). It is in the competing early evening and main bulletins that they are most likely to appear. In the early evening bulletins, ITN used them 12.2 per cent of the time as against the BBC's 10.4 per cent; and in the main bulletins ITN used them 13.4 per cent as against the BBC's 8.3 per cent. But this seeming discrepancy wherein ITN appear to be more 'talking head' orientated than the BBC, must be read against the other main correspondent input category – that is, their use via radio circuit. This is a cheaper way of having correspondent input, if the person concerned cannot be brought to the studio. Here we find that in the early evening bulletins the BBC used radio circuit captions 6.3 per cent of the time as against ITN's 4.1 per cent. This gives a total for correspondent inputs as a whole of 16.7 per cent for the BBC and of 16.3 per cent for ITN (with ITN relying less on the use of radio captions and more on the correspondent as 'talking head – a significant utilisation of resources since the radio caption is the slowest and least changing of all visual categories, whether moving or still). ITN in *News at Ten* used only 0.9 per cent of radio circuit captions as against the BBC's 2.7 per cent. This means that ITN used its correspondents 14.3 per cent of the time as against the BBC's 11 per cent.[9] These figures do not include further correspondent and reporter input in terms of voice-overs other than radio captions or further to camera appearances on film, tape or live from an outside broadcast (OB).

The average duration of shot in both the correspondent categories now being discussed was longer than for other inputs including newscaster to camera. But (with the exception of ITN's early evening bulletin) the BBC tended to allow correspondents, whether over the radio circuit or in the studio, to talk for longer uninterruptedly than ITN, although ITN overall used them more.

The correspondent, in the studio, can be instantly differentiated from the

Figure 7.21 Correspondents: *Chromokey* as backing

newsreader because he almost always appears with a visual backing. This is normally achieved by the use of *Chromokey*. A suitable image is matted-in behind the correspondent (Figure 7.21). On only 6 occasions during the week did correspondents appear without a full *Chromokey* backing: 2 appeared on the BBC against plain backings; 2 appeared on ITN against a special 'flat' with a map of Europe with Britain as a missing jigsaw piece in bas-relief; 1 appeared in the *First Report* set and 1 against a *Weekend Sport* flat. (These appearances can be found in Table 7.1, p. 227, entries 12, 28, 29, 32, 36 and 43.) In contrast to the use of *Chromokey* behind newscasters, here it was used not as a screen, but as a complete backing.

As we have already noted in connection with newscasters, British television is restrained in its use of *Chromokey*. Behind the newscasters it pretends that it is a projection screen; but there is no technical limitation on the size of the matted-in picture. On the other hand, except in the *News Extra* and *First Report* sets, it never uses moving images on the screen although, again, there is no technical limitation to so doing. All British television news services impose upon themselves the identical set of limitations in the use of *Chromokey*; just as the *Nine O'Clock News* and *News at Ten* used *Chromokey* identically as a mock screen, so both BBC and ITN used it similarly as mock backing for correspondents. The only difference between services is that the BBC, in the main bulletin, adds a written identification to the area the correspondent is covering ('BBC NEWS PARLIAMENT' in Figure 7.21) whereas ITN does not (Figure 7.26, p. 263).

The use of these backings requires decoding work on the part of the audience since they are always symbolic of the area being reported on by the corespondent. Figure 7.21 is perhaps the most obvious. Parliamentary reporting is signified by a colour still photograph of parliament. If it is a night-time bulletin then a night exterior photograph is used, but if it is day outside, the backing photograph is a day exterior. The relationship between the substance of the report and the backing image can be more attenuated than this. For example, in the BBC main bulletin on the Monday night, Harrod's piece was primarily about the exchange rate (Figure 7.22). This is concretised (as we shall see below when we discuss film) by images of the main exchange dealing rooms of the central clearing banks. For this report the *Chromokey* backing image was a still photograph of dealers. However, it should be noted that there is little in the backing icon itself to tell the viewer what is being talked of. There are two clear and two obscured figures in shirt-sleeves and ties at desks, one with a telephone in his hand. There is a woman back to camera, leaning over an obscured object in the far background. This general view has to be located, first, by the 'BBC NEWS ECONOMICS' written identification. Then, at a second level what Harrod is saying becomes crucial. But Harrod broadens his remarks from the particularity of the exchange rate story to general comments on the economy (Example 7.10) so that this already generalised icon of white-collar workers becomes a symbolic image of 'inflation in this country'.

Figure 7.22 Correspondents: *Chromokey* as backing

Finding icons for intangibles is a major problem in visualising the news. We have previously argued that the search for such icons does not affect the order and importance given to items, except perhaps towards the end of the bulletins. But assumptions are made by the newsproducers as to the audience's visual vocabulary which are not matched by the assumptions made as to the audience's overall attention-span or grasp. For instance, when reporting the TUC on Wednesday in the BBC's early evening bulletin, Ian Ross, the industrial correspondent, appeared before a medium general view of the front of Congress House on which there was no written identification at all (Figure 7.23). Examples 7.11a and 7.11b reveal that the newsproducers were expecting a considerable level of visual understanding on the part of the audience to decode the icon behind Ross in terms of his verbal statement. The audience had 60 seconds in which to work it out. Is Ross here struggling with a viewers' maxim that might state, 'See the background in terms of what is said' in general, and 'See the background building in terms of the first building mentioned' in particular? If this is so, it is possible to adduce the change in Ross's language to a need, at least in part, to make some sense of the visual element in the presentation. This problem is not confined to correspondents. In the areas of industrial and economic life the *Chromokey* screen behind the newscaster presents the same problems. It is at its most extreme when images are juxtaposed graphically to form semantically significant statements without any comment being needed from the news

Figure 7.23 Congress House background

Figure 7.24 The 'crystal ball'

personnel. Perhaps the best example of this during the week was the repeated 'crystal ball' icon used by *News at Ten* (Figure 7.24). This is an extremely complex image. The icon of the crystal ball is used symbolically in terms of generally established cultural codes to signify the future and the flag signifies the nation. The written information localises the image a little by referencing the economy (Example 7.12). On occasion in Figure 7.24, Parkin was reading a news story about the pound's slippage against other currencies. Since Parkin's text dealt exclusively with past incidents (the day's fall, the Prime Minister's remarks of the previous day) how was the viewer to decode the futuristic implication of the backing image?

On the following night the same image was used to back the CBI report story (see Example 7.13). It is difficult to see how the 'crystal ball' aids the viewer in either of the two examples.

To return to the correspondents, there is a further problem using *Chromokey* as a whole-screen backing. Since the correspondent is the main foreground part of the image, he perforce obscures much of the *Chromokey* picture – which does not occur if the *Chromokey* is used sparingly as an inserted false projection screen. Few pictures lend themself to being thus obscured. Perhaps the image of the Houses of Parliament with Big Ben is among the most convenient for this purpose. But when this basic design constraint is coupled with a desire to make the image as indexical as possible, some results are, in design terms at least, awkward. The backing used in reporting the armed services' pay increase on BBC has Luton before a photo-

Example 7.12 ITN, 22.00, 12 May 1975

	2.11 *PARKIN (Newscaster) TO CAM*
8 Parkin MS CSO (SCR LFT) *Graphic*: Union Jack in crystal ball CU + 'The British Economy' CUT 0.17	At home the pound has fallen to another record low. It's now lost a quarter of its value against the world's major currencies since December 1971. Its fall on the foreign exchange markets came despite support from the Bank of England and despite the Prime Minister's strong remarks about the economy at the weekend. /
9	*PARKIN VOICE-OVER* The pound's fall by 25 per cent against its 1971 value marks the sixth day of successive low points for sterling.

Example 7.13 ITN, 22.00, 13 May 1975

	10.18 /
48 Gardner MS CSO (SCR RHT) *Graphic*: Union Jack in crystal ball + 'The British Economy'	*GARDNER (Newscaster) TO CAM* A report from the Confederation of British Industry shows manufacturing industry moving very rapidly into recession, and the report suggests that the recession will be much deeper than those we've experienced in recent years. The survey, which covers several hundred firms and acts as a kind of industrial barometer, forecasts rising costs and unemployment and a decline in output and investment. It blames the recession on pay increases and gives a warning that firms will be forced to cut back on jobs . . .

montage of members of each service crudely laid across one another and the whole arranged to balance his position in the frame (Figure 7.25). While this icon is admittedly easy to decode, it nevertheless owes little to the aesthetics of the golden mean.

Another problem with whole-frame *Chromokey* can be seen in the sequence of Figures 7.26 to 7.28. The image of the supermarket, one of the generalised images of consumerism specifically used to indicate inflation as it affects the cost of living (as opposed to pound notes, £ symbols, crystal balls and flags, etc., which related to the national economy and inflation) is backing Sissons (Figure 7.26). Cutting to the source which has the actual inflation statistic on it (Figure 7.27) and superimposing that on the same image that has been backing Sissons, means that he, in effect, disappears. This occurred in the early evening bulletin but it was changed for *News at Ten*. Then Sissons

Figure 7.25 The armed forces

Figure 7.26 Sissons and the supermarket

was backed by pound notes (Figure 7.28). The image in Figure 7.27 was cut-in again in this bulletin but this time without any violence to Sissons.

We have suggested that the range of images in the news is restricted and we have begun to substantiate that claim in some detail. Table 7.1 (p. 227)

Figure 7.27 Sissons disappears

Figure 7.28 Sissons' new backing

offers some evidence in this matter. Of the 26 opening images (in changing image bulletins), 4 were still portraits of the then Prime Minister, Harold Wilson, and 1 was a still portrait of Jack Jones. Graphics involving signs were used twice and maps 3 times. Company logos and still photographs of company buildings were used 3 times. Shopping precincts and supermarket interiors were used twice. The aftermath of a factory disaster was used once, marching soldiers were used once, and the *Mayaguez* affair took up the rest – the black-and-white image of the ship 3 times, the ship at Singapore 4 times, the ship on tow twice and the marines on Ko Tang once (1 photograph of a company building was in a montage with a photograph of the Prime Minister).

Turning to the 'bongs' (Examples 7.2a–e, pp. 234–7), we find portrait stills of President Ford, Michael Foot, Ilie Nastase and Roger Taylor (mounted together) and an identikit picture of the Cambridge rapist. For industry we had the Chrysler strikers voting, the Dunlop logo, a still photograph of the Ryton factory gate, a photograph of a dockside, the cover of a CBI report and the crystal ball mentioned above. We had, in addition, British soldiers, American marines on Ko Tang, Flixborough being rebuilt, ancient Japanese football, a ballot box, one map, Orantes in action and four uses of the black-and-white *Mayaguez* photograph.

The icons used as background to correspondents, which are listed in Table 7.2 on pp. 273–6, share a number of characteristics with these groups. First, only two are iconic – the news picture of Vice Premier Teng in Paris and the colour picture of Flixborough after the explosion (Entries 11 and 14, Table 7.2). Most are indexical and largely avoid close-ups of particular people. The Ali portrait in the BBC2 sports package on Saturday is the only exception. The buildings are No. 10 Downing Street (with policeman), Chequers, Parliament, the White House, the Pentagon, Congress House, Ferranti's headquarters, the front of a bank and the Capitol building. It should be noted that all of these are exteriors and some are aerial views. In other words, no assumption is being made that the correspondents should be seen by the audience to be physically before these buildings. The parliamentary correspondents would be sited somewhere above the Albert Embankment, for instance, if this were the case. (Yet night reports have a night photograph to back them.) These images are iconic of themselves but indexical of the subject matter of the reports: the American army is the Pentagon, Congress is the Capitol, the Prime Minister is No. 10 Downing Street or Chequers, and so on. This indexical quality is increased with the exchange dealers, the dockside, soldiers, interiors of supermarkets, people on a pavement, children in a classroom. Apart from the images of soldiers, which relate indexically to armed forces' pay, and of children, which relate to education, the rest of these all back economic stories. The *Mayaguez* photograph is also in this group. Throughout the week, wherever the ship was (and for some hours it was completely missing), this icon stood indexically for the story. More symbolic were the graphics – splayed notes, the European jigsaw puzzle, the Far East maps. More use was made of the covers of reports to stand indexically for the reports' contents than in the opening image or 'bongs' group. The CBI report and armed forces' pay review were both used in this way.

Both TV news services responded to the same problems of visualisation with similar solutions. Parliament was Big Ben on all channels. On the Monday, Harrod had the CBI cover and so did Green. On the Tuesday, Harrod had the dockside and so did Green. Brunson had the White House and so did Humphrys.

The same basic tendencies can be seen in the choice of background images: the majority were indexical, a few were symbolic (although, as in Example 7.10, the report can render an indexical image symbolic), and, surprisingly for a visual news service, an equal few were iconic. The tendency to avoid portrait stills (an image difficult to mesh with the foreground correspondent figure) and the use of report covers, were the only differences between these backgrounds and the other groups of images discussed in the previous chapter.

CORRESPONDENT REPORTS

The correspondents appeared in three main modes – long pieces, uninterrupted; by visuals but not on the sound track because the correspondent talks over the interrupting image (these visuals being either graphics of various sorts and/or *non-sync.* film); pieces interrupted visually and on the sound track, i.e. *sync.* pieces from other speakers.

The correspondents (a category which, it should be remembered, also includes reporters appearing in studio to camera with full *Chromokey* backing) made 43 appearances in these modes. On 11 occasions during the week they delivered uninterrupted pieces to camera (Mode A, Table 7.2). On 15 occasions they delivered their pieces uninterruptedly on the audio track but voiced-over other visual inputs (Mode B, Table 7.2). On 5 occasions they introduced segments from *sync.* film or tape (Mode C). In addition to this, on 7 occasions they appeared in a combined mode both voicing-over other inputs and introducing other *sync.* (Mode D) and on 5 occasions reporters or correspondents read introductions to *sync.* but did not then reappear after the *sync.* was finished (Mode E).

The uninterrupted mode occurs most often, as would be expected, in the economic and parliamentary categories. But what is less expected is that it never occurred on ITN. In other words, ITN, in this sample using its correspondents more than does the BBC, made a greater effort to add visual variety to that use.

All these 11 appearances lasted upwards of 1 minute or more each, the shortest being pieces from Colebourne on the BBC1 early evening bulletin on 15 May at 45 seconds (29, Table 7.2) and from Harrod in the same bulletin the following day at 58 seconds (32, Table 7.2). (These were the only two correspondent appearances in the week with a plain background flat.) The longest appearance was an update from Jones on a commons debate in *News Extra* on Monday which lasted 1 minute, 40 seconds. Biddulph on the night of the seizure of *Mayaguez*, Curtoise and Ross were the other correspondents allowed these sorts of durations.

Example 7.14 BBC1, 17.45, 14 May 1975 (Table 7.2, Item 19: Mode B$_1$)

$3.49\frac{1}{2}$ /

10 Harrod MCU (top of   *HARROD (Correspondent) TO CAM*
     pocket) (SCR CENTRE)   The London dock strike hit imports in March,
     B/G = ship unloading at   producing very good figures and exports in
     dock *Colour photo*   April. But as these figures show there was
                           no/

· ·

     10a *Super* 'Dominic   rebound in imports so the result was a good
         Harrod, Economics   deal better than expected. /
         Correspondent' lose
         super

· ·

                           Indeed after allowing for those invisible
                           earnings, from dividends and interest, tourism
                           and the like, which have been running at about
CUT 0.20 $4.9\frac{1}{2}$ £120 million a month, /

11 *Graphic*: Balance of   *HARROD (Correspondent) VOICE-OVER*
     Payments Current Account   the current account of the foreign balance has
     Nov., Dec., Jan., Feb.,   been improving steadily since last year. Even
     Mar., April on black B/G –   after the April setback the average deficit for
     169m on red B/G   the past three months has been about £112
                           million. Bad, but nothing like the deficit of more
                           than £300 million a month at the end of last
CUT 0.16 $4.25\frac{1}{2}$ year. /

12 Harrod as 10   *HARROD TO CAM*
                           So there's been an improving trend and in
                           recognition of the figures the pound rose on
                           foreign exchange markets this afternoon for the
                           first time since the steep slide began. The slide
                           had brought the pound down by more than 4
                           per cent in three weeks but this evening it was
                           the dollar that came under strong pressure on
CUT 0.19 $4.44\frac{1}{2}$ the latest news from Cambodia. /

In the second mode it is necessary to differentiate between the long piece interrupted visually at most twice (Mode B$_1$, Table 7.2) and the complex illustrated pieces that characterised, for instance, ITN's coverage of the *Mayaguez* (Mode B$_2$, Table 7.2). Of the 15 instances in this mode, 5 consisted of piece to camera, voice-over still, piece to camera sequences (B$_1$). ITN had 3 and BBC 2 of this type (see Example 7.14).

More complicated were sequences which appeared on 10 occasions (Mode B$_2$) each as that in Example 7.15. These consisted in the sample week of at least 7 shots up to (as in the example) 23 shots. The correspondent could appear either at the beginning and end of the sequence or in the middle as well

Example 7.15 ITN, 22.00, 15 May 1975 (Table 7.2, Item 30: Mode B$_2$)

		1.4½	*WAIN (Correspondent) TO CAM*
2	Wain MCU (top of pocket) (SCR CENTRE) B/G = *Mayaguez* at dock B&W photo		So the great rescue has ended successfully but at considerable cost./

	2a	*Super* 'Christopher Wain, Defence Correspondent' lose super	The *Mayaguez* incident had started on /

CUT 0.8   1.12½ Monday when the ten/

3	*Map*: Hong Kong Hanoi Laos Thailand Cambodia Settapao Ko Tang Seized here	*WAIN VOICE-OVER* thousand ton container ship was seized by a Cambodian gunboat while steaming through the gulf of Thailand en route to Settapao. It was
	CUT 0.7½ 1.20	an act of pir/

4	Ford *Portrait still* (bottom of tie) CU flag B/G	acy said President Ford. He ordered a task force from the seventh Fleet to go in and get the prisoners out /
	CUT 0.6½ 1.26½	

5	Wain as in 2	*WAIN TO CAM* It all took time. On tuesday two battalions of US
	CUT 0.5 1.31½	Marines, 1,100 men, arrived at/

6	*Map* Ream Phnom Penh Utapao Bangkok Ko Tang Cambodia Gulf of Thailand	Utapao air-base in Southern Thailand. Meanwhile the aircraft carrier *Coral* /
	CUT 0.4½ 1.36	

7	*Coral Sea* aerial GV *B&W film*	*Sea*, a 50,000-tonner carrying seventy-five aircraft,/
	CUT 0.3½ 1.39½	

8	Pan plane GV forward flight deck – takes off (sea to sea) *B&W film*	was moving to a point midway between Utapao and the island of Ko Tang, where the /
	CUT 0.4½ 1.44	

9	Plane takes off top shot *B&W film*	*Mayaguez* was lying. By Wednesday the battle plan was ready. A US navy Corsair /
	CUT 0.5 1.49	

10	Corsair GV on ground *Colour photo*	fighter bomber sank three Cambodian gunboats and immobilised four others. And as
	CUT 0.7½ 1.56½	darkness fell, the aircraft direct /

Example 7.15 continued

| 11 | *USS Holt* (aerial) GV *B&W photo* | | ion-destroyer, *Holt*, moved into the area. Her task was to guide the marine assault |
| | CUT 0.7½ | 2.04 | helicopters into Ko Tang. According to so/ |

| 12 | *Map* as in 6 | | me reports the first wave of 135 marines flew into the attack direct from Thailand, but that's not likely. The aircraft almost certainly stopped to refuel on board the *Coral Sea* before the |
| | CUT 0.13 | 2.17 | dawn attack. They went in at mid/ |

| 13 | Wain as in 2 | | *WAIN TO CAM* night our time last night. They were flying in on |
| | CUT 0.3 | 2.20 | CH/ |

| 14 | GV chopper turning – track (ground to air) SCR RHT *Film* | | *WAIN VOICE-OVER* 53D heavy assault helicopters |
| | CUT 0.2 | 2.22 | |

| 15 | CU chopper turning – track: (ground to air) SCR LFT *Film* | | each one carrying 37 marines and 3 crew. One helicopter apparently landed on the *Mayag* |
| | CUT 0.6 | 2.28 | |

| 16 | Wain as in 2 | | *WAIN TO CAM* *guez*. The marines hurriedly searched the ship but found she was empty, the others stormed ashore and it was here thay they started taking casualties. According to the reports from |
| | CUT 0.10 | 2.38 | Washington, three heli/ |

| 17 | GV belly flopped chopper *B&W News picture* | | *WAIN VOICE-OVER* copters were lost. One was shot down, the others crashed into the sea just off shore. The |
| | CUT 0.6 | 2.44 | marines were/ |

| 18 | 4 marines LS chopper *B&W News picture* | | pinned down by gunfire from the waiting Cambodians, but those ordered to search for the missing sailors, couldn't find a sign of them. |
| | CUT 0.8 | 2.52 | Meanwhile jets from the *Coral* / |

| 19 | Wain as in 2 | | *WAIN TO CAM* *Sea* had attacked the Cambodian airbase at Ream. At 10.00 in the morning, four hours after the marines had hit the beach at Ko Tang, a Thai fishing boat came out from the Cambodian mainland flying a white flag and according to the reports from Washington all 39 of the missing crew members were on board |
| | CUT 0.19½ | 3.11½ | the ship. They were transferred/ |

| 20 | *GV Wilson* (ship to ship) *B&W photo* | | to the destroyer *Wilson* and President Ford announced that the operation was over and |
| | CUT 0.5½ | 3.17 | was a success/ |

Example 7.15 continued

21 *Map* Ko Tang (large scale)	But the marine task force was still on Ko Tang and under heavy Cambodian fire. There was no need for them to be there and so orders were given to evacuate them. But this was much easier said than done. For one thing, they had to wait until the *Coral Sea* had
CUT 0.17 3.34	approached close enough for the heli /

22 *Coral Sea* aerial GV *Colour photo*	copters on board to be sent in. And when they did attempt to land they were beaten back by
CUT 0.7 3.41	Cambodian ground fire. So it wa/

23 LS marines (no chopper) B/G *B&W News picture*	sn't until 8.00 this evening, local time, that the marines were pulled out and the helicopter evacuation by darkness under fire was even
CUT 0.10½ 3.51½	more dangerous than this morning's landing./

24 Wain as in 2	*WAIN TO CAM* The last known survivor was lifted out at two minutes past 8.00 but the destroyers, *Holt* and *Wilson*, stayed close inshore searching for other survivors. The known casualties are 2 dead and 8 wounded but 14 men are missing. Their chances of survival are slender. So it all adds up to about 10 per cent casualties amongst the marines who took part and that's a rough indication of how hazardous a rescue
CUT 0.22½ 4.14	this was. /

Key: sea to sea = shot from one boat to another
       aerial = taken from the air
       ground to air = shot from the ground of aircraft

(as in the example). Of these sequences 7 were on ITN and 3 on the BBC. The example is particularly instructive in that it was the most visual of all the accounts given of the *Mayaguez* affair.

This sequence contains practically every available image in the story.[10] In the following days, only some official film of the raid, the ship being towed and its arrival at Singapore, were added. In fact only three shots were actually taken in the course of the rescue – shot numbers 17, 18, 22 – used for a total of 24.5 seconds out of a report running for 3 minutes, 16.5 seconds. This must be seen as an achievement because Wain, the most readily available image as it were, talked to camera for only 1 minute, 8 seconds. Thus over half the story was illustrated by indexical photographs, library film and maps. Of this material, most had already been seen (the black-and-white footage of the Coral Sea was new but the BBC had colour footage of the ship two days before). The time span of the story (at this point in its fourth day) helped this presentation.

Yet the sequence also points up the visual limitations of the television journalist in such situations. The icon of the shot-down helicopter stands indexically for 'the others crashed into the sea'. The icon of the running marines stands indexically for marines 'pinned down by gunfire' or 'the helicopter evacuation by darkness'. Thus even the 24.5 seconds of imagery actually emanating from the Far East must also be made to work indexically for the journalists' needs to be met.

The tendency for correspondents on ITN to break up the reports with other visual material is yet another indicator that we have found which could contribute to the audience's perception of the service as being 'livelier' than the BBC's.

The use of correspondents to introduce other pieces of *sync.* is less likely to contribute to 'liveliness' because each segment of the *sync.* (apart from being by definition 'talking heads') has to be separately cued (i.e. the video-tape or Telecine projection machine, in the case of film, has to run up to and stabilise at the correct speed). Thus the 5- and 3-second shots (shots 5 and 13 in Example 7.15) are not easily possible with *sync.*

Of the 5 entries in this mode (C), 3 are ITN's and 2 BBC's but it should be noted that 4 of the 5 are from America and in each case the report is from the service's Washington correspondent. In other words, in this week of a major United States story the pattern was to have the correspondent introduce *sync.* material gleaned from American television. The shared language is a major factor facilitating this. The odd value out here is the analysis by Haviland, ITN's political editor, of the Prime Minister's interview on the Sunday. This was carried by the BBC but not at such great length – perhaps because it emanated from an ITV source.

Modes D and E account for the rest. These tend to be lengthy inserts and because of the status of the interviewees and the length of their contributions the cutting rate is much slower than in Example 7.15. Mode D can be characterised as having an insert or inserts with an interrupted illustrated introduction or payoff. Item 8, in Table 7.2, introduces the *sync.* and then voices over one shot in the payoff. Item 12, in the same table, has an illustrated introduction followed by a sequence of *sync.* inserts interspersed with to-camera pieces by the correspondent. Item 25 has an illustrated payoff. (On the third day of the *Mayaguez* incident the ITN Washington correspond-ent began his report with film of himself standing before the Pentagon. The previous evening he had been suspended above it – because of the combination of his studio seat and the aerial photograph backing him.)

In Item 39 the *sync.* butt-joins the correspondent's voice-over. Item 41 has an illustrated payoff while the two sports packages are too complex to analyse in this way.

The E mode has five entries (1, 11, 16, 18, 28). What distinguishes these from the above is simply that the reporter or correspondent does not reappear after the *sync.*

Only 11 of the total number of correspondents-to-camera shots (not reports, as above) were under 10 seconds and 27 of them were over 40 seconds. It is therefore likely in the code of television news that once correspondents appear, they will remain on screen for periods that can only be described as lengthy in bulletin terms. Only in complex sequences (Mode B_2) will they normally get less than 10 seconds in any one shot and usually they get much more.

INTRODUCING CORRESPONDENTS

This high-status uninterruptibility of the correspondents is reinforced by the way in which they are supercaptioned. On only five occasions did correspondents or reporters appear in the studio without supercaptions; Jones on *News Extra*, Wain on *First Report* and Colebourne from the Midlands and Delahaye from the North, Luton and Blackie. Thus most of these non-captioned appearances were on the BBC, the one on ITN being of itself a somewhat unusual event; i.e. a correspondent's appearance in *First Report*. It is fair to say that correspondents are more regularly captioned than any other group. In addition, on only nine occasions was this caption not reinforced by a verbal announcement and significantly all these occasions are on the BBC. In other words ITN never failed verbally to introduce the correspondent and, with the one exception (Wain's appearance on *First Report*), also never failed to caption them. This greater care on ITN's part to identify its own personnel is repeated when supercaptions on film or tape are examined. Of these verbal announcements only one, again on the BBC, failed to mention the name as well as the status of the person. This was Item 32, Table 7.2, on BBC1, when Harrod was introduced with just a 'Here's our economics correspondent'.

Eight forms of introduction can be found in the week's sample (see Table 7.3, p. 277). The first type in Table 7.3 dominates the verbal hand-over. It was used 16 times during the week. The second, used only on ITN, was employed 3 times to introduce background or feature pieces from the correspondent concerned. The third was used 4 times, on each occasion to hand over to an American report. The fourth was used once by ITN and the fifth once by BBC (to hand over to Jones in the Westminster studio). The sixth was used 3 times to introduce reporters and the seventh twice – once for Colebourne and once for Luton. Only Blackie on Saturday's BBC2 sports package had the details.

Reporter is thus not a job that warrants verbal identification. 'Here's our reporter' was not used in the sample week. A further clue as to the status of correspondents can be seen in the combination of name and job description in types 1, 2 and 4 (Table 7.3). Reporters are not so introduced. Further, 'over to' and 'from' seem to mean that the correspondent is in another studio either at home or abroad.

The combination of caption and verbal identification reflects the organisational hierarchy within the newsrooms. Together, they constitute the

Table 7.2 Correspondents and reporters in studio (Index 11)

	Date	Channel T/X	Name	Chromokey backing	Pattern & duration of shots	Identification	Mode
1	11/5	BBC1 18.05	Curtoise	No. 10 (door) + policeman *Colour photo*	1'05" ↑ (Wilson 0.21")	Political correspondent	E
2		BBC1 21.30	Curtoise		1'22"	Political correspondent	A
3		ITN 22.00	Haviland	GV Chequers *Colour photo*	44" ↑ (Wilson 44½") 15" ↑ (W 35") 18" ↑ (W 67") 20" ↑ (W 37") 13"	Political editor	C
4	12/5	BBC1 17.45	Harrod	GV bank building *Colour photo*	1'21"	Economics correspondent	A
5		BBC1 21.00	Biddulph	Cambodia *Map*	1'05"	BBC News/diplomatic	A
6		BBC1 21.00	Harrod	Exchange dealers *Colour photo*	24" (9") 36"	BBC News/economics	B_1
7		BBC1 21.00	Jones	Big Ben GV night *Colour photo*	1'23½"	BBC News/parliament	A
8		ITN 17.50	Green	Splayed £s *Graphic*	55½" ↑ (Kleinwort/Kee 57") 39" (6") 16"	Reporting	D
9		ITN 22.00	Sissons	Splayed £s *Graphic*	44" (10") 7½" (8½") 27½" (6½") 26"	Industrial editor	B_2
10		ITN 22.00	Mathias	Big Ben GV night *Colour photo*	14" (8") 23½" (10") 20½" (7") 10"	Political correspondent	B_2
11		ITN 22.00	Hatfield	GV Flixborough after *Colour photo*	42" (50"/12 shots) ↑ (Locke/Hatfield 1'13½"	Keith Hatfield	E

Table 7.2 continued

No.	Date	Channel	Time	Lander	Description	Measurements	Role	D
12		ITN	22.00	Lander	Europe jigsaw (flat)	22" (17") 4½" (13") 51" (30") ↑ (Williams 34") 13" ↑ ↑ (Winnifrith 35") 27½" ↑ (Wil + Win 17") 39¼"	European political correspondent	D
13		BBC2	22.20	Jones	Big Ben GV night Colour photo	148"		A
14		BBC2	22.20	Biddulph	Teng + Guard	1'10"	Diplomatic correspondent	A
15	13/5	BBC1	21.00	Harrod	CBI report cover Graphic	39" ↑ (McDougall/Harrod 1'15") 37½"	Economics correspondent (used twice, both shots)	C
16		ITN	17.50	Green	CBI report cover Graphic	20" (30") 40" ↑ (McDougall/Green 46")	Industrial correspondent	E
17		ITN	22.00	Brunson	White House GV aerial GV Pentagon/White House bis Colour photos	25" ↑ (Javits 29") 20" ↑ (Pentagon spokesman 20") 26" ↑ (Buckley + Humphreys 45") 28½" ↑	Washington correspondent	C
18		ITN	22.00	Green	CBI report cover Graphic	24" (36") 8½" ↑ (MacDougall/Green 1'12")	Industrial correspondent	E
19	14/5	BBC1	17.45	Harrod	GV dockside unloading Colour photo	20" (16") 19"	Economics correspondent	B₁
20		BBC1	17.45	Ross	Congress House ext. Colour photo	1'		A
21		BBC1	21.00	Humphrys	White House Colour photo	29½" ↑ (Laitkin 42") 22" ↑ (Goldwater + Clark 1'37") 52½"*	*	C
22		BBC1	21.00	Delahaye	Ferranti HQ GV Colour photo	19½" (10") 11" (38½")'7 shots) 22½"		B₂

Table 7.2 continued

		Channel	Time	Name	Description	Timing	BBC News/Industry	
23		BBC1	21.00	Ross	Congress House ext *colour photo*	1'17"		A
24		ITN	17.50	Green	GV dockside *Colour photo*	47" (4½") 23"	Industrial correspondent	B₂
25†		ITN	22.00	Brunson	(On film Pentagon GV) White House	(TO CAM on film 29" ↑ (Laitkin 1') (47½'/3 shots)) 41" (11½") 10½"	Reporting from Washington	D
26		ITN	22.00	Wain	*Map:* Thailand Cambodia Bangkok Utapao Phnom Penh	9" (7½") 13½" (44½/7 shots) 12½" (6½') 7½"	Defence correspondent	B₂
27		ITN	22.00	Green	GV dockside *Colour photo*	31" (10½") 37½"	Industrial correspondent	B₁
28		ITN	22.00	Mathias	Europe jigsaw (flat)	32" (13½/3 shots) 32" ↑ (Allen/Mathias 1'21") 45"	Political correspondent	E
29	15/5	BBC1	17.45	Colebourne	Plain beige B/G			A
30		ITN	22.00	Wain	'Mayaguez' *B/W photo* at dockside	8" (7½") (6½") 5" (46½/8 shots) 3" (8"/2 shots) 10" (14"/2 shots) 19½" (40"/4 shots)	Defence correspondent	B₂
31		ITN	22.00	Brunson	Pentagon aerial GV/Capitol dome/White House GV *Colour photos*	46½" ↑ (40" Ford) 11" ↑ (McGovern/Sparkman 17½") 26" ↑ (Schlesinger 46") 44" 58"	Washington correspondent	C
32	16/5	BBC1	17.45	Harrod	Plain blue B/G	20" (1'0½"/9 shots) 12"	Dominic Harrod	A
33		BBC1	17.45	Luton	Montage soldiers, etc. *Colour photo*			B₂
34		BBC1	21.00	Harrod	£s	1'11½"	BBC News/Economics	A
35		BBC1	21.00	Luton	Montage soldiers, etc. *Colour photo*	20" (1'0½"/9 shots) 11½"		B₂

Table 7.2 continued

				First Report B/G			
36	ITN	13.00	Wain		14½" (50"/6 shots) 12" (7") 20"		B₂
37	ITN	17.50	Sissons	GV int. Supermarket Colour photo	48" (8")1'30"	Industrial editor	B₁
38	ITN	17.50	Wain	Review body cover Graphic	18" (51"/10 shots) 4"	Defence correspondent	B₂
39 15/5	BBC1	21.00	Humphrys	Capitol/White House Colour photos	36" ↑ (Dole 27") (26½"/2 shots) 29*	Washington (2) correspondent	D
40 16/5	ITN	22.00	Sissons	GV people on pavement Colour photo	45" (13") 6" (9") 41" (31"/2 shots) 1'9"	Industrial editor	B₂
41 17/5	BBC1	21.35	Buerk	GV children in class Colour photo	34½" ↑ (Prentice 36") 7½"* (12") 6½"	*Michael Buerk	D
42	ITN		Parker	Saturday sport + /portrait still Ali	37½" (16½") ↑ (Moore v/o) 10" (9½") 10" (2½") 22½" (39"/6 shots)	Sports correspondent	E
43	BBC2	19.30	Blackie	Sport on 2 (flat)	13" (2'38"/38 shots) 29" ↑ (Waring v/o 33½"/4 shots) (18½"/2 shots) 15½" (20½"/2 shots) 10" (14"/2 shots) 13" (25½"/3 shots)		E

Key:

Flat: a piece of setting: a set

Timing pattern: figures outside brackets refer to camera shot lengths. If followed immediately by () indicates voice-over. () with timing figure/no. shots = voice-over a number of continuous shots. ↑ before () = *sync.* insert. Name within bracket = interviewee, followed by name of interviewer. Two names within such brackets = two *sync.* pieces butt-joined.

All supercaptions (*) include name unless otherwise stated.

Name alone = only the name appeared without title

* = shots where super appeared. If no * then super appeared in first shot. If no name then no super.

A = Uninterrupted pieces to camera

B₁ = Pieces with one single shot interruption voiced-over by correspondent

B₂ = Pieces with more than one single interruption voice-over by correspondent

C = Pieces with one or more *sync.* inserts (or inserts with voice-over from other personnel)

D = Pieces combining voice-over shots with *sync.* inserts

E = Uninterrupted pieces leading to *sync.* (correspondent does not reappear after *sync.*)

† Item 25: this introductory shot on film is also listed in the film indices.

Table 7.3 Newscaster to correspondent/reporter hand-overs (studio)

1   Here's our X editor/correspondent (Tony Other):
2   Our X editor/correspondent Tony Other has been looking at Y. Here's his
    report:
3   (And now) from Place Z, Tony Other reports:
4   Our X editor/correspondent Tony Other reports:
5   Over to Tony Other:
6   Here's Tony Other:
7   Tony Other reports:
8   Here with the details, Tony Other:

equivalent of the press by-line and they seem to reflect press practice in that, just as the by-line is a mark of seniority and status, so too is the combination verbal hand-over and caption, providing a job description is used.

In terms of pay-offs, there is a distinction between the services since ITN has adopted the American practice of signing off a story – thus, 'This is Tony Other *First Report/News at Ten* (etc.), Place Z'. The BBC does not do this. Neither does ITN do it in the studio. Therefore in the correspondents' list, only Michael Brunson signed off in this way, from Washington.

All in all, ITN was more systematic in naming its personnel than was the BBC, but both services were thorough about the use of captions in the studio context. This tendency carefully to name the staff and their jobs not only confers high status on them (we would argue), but also of course serves to legitimise what they say. It is in contrast, as we shall see below, to the more haphazard treatment given to others who appear in *sync.* in the bulletins.

The normal point at which the supercaption appears is during the first piece to camera. The latitude is comparatively wide (as can be seen in the examples) but, obviously, if the piece to camera is short then the supercaption must appear closer to the start of the piece than otherwise. On only three occasions during the week did the supercaption appear after the opening piece; twice when John Humphrys was reporting from the United States and once on Saturday with Michael Buerk. This last occasion looks like nothing but oversight: the caption was not used during his opening 34.5 seconds but was inserted into his illustrated payoff in a shot lasting only 7.5 seconds. The Humphrys examples are more complex. In his longest piece on the Thursday, he began by voicing-over film. This was covered by a 'John Humphrys reporting' caption. He then appeared in the item numbered 39 in Table 7.2. Each time he appeared to camera he was captioned 'John Humphrys, Washington'. On the Wednesday despite his two appearances to camera in the item, the caption was saved until this third and last appearance. However, he was verbally introduced on this occasion.

Again, ITN appears to be marginally more regular in its use of these devices than does the BBC. The rule seems to be that supercaptions appear only once, normally at the first opportunity in the first piece to camera of a sequence.

VOICE-ONLY

The use of correspondents and reporters appearing in the bulletins in sound only displays the same range of characteristics as those outlined above. We are not here discussing sound tracks of film that might have arrived via radio circuits but only those appearances that combine reporter/correspondent voice with radio circuit captions.

This sort of input is not used by the two short bulletins but it accounts for 2.7 per cent and 3.3 per cent of the total durations of *News Extra* and *First Report* respectively. It accounts for 4.1 per cent of the ITN's and 6.3 per cent of the BBC's early evening bulletins. But it accounts for less than 0.9 per cent of *News at Ten* and 2.7 per cent of the BBC's *Nine O'Clock News*.

Since there is no particular inhibition about the lengths at which this input is used – correspondents are allowed as long to talk over the radio circuit caption still as they are allowed to talk in the flesh – these figures represent comparatively few actual reports during the week. This input was used on seventeen occasions (see Table 7.4). The discrepancy between the main bulletins can be accounted for as the obverse of the previous discrepancy in the use of correspondents in the studio. Specifically, ITN opened the satellite for Brunson to do a piece to camera on the Tuesday whereas the BBC did not do the same for Humphrys. On the other hand the BBC had Humphrys on radio circuit that night but opened the satellite for him to be interviewed by Angela Rippon on the Wednesday. In other words, although the BBC used Humphrys more on the cheaper radio circuit in terms of the *Nine O'Clock News*, over both its services it used satellite as much as ITN did.

The shot durations in these radio circuit inputs last longer than any other group of still images in the visual vocabulary of the news. In terms of the competing early evening bulletins they last longer than do shots of correspondents in the flesh; and in terms of the BBC's *Nine O'Clock News* that remains true. Only *News at Ten* breaks them up to bring down the average duration, but even then it is still true that on average a radio circuit caption will last a full 9.35 seconds longer than a portrait still, the most common of non-moving inputs.

The phenomenon here noted is that we are dealing with a class of still images which are treated in the length they can be permitted to remain uninterruptedly on the screen as if they were moving images. Nowhere, therefore, in the bulletins is the visual imperative less in evidence.

Unlike actual studio appearances the radio circuit appearance was not used, during the sample week, to introduce *sync.* inserts. Therefore there are no examples in Table 7.4 of the Modes C, D and E shown in Table 7.2. Otherwise the range of modes distinguished for correspondent studio appearances also

Table 7.4 Correspondents and reporters via radio circuit (Index 10)

	Date	Channel	T/X	Name	Radio circuit caption details	Timing pattern	Mode	Overall duration
1	12/5	BBC1	21.00	Humphrys	PS + White House 'JH reporting'	26" (17") 50"	B₁	1'33"
2	12/5	ITN	13.00	MacDonald	PS + Chrysler gate 'First Report: TM reporting'	1'33"	A	1'33"
3	12/5	BBC1	22.20	Humphrys	PS + White House 'JH reporting'	24" (9½") 52½"	B₁	1'16"
4	12/5	ITN	22.00	Selvin	White House 'DS reporting'	19" (12") 23"	B₁	54"
5	13/5	BBC1	17.45	Humphrys	PS + White House 'JH reporting'	40"	A	40"
6	13/5	BBC1	21.00	Humphrys	PS + White House 'JH reporting'	1'05"	A	1'05"
7	13/5	ITN	17.50	Brunson	Capitol 'MB reporting from Washington'	49½"	A	49½"
8	13/5	BBC2	23.05	Humphrys	PS + White House 'JH reporting'	1'04"	A	1'04"
9	14/5	ITN	17.50	Brunson	Capitol 'MB reporting from Washington'	1'25"	A	1'25"
10	14/5	ITN	22.00	Seymour	PS + Map (Ko Tang/Cambodia/Bangkok/Utapao/Thailand) 'GS reporting from Bangkok'	9" (22½") 11" (13½") 20"	B₂	1'16"
11	15/5	BBC1	21.00	Humphrys	PS + White House 'JH reporting'	48"	A	48"
12	15/5	ITN	13.00	Seymour	PS + Map (Utapao/Gulf of Thailand/Phnom Penh/Kompong Som/Ko Tang/Mayaguez (in box) 'First Report: GS reporting'	15" (9") 8½" (4½") 31½" (7½") 16" (4½")	B₂	1'40½"
13	16/5	BBC1	17.45	Humphrys	PS + White House 'JH reporting'	48"	A	48"
14	16/5	BBC1	21.00	Humphrys	PS + White House 'JH reporting'	30" (9") 30½"	B₁	1'09½"
15	16/5	ITN	13.00	Alick	Aerial GV Port of Spain 'First Report: Vernon Alick reporting from Trinidad'	52"	A	52"
16	16/5	BBC2	23.05	Humphrys	PS + White House 'JH reporting'	16" (40½"/3 shots) 12½"	B₂	1'07"
17	17/5	ITN	13.10	Seymour	PS + Newspic. Mayaguez at dockside Singapore 'GS reporting from Singapore'	(32") 35" (18") 11"	B₂	1'36"

Key: PS = portrait still

exists for radio circuit inputs, with the radio circuit caption taking the place of the to-camera shots.

On this basis, 9 entries in Table 7.4 are uninterrupted pieces (Mode A), 4 are in Mode B_1 and 4 are in Mode B_2. The uninterrupted (Mode A) pieces last as little as 40 seconds or as long as 1 minute 33 seconds. The 5 appearances for the BBC in this mode all involve Humphrys broadcasting from Washington, 3 times into the early evening bulletin, once into the *Nine O'Clock News* and once into BBC2's *News Extra*. Of the 4 ITN appearances, 2 are reports from Brunson in Washington, both broadcast in the early evening. The other 2 appearances are from *First Report*: one, the week's longest, coming from MacDonald in Coventry and the other coming from a stringer in Trinidad.

The visually interrupted piece at its simplest involves voicing-over one still. In the radio circuit input category this takes the form of cutting from the radio circuit caption to another still and then back to the radio circuit caption. This happened on 4 occasions during the week (Mode B_1, Table 7.4); 3 of them occurred on the first night of the *Mayaguez* (Monday). Humphrys' initial report from Washington in the *Nine O'Clock News* lasted 1 minute 33 seconds, 17 seconds of which he talked over a photograph of the USS *Pueblo*. The piece he did for *News Extra* that same Monday night lasted for 1 minute 26 seconds and the USS *Pueblo* was seen for 9.5 seconds. ITN took a piece lasting in all 54 seconds from Selvin in Washington, which it illustrated with a map of Cambodia showing Kompong Som and Phnom Penh for 12 seconds. Humphrys' piece into the *Nine O'Clock News* on Friday lasted 1 minute 9.5 seconds and used a portrait still of Kissinger for 9 seconds.

Of the 4 rather more complex pieces, 3 were in ITN bulletins and 1 in the BBC. The pattern previously established was thus repeated. The more visually complex the mode, the greater the percentage of ITN pieces in the mode.

In the case of the B_2 values in Table 7.4, 3 were from Seymour reporting from Bangkok. On the Wednesday (10) Seymour's report lasted 1 minute 16 seconds. He talked over six film shots arranged on either side of a portrait still. On the Thursday (12) he talked for 1 minute 40.5 seconds, interspersing still photographs with the radio circuit caption, a pattern repeated rather less elaborately in (17) on Saturday. The Humphrys piece into the *Nine O'Clock News* illustrated by one still of Kissinger became for *News Extra* two colour news pictures plus a map rather than this file portrait still.

The length of these appearances overall varied little whether they were illustrated or not. They averaged out overall at 1 minute 8 seconds. Most of the unillustrated appearances were shorter than this average. A complex hidden assumption about viewers' tolerance levels for unchanging images can perhaps be discerned here. On the one hand, radio circuit captions were not treated as still images at all when the durations on the screen are compared with durations for other still inputs. On the other hand, however, an interrupted radio circuit caption could sustain a longer piece from the correspondent than an uninterrupted one. The only exception to this was the 1 minute 33 second unillustrated piece from MacDonald in *First Report*. Otherwise unillustrated pieces are shorter overall than illustrated pieces, however limited that illustration might be.

This leaves a residual group of inputs with two entries. In one, in the early evening bulletin on Wednesday, the BBC allowed a Pentagon spokesman to talk for 56.5 seconds over an aerial photograph of the Pentagon with the words 'Pentagon spokesman' superimposed throughout. The visual to this audio track caught up with it, as it were, in a *sync.* insert into *News Extra*. In the second entry on the same day, ITN used a portrait still of Premier Bourassa of Quebec and his voice over it for 19 seconds in the middle of a film report on the readiness of the Montreal Olympic site.

The radio circuit caption is among the more sophisticated images regularly used on the news. It consists of three distinct elements (Figure 7.29). First, there is a background image of the place from which the report comes. Second, there is a portrait still of the person making the report; and, last, there is written identification. In the case of the photograph, the BBC *Nine O'Clock News* identification of service and area is worked into the caption 'BBC NEWS WASHINGTON'. With stringers the portrait still can also be omitted but some written identification of the place is present normally in the form 'Tony Other reporting from Z'.

Thus, we decode the image by reading the name of the man portrayed as being his name (although it is not under his face) and we hear the voice as being his voice (although by definition, in the still portrait, he is not talking); and finally we hear the voice attached to the silent face as coming to us from the place in the background. ITN add to the complexities of this by having their man in the portrait holding a telephone. This clearly signifies how the sound is reaching us – but, often, as in Figure 7.30, the correspondent/reporter has been caught by the photographer listening, not talking. Thus we decode a picture of a man listening in terms of his voice being listened to. Could it be that ITN do not want portrait stills of their staff caught in the act of speech?

This image consists entirely of various indexical elements, the montage of which symbolically signifies reporters/correspondents talking to us from the site of the event they are talking about. It is used to expedite reports into the bulletin in the case of domestic stories or, more generally, to obtain foreign reports in the cheapest way possible. Needless to say, there are almost no iconic images of any kind in these reports – the two photographs of Kissinger and the *Mayaguez* at Singapore being the exceptions.

The correspondent, paradoxically, when he is most out in the world appears in the bulletins most symbolically.

Figure 7.29 Radio circuit caption

Figure 7.30 Listener as talker

GOOD NIGHT

We have discussed in this chapter the basics of the bulletins – the opening and closing titles, the studio settings and the appearances of news personnel in those settings.

Not only do news personnel dominate the bulletins in terms of overall durations but also they appear uninterruptedly at great length (given average shot durations), and are accorded the maximum status of supercaptions and hand-overs.

Such a dominance must obviously raise questions as to the possibilities of editorialising. The very length at which correspondents appear means that their interpretive role can be allowed to flourish. It also means that reports in the economic and parliamentary areas, which themselves dominate the bulletins, are overwhelmingly illustrated by the talking heads of these correspondents. For television news, the journalist appears to remain as important as he or she is for print journalism. All the visual apparatus available for reporting the world without the overt mediation of the journalist has in the twenty-plus years of broadcast journalism hardly affected the journalist's centrality in the news presentation process. The close analysis laid out above simply documents the extent to which the traditional role of correspondents has been taken over by television; and how the use of correspondents is a major factor in avoiding the visual imperative – in allowing the bulletins to report on intangibles for at least the same duration as they use to report on filmic events.

NOTES

1 *Television News*, BFI Television Monograph 5, London, 1976, p. 36.
2 *Ibid.*, p. 36.
3 Although the use of Alastair Burnett and the arrival of Anna Ford might indicate that, at least on ITN, this might be changing.
4 *Report of the Committee on the Future of Broadcasting* (Annan Committee), Cmnd 6753, London: HMSO, 1977, p. 282.
5 Except possibly on Tuesday. The Archive tape is damaged.
6 See below, p. 261.
7 *New Yorker*, 21 February 1977, p. 70.
8 Christine Eade, a member of the BBC's political staff, was the only woman in this group, but she does not appear in the sample.
9 These figures do not include further correspondent and reporter inputs. These can include voice-over film or tape, to camera appearances on film or tape or live from an OB. The one exception to this is the shot of Brunson on film listed in Table 7.2.
10 Footage of marines in Okinawa and Utapao had been used on earlier bulletins. The remark is intended without prejudice to any other footage that might have been available but relates only to what was shown on British television.

Chapter 8

Case studies*

I Access to television

Access to the news is given mainly to the powerful. The view of social and political life that informs news production limits who is able to appear to put his or her case. It is a view of the world from the top downwards, in which those at the top do most of the talking. Restriction of access to a small minority of powerful people cannot be explained, in terms of 'shortage of time', mistakes by individual journalists, or difficulties of putting together a live news programme. These arguments may apply to an individual bulletin – but our evidence underlines that restriction of access occurs regularly over hundreds of hours of news bulletins. Over such a long period, arguments such as the shortage of time simply will not hold. They cannot explain the consistently one-sided nature of access.

'IT'S A LOT OF RUBBISH'

The case of the Glasgow dustcart strike pinpoints how television's view of the industrial world affects who is allowed to appear on the news, as well as the kinds of questions asked and the legitimacy and status given to different views.

The news established that the story of the Glasgow dustcart drivers was about the piling up of uncollected rubbish, the eventual official declaration of a health hazard, and the calling in of troops to break the strike and clear the rotting refuse. But the most remarkable feature of this coverage was that the workers who had apparently caused all this never appeared on the screen to explain their actions. The coverage began with reports of the decision of the dustcart drivers to go on strike. Yet the dominant television theme was never

---

*Sources: GUMG, *Really Bad News*, London, Writers & Readers, 1982, pp. 113–26; GUMG *More Bad News*, London, Routledge & Kegan Paul, 1980, pp. 69–96; GUMG, *War and Peace News*, Milton Keynes, Open University Press, 1985, pp. 196–214, 247–61.

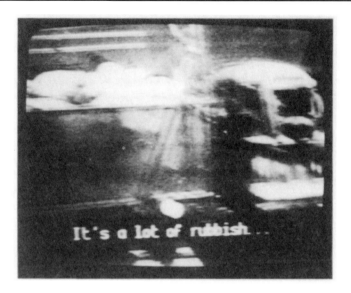

Figure 8.1 BBC2, 22.15, 23 March 1975

the dispute between the drivers and their employers (Glasgow Corporation), but rather its effects. From the very first day the frame was set that would exclude the strikers themselves and their case. That day (Saturday, January 11 1975) the BBC early evening bulletin carried a film report from Glasgow showing men leaving a meeting, over which it was stated that the decision to strike had been taken. We were then shown *library film* of piles of uncollected rubbish from a strike the previous year as the report continued: 'It was only last October when rubbish piled up in the city streets for four weeks since Glasgow's dustmen staged their last strike for higher wages' (BBC1, 17.45, 11 January 1975). Other BBC bulletins that day showed similar cuts of old footage without including the new film of the break-up of the strike meeting. In each case the newscaster's message was equally sombre: 'The decision to stop work from Monday was bringing fears of a repeat of the situation last October when rubbish piled up in the streets causing a health hazard' (BBC2, 22.30, 11 January 1975). This editorial speculation and forecasting was not restricted to the BBC. ITN also used old film on January 11 of the previous autumn's rubbish. The following day it reported: 'The strike means that Glasgow faces another pile-up of rubbish on the pavements as happened for four weeks last autumn' (ITN, 22.00, 12 January 1975). Overall, a total of six national bulletins that day used library film to highlight the 'effects' of a dispute that had not yet begun.

The use of old film in this manner raises some important questions. Is news a depiction of reality at a point in time or is it an attempt to persuade the viewer that the events selected have definite implications? In a sense these aspects cannot be separated. News is never 'the facts' pure and simple; it necessarily involves a selection, an analysis and, crucially, an evaluation of reality. This is the work journalists do when they 'present the news' to their audience. Yet critics such as John Birt and Peter Jay have suggested that a 'bias against understanding' exists in television news partly because of the lack of background information in normal bulletin presentation. In answer to this, the newsroom editors may have congratulated themselves on the speed with which they contextualised the Glasgow strike story by linking it to its previous history. In this instance it is clear that the television news did provide background information and understanding. However, such information was selected from within a partial viewpoint. The manner of the linking serves to provide a very clear understanding – one might say a 'biased understanding' – of the story, as being predominantly about another health hazard. The fact that the old film carried a superimposed caption stating the date of the events which it portrayed entirely misses the point. We are not arguing that the journalists attempted to mislead viewers into believing that the rubbish actually existed then, in January. The point is that such presentation could only lead to the conclusion that the main issue of the current dispute was nothing more than a danger to health caused by workers.

Figure 8.2 ITN, 22.00, 17 March 1975

It was not until seven weeks later that Glasgow Corporation announced that a health hazard existed. By this time there were real rubbish piles to film. Shots of black plastic bags lining the streets and piled on open dumps became the familiar visual image which symbolised the running story. What began as a dispute between the dustcart drivers and their employers became quite simply, 'The Glasgow rubbish strike' (BBC1, 17.45, 14 March 1975), 'The Glasgow rubbish' (BBC1, 17.15, 15 Marsh 1975), and headlined on *News at Ten* as 'And now rubbish' (ITN, 22.00, 21 March 1975).

REPORTING THE FACTS

If the news was so concerned to provide a context and background to the dispute, why could more pertinent facts not have been given? We have shown that the kinds of information and explanation that appear in the news essentially flow from the dominant view. Alternative facts and explanations, where they emerge at all, appear in fragmentary and sometimes contradictory form. This is no less true in the reporting of this dispute. What then was this strike really about?

The Glasgow Corporation drivers went on strike in the autumn of 1974 in pursuit of pay parity with other Heavy Goods Vehicle drivers. They were claiming an extra payment to bring them in line with the minimum wage earned by drivers in other industries. After four weeks the issue was still unsettled but the drivers returned to work. This was on the understanding that if national negotiations failed, then a local agreement would be discussed. These facts are straightforward and were available to anyone interested. The present authors when speaking to the strikers during the 1975 dispute were readily shown a photocopy of a letter from the Corporation to the drivers' representatives giving just such a promise of local negotiations. This matter was covered on the regional news programmes on March 11. In *Scotland Today* and *Reporting Scotland* a spokesman read a statement giving the reasons for the strike action:

The committee are still firmly of the opinion that they have a genuine grievance. They believe that the Corporation clearly promised to discuss the issue of a suitable payment at local level if national negotiations failed to provide an acceptable solution. The basic wage of HGV drivers with Glasgow Corporation is £32.50, the earnings referred to in last night's programme included bonus and at least 10 hours' overtime payment. And there are Corporation drivers who only receive minimal bonuses. The lowest rate for a HGV driver in road haulage is £37.00. The committee are conscious of the effect of the strike on the public and would hope that the discussions they are now engaged in can provide the possibility of rapidly clearing the mountains of refuse now lying around the city.

(*Reporting Scotland*, 11 March 1975)

The closest the national television news came to the reason for the strike was on one bulletin on BBC. Speaking over film of parked dustcarts in a shed, it was reported that: 'The men say their basic pay is £2.30 less than road haulage drivers and accuse the Corporation of going back on a promise to negotiate a local agreement' (BBC1, 21.00, 13 January 1975). This is not specialised or privileged knowledge – the journalists had the facts. Yet information of this kind was not generally given and was never used to organise or give coherence to reports.

Both channels emphasised that this was the second dispute in three months, without saying why this should be so. The effect was to give a picture of workers producing random chaos. This was mentioned in 13 of the first 14 bulletin reports following the strike decision and was still being mentioned in ITN reports about a fortnight later. Information concerning the earlier dispute was processed in terms of the dominant view. It merely strengthened the suggestion that the 'health hazard' was on the cards again. *News at Ten* on the second day of coverage repeated the showing of last October's rubbish; *Nine O'Clock News* was still showing library film on the third day.

The chosen angle governed the flow of news information. Whilst reporting 'health hazards' and rubbish where they did not yet exist, the current dispute that was supposed to have caused them was not itself always mentioned. The dispute and its causes almost disappeared from view. After several weeks of the strike the City Authorities declared that a health hazard existed and troops were brought in on 16 March. That day their expected arrival was reported on the BBC lunchtime bulletin but the strike itself did not warrant a mention. The

Figure 8.3 BBC2, 22.15, 23 March 1975

BBC lunchtime news the following day reported the arrival of the troops yet made no mention of the dispute except by reference to 'the dustmen who aren't involved in the strike'. Similarly, on March 20 ITN's *News at Ten* and BBC's early evening bulletins both chose to focus on the difficult and unpleasant task facing the troops without mentioning the strike. From this point on, the progress of the army in clearing the rubbish became a major preoccupation of news coverage. Much use was made of film of heavy machinery, protective clothing, the good humour of the troops facing picket lines and chasing rats with sticks. Such exciting visual material was good news for television. Soldiers even held up rats by their tails for the cameras. These events fitted easily into the health hazard angle.

When the dispute was included in reports, however, it was with information that was confused and contradictory. The causes and the men involved were very much in the background. Who exactly was on strike and how many were involved varied bewilderingly. For example, on March 4 the BBC reported rubbish accumulated during 'the strike by dustmen' (not by dustcart drivers). ITN suffered similarly revealing confusion: 'In Glasgow where the dustmen's strike, or rather the strike by dustcart drivers ...' (ITN, 13.00, 10 March 1975). Meanwhile the news had reported the fact, and showed film to prove it, that the men who picked up the bins were not in dispute and were working alongside the soldiers. The account of who was on strike and the numbers involved varied from bulletin to bulletin. Thus the news spoke of '350 dustcart drivers', '550 men', '550 dustmen' and '500 dustcart drivers'.

Other aspects of the dispute such as the facts of the men's claim were similarly affected by this coverage, either not appearing at all or being misreported. Of a total of 40 bulletins on the BBC, only 4 mentioned a parity claim. An additional 7 bulletins referred to an 'interim offer' or an explanation of the dispute such as 'over pay'. Of 19 reports on BBC2, only 2 mentioned a parity claim. Three others reported the issue as 'over pay' and one as over a 'regrading structure'. Of a total of 43 ITN bulletins, only 8 carried reports of a parity issue and a further 11 described the cause of the dispute as 'over pay', etc. The narrow and restricted framework provided by the dominant view that produces such 'bad news' thus often leads quite simply to bad reporting.

A HIERARCHY OF ACCESS

By news journalism's own standards, perhaps the most glaring omission was that during the whole of the dispute not one of the strikers was interviewed on the national television news. In all, 10 people were interviewed, some of them appearing several times. The three news services together produced 20 national bulletins which included interviews with the following:

Figure 8.4 BBC2, 22.15, 23 March 1975

- a professor of community medicine (4 appearances)
- a fire brigade officer (1 appearance)
- the Lord Provost of Glasgow (2 appearances)
- the Secretary of State for Scotland (4 appearances)
- a Glasgow Labour MP (1 appearance)
- a Labour councillor (1 appearance)
- a lieutenant colonel (2 appearances)
- a second lieutenant (1 appearance)
- 2 TGWU officials, Alex Kitson (4 appearances) and
- George McGredie (1 appearance)

This selection of interviews indicates whose views were deemed to be important. These are the legitimate and authoritative voices in terms of the dominant view. Once inserted into the logic and flow of coverage, they constitute what amounts to an 'official view'.

The chosen definition of the news story provides the structure for the routine coverage and determines who will appear. It also frames the questions that are seen as important: 'Is there a health hazard?', 'How serious is it?', 'When is the Corporation going to act?', 'When are the troops being sent in?', 'How are they coping with the unpleasant task?' Given these priorities, there is a hierarchy of access which logically excludes unofficial strikers.

As this was an unofficial dispute the interviews with the two union officials in no way represent a balanced coverage of 'both sides' of the issue. Only on the day the strike ended in defeat were the drivers allowed to comment on their lost cause. ITN reported that the 350 men were back at work 'after their abortive 13-week strike' and at last interviewed one of the drivers. The report claimed that the drivers would 'happily go through it all again'.

> TOM DOCHERTY: I would go on strike for the same cause again because we're qualified drivers ... We're experienced and we're professionals ... we are entitled to this money...
>
> REPORTER: But going on strike doesn't appear to have achieved anything because the army can come in and do your work?
>
> DOCHERTY: Certainly, because we didn't have union backing this time.
>
> REPORTER: So why go on strike again?
>
> DOCHERTY: We'll go on strike on principle and we're still entitled to this money. And there's nobody saying we won't go on strike, we definitely will, if it comes to the cause again, and it's a justful cause, we must go on strike for it again.
>
> (ITN, 22.00, 14 April 1975)

The television news, however, did not seem to think it was a cause worth reporting.

This is not an isolated or unrepresentative instance. The routine restriction of access if further evidenced in our study of economic coverage. Throughout the period ITN's *News at Ten* and BBC's *Nine O'Clock News* kept the range of views and opinions within a very narrow section of the social and political spectrum. In news items dealing with the Social Contract and its relationship to wages, prices and the economy, there were twenty-three different people interviewed, these were:

- the Prime Minister
- three government ministers
- the President and the General Secretary of the CBI
- the heads of two nationalised industries
- two MPs
- the General Secretary of the TUC
- eleven leaders from national trade unions.

Among all these people there was only one 'ordinary' member of the public: a senior consultant surgeon at Leyton Hospital, Crewe. By contrast no miner, railway worker, power engineer, electrician, doctor, postal worker, shop assistant or nurse was offered the opportunity to give their views about the workings of the social contract.

Apart from being interviewed or filmed whilst addressing a meeting, there are other ways of being featured on television news. Without appearing in person, one may be quoted directly, from a speech, or from answers to journalists' questions. Such 'reported statements' are less powerful or prestigious than an appearance on the screen but nevertheless indicate that serious attention is being given. An analysis of these also shows a restricted access to news. Such statements come mainly from a narrow group. In this period, 35 per cent of all reported statements on both BBC and ITN came from those interviewed in other bulletins. Within this select group the Chancellor of the Exchequer provided approximately 40 per cent of the statements.

Taking all reported statements, including those from people not interviewed elsewhere, the Chancellor's share was still 14 per cent on the BBC and 13 per cent on ITN. Reported statements in general were mainly taken from members of the same narrow grouping:

- 12 from 5 government ministers
- 11 from 6 named Labour MPs
- 13 from other Labour parliamentary groups and sources
- 18 from 8 named Conservative MPs
- 7 from other political (parliamentary) parties and groups
- 6 from 5 other named trade-union leaders.
- 16 from other official trade-union bodies and executives
- 21 from government bodies and nationalised industry managements
- 5 from employers' groups, and 6 from the CBI
- 3 statements from the AA, a firm of stockbrokers and 'financial observers'
- 3 statements attributed to 'left-wing miners', 'moderate miners' and 'shopkeepers'.

SHORTAGE OF TIME?

It is often argued by journalists that they do not have the time and space to include all the views and information that surround a news story. While there are finite limits on what can be included, the selection process is consistently one-sided. What is involved here is not something that can be explained by errors, lapses of judgement or shortage of time. The Glasgow dispute was featured widely and prominently over a long period. It involved the professional judgement of several reporters and numerous editors in the newsrooms of all three channels. Rather the coverage consistently focuses on one view, while routinely downgrading, or excluding others.

Television news does not merely restrict access, it also organises the flow of coverage around its preferred views. We have shown how statements from Healey as Chancellor, calling for wage restraint, were accompanied by information and explanation that render such a view 'coherent' and 'reasonable'. Other alternative viewpoints are often excluded, but even when they are aired on television news, they appear as disembodied fragments. The effect of such coverage is to accord status to some views as 'rational' and 'legitimate', while others appear as 'irrational', 'disruptive' and 'against the national interest'.

ACCESS TO POLITICAL DEBATE

In the coverage of the 1979 Labour conference (limited to the BBC since ITN was on strike), the group that was selected to speak on the news was very narrow in its composition. There were 100 occasions when people were interviewed or were shown speaking. Of these, 86 were either the Leader of the Opposition, Members of Parliament, or trade-union leaders. In a conference which was explicitly questioning the relation between these groups and the party's grass roots, the news endorsed the view that it is the hierarchy who has a special right to be heard. All through this period and later in the leadership election, a major debate was being conducted in the party branches and in the unions, concerning their future role in the party. The main issues were as follows. Should the leadership and MPs be accountable to party members? What was to be the relationship between conference decisions and the policy of the parliamentary Labour Party and any future Labour government; and should the election of the party leader be the exclusive right of MPs?

The parliamentary Labour Party was itself divided on such issues, and it is reasonable to expect the media to seek out the opinions of MPs involved in this debate. It is quite clear, however, even by the media's own account, that the debate taking place outside parliament in the constituencies was central to the leadership issue. Thus a journalist on BBC2 noted:

> For many in the Labour movement, next week's election, confined as it is to the parliamentary party, is just a stop-gap measure to pick a leader until new arrangements can be introduced to extend the vote to an electoral college representing the whole party. So already, therefore, there is an intense debate going on in the constituencies, not just about who should be selected but who should do the selecting and what sort of party he should lead.
>
> (BBC2, *Newsnight*, 30 October 1980)

Clearly there is a wide diversity of opinions in the constituency parties on the issues indicated by *Newsnight*. The coverage of the leadership issue took place against a backcloth of allegations concerning 'left-wing dominated constituencies'. But rank-and-file members of the Labour Party were rarely allowed to emerge from 'smoke filled rooms' into the clear light of the television studio – certainly not in the case of ITN and BBC1. The familiar cast of interviewees included Healey, Foot, Silkin, Shore, Owen and Shirley Williams. We have already shown that even with this limited range of interviewees, questions put to them featured the alleged 'threats' and 'intimidation' said to be occurring in the constituency parties. Yet in the two main news services only *one* individual is interviewed as a member of a constituency party. Enter stage left – the Barnsley constituency party chairman. Having established that the Barnsley party attempted to order their

Figure 8.5 BBC2, *Newsnight*, 30 October 1980

MP to vote for Foot, the only question put to the chairman was: 'Did Mr Mason give you any indication at all which way he is prepared to vote?' This pattern of neglect was paralleled in BBC1's and ITN's selection of reported statements. A debate which is about the relationship between the grass roots of the party and MPs is thus channelled almost exclusively through the opinions of the latter.

Those interviewed and the number of appearances on BBC1 and ITN news in our sample were as follows:

Table 8.1 TV interview frequency of key political figures

Interviewee	BBC1	ITN
M. Foot, MP	5	12
P. Shore, MP	5	3
J. Silkin, MP	3	4
D. Healey, MP	8	6
J. Lestor (NEC)	1	–
S. Williams (NEC)	1	–
D. Owen, MP	1	1
N. Kinnock, MP	1	–
R. Mason, MP	1	–
Barnsley constituency party (Chairman)	1	–
T. Benn, MP	–	1
Unidentified speaker	–	1

This hierarchy of access was routinely followed on BBC2 with two notable exceptions. In the aftermath of Foot's election, the reactions of constituency members on the Left and Right of the party were sought. On October 30, *Newsnight* went to the constituency meeting in Islington and filmed, without comment, a discussion on the leadership. It showed an intense debate on the nature of the party, and questions were raised from Right and Left which were absent from the rest of the news. Ordinary party members felt quite able to indicate, for example, that they had never heard of John Silkin and could not see why he was standing. What struck us most about this particular coverage was simply that it was so rude and so honest. People on both sides said things about the candidates, about politicians in general and about our history which 'official' spokesmen and 'trained' journalists would simply not choose to say. The normal pattern of access is a product of the narrow understanding of social and political life around which television news is organised. It is quite 'natural' in this context for the news to exclude the voices of the powerless in our society.

II Pointing the finger: evaluations and judgements

Broadcasters do not represent adequately the industrial and commercial life of the country.

(Report of the Committee on the Future of Broadcasting)[1]

A further dimension to the organisation of the industrial and economic coverage remains. This was the systematic evaluation of individuals and organisations such as trade unions from within the partial and limited viewpoint that the television news had established. This process of evaluation follows from what we have said about the media's control of explanation. It may be implicit only because whether people's actions appear rational or reasonable will depend very much upon how the world in which the actions are occurring is portrayed and understood. If wage increases are thought to be the source of economic problems then the demands for these may be seen as irrational. The control which the media exercise over the flow of information and explanation grants them an enormous power over how individual and group action is evaluated and judged. In the following example from ITN in February 1975 the reported statements of two trade unionists were juxtaposed. The first is Arthur Scargill, who is reported as having spoken at a rally in London:

It was addressed by the Yorkshire miners' leader, Mr Arthur Scargill, who said that the Social Contract had been smashed by the latest miners' pay settlement, and, he added, my advice to the trade unions is to press through the breach. But another union leader, Lord Allen, speaking at another conference in London, said that the worst thing the unions could do was to endanger the Social Contract by taking a 'go it alone' attitude on pay claims.

(ITN, 18.05, 23 February 1975)

The apparent neutrality of the news is sustained by the formal 'balance' of the two speakers, which is a familiar feature of news coverage. But such an apparent balance appears within an already established context of social and economic explanations. This taken-for-granted background context influences how each statement is 'heard' and 'understood' and how the alternatives proposed by each speaker are to be evaluated.

The language used in the description and assessment of pay claims was often quite explicitly critical. The following example is taken from an interview between a trade unionist and an ITN newscaster. Here, the newscaster argues consistently from within the economic assumptions of the television news. In two of his questions, he equates 'rational' and 'reasonable' behaviour quite explicitly with the acceptance of wage restraint. The first of these follows the introduction to the item:

NEWSCASTER: Bank employees, who've just had a 30 per cent pay rise, have put in a claim for 20 per cent more. Their leader, Mr Leif Mills, in fact said, 'we broke the contract last year and we intend to break it again'. Of course it's possible – reasonable – for him to say that because the bank employees' union is not in the TUC, whose Social Contract this is meant to be. However, I now say, turning to the Assistant Secretary of the National Union of Bank Employees, Mr David Dines, who's in the studio with me now, you can opt out of your responsibilities to the TUC all right, but can you really opt out of your responsibilities to the national economy as a whole?

(ITN, 13.00, 24 February 1975)

Later in a follow-up question, the theme is made even more explicit:

INTERVIEWEE: Our job as a trade union is to maintain the purchasing power of our members' salaries and that's all we're trying to do with the pay claim we've now formulated.

NEWSCASTER: But as reasonable men and responsible citizens can you say that's all you are trying to do and all you are interested in when you hear warnings from the Chancellor to the effect that increases of this sort are going to wreck the national economy?

(ITN, 13.00, 24 February 1975)

Throughout this period the news consistently spoke on behalf of the values and beliefs which followed from its analysis of the nature of the economic crisis. It appealed to a restricted system of values about the common good and the benefit of everyone in the society. It then established by its limited account of the workings of the economy what people ought to do to produce this common good. This view of how society works and of what ought to be done was assumed to characterise the beliefs of a vast majority, except, of course, those who were creating problems, such as the coalminers. Thus in the following description from ITN of the miners' pay negotiations of February 1975, we were told that there were 'fears' about what the miners would do. The 'fears' at this point were presented as general and were not related to any specific group:

> It is almost certain that they [the miners' leaders] will then formally tell the Coal Board that the offer is unacceptable – probably it will be on Tuesday afternoon. The Board's offer was within the framework of the Social Contract, but there are now fears that the miners' pay target will force a breach in the Social Contract.
>
> (ITN, 22.00, 6 February 1975)

The miners as an industrial group have, of course, in recent years attracted a huge amount of media coverage. In the period of our study, they were treated by the television news as perhaps the most significant trade union in the success or failure of the Social Contract. It is therefore important to assess how their pay negotiations and eventual settlement were covered by the newsrooms. A detailed account of this now follows.

THE MINERS' PAY NEGOTIATIONS AND THE SOCIAL CONTRACT

The miners' pay deal in February 1975 was followed closely by both BBC and ITN, mainly from 5 to 16 February. The sequence in its simplest outline was is shown in Table 8.2. The whole of this sequence is framed against the relevance or supposed relevance to the Social Contract of the miners' pay claim and how this was perceived by various participants or media commentators.

5 February 1975

In the two BBC1 bulletins where the subject was raised on 5 February, there was a brief newscaster introduction followed by an extended comment from Ian Ross, the industrial correspondent. In the first newscast (17 April 1975) the point was made by the newscaster and the correspondent that the offer was within the terms of the Social Contract but that dissatisfaction with the offer was to be expected.

> NEWSCASTER: Miners' leaders got details today of the Coal Board's full pay offer. The proposals, which conform with the terms of the Social

Table 8.2 The miners' pay deal, 1975

Date	BBC1	BBC2	ITN
5 Feb.	NUM receive NCB offer		
6 Feb.	NUM reject NCB offer		NUM reject NCB offer
9 Feb.		*News Review* résumé	
10 Feb.	Threats of industrial action from Yorkshire and Scotland		
11 Feb.	NCB increase offer		NCB increase offer Inter-union conflict
12 Feb.	NUM pay and the railwaymen		NUM reject new offer
13 Feb.	NUM accept latest offer		NUM and railwaymen CBI views Miners accept latest offer
14 Feb.	Reactions to pay deal: Foot and railwaymen		
16 Feb.		*News Review* résumé	

Contract, seem certain to cause a row among the union's left wing when its full negotiating committee meets tomorrow morning. Here is our industrial correspondent, Ian Ross.

IAN ROSS: The Board is offering increases of between £7 and £10 on basic rates, about 22 per cent, which is rather more than prices have risen in the past year. But, as the Social Contract stipulates, the offer does take account of what the miners have been getting under threshold cost-of-living payments and that is £4.40 per week per man.

The correspondent then gave some information, saying that the effect of the deal would be to raise the basic wage of face workers from £45 to £55; of other underground workers from £36 to £44; and of surface workers from £32 to £39. He also indicated that this had the effect of widening differentials between face workers and surface workers and that there was also a new production bonus related to quarterly output figures. He concluded:

Some of the union's negotiators won't regard this offer as a satisfactory answer to a pay claim which demanded substantial pay increases, and there is bound to be a move to reject it, but the union is still likely to go along and see the Coal Board as arranged tomorrow afternoon.

So, here was an offer within the terms of the Social Contract and even a little generous, since the 22 per cent was 'rather more than prices have risen in the past year', although this was in fact a very dubious conclusion. It could have been argued that the 22 per cent, had it been accepted, would have represented a cut in real income. The *Nine O'Clock News* item contained similar information and comment to that of the early bulletin, with a slightly different gloss. The 22 per cent was now in the newscaster's introduction: 'Miners' leaders got details today of the Coal Board's full pay offer. The offer will mean increases of between £7 and £10 on basic rates, or about 22 per cent.' The correspondent then adjusted his earlier piece at the beginning and the end. He began:

> The wages side of the Social Contract is all about making sure that wages rise no more than prices and the Coal Board, faithful to the government's dictate, has offered 22 per cent, which, in fact, is rather more than retail prices have risen in the past year.

Here, then, was the Coal Board keeping to the wages side of the Social Contract. What other side was there to the Social Contract? The bulletin was silent on the matter, but referred to union negotiators who would not see this as a substantial increase, adding, 'especially those who not long ago were talking about only being satisfied with an extra £30 per week: the same people who have no time for the Social Contract'. The scene was set whereby the rejection of this award, already presented as slightly generous in Social Contract terms, would be interpreted as a threat to the Contract by those who wanted to breach it anyway.

6 February 1975

On this day the NUM rejected the NCB's pay offer and this was reported on BBC1, BBC2 and ITN. With the exception of BBC's *Nine O'Clock News*, the rejection of the offer referred to the 22 per cent in the opening sentence:

> Miners' leaders have rejected the Coal Board's pay offer which would give them a 22 per cent increase in basic rates.
>
> (BBC1, 17.45, 6 February 1975)

> Miners' leaders have rejected a 22 per cent pay increase offered by the Coal Board: instead they want an increase of around 40 per cent on basic rates.
>
> (BBC2, 23.05, 6 February 1975)

> Leaders of the miners' union have recommended that a 22 per cent pay package offer should be turned down.
>
> (ITN, 17.50, 6 February 1975)

> The miners' leaders have unanimously decided to recommend that their members should reject a 22 per cent pay offer made by the Coal Board.
>
> (ITN, 22.00, 6 February 1975)

In each case this is followed by the information that the union had called off its arranged meeting with the NCB.

The BBC's treatment of the NUM's attitude on the preceding day had been to distinguish between the left wing of the NUM and the rest of the negotiating committee and to make specific reference to those 'who have no time for the Social Contract'. In the light of the unanimous rejection of the pay offer by the negotiating committee, some adjustment was called for. On BBC1, 17.45, the industrial correspondent commented as follows:

> Even moderates among the miners' leaders are unhappy about the offer and the Left is positively contemptuous. The militant Mr Arthur Scargill, the Yorkshire miners' leader, likened the offer to a 'bag of crisps'. 'We should serve notice of industrial action on the Coal Board right now,' he said. Well, they won't, because the offer is still negotiable. The Board is prepared to look again at the question of pay differentials, widening the gap between the surface worker and the man right down at the coal face, who could end up getting more than the basic £55 per week that is on offer now. That would be permissible under a clause in the Social Contract which refers to reforming outdated pay structures. But what is really at issue here is the miners' attitude to the Social Contract. Although the union was the first to speak in its support at the Trades Union Congress last September, to many of its leaders it no longer matters and they are now looking for the kind of pay rises which could in no way be reconciled with the Contract.
>
> (BBC1, 17.45, 6 February 1975)

A distinction was made here between moderates and militants on the NUM. The latter are 'left-wing'. To juxtapose 'moderates' and 'militants' in this way in the context of an analysis of the economy which was organised around 'wage inflation' and the necessity of wage restraint carried with it an implicit judgement. The force of this stereotyping came through with the opening phrase: 'Even moderates ... are unhappy'. Second, Ross, in saying that the NCB was still negotiating and was still looking at pay differentials, recognised that this was permissible under a clause in the Social Contract which relates to the reform of outdated pay structures. This was, however, immediately followed by a *but*. The correspondent was concerned to tell us 'what is really at issue'. He then compared the attitude of the union, which was 'the very first to speak' in support of the Social Contract at the September TUC Congress, with the assertion 'and they are now looking for the kind of pay rises which could in no way be reconciled with the Contract'. Given the subtleties of the Social Contract taken as a whole and given that negotiations were still in progress at the time of the assertion, this was an imputation that prejudged the outcome. This may be a point of view, but it was scarcely a 'fact' which the correspondent had conclusively demonstrated was the case.

The BBC's *Nine O'Clock News* was organised on similar lines. The contrast between the Board's 'offer' and the miners' 'demands' was developed in two consecutive sentences:

> The Board's offer was for a 22 per cent pay increase on basic rates; that is, between £7 and £10 a week more excluding a production bonus, an improved sick pay scheme and free working clothes. The miners are demanding between 37.5 per cent and 41 per cent increases on their basic rates and improvements in the bonus for productivity.
>
> (BBC1, 21.00, 6 February 1975)

The picture now drawn was of a generous offer spurned as 'a bag of crisps'. The continuing reference to Mr Scargill was surprising, for he was not the spokesman for the NUM negotiating committee. Ian Ross in his comments supplied us with an answer: 'Mr Scargill and the Left . . . have highlighted the real issue here, and that is the credibility of the Social Contract, which may stand or fall according to what the miners settle for.' He went on to say: 'Certainly it is impossible to reconcile a claim for increases of 40 per cent with even the very flexible terms of the Social Contract.' This general point was reiterated when Ross acknowledged again that reforming an outdated pay structure was compatible with the Social Contract and that Mr Foot might have recognised a special case for pay rises but not to the tune of 40 per cent. The miners' pay claim was, says Ross, 'the acid test of the Contract'.

The BBC2 *News Extra* report followed closely the *Nine O'Clock News*. In addition to concluding that this was the acid test of the contract, Ross's opening comment assured us that another miners' strike was not likely, despite left-wing pressure:

> No, it is a battle between the miners and the Social Contract, with the Coal Board and the government waiting in the wings. What the miners finally accept as a pay settlement will, to a very large extent, make or break the Social Contract.
>
> (BBC2, 23.05, 6 February 1975)

If we turn now to ITN's coverage on the same day there was a reference to the 22 per cent and the newscaster said on the early evening bulletin that the miner's pay target would 'impose a serious threat to the government's Social Contract' and in *News at Ten*, that 'there are now fears that the miners' pay target will form a breach in the Contract'. Michael Green, the industrial correspondent, agreed with the BBC's correspondent when he began by saying: 'There is no doubt that the miners' pay negotiations can make or break the Social Contract as it stands.' However, there were some noticeable differences in tone and content. For example, apart from the newscaster's mention of a '22 per cent pay package offer', there was only one further reference to the 22 per cent by Green on the 17.50 bulletin and none at 22.00. There was no reference to the miners' 'demands' for 37.5–40 per cent increases. In fact, it was easy to set the NCB's offer against the miners' claim with the information we were given (see Table 8.3). Green also calculated that

Table 8.3 The miners' claim and the NCB offer (in £)

	NC offer basic weekly rate	Increase on present rate	NUM target basic weekly rate	Increase on present rate
Face workers	55	10	63	18
Other underground workers	44	8	50	14
Surface workers	39	7	44	12

the difference in the total wage bill between these two positions was £70 million for the NCB and a further £80 million for the NUM. The fact that the negotiations had to do with offers and counter-claims and that first offers and replies are the beginning of the bargaining process was clearly presented by Green:

> The negotiating committee which met this morning turned down the Coal Board's offer without so much as a vote, and, to be frank, that won't surprise the employers a bit. They have been criticised in the past for offering too much too soon, and this time they were determined to keep something in reserve.
>
> (ITN, 22.00, 6 February 1975)

Another significant difference in presentation was this. While the BBC reported the language of Mr Scargill in his attitude to the offer – 'a bag of crisps' and 'disgusting' – no reason for this was advanced other than the implication that he was opposed to the Social Contract. But since the rejection by the NUM was unanimous, surely there was more to be said? Green made a crucial point which the BBC report ignores:

> Part of the dissatisfaction with the current offer is that it includes the consolidation of threshold payments of £4.40 which all the miners already get. So in new money terms the men would only get between £2.60 and £5.60 more on basic rates.
>
> (ITN, 22.00, 6 February 1975)

9 February 1975

The Scargill words 'disgusting' and 'a bag of crisps' were given a further airing on BBC2's Sunday *News Review*. In fact, the interview with the Chancellor of the Exchequer, Denis Healey, was structured around them:

NEWSCASTER: A new pay offer from the Coal Board to the miners this week: 22 per cent extra, which means a weekly increase of £7 and £10. It was rejected and described by Arthur Scargill, leader of the Yorkshire miners, as 'disgusting' – 'a bag of crisps'.... Are the miners seeking a fight with the government?

HEALEY: I don't think so – I don't think there are many miners and certainly very few people outside mining who would regard £10 a week as a bag of crisps, certainly none of the nurses that I know, or the postmen, or the farm workers who produce our food, would take the view and I think the miners appreciate what the present government has done for them in increasing the social wage, which has gone up, you know, 10 or 12 per cent in the last year after you've taken prices off.

INTERVIEWER: But the miners and other groups of workers are still wanting to settle outside the TUC guidelines. Does this worry you?

HEALEY: I'm very concerned. In recent weeks a quarter of the people who've had settlements have had them outside the guidelines. That's far too many. If we go on like that we shall price the country out of jobs and that could mean mass unemployment.

(BBC2, 18.50, 9 February 1975)

So the reference to the pay offer in the above interview was followed by the phrase: 'It was rejected and described by Arthur Scargill, leader of the Yorkshire miners, as "disgusting" – "a bag of crisps".' Not only was the phrase repeated on several bulletins on BBC, but the drafting of the sentence could convey the impression that it was Arthur Scargill who had rejected the pay offer, whereas the reference should properly be to the miners' political standpoint. It is, however, relevant to comment that Healey's statement is not easy to understand: 'I think the miners appreciate what the present government has done for them in increasing the social wage, which has gone up, you know, 10 or 12 per cent in the last year after you've taken prices off.' It certainly depends on understanding the concept of 'social wage'. Obviously one cannot assume that everyone who watches television news has read the Social Contract.

10 February 1975

This was the day before negotiations were to be resumed between the miners and the NCB, and BBC1 gave further coverage on the theme of calls for industrial action from Yorkshire and Scotland in support of higher wages. The item was once more introduced with another comment from Arthur Scargill, who described the NCB's offer as 'bloody daft'. Scargill then in interview said:

SCARGILL: It appears to me that there are far too many people intent on a collision course with the miners and many people in this industry have been accused of being saboteurs. Well, if there are any saboteurs on this occasion it's certainly not on the National Union of Mineworkers' negotiation table. It must be on the negotiation table of the National Coal Board. And I would ask the question why they're sticking so rigidly to a ridiculous offer of 8 per cent, which after all is a net reduction in real terms on the inflation rate of about 20 per cent.

(BBC1, 17.45, 10 February 1975)

The 8 per cent was a new figure to appear and no discussion or comment flowed from it.

The news had already established what the 'facts' and 'figures' of current wage claims were. The firm link had been made between wage increases, inflation and the economic crisis. To have seriously considered Scargill's new figure of 8 per cent at this juncture in the coverage would have made a severe dent in this dominant framework. In the event, and this is not untypical of such alternative frameworks, it passed without comment. Subsequently, in the same bulletin, the industrial correspondent stressed the dominant frame: 'Scotland and Yorkshire are merely banging the drum without any real hope of attracting much support. The £30 demand from Scotland would mean increases of up to 94 per cent, alongside which Yorkshire's £20 seems almost moderate' (BBC1, 17.45, 10 February 1975). The BBC's correspondent went on to speak of the NUM's 41 per cent claim and the NCB's 22 per cent offer. Having stated that there was a big gap between their two positions, his prediction was that

where the Coal Board might go further tomorrow without bending the Social Contract too much, is a widening differentials to the advantage of the man working at the coal face and improving the terms of the production bonus. Beyond that, and anything approaching the union claim, would be right outside the Social Contract.

This kind of media judgement is not a matter of unadorned factual information. It is a mixture of prediction and opinion which takes its evaluative strength from the systematic trading upon limited frameworks of analysis.

11 February 1975

The report on negotiations between the NUM and the NCB was organised in BBC1's main news around a speech by Chancellor Healey on 'excessive wage increases':

The Chancellor of the Exchequer, Mr Healey, has warned again of excessive wage increases as the miners start negotiating on their claim for up to 43 per cent. Mr Healey said in London tonight that Britain could be bankrupt if the national wage bill were too high this year – but it needn't happen if the workers stuck strictly to the Social Contract. During the day

the Coal Board twice increased their offer to the miners, mainly to the
benefit of those working underground.

(BBC1, 21.00, 11 February 1975)

This report was very clearly organised to link the themes of wage inflation,
as a problem, with the miners' pay negotiations. There was no question of this
being a random juxtaposition in the news, since the two themes were
presented in the form of a 'double sandwich': i.e. references to them followed
alternately in quick succession. The miners' claim was effectively defined as
excessive and was linked with a threat of national bankruptcy should it
succeed.

If one collates the percentages that have now been given an airing on this
claim, it amounts to quite a list: 8 per cent, 22 per cent, 25–30 per cent,
37.5–41 per cent, 43 per cent, 94 per cent. References to 25 per cent and 30
per cent, which also came in the passage quoted above, were somewhat
ambiguous. They presumably related to an increase on the present basic wage.
In his ensuing comments the BBC's correspondent stated that the Coal
Board's offer was 'certainly not the strict interpretation of the Social Contract
that Mr Healey is insisting on'. He organised his commentary on a Healey
versus Scargill basis:

> In his speech tonight Mr Healey took a swipe at the militant Yorkshire
> miners' leader, Arthur Scargill, over his philosophy of damn the Social
> Contract. The contract, said the Chancellor, has two sides. The govern-
> ment's ability to avoid mass unemployment, improve social services and
> the like depended on keeping wage settlements within the spirit not just the
> letter of the Social Contract. Mr Healey, whose Department has kept in
> close touch with the miners' pay talks today, can't be pleased that there is
> likely to be a miners' settlement, without a strike, when that settlement
> looks like being without and not within the spirit of the Social Contract.
>
> (BBC1, 21.00, 11 February 1975)

Our concern here is not with the Healey position, but with the media
presentation. Throughout Mr Scargill was portrayed more and more like a
devil in a morality play, a man who exclaims, 'disgusting', 'ridiculous',
'bloody daft', and 'damn the Social Contract' and who by implication was
bringing the country to the verge of national bankruptcy. The bulletins gave
Mr Scargill's *attitude* to the Social Contract, but never the rationale which
underlay it. His statements were not explained as being linked to an
alternative position on the nature of the economy and inflation, which might
make more sense of them. His appearances had the status of token references
to the 'extremes' of political opinion – in reality they amounted to little more
than downgrading a position by isolating it, and indicating by absence that it
did not fit the economic model assumed as correct by the broadcasters.

ITN's treatment of the negotiations on this day was differently organised.

Table 8.4 NCB offer in relation to miners' current wages and the NUM claim (in £)

Miner categories	Present wages†	NCB's old offer*	NCB's new offer	NUM's claim
Face workers	49.40	55	58.50	63
Other underground workers	40.40	44	46	50
Surface workers	36.40	39	40	44

Notes: *Information in this column was given only in the early evening bulletin.
†This column includes £4.40 threshold payments.

On *First Report* an account was given of the NUM's meeting prior to its negotiation with the NCB. The Yorkshire miners' claim for a £30 increase on the basic rate (including the threshold payments) was 'narrowly rejected'. Michael Green reported: 'There were only 4 votes in it, in fact.' The vote was 15 against, 11 in favour, and 1 abstention. In an exchange of questions with the newscaster Robert Kee, there was a discussion of the significance of the 'militant noises' and of the possibilities of unofficial strike action. Green stated that the hands of Scargill and the Scottish miners are tied by this executive decision. The closeness of the vote did not accord very well with the dismissive comment of BBC's industrial correspondent the day before: 'Scotland and Yorkshire are merely banging the drum without any real hope of attracting much support' (BBC1, 17.45). As with BBC coverage, the terms 'moderate' and 'militant' were used as descriptive categories for groupings within the NUM – the militants being 'left-wingers' and personified in Arthur Scargill.

Both ITN's early evening bulletin and *News at Ten* began with a presentation of the NCB's new pay offer in relation to miners' current wages and the NUM's claim. This was done for the three main groupings noted before and can be clearly itemised (see Table 8.4). There was far less emphasis on percentages in ITN's coverage. An ITN correspondent concentrated on the actual wage figures and only once employed percentages – at the close of his *News at Ten* report: 'The offer, the Coal Board maintains stoutly, is still within the Social Contract, even though it adds between 25 and 30 per cent to basic rates' (ITN, 22.00, 11 February 1975).

12 February 1975

The on-going negotiations continued to be reported on both channels. The main evening bulletins on BBC1 and BBC2 both consisted of a newscaster reporting that the Coal Board had 'again narrowed the gap between what they're prepared to offer and what the Union want'. This was specifically linked to face workers – 'this time a rise of 33 per cent, putting the men in the £3,000 a year bracket' – together with an improved production bonus. There was then a comment from the BBC's correspondent incorporating a brief interview with Joe Gormley, the NUM President. The main negotiating problem was now said to be the pay of surface workers. On both bulletins Ross asked Gormley: 'Do you claim you are still working within the Social Contract?' Gormley replied: 'We always work within the laws of society, within the TUC's figures. We will do that all the time and feel we came out with a good settlement which will still be able to be portrayed as being within the Social Contract.' The industrial correspondent was prepared to contradict this: 'Despite what Mr Gormley says, the offer is already well outside the Social Contract' (BBC1, 21.00, 12 February 1975).

ITN's coverage, while briefer, covered similar ground to the BBC's. Both the newscaster and the industrial correspondent refer to the £3,000 a year offer. On this occasion ITN made more play with percentage. Peter Sissons, said:

> What is being scrutinised with some unease in Whitehall are the percentages: 33 per cent for miners at the coal face, taking them to £60; 28 per cent for other underground workers, making their basic pay £46; and 25 per cent for surface workers – a deal which would give them a basic £40.
>
> (ITN, 22.00, 12 February 1975)

He then pointed out that the remaining negotiating point centred on surface workers and said that this was relevant to pay negotiations in other industries such as electricity supply and the railways. There then followed a question from Giles Smith to Joe Gormley as to whether these percentages were compatible with the Social Contract – to which Gormley's answer was yes. As with the BBC report the industrial correspondent permitted himself some scepticism on this topic. Here, attention was drawn to what was claimed as the scant regard which the miners were paying to the Social Contract and the principle of wage restraint:

> Without doubt the Social Contract has some fairly vague provisions, but for this key economic policy to succeed, as Mr Healey insisted last night, everything depends on keeping wage settlements within the spirit and not just the letter of the TUC guidelines. What the Contract's supporters will find disturbing is that there's little evidence during these negotiations to suggest that it ever figured seriously in the miners' thinking.
>
> (ITN, 22.00, 12 February 1975)

The content and manner in which the news is organised sets the context for the understanding and evaluation of the social world. It may well have been 'true' that some of the miners' leaders did not give much thought to keeping within the Social Contract, but what gave this piece of news its significance was the previously established context from which the evaluation follows:

that the miners *ought* to have been thinking about wage restraint. This context was set by consistent references on the news to the limited body of social and economic explanations which it favoured. The significant absence is any explanation of why they should want to reject the Contract.

13 February 1975

This was the day the miners agreed upon a wage settlement to recommend to their members. Matters had not been agreed by the time of ITN's *First Report* and the Industrial Editor began his piece in an informal style: 'Well, the National Union of Mineworkers are still shaking the gravy train here at the Coal Board. So far this morning nothing really substantial has yet fallen out (ITN, 13.00, 13 February 1975). He went on to predict that the offer to surface workers, who were now defined as the difficult category, would move from £40 to £41. By early evening the settlement was concluded (see Table 8.5).

The figures given in Table 8.5 were the 'hard facts'. There is a difference of £5 million between ITN's and BBC's costing of the offer. Further, the use of percentages is deployed with different degrees of generality. The BBC generally reported increases of up to 35 per cent, whereas ITN related percentages to particular categories of workers. It was also the case that whereas BBC simply announced what the new basic rates would be, ITN said what the old basic rate was.

In both presentations, however, there was an important and significant omission. The settlement could have been portrayed in standard negotiating terms relating the NCB's original offer, the NUM's claim and the final

Table 8.5 TV coverage of miners' settlement package

ITN, 17.50 and 22.00	BBC1, 17.45
1 £185 million offer	1 Face workers basic £61 per week
2 Increase of between 28 and 35 per cent	2 Other underground workers £47
3 New basic rates between £41 and £61	3 Surface workers £41
4 32 per cent to basic wage bill	4 Increase in basic rates up to 35 per cent
5 Coal face workers go from £49.50 including threshold of £4.40 to £61; i.e. 35 per cent increase	
6 Other undergound workers £40.40 to £47; i.e. 30 per cent increase	*BBC2, 22.35*
7 Surface workers £36.40 to £41; i.e. 28 per cent increase	1 Increase up to 30 per cent
8 Productivity deal – extra pay for all once an average weekly target reached	2 Cost of £190 million in a full year
	3 Face workers £61 per week
	4 Other underground workers up to £47
	5 Surface workers up to £41

Table 8.6 The NCB's offer, the NUM's claim and the agreed settlement (in £)

Miner categories	Basic weekly rate NCB's original offer	NUM's claim	Agreed settlement
Face workers	55	63	61
Other underground workers	44	50	47
Surface workers	39	44	41

outcome (see Table 8.6). In the case of other underground workers and surface workers, these were typical 'split-the-difference settlements', familiar to wage bargainers and arbitrators, with the surface workers pegged down somewhat. The shape of the overall settlement did widen the differentials to the advantage of face workers. Despite constant reporting on television news, the character of the settlement was not precisely stated within such an explicit frame of reference.

ITN, 17.50 and 22.00

INDUSTRIAL EDITOR *(Peter Sissons)*: So, is the settlement within the spirit of the Social Contract? Have the miners shown restraint?

GORMLEY: We've shown tremendous restraint I think in the last two and a half days. I think we've been very patient with one another and there has been real restraint in the way we have tried to negotiate.

SISSONS: But what if others, other groups of workers, got between 28 per cent and 35 per cent – the Social Contract would mean nothing?

GORMLEY: Well, I remember what you said at another meeting that nowhere within the Social Contract does it lay down that you can only get this percentage or that percentage. And if as a result of the whole exercise that we have been involved in, it comes up to a

BBC1, 17.45

NEWSCASTER: The agreement would increase basic rates by up to 35 per cent but Joe Gormley, the miners' President, says it's not damaging to the Social Contract. Here's our industrial correspondent, Ian Ross.

ROSS: Well, it must damage the Social Contract and it must put into question what relevance the Social Contract has now to controlling inflation.... The miners' leader, Mr Gormley, when claiming that the deal fell within the spirit of the Social Contract, justified this on the grounds that they had reorganised the pay structure which the Contract allows for.

BBC1, 21.00

ROSS: Both sides deny that throughout the talks they were under any kind of pressure from the TUC or

ITN, 17.50 and 22.00

certain percentage I don't think anybody can then just say – well, that drives a coach and horses though the Social Contract. If you view the Social Contract as we know it correctly, in order to put some of these injustices that were apparent in the – in any industry – which would have to be dealt with whatever the government policy, then I don't think you can be criticised.

SISSONS: Mr Siddell, in these negotiations did you detect any element of restraint by the National Union of Mineworkers?

SIDDELL: Well, I think restraint is a peculiar term to apply to the National Union of Mineworkers, but if one can look at that in the context of a talk about a £30 increase, and indeed when we came to negotiating around the table a minimum claim of £44 on the surface was settled at £41, I think one could detect restraint.

BBC1, 21.00

government ministers to settle at a particular level and both claim that they had been influenced by the terms of the Social Contract, or at least the escape clause in it which makes a special case of a pay deal that reorganises the wage structure and widens differentials. The very flexibility of the Social Contract was their ally. I suggested to the Coal Board's chief negotiator that their original pay offer had been in line with the Social Contract and then they'd thrown the Contract away.

SIDDELL: No, we didn't throw it away. In fact, I've been reciting it right throughout and right up to today.

ROSS: Can you claim then that this agreement falls anywhere within it?

SIDDELL: Well, we've done a restructuring exercise which was particularly vital in my view to this industry because of the events of the past few years, when we've had settlements virtually imposed upon us, and the differentials between grades that really eliminated the incentive for men to work through the surface, underground, right up to the producing category, which is our important place of course. And therefore we have restored that within this agreement. The difficulty has been the minimum surface rate, which is, I suppose, a place where people can

BBC1, 21.00

mostly point the finger against us. We have discussed the Social Contract. As I say, I have read it out many times. I can recite it by heart almost now. In terms of percentages it is quite difficult to reconcile what the strict interpretation is. But having regard to other settlements that have been made in the public sector even, the amounts of increases on the basic rate aren't very far outside the sort of settlements that have been made.

While the negotiators are here given a chance to explain the pay deal, this must be seen in the context of the continuous coverage analysed above, which had emphasised in turn the NCB's concession and a sequence of new offers to the NUM, as well as the size and scale of the eventual offer and an expressed scepticism that the deal was within the Social Contract. The BBC's correspondent was prepared to contradict flatly any assertion that it was within the Contract. His opening question to Mr Siddell contained his own judgement on the matter, which he had continuously reiterated from 5 February. Even his references to the restructuring element in the pay deal he described as 'the escape clause' in the Contract, which was only one way of looking at it. Either such an arrangement was within the framework of the Contract or it was not. It was incorrect to call it an 'escape clause'. By the same token, in his comment 'the very flexibility of the Contract was their ally' the BBC manages to imply that negotiators were acting together to take advantage of a 'flexible' Contract.

While both channels clearly used the Social Contract as an organising device in presenting the miners' pay deal, some differences in tone and content have already been indicated. Comments after the settlement also reflected some differences:

ITN, 17.45, 13 Feb. 1975	*BBC2, 18.50, 16 March 1975*
SISSONS: Britain's most crucial wage claim, the pursuit of which has previously brought down a government and led to damaging strikes, is all but settled and settled quite amicably.	NEWSCASTER: The miners through their negotiators put the Coal Board out of its misery this week by accepting a large pay offer. After some haggling the offer crept pound by pound closer to the miners' own demands.

14 February 1975

The day after the miners' negotiations were settled, the Secretary of State for Employment, Michael Foot, gave a speech in his constituency at Ebbw Vale. Compare the opening of BBC1's *Nine O'Clock News* with ITN's *News at Ten*:

ITN, 22.00	*BBC1, 21.00*
NEWSCASTER: Good evening. The Employment Secretary Mr Michael Foot tonight justified the miners' pay offer, but he warned that other workers mustn't expect similar treatment.	NEWSCASTER: The Employment Secretary Mr Foot has admitted that the miners' settlement goes well beyond the Social Contract's guidelines on compensating for rises in the cost of living.

Whereas ITN's announcement suggests that the settlement was a one-off, the BBC's version was simply that the Contract was broken. The BBC's interpretation continued strongly:

> Throughout today no single cabinet minister has attempted to claim that the miners' 32 per cent settlement is within the Social Contract. What they've been intent on doing is warning that other groups of workers shouldn't fall behind the miners. Mr Foot in his speech tonight denied that the Social Contract had now vanished into thin air. With what many will dismiss as verbal gymnastics, he attempted to justify the miners' pay deal as a much-needed and long-overdue reform of an outdated pay structure which was consistent with the terms of the Social Contract. And yet in the next breath he said it is undeniable that a settlement of over 30 per cent goes well beyond the figure required to compensate the rise in the cost of living, and if other settlements followed this pattern, he went on, Mr Denis Healey's warning on the economic consequences would come true.
>
> (BBC1, 21.00, 14 February 1975)

This commentary contained the following features. First there was the argument from silence: 'No single cabinet minister has attempted to claim that the miners' 32 per cent settlement is within the Social Contract'. This was a factually doubtful form of argumentation as Mr Foot (a 'single' senior cabinet minister) was justifying the settlement as *within* the Contract. Second, the crude depiction of the deal as a 32 per cent wage settlement was inadequate. There was by now enough information available to do better than that, as ITN had done the day before. Third, there was the appeal to a multitude of unnamed critics of Mr Foot, linked with the inference that he had not succeeded in what he was claiming: 'With what many will dismiss as verbal gymnastics, he attempted to justify the miners' pay deal as a much-needed and long-overdue reform of an outdated pay structure which was consistent with the terms of the Social Contract ...' All of this came *before* any interview with Mr Foot and therefore established a framework for viewing such an interview. Whatever else it was, this was not neutral news. It was not for that matter 'balanced' news in the sense of fairly listing the pros and cons. It was a particular and partial perspective on industrial relations and wage policy. For the record, rightly or wrongly. Mr Foot did say in his interview with Roy Roberts on the BBC bulletins that the settlement was within the Social Contract.

> The settlement's taken into account the need to get coal, it's taken into account the need to get miners, who are the only people who can get us to the coal, *it's taken into account also the fact that the National Coal Board's offers were made within the Social Contract.* All these factors have been taken into account in reaching this settlement and all in all I think it's a settlement that is beneficial for the country. Of course it's true that the figures go beyond the figures that would be required to keep up with the cost of living, and that is due to the factors I've mentioned – those have got to be taken into account. If this pattern was followed generally in other settlements then it would be damaging to the Social Contract and that is why we want people to take into account these factors.
>
> (BBC1, 21.00, 14 February 1975; our italics)

In this respect, then, the introduction to the ITN main bulletin would seem to be a more accurate description of Mr Foot's views than that of the BBC bulletin. However, this only reflected the more extreme and idiosyncratic stance of the BBC with regard to this pay claim and settlement.

Overall, the story of the miners' pay deal as presented by the media was told in the language of a 'battle' and an 'acid test' for the Social Contract. It was spiced with a bewildering array of percentages; with threats of industrial action and 'militant noises'; with fears of national bankruptcy. It saw in very truth the advent of some £3,000-a-year basic rate miners and a £41-a-week surface worker. The negotiations were under journalistic scrutiny but they were reported in a way that revealed more about the journalists' assumptions than the texture of the negotiations. While some of the participants to the negotiations were able to comment, explain and justify what was happening, this was typically within the highly structured conventions of interviewing and accommodated within the more general dominant framework provided by the television coverage.

'INSIDE' – 'OUTSIDE'

The link between the explanation of the economic crisis and the evaluation of the miners' claim was at times generalised to warn of the actions of other groups of workers. In the following example, the BBC industrial correspondent gave his view of the final settlement which the coal miners reached:

Well, it must damage the Social Contract and it must put in question what relevance the Social Contract now has to controlling inflation. Particularly when other groups of workers like the men in the power stations and the railways, use the 28 per cent increase for the surface workers as the target for their pay negotiations.

(BBC2, 17.45, 13 February 1975)

There was no comparable monitoring of the activities of employers. On only one occasion in this whole four-month period did a news journalist suggest directly that the Confederation of British Industry had some responsibility for the resolution of the crisis. This was in a BBC2 bulletin of January, which dealt with proposed talks between the Prime Minister and the CBI:

They [the CBI] said that with prolonged high inflation on top of price controls and high corporation tax, many more companies are, and will continue to be, forced to seek financial aid from the government. They accepted that management have some responsibility for reducing inflation but they needed union and government help. Without it, they said, unemployment would rise very fast.

(BBC2, 22.25, 7 January 1975)

What the responsibility was and how well it was being discharged was not expanded upon. There was no sense in which the news coverage was organised systematically to give this information, or in which it routinely examined the managerial workings of private industry. Rather, the news relayed in great detail exactly what unfortunate consequences could follow from the 'demands' and 'claims' of trade unions, while the 'offers' of the 'other side' of industry remained largely ignored or were left in large part unexamined. Often the concentration moved away from 'negotiations' to the probable effects if agreements were not reached. For example, at the time of the coalminers' pay settlement, we were informed of the effect it would have upon coal prices:

The deal gives them new basic rates of between £41 and £61 and was accepted 15 votes to 11, by the union's executive. It will mean increases in the price of coal to consumers. The Coal Board's Deputy Chairman, Mr Norman Siddell, said they would have to be fairly substantial and fairly soon, but he wouldn't suggest whether the main burden would be on private consumers or on industry.

(ITN, 17.50, 13 February 1975)

We are not suggesting that such news should not be reported. What we are highlighting is that only some actions and their consequences are systematically explored and critically examined in this fashion. The actions of other groups in our society were not balanced by such routinely critical coverage.

For example, there was no similar detailed examination or reporting on the news of what many saw as the key problem facing British industry; namely, the failure of substantial sections of private industry over a thirty-year period to mount adequate investment programmes. As we have noted, references to the causes of this problem did occasionally appear in the news, but it is significant that they came normally as interview responses rather than from media personnel. Thus both Ray Buckton (General Secretary of ASLEF) and Ian Mikardo, MP, appeared in interviews and called for exchange controls to stop the movement of capital from Britain (Buckton, ITN, 13.00, 16 April 1976). At other times, there were fragmented references to the movement of capital into speculative areas such as land and property, with its consequent effect on price inflation (Ian Mikardo, MP, quoted above, ITN, 13.00, 13 April 1975).

However, the overwhelming emphasis of news bulletins dealing with the economic crisis during this period related to the activities of the trade unions. This included the evaluation of wage negotiations and settlements, which was a major theme in news coverage. Individual pay claims, offers and settlements were routinely monitored to an extent quite unlike any other phenomenon in this period. In addition, this reporting was organised principally in terms of the supposed effects on the Social Contract. In the period of our study the pay negotiations of doctors, power workers, railway workers, Civil Service staff, engineers and miners were all reported – often simply in terms of whether the sums in question were 'inside' or 'outside' the Social Contract. This concern to point out the significance of pay claims and settlements to the 'wages side' of the Social Contract (itself a significant one-sided view of the Contract) is indicated by the inclusion in each case of reported statements, interview questions and responses directly relating to the question of whether the Social Contract could be said to have been broken. Moreover, in a significant number of cases the media institutions took it upon themselves to judge the issue in the form of direct media statements, irrespective of the number of interview responses or reported statements that may have contradicted this, Often, however, the reported statements chosen for inclusion in the bulletins were of the view that the pay in question was 'outside' the Social Contract (see Table 8.7).

Table 8.7 Pay settlements and the Social Contract: direct media judgements

	Number of media statements	
	Within the Social Contract	*Outside the Social Contract*
Miners	–	8
Railway workers	–	5
Dockers	–	4
Power workers	–	2
Civil Service staff	–	1
Engineers	1	1
Building workers	2	–

The interpretation of the Social Contract as being primarily about wages was criticised at this time by both trade unionists and members of the government. Mr Michael Foot, for example, spoke at the Scottish Trade Union Congress in April 1975 against the limited view that some people had of the Social Contract. His speech was reported on BBC1 as follows:

> FOOT: However some people, of course, when they talk of the Social Contract, wish to disguise the fact that it's not only a question that deals with wages at all; the Social Contract was an understanding reached between the political leadership of the Labour Party, and the representatives of the trade-union movement – an understanding reached about common economic and political objectives covering a much wider field than anything that is solely concerned with incomes or wages. It is for that reason, first of all, that I say as clearly as I possibly can to this Congress and to anybody else who might be overhearing what we have to say, that we deny that the Social Contract is dead and destroyed for the very first reason that we've got a lot of unfinished business to deal with under that Social Contract.
>
> (BBC1, 21.00, 17 April 1975)

One of the groups which focused largely on the 'wages' part of the Contract at this time was the television news personnel. The report of this speech which criticised the exclusive focus on wages was actually linked twice on the BBC news with references to a current wage claim. The above bulletin continued:

> The unfinished business Mr Foot went on to list included the repeal of the Conservatives' Industrial Relations Act, putting into law the Employment Protection Bill and moves like the setting up of the National Enterprise Board and for dealing with North Sea Oil.
>
> As Mr Foot was making his speech, leaders of 100,000 workers in the shipbuilding industry were accepting pay rises of over 30 per cent to their members. The deal follows the recent rise for engineering workers and it affects basic rates.
>
> (BBC1, 21.00, 17 April 1975)

The late-night BBC2 bulletin that day actually sandwiched a reference to the pay rises into the middle of its report of the speech:

> Speaking at the Scottish TUC, where the Budget is being fiercely attacked, Mr Foot said the government remained determined not to reintroduce wage controls, the alternative to the Social Contract. As Mr Foot was speaking leaders of 100,000 shipbuilders were accepting a pay rise of over 30 per cent for their members. Mr Foot also spoke on the Common Market. He believed that Britain's dependence on the bankers of Europe was a humiliating state of affairs.
>
> (BBC2, 22.00, 17 April 1975)

The news reporting of the wages side of the Social Contract was reduced substantially to the question of whether it was being 'broken'. The implication was frequently made that wage settlements were in advance of price rises.

In the following example from ITN in April, the pay settlements of the power workers and the railwaymen were discussed in this fashion. An agreement had just been reached for the power workers.

> The damage now is the size of the settlement, which deals yet another blow to the government's hope of keeping wage increases on a par with rising prices. It's bound to increase the aspirations of other workers with pay claims in the pipeline, and it seems difficult for the government to avoid allowing a similar-sized pay rise to the country's railwaymen; and if the railwaymen get around 30 per cent too, the credibility of the Social Contract, already under severe strain as a result of tonight's settlement, may be damaged beyond repair.
>
> (ITN, 22.00, 3 January 1975)

From the trade-union point of view, the 'other side' of the Social Contract at this time was the defence of living standards. This was referred to quite clearly by news journalists on a number of occasions, as in the following example from the BBC news of January 1975.

> INDUSTRIAL CORRESPONDENT: Well, as the trade unions see it, the Social Contract is all about making sure that wages don't fall beneath the rise in the cost of living and that there is no cut in the amount of money they have to spend. The TUC insists on maintaining living standards and even on increasing wage demands, if unemployment rises.
>
> (BBC1, 21.00, 10 January 1975)

If there had been any serious attempt in the television news to consider the point of view of these trade unions, then we might have expected some media personnel to evaluate wage settlements in terms of how they affected living standards. But, as we have indicated, the focus in the news within this area was on the 'breaking' of the Contract in the sense that some settlements were allegedly 'excessive'. There was no comparable focus or even comment on wage negotiations and settlements which were the opposite of this in the sense that they represented cuts in the living standard. They were merely reported as being 'inside' the Social Contract. At no point have we found an evaluation or even a comment from media personnel to suggest that any of the settlements or wage offers from employers were below the rate of inflation or were 'too low' to be inside the Social Contract from the trade union point of view. There were no 'fears' expressed by media personnel on such occasions. A clearer expression of value commitment would be difficult to unearth. The inferential framework of reporting sees wage negotiations as 'threatening' or 'demanding', never as part of continuing process in which both sides sometimes gain and sometimes lose. No union ever 'accepts' too little – but some managements or boards are judged to 'offer' too much.

III Breaching the peace at Greenham Common

TV NEWS COVERAGE OF GREENHAM COMMON AND THE WOMEN'S PEACE MOVEMENT

The women-only peace groups throughout the country, and particularly the women's peace camp at Greenham Common airforce base, form a distinctive part of the British peace movement. We have taken them as a key example not because we believed they were particularly badly treated but because they provide the media as a whole with a reason to feature a series of stories. At the same time they are outside the main stream of sources for news journalism and do not 'fit' well into the routine way in which stories are assembled. In addition the women's movement has its own press which runs parallel to the rest of the media and offers its own account of events. There are also statements issued from other sources such as the police. As such it was important to lay out the range of perspectives which were available on the Greenham issue, to examine how each was treated in news accounts and to suggest why the coverage was as it was.

By the end of 1983 the women's peace movement had become highly visible in the media, the Greenham women in their woolly hats a familiar sight on our screens. BBC1's evening news on Christmas Eve 1983, for example, carried a film report about the women celebrating their third Christmas at the peace camp. We hear about donations arriving at the camp; about the women giving excess Christmas puddings to local children's homes; and a woman describing a campaign of attacks by local vigilantes; by now Greenham Common is well enough established to provide a seasonal news story without a mass demonstration or any arrests. The women even have the status of their own logo appearing behind the newscaster. Although the forms of protest varied, the television reporters seem to become quickly accustomed to them:

> Such scenes have become a familiar sight outside this particular court building.
>
> (BBC1, 21.00, 15 February 1983)

> ... members of the women's peace camp staging their now familiar demonstration outside all seven of the entrances to the base.
>
> (BBC1, 21.00, 21 March 1983)

> Then they did what they often do: they sat down and started to sing.
>
> (BBC1, 17.40, 8 July 1983)

Greenham Common was not always so well covered on the news. It came out of relative obscurity in December 1982, when 30,000 women were seen on television 'embracing the base'; by then the camp had already been in existence for over sixteen months, virtually ignored by the media (although the fact that it attracted large numbers of women *before* it attracted much media coverage indicates that the camp and the national women's peace movement were already very active). In the earlier days, Greenham Common was not treated so seriously. In a brief report on BBC news of an incident not covered at all by ITN, it was dismissed as a 'so-called peace camp':

> Four women campaigning against nuclear weapons were arrested this afternoon after bailiffs arrived to demolish their *so-called peace camp* at Greenham Common near Newbury in Berkshire.
>
> (BBC1, 21.30, 25 May 1982)

After the first sixteen months the Greenham Common camp did start to receive more coverage, but many events still were unreported. For example, on 25 June 1983, a large number of women arrived and put together a four-mile banner made up of embroidered sections from all over the world. Participants claimed that over 300 women entered the base but this was not covered on TV. Nor did the news report the regular break-ins, with small groups of women breaching security and entering the base, which continued on a daily or weekly basis throughout 1983. Another example of editorial selection was the treatment of International Women's Day for Disarmament on 24 May 1983. As the main BBC1 news reported:

> Thousands of women in Britain have been holding anti-nuclear demonstrations, they've been marking International Women's Day for Disarmament with protests in city centres and outside military bases ... the organisers claiming that up to one million women had taken part nationwide.
>
> (BBC1, 21.00, 24 May 1983)

Women were shown linking hands around the Ministry of Defence in London, protesting in a Kingston-upon-Thames supermarket, rallying in Glasgow, being dragged out of a military base in Devonport, and lying down in the main road in Bristol. The BBC report, lasting 1 minute 15 seconds, did not invite any of the women involved to explain their protest, and did not tell us about the full number of demonstrations across Britain (over 100) or about the simultaneous action in fourteen other countries; but it at least recognised that thousands of women participating in over 100 co-ordinated anti-nuclear and anti-military protests were making news.

By contrast, the Channel 4 and ITV news bulletins on the same night did not mention the women's actions at all. The absence of coverage of International Women's Day for Disarmament is even more striking, since both ITN evening bulletins led with long items on defence and disarmament (discussing Labour's plans to scrap Polaris and the MX vote in Washington).

Channel 4 news even appeared to run out of stories for its hour-long bulletin. Before the final item the newscaster is reduced to asking, 'Is there anything else out there?' The reply is a two-minute 'light' report on summer, beginning: 'It was just one of those great ideas that news editors sometimes pass on to reporters: has summer finally arrived?' before the closing news summary, 'and that's Channel 4 news tonight, a day when the election campaign was dominated by defence' (Channel 4, 19.00, 24 May 1983). ITN and Channel 4 chose to feature only debates within political parties or in the US Congress. So however 'familiar' Greenham Common's songs have become, the TV news can still leave out the women's peace movement.

We analysed the coverage of six women's peace demonstrations that appeared on the news between December 1982 and December 1983, in a total of thirty-eight bulletins; and compared it with other reports including some from the women who participated. We found that many features central to the camp were not covered in the news. First, why is the camp all-women? This is a fairly obvious question, asked by many visitors to the camp except apparently TV journalists; it does not seem to be prevalent in news reports and was not explained or raised in any of the coverage in our sample.[2] How is the camp run? The women's peace movement has developed its own form of organising, based on collective decision-making and individual responsibility, run without leaders or any formal structure of bureaucracy. It's an exceptional method, quite distinct from the way CND, for example, or any political party works; but again the TV did not tell us about it. Instead, it gave the impression that the women's peace camp is run by the better-known disarmers of CND:

> At Greenham Common today women peace protesters have started a five-day attempted blockade. It's one of a number of events organised by CND to coincide with US 4th of July celebrations.
>
> (BBC2, 19.35, 4 July 1983)

> Once again demonstrators from all over Britain converged on Greenham Common, and CND's hopes of a big turnout were fully realised.
>
> (BBC1, 22.15, 11 December 1983)

The camp has always been independent from CND, and there are many differences between the two.

A further question is, what exactly is the political protest the camp is making? The broadcasters have grasped the fundamental idea that the camp is opposed to Cruise missiles – although even this is not always made clear. Coverage on the two ITV evening bulletins and BBC2's *Newsnight* of the opening of the five-day blockade at Greenham Common avoided giving any reason at all for the women's action. The full BBC2 report ran:

> Women peace compaigners have been trying without success to prevent workers entering or leaving Greenham Common air base. Police were there in strength and cleared a passage to allow workers in and out. There was

one arrest. The protest began today on American Independence Day and is expected to continue until Friday.

(BBC2, 22.25, 4 July 1983)

On ITN the newscaster began: 'At Greenham Common police broke up an attempted blockade by women peace protesters' (ITN, 17.45, 4 July 1983); and the correspondent concentrated on how the women were dragged away rather than why they were there. The BBC1 news did state that the protest was against Cruise. This is the full text of a BBC1 report:

American Independence Day has been marked by more protests *against the siting of Cruise missiles* in Britain. The largest demonstration was at Greenham Common air base. Several dozen women tried to block coaches carrying base workers into the compound. There have been no reports of arrests.

CORRESPONDENT: There are fewer protestors than previously at Greenham. Too few to succeed in their aim of blockading the base. A large force of police is apparently prepared if many more arrive as the five-day protest goes on. The main aim is publicity which helps explain the choice of today, American Independence Day.

(BBC1, 17.45, 4 July 1983)

Note the claim that 'the main aim is publicity'. The same point was made on International Women's Day for Disarmament: 'The women were more interested in putting across their anti-nuclear message than in inconveniencing the public' (BBC1, 21.00, 24 May 1983).

The news does not give any publicity to the women's case. Opposition to Cruise is mentioned, and some 'anti-nuclear message' is referred to, but the women have no chance to explain exactly why they oppose Cruise, why they are anti-nuclear. In particular, the broader anti-militarism of the women's peace movement, and the links they make between male supremacy, male violence and nuclear weapons are buried. Of course 'putting across their anti-nuclear message' is not the broadcaster's job; but they are falling down on the job of providing informative reporting if they cover the demonstrations without explaining (or allowing the demonstrators to explain) what they are trying to say.

Moreover the broadcasters do find space to give a full and proper explanation of the official pro-Cruise message. The BBC2 news story *Countdown to Cruise* on 9 November 1983 reports on:

1   (50 secs) Mrs Thatcher's speech in Bonn urging the Soviet Union to accept the 'zero option'.
2   (18 secs) The 24-hour peace camps set up at all the 102 US bases in Britain (through the newscaster adds that 'the government says they got their sums wrong and their are only 74').
3   (27 secs) 'The effort of a group of Greenham women to take their action

to the other side of the Atlantic' with their court case against President Reagan for acting illegally in deploying Cruise.

4   (30 secs) The visit of fourteen Labour MPs to the Greenham peace camp 'to show solidarity'.

5   (10 secs) The government announcement that policing Greenham had cost £1.5 million over the past year.

6   (12 mins 25 secs) The correspondent's own story of how 'this morning I went down to Greenham to look as it were behind the wire'.

This is the background he gives to the decision to site Cruise in Europe:

> These missiles, planned for Britain, Holland, Belgium, Germany and Italy, are intended to tell the Russians: Just in case you are tempted to try any attack, the West can now strike back from European soil, at selected military targets as far away as Kiev and Minsk, without having to risk certain annihilation by calling in America's intercontinental strategic system.
>
> So the argument runs, these new Cruise missiles here at Greenham Common will actually make war *less* likely', by demonstrating to the Russians that if they attempted to lop off Western Europe from America, there would actually be a credible and still very demanding Western nuclear response.
>
> Well, there's debate about the cogency of that nuclear strategy.
>
> (BBC2, 23.00, 9 November 1983)

At this point the reporter goes into the technical details of deployment – the training and organisation of missile crews; the composition of missile convoys; the construction of missiles; the timetable for deployment: (If all goes well, and all these tests are successfully passed, then the 501st will be awarded its Initial Operational Capability, its IOC. By the end of the year, Greenham will be a fully active nuclear weapons base (BBC2, 23.00, 9 November 1983). This is followed by an account of the use of the silos, and the programme for convoy dispersal. Finally, he interviews a military specialist in a wood – 'an extremely good dispersal area' – about how the missiles would be fired. The official justification for Cruise which rests on the assumption of a Soviet threat ('to tell the Russians: "Just in case you're tempted to try an attack"'), and the deterrence arguments ('these new Cruise missiles here at Greenham will make war *less* likely') are presented in detail as 'news'.

The reporting is scarcely in neutral terms, using such phrases as '*if all goes well* ... Greenham will be a fully active nuclear weapons base'. Meanwhile, the case against Cruise is reduced to the single sentence: 'Well, there's debate about the cogency of that nuclear strategy', even though the whole item is based on reports of active *opposition* to Cruise. In all, 1 minute and 15 seconds are devoted to the protest, and 12 minutes and 25 seconds to the 'technical background'. If it were not for the peace camp, the Greenham Common base would probably not be news at all, yet the political reasoning of the camp is virtually silenced.

The broadcasters sometimes argue that the business of TV news is to tell us about each day's events, and that 'background' issues and 'in-depth' explanations are properly left to current affairs programmes. However, it could be countered that the huge growth of a women-only movement, its unusual form of organisation, and the developing arguments against Cruise are all integral parts of the news about particular events, essential for allowing the viewers to come to an understanding of them. It is untrue to say that the news always confines itself to reporting merely 'what happened'; it does attempt to explain the background to *some* issues. Consider, for instance, not only the 'in-depth' justification for Cruise missiles on BBC2 quoted above, but also the normal reporting of Westminster politics, with political correspondents offering their analyses of the arguments and the internal working of the parties.[3] The problem is neither lack of space nor the news/current-affairs split – it is the journalists' assumption that Westminster politics are more important than the politics of grass-roots opposition movements like the peace movement (which perhaps explains why BBC1 and BBC2's evening reports from Greenham Common on 9 November 1983 both carry an interview with a visiting, male MP, rather than with any of the peace women). This may seem a 'natural' value judgement to the broadcasters, but it is a value judgement none the less.

Perhaps one of the reasons why the news captures so little of this innovative work is the women's refusal to tailor their activities to the needs of the media. A film about the camp[4] records an incident of a TV journalist having difficulty coping with their obvious lack of respect for professional journalistic practices:

JOURNALIST: For God's sake, I'm doing a piece to camera to put your protest in a logical – in a way that people will understand – and make out that you're making some sense, and you go and clown around in the background and that doesn't do your case any good at all. . . . The bloody thing won't be used if you're doing cartwheels in the background because it will be distracting.

PEACE CAMPER: But why should it be distracting? We're doing all kinds of things here.

JOURNALIST: I know you are, and when we film you doing them that's fine but when I'm doing a piece to camera . . . You were deliberately doing cartwheels in the background and you must know – all right I'm sorry I called you a tit.

PEACE CAMPER: But there's a way of speaking to people . . .

JOURNALIST: I know there's a way of speaking to people – I've got a job to do and my job is completely messed up.

PUBLIC OPINION AND SUPPORT

Another aspect of the Greenham Common peace camp not really dealt with in the news is the question of how much public support it has for its call that Cruise missiles should not be sited in Britain. There are hints given that, although the peace women themselves are sincere and confident, the television journalists from their position can see that they ought to pay more attention to 'criticism of their cause' and the fact that there is 'no hope':

> They left tonight having spent two days somewhat detached from dispute about and criticism of their cause, but full of confidence in it.
>
> (BBC1, 21.00, 12 December 1982)

> [INTERVIEW QUESTION] Are you surprised by the level of support, given that there seems to be really no hope now of stopping the Cruise missiles?
>
> (Channel 4, 19.00, 8 July 1983)

From this point of view, support would indeed by a surprise. On a BBC World Service radio programme answering listeners' letters, we hear that:

> Our news editor's view is that it's obvious that the Greenham Common women are protesting against the views of the established majority. After all, if the Greenham Common women were supported by the majority, they'd have nothing to protest about, would they?
>
> (BBC World Service, 25 November 1983)

In fact, though, as a range of public opinion polls over a period of time consistently showed, more people were opposed to Cruise than in favour of it; and most polls showed an absolute majority against Cruise (See Table 8.8).

Table 8.8 Siting Cruise in Britain: 1981–3 opinion polls[1]

	% against	% for	Don't know
April 1981 Marplan for *Guardian*	59	41	9
December 1982 Gallup for *Sanity*	58	31	11
January 1983 Marplan for *Guardian*	61	27	12
January 1983 MORI for *Sunday Times*	54	36	10
February 1983 Gallup for *Daily Telegraph*	54	36	10
May 1983 Marplan for *Guardian*	54	34	12
May 1983 Harris for *Observer*	55	32	13
October 1983 Marplan for *Guardian*	48	37	15
October 1983 MORI for *Sunday Times*	51	43	6
November 1983 NOP for *Daily Mail*	47	37	16
November 1983 Marplan for *Guardian* and *Panorama*	47	42	11
November 1983 Gallup for *Daily Telegraph*	48	41	11
December 1983 Marplan for *Weekend World*[1]	66	28	6

Notes: [1]Some of the variations in results are attributable to variations in the sampling techniques and in the wording of poll questions, but the underlying trend is clear.
[2]This poll question was about deployment rather than siting, as Cruise missiles had arrived by December 1983.

In other words, the repeated demonstrations at Greenham which the TV news (sometimes) covers are in some respects voicing majority opinion, and not the lost cause of a 'detached' few. The fact that the cause commands such widespread support could well be important in the viewers' perception of the Greenham demonstrations, but the TV news almost always fails to mention it.

We found only two cases in our sample when the TV news mentioned public opinion in conjunction with women's peace protests. One was on 9 November 1983, in the coverage on Channel 4 news of the Greenham women's court case and the 102 peace camps across Britain. It was a straightforward report on the latest poll, backed up with animated block graphs on the screen:

> An NOP poll published in this morning's *Daily Mail* shows that 94 per cent of people want dual key control of Cruise missiles and an increasing number of people are against Cruise being deployed at all here. Now only 37 per cent of people favour the deployment of Cruise, while 47 per cent oppose it.
>
> (Channel 4, 19.00, 9 November 1983)

However, none of the ITV or BBC bulletins that evening mentioned the poll. Why was it relevant news at seven o'clock but not at nine, ten or eleven?

The second case was on 11 December 1983, the day following screening of the nuclear war film *The Day After*, and the day that 20,000–40,000 women encircled the base at Greenham Common. Both ITN evening bulletins used the Marplan poll commissioned by ITV's current affairs programme *Weekend World*, as a link between the opening item on Greenham Common and the item on reactions to the film *The Day After*: 'An opinion poll shows just under two-thirds of people in Britain think a nuclear war is becoming more likely' (ITN, 18.30, 21.45, 11 December 1983). Public opinion on the likelihood of nuclear war is picked out as the only relevant question. There were other results from the same poll, showing clear majorities against the deployment of Cruise and disapproving of the government's handling of the issue, which were screened in *Weekend World*:

> Do you approve of the government's handling of the Cruise missile issue?
>
> Yes   36%
> No   52%
> Don't know   12%

> Should deployment of Cruise missiles go ahead even without arms negotiations talks in progress? [Arms negotiations talks were *not* in progress at this time.]
>
> Yes   28%
> No   66%
> Don't know   6%
>
> (*Weekend World*, ITV, 12.00, 11 December 1983)

These results were not given on the news, although the reports on the poll immediately followed items on the demonstration against Cruise.

So in spite of readily available evidence, TV news here failed to make clear the extent of public support for the campaign against Cruise missiles. It also seems to be confused about the support given to individual demonstrations. During the blockades in July 1983 covering all eight entrances to the base for five days, the peace camp estimated that several thousand women participated altogether, with over 1,000 on the first day (4 July) and over 2,000 on the last day (8 July). There were about 100 women already living at the camp at that time. Table 8.9 shows the numbers given on the television news. Even with some cynicism about the participants' own count, the TV news figures, as well as being inconsistent, seem rather low. Even the highest TV figure for 4 July – 'less than 300' – would scarcely be enough to maintain the eight blockades; and the BBC's 'several dozen' would be accounted for by the permanent peace campers alone, without the coachloads of supporters. Three of these came from Glasgow alone.

The TV figures also compared oddly with those given in the press. The *Daily Telegraph* (5 July 1983) gives no overall total but says that 150 had assembled at a single gate by 06.00; and the *Daily Express* says 'only 500 supporters attended', which is over 200 more than the very highest TV figures. Neither paper is particularly supportive of the peace camp.

On 12 December 1983, the nine-mile perimeter fence was ringed with women; the camp estimated over 40,000. The majority of newspapers said 30,000. The BBC conceded 'nearly 30,000', while ITN gave 'some 20,000', differing from the camp's estimate by over 20,000 and once more undercutting even the *Daily Telegraph*, which gave the lowest newspaper figure of 25,000.

Table 8.9 TV reports of numbers of demonstrators at Greenham Common, July 1983

4 July 1983		8 July 1983	
ITN	13.00 – less than 150	ITN	13.00 – no figure
	70 at one gate*	ITN	17.40 – about 600
ITN	17.45 – less than 300	ITN	22.00 about 600
ITN	22.00 – less than 300	C4	19.00 – a few hundred
C4	19.00 – about 40 at one	BBC1	13.00
	gate*		17.40 – no figures
BBC1	13.00 – several dozen	BBC1	21.00 – about 600
BBC1	17.40 – several dozen	BBC2	22.50 – about 600
BBC1	21.00 – 'too few to succeed against a highl yorganised force of police'		
BBC2	19.35		
	22.25 – no figures		

Note: *These two numbers were given over the same piece of film of the same gate.

VIOLENCE

The coverage of violence at Greenham Common is crucial as there are at least two very different perspectives at stake. From the official perspective of the police and military, they do have to use force, but only the minimum necessary to maintain public order; and the military need to keep nuclear weapons in order to deter their use. The 'trouble' therefore stems from demonstrators, particularly the hard core of troublemakers amongst them, many of whom have overstepped their democratic right to protest and have had to be convicted and imprisoned for breaching the peace and other offences. From the women's peace movement perspective, on the other hand, the camp exists to oppose state violence, specifically the nuclear defence policy, but increasingly drawing in the less extreme levels of 'normal' state use of violence in the military, police and prisons.

One of the camp's own central principles is its commitment to *non-violence*, which the women feel is the basis of their demonstrations. For instance, when the police break up a blockade, the women say that they resist passively instead of struggling physically, to make it clear that the force or violence originates from the police. Here is typical news description of such an occasion:

> The police returned as more men and supplies turned up and had to get inside. Again the women linked arms and were dragged away, this time encountering slightly rougher handling from the police. But again there were no injuries and no arrests. The road clear, the convoy rushed inside, and the police dispersed at speed to avoid any further confrontation.
>
> (ITN, 22.00, 4 July 1982)

This is very different from the accounts given to us by the women involved in this blockade. They all stressed the police use of force. According to the participants, 'slightly rougher handling' included women being pulled by the hair or by the neck, having their arms twisted up their backs, and being thrown on top of one another into a ditch. On other occasions women said they had suffered concussion and broken bones at the hands of the police and soldiers. The TV report, while acknowledging the rougher handling, is more from the police point of view: the men and supplies 'had to get inside' (the women felt they 'had to' stop them); there were 'no injuries' reported by the police (the TV journalists did not ask the women if they had been injured); and the police were 'avoiding confrontation'.

The women's non-violence in the face of this is sometimes referred to on the news – 'For the Greenham Common women, it is what they term non-violent direct action' (BBC1, 13.00, 8 July 1983) – but their approach is neither explained nor compared with that of the police. There is a contradiction in the coverage here: although the words are deadpan, as in the example above, or the caption below, the *film* shows women being treated

Figure 8.6 'There were scuffles as women were dragged from the roof of one of their vans' (BBC1, 21.00, 8 July 1983)

roughly, having their hands battered by soldiers with sticks, and mounted police galloping straight for them; so such violence does get some TV exposure. The women at the peace camp reported other forms of harassment which don't appear on the news, such as soldiers throwing stones through the fence and slashing their tents, and strip-searches in police custody. But still the TV news tends to play down the authorities' use of force to counter the women's protest.

The arrival of soldiers to back up police, an important escalation which was headlined in *The Times* ('Greenham Women Face Army', 5 July 1983), was not commented on by the TV. The five BBC bulletins and Channel 4 news that day do not mention the army at all, while on ITN they appear only in passing: 'This Independence Day blockade started forming up long before dawn but not in strong enough numbers to worry a heavy police and army presence' (ITN, 17.45, 22.00, 4 July 1983). The only time the question of the use of force against the women made a big splash on TV news was when Mr Heseltine announced in parliament on 1 November 1983 that they could be shot by US servicemen if they ventured inside the final fence around the silos housing the missiles. The stir this caused only underlined the media's general lack of awareness about violence used against peace protesters: the risk of getting shot near nuclear weapons stores had been common knowledge in the peace movement for years. It had even been mentioned in press reports earlier in the year ('Two Greenham women who claimed they got into the base on Wednesday night said they saw notices warning that people went in at their own risk of being shot' – *Guardian*, 26 June 1983).

The TV news appears to assume that a nuclear weapons base is on the whole a peaceful place, disturbed only when crowds of protesters arrive. Thus two reports close with:

As the demonstrators headed for home, local residents were hoping for some peace and quiet.

(BBC1, 21.00, 8 July 1983)

Tonight the day of action ended ... and peace returned to Greenham Common.

(BBC1, 22.15, 11 December 1983)

Violence against women and accusations against the police do not seem to make news; but the story was different when a policeman was injured and the women could be accused. On 11 December 1983 some of the women standing at the Greenham perimeter fence started to rock it rhythmically with their hands, and the fence posts swayed. One of these posts hit an unfortunate policeman, who was knocked unconscious. This incident (and three other 'slight injuries') became the focus of the TV reports:

HEADLINE: The Greenham women attack the camp's perimeter fence, nearly sixty are arrested and four policeman are hurt.

REPORTER: There were fewer police on the side nearer the missile bunkers, and it was here that the women launched an assault. Inspector Michael Page from Reading was hit on the head by a concrete post. He was unconscious for half an hour, and the crowds delayed an ambulance taking him to hospital. Three other policemen were slightly hurt.

(BBC2, 20.35, 11 December 1983)

NEWSCASTER: Good evening. The Greenham Common peace women today pulled down the perimeter fence at the Berkshire air base during the biggest demonstration since American Cruise missiles arrived last month. 20,000 or more joined the protest, forty-two were arrested. A police inspector was knocked unconscious by a toppling fence post. He is in hospital. Three other police were hurt....

REPORTER: The peace protestors came from all over the country.... At a gate on the east of the camp, words changed to action as the women made concerted attacks on the perimeter fence. Concrete posts wobbled under the weight. The police inspector was knocked out when one hit him.

(ITN, 21.45, 11 December 1983)

HEADLINE: Greenham under attack again – seventy arrests and policemen are hurt.

NEWSCASTER A peaceful day of protest by nearly 30,000 demonstrators at the Greenham Common air base in Berkshire turned to violence just before dark.... Just after three o'clock the nine-mile perimeter fence was attacked at several points. There were seventy arrests and four policemen were hurt.

REPORTER: ... Elsewhere women protesters were doing their best to tear down the airfield's perimeter fence with their bare hands, and in one or two places almost succeeding. Four policemen were hurt. One, Inspector Michael Page, was knocked out when a concrete post fell on him.

(BBC1, 22.15, 11 December 1983)

BBC1 and 2 did report the women's statement that they regretted the accident; BBC2 added that they 'claimed that one of them had her fingers broken by soldiers', and ITN said that 'two peace women were injured'; but the stress was firmly on the police injuries, which were blamed on violence from the women. The language used to describe the women's actions shows the perspective of the news: 'attack ... assault ... concerted attacks ... attack ... turned to violence ... tear down'. This is not how the participants saw their rocking of the fence. Compare the accounts in the women's press:

GREENHAM WOMEN FACE VIOLENT ATTACK
Soldiers, armed with huge wooden sticks and metal bars reached out across the barbed wire and started bashing women's hands, some had their fingers crippled. A women got entangled in the barbed wire, soldiers pulled her through without allowing her to disentangle herself.

Outwrite, January 1984

THE CHANGING FACE OF GREENHAM
Hundreds of women were injured by police wrenching women's hands from the fence or soldiers hitting their hands with sticks ... women got into the base and were wrapped in barbed wire and beaten up. The soldiers then tied the women to concrete fence posts and masturbated in front of them before letting them go.

Spare Rib, February 1984

Women at the camp reported that seventeen demonstrators were treated in hospital in Newbury that night. They also stated that one of a group of thirty who entered the base was 'kicked unconscious' by MoD police. The TV news did not ask if any women got into the base or if any were hurt. If the broadcasters faced a choice of perspectives on the responsibility for violence at Greenham Common – it is fairly clear which one they adopted.

BALANCE

Two very eloquent groups of campaigners.

(BBC1, 21.00, 4 July 1983)

One of the things that stands out in the expanding TV news coverage of the women's peace movement is the ingenuity of the broadcasters' attempts to find 'balancing' stories, i.e. stories putting the other side of the argument. Sometimes they are provided by straightforward government statements (which may be timed specifically to counter disarmament demonstrations.) On 9 November 1983, when the Greenham women started their case against Reagan in the US courts, and peace camps were set up at all US bases in Britain, the Prime Minister made a speech in Bonn urging the Soviet Union to accept the 'zero option'. All the evening news bulletins linked the two stories together. BBC1's headlines ran:

No to Cruise – Greenham women go to court in America.

No to the SS-20s – that's my Christmas wish, says Mrs Thatcher.
(BBC1, 21.00, 9 November 1983)

Announcements by other public figures have also been used. On 4 July 1983, the day of a series of anti-nuclear protests at Greenham Common and elsewhere, a group of trade-union leaders held a press conference on the question of the Labour leadership contest, at which Frank Chapple and Terry Duffy underlined their rejection of Labour's policy of unilateral nuclear disarmament. The main ITN news reported this before their item on Greenham Common:

Electrical and engineering trade-union leaders formally rejected unilateral disarmament today .... On the other side, the Greenham demonstrators marked American Independence Day with what they called the start of a four-day blockade.

The Greenham report proceeds, without any interviews or statements from the women. At the end we return to Frank Chapple and Terry Duffy, who make speeches to the camera. The framing is complete:

The supplies and personnel to get this Cruise missile base operational before the end of the year are still getting through. Trade-union leaders who do not support the Labour Party's stance on disarmament declared their hand.
(ITN, 22.00, 4 July 1983)

The BBC news also links the two:

There was criticism too for the Greenham Common anti-nuclear protestors. Electricians' leader Frank Chapple said they should thank their lucky stars they're living in a society which allows them to demonstrate without being put in gaol. American Independence Day has been marked by more protests against the siting of Cruise missiles.
(BBC1, 17.45, 4 July 1983)

A group of trade-union leaders has said Labour should move away from its unilateralist policies. . . . And the electricians' leader Frank Chapple had criticism for the Greenham Common protesters. He said they should be glad they lived in a society which didn't goal its dissenters. And at Greenham Common today, women peace protesters have started a five-day attempted blockade.

(BBC2, 19.35, 4 July 1983)

On days when there were no press conferences putting the other side, the news proved itself able to generate its own balancing stories. For example, on 15 February 1983, forty-four women went on trial in Newbury for breaking into the base, while a further sixty broke in but were not arrested. ITN followed its report on these events in Greenham Common with a report on another Cruise missile base in the United States, beginning 'It's easy to love your local missile base', and using interviews with local residents to show that they were not worried by Cruise. This was the newscaster's link in the first bulletin:

Well, one missile base where there's no problem with demonstrators and trespassers is Griffiths air base near the town of Rome in New York State. Even the proximity of Cruise missiles doesn't worry the local population, as John Suchet reports.

(ITN, 13.00, 15 March 1983)

By the evening it was:

In the United States some communities have learned to live with Cruise missiles, at a profit. People in the town of Rome, in New York State, say their local missile base has helped the economy.

(ITN, 22.00, 15 March 1983)

There was no 'news' in the normal sense in the report from the USA; the apparent reason for showing it was to 'balance' the women's protests.

Lady Olga Maitland's organisation, Women and Families for Defence, seems tailor-made for supplying copy to 'balance' news from Greenham Common with a firm pro-Cruise line. It was set up in March 1983 with mainly this in mind: 'We do a lot of counter-activities,' as a spokeswoman in their London office told us. The spokeswoman said it was 'hard to calculate' how many members they had, but quoted 'up to 300' as the largest attendance at any of their rallies. They concentrate their energies on 'being the other point of view' and countering what they perceived as a bias towards CND in the media, particularly television.

The startling success of Women and Families for Defence can be shown by looking at the BBC1 coverage of the blockades at Greenham Common on 4 July. The lunchtime bulletin concentrated straightforwardly on the blockades themselves. This was the newscaster's introduction summarising the film report:

> Women peace protesters have begun a five-day blockade of the Greenham Common air base in Berkshire. They're demonstrating against plans to site American Cruise missiles there. At daybreak several dozen women tried to block coaches carrying base workers into the compound, but police dragged them away.
>
> (BBC1, 13.00, 4 July 1983)

During the afternoon Lady Olga Maitland visited the camp, and after that the whole focus of the news coverage changed. The headline was: 'The nuclear debate in full cry at Greenham Common', with a short clip showing Lady Olga speaking in front of a singing crowd of peace protesters blockading a gate: 'With American aid NATO has acquired a strength which has made it imperative ...'). When we come to the item itself, the 180-word description of the blockades given at lunchtime is cut down to 100 words, and the correspondent now continues:

> CORRESPONDENT: But not all the women at Greenham today were against Cruise missiles in Britain. Lady Olga Maitland and the women for defence were there to make sure of their fair share of the attention and to try and make themselves heard arguing in support of NATO policy.
> LADY OLGA MAITLAND: With American aid NATO has acquired a strength which has made it imperative. . . .
> CORRESPONDENT: There was real dialogue. The discussion was ordered and peaceful.
> DEMONSTRATOR: As an American I have to say that it is my country that has taken every step in the arms race, and Russia has played catch-up, and historically please get your facts right.
> LADY OLGA MAITLAND: It is the Russians all the way have led the arms race.
> DEMONSTRATOR: That's not true.
> CORRESPONDENT: But at the end of a long hot day, no sign that two very eloquent groups of campaigners had narrowed the difference between them in the nuclear debate.
>
> (BBC1, 21.00, 4 July 1983)

A story about a mass protest has been transformed into an 'ordered dialogue' between 'two very eloquent groups of campaigners', with the small pressure group Women and Families for Defence presented as equivalent to the women's peace movement. The concept of 'balance' is operated within a structure of power and access, which the broadcasters accede to in practice, but are unwilling to acknowledge.

IV The Church and the Bomb: framing and reporting a debate

THE BISHOP'S MOVE

The way forward which the report took was to say that if nuclear weapons are not morally acceptable, then it is of the first urgency to get rid of them. What would be the safest way of doing that, and the one most likely to succeed? Contrary to the popular impression given by the media and never eradicated, we did not advocate unilateral nuclear disarmament. The report recommended a modest unilateral reduction by the West, which would not in any way endanger security. We accepted that the nuclear deterrent had played a part in keeping the peace since 1945. What we urged strongly was that new developments were eroding the stability of the present equilibrium and that it could not last for ever. Balanced force reduction had not so far delivered the goods. Had not the time come for independent initiatives which were carefully calculated not to tempt anyone to the gamble of war? I still firmly believe that this idea has not been defeated by argument. It has only been distorted by misrepresentation.[5]

(John Austin Baker, Bishop of Salisbury)

The Church and the Bomb, subtitled 'Nuclear Weapons and Christian Conscience', was published on 18 October 1982. As part of its continuing concern about the issue of war and disarmament, the Church of England Synod in 1979 asked its Board of Social Responsibility to set up a working party. Its brief was to study the implications for Christian discipleship of the acceptance by the major military powers of a role for nuclear weapons in their strategy and to consider the bearing of this on the adequacy of past Christian teaching and ethical analysis regarding the conduct of war. The working party was ecumenical in composition. Its members were mainly theologians, including pacifists and non-pacifists, but also included a lecturer in War Studies from Kings College, London. It was chaired by John Baker, who in 1982 had become Bishop of Salisbury. From 1978 to 1982 he had served as Rector of St Margaret's, Westminster, and Speaker's Chaplain.

The report, a substantial document, was published in book form. In succeeding chapters it looked at the technological, strategic, political, legal, moral and theological aspects of the possession and use of nuclear weapons. It went on to analyse the principal policy options which nuclear states might, or do, pursue to maintain peace: negotiation from strength, balanced force reductions, multilateral disarmament with unilateral stages and unilateral renunciation. It concluded that 'there are fundamental objections on the basis of ethics and faith both to the use of and the conditional intention to use nuclear weapons'.[6] The final chapter contained twenty-two recommendations based on its conclusion that 'the nuclear element in deterrence is no longer a reliable or morally acceptable approach to the future of the world'.[7]

The working party advocated discriminating support for the United Nations in its work for peace. It thought that pressure should be brought to bear on the British government to ensure that the debate on defence and disarmament is a real one and commented:

> We welcome the recent increase in the availability of information. It must be said, however, that the government's counter-offensive against the peace movements, however understandable, has often not improved upon the level of some peace movement propaganda.[8]

The role and responsibilities of the media were also explicitly commented upon, including the need for an informed understanding and an appreciation of how other nations see the issues of defence and disarmament. The need for constant vigilance in the use of language was noted:

> Commentators need also to warn us again and again about the vague terminology that springs from woolly thinking and begs questions – for example, the constant tendency to use bland expressions like 'take out' when what is meant is the destruction of a city and its inhabitants, or words like 'strength' or 'power' to mean more and better nuclear weapons, thus predetermining the outcome of the argument.[9]

More specifically, the report recommended the cancelling of the Trident programme and the phasing out of Polaris and Chevaline; the phasing out of other nuclear weapons in Britain including US air and submarine bases and the refusal to accept Cruise missiles in Britain.

Even before it was published there were press accounts of what the report was proposing. David Fairhall and Martyn Halsall, respectively defence and religious affairs correspondents, wrote the lead story in the *Guardian* under the headline: 'Whitehall salvo at Church arms plan' (15 October 1982). They refer to the alarm bells which the report set ringing in Whitehall:

> Officials have reacted by reiterating the official view that successful multilateral negotiations to reduce nuclear arms are only likely to be achieved from a position of nuclear strength; an 'independent' deterrent is an asset to NATO as well as to Britain if she were ever on her own; and that we cannot honestly shelter under the American nuclear umbrella while refusing to take the risk of having American nuclear bases on our soil.

Conservative MPs were reported as fearing that the Church of England was falling into the lands of 'trendies'.

The next day Winston Churchill MP described the report as representing 'the workings of a narrow activist group, inspired in some quarters with a political motivation. There could be nothing more immoral than if the government of this country were fecklessly to pursue the unilateralist policies advocated by this report and CND' (*Guardian*, 16 October 1982). This was interpreted as the opening of a government campaign against the report in which the Prime Minister was expected to get involved. In the House of Commons on 19 October she rejected the report's advocacy of a non-nuclear policy for Britain: 'Nuclear weapons are an essential part of our security. If there was any suggestion of unilateral disarmament it would threaten the peace and security we have enjoyed in this country for the past thirty seven years' (*Guardian*, 20 October 1982). This followed the accusation in the House from the Tory MP Robert Atkins, who referred to the group 'supposedly eminent and certainly unrepresentative clerics [who] seek to undermine the defence of the United Kingdom' (*Guardian*, 20 October 1982). This comment came the day after London Weekend Television reported a survey finding that 40 per cent of the Church of England clergy thought Britain should abandon its nuclear deterrent.

The *Guardian* did take up the issues raised by *The Church and the Bomb* with some vigour. The publication date, 18 October, was the occasion for a long editorial – 'Which path back from the brink?' – and was linked to a sympathetic reference to Jonathan Schell's *The Fate of the Earth*: 'For if there is even a chance that Schell's glimpse of Armageddon is right, then the framework of strategy and doctrine that locks together conventional and nuclear war is shot to pieces' (*Guardian*, 18 October 1982). Mrs Thatcher's often-repeated statement that nuclear weapons have kept the world at peace for thirty-seven years (she said it again the next day, as we have seen) was put in an alternative perspective: 'That is a pimple on the face of history. Can they so work for millenniums to come? If human frailty, miscalculation or dementia puts the logic at risk, then how can that risk be diminished?' The failure of multilateral disarmament to make progress in the light of the continuing escalation of the arms race was noted and a call to the West to pursue more actively nuclear disarmament policies was made.

On the same day the Bishop of Durham, John Habgood (now Archbishop of York), wrote about the report on the Agenda page: 'Morals of the Bomb'. His comments and intervention are of particular interest since he had chaired a World Council of Churches Hearing in November 1981 on Nuclear Weapons and Disarmament. This was subsequently published under the title *Before It's Too Late*. Habgood commended the report as an example of Anglican sanity at its best. However, while he took the view that the moral argument against nuclear weapons is unanswerable, he was not happy with the way this was connected in the report to what he saw as pragmatic political arguments:

> I am not at all sure that the Church as a corporate body would be wise to identify itself too closely with a particular political programme. It is not that churches have no right to make political judgements. Sometimes they have to. In a case of this complexity the problem is that decision-making must depend on a host of subtle factors which those not directly engaged

in the business of politics have difficulty in estimating.[10]

He argued, therefore, that the role of the Church here is to set a moral direction and put pressure on the political process, whilst recognising the imponderables surrounding the process which make movement in the desired direction difficult to accomplish.

The following week, Peter Jenkins, one of the *Guardian*'s senior writers, used the report as a springboard for further thoughts: 'Widening the constituency of concern' (27 October 1982). He also commended the report as exemplifying the enquiring spirit of the times so far as the nuclear issue is concerned. He set this alongside other challenges to nuclear orthodoxy. These include Robert McNamara, McGeorge Bundy, Gerard Smith and George Kennan's challenge to NATO's strategy of 'flexible response'; Lord Carver and Lord Zuckerman's disbelief in the feasibility of 'limited nuclear war" and the Palme Commission's call for a zone free of battlefield nuclear weapons. Received nuclear wisdom is losing its sway over the public mind:

> The paradox of deterrence becomes too paradoxical for sensible minds when it reaches the point at which war-fighting and *'war-winning'* capability is deemed necessary for the credibility of deterrence. This is not thinking about the unthinkable but double-thinking about the unthinkable.

Following a strong critique of the Reagan administration' Jenkins suggested that unilateral nuclear disarmament in Britain is too parochial a solution and offered a threefold list of priorities: first, a verifiable nuclear freeze; second, a no-early-use NATO strategy involving the use of battlefield nuclear weapons; and third, political policies of détente or managed coexistence backed up by simple deterrence.

Elsewhere in the media the report also gained attention. Professor John Vincent examined the arguments in his piece 'Church against Bomb':

> It can be recommended with confidence to anyone new to the study of the question. It is not ... a unilateralist tract and anyone who denounces it as such without having read it will come badly unstuck. ... The sentences are crisp, intelligent and unemotional. The Church has taken a lurch towards reality.
>
> (*Sunday Times*, 24 October 1982)

His main reservation was that the effects on Western Europe of creating a nuclear-free Britain within NATO were problematical. Moreover, in order to make war less likely, we need to know more about the behaviour of the two superpowers. This, in Vincent's view, the report did not do with sufficient thoroughness, although he readily admits it is a difficult task.

In the *Observer*, Conor Cruise O'Brien wrote two articles on successive weeks, which prompted a response from the Bishop of Salisbury (24 October

1982; 31 October 1982; 7 November 1982). According to O'Brien, what's wrong with the report was that:

> Its political conclusions are incompatible with its central, ethical conten-
> tion, which does point in the direction of withdrawal from a military
> alliance based on the concept of nuclear deterrence. You can't be against
> nuclear deterrence and in favour of NATO.

Nevertheless, O'Brien went on to suggest:

> because of its ethics and irrespective of its comparatively Mickey Mouse
> political conclusions, *The Church and the Bomb* is a profoundly subversive
> work. Mrs Thatcher is said to be very angry about this report, and from her
> point of view she is right to be angry. If the Church of England adopts this
> report, it will be saying that the strategic thinking of the Western alliance
> is ethically intolerable.

The Bishop's reply was one which also had relevance for the Habgood argument already cited. It was to stress the importance of going beyond ethical principles to practical recommendations on the grounds that this was an appropriate way of stimulating debate not pre-empting eventual conclu-sions. He was looking for discussion that could have real consequences. This form of pragmatism was seen as necessary in the light of the fact that orthodox claims for the realistic (that is, peacekeeping) character of mutual balanced force deterrents were themselves highly disputable: 'Mutual balanced force deterrence is said to be "stable" while suggestions of even modest unilateral reductions are dismissed as "seriously destabilising". This is almost the exact reverse of the truth' ('The freedom not to be afraid', *Observer*, 7 November 1982).

The importance of the 'Church and the Bomb' debate to which the report gave rise was, then, clearly recognised by the quality press. The potential rift between Church and state was identified. But in addition, the internal differences between bishops of the Church provided another element in the story. 'Bishops will clash in debate on bomb' was the title of Judith Judd's piece in the *Observer* (6 March 1983). She outlined the varying positions of the Archbishop of Canterbury and the Bishops of London, Salisbury, Durham and Birmingham. The piquancy of Salisbury's position was savoured: a Thatcher appointment to the Bishopric, he had been converted, as he saw it, by the reasonableness of the arguments of his colleagues on the working party. He had, suggested Judd, 'startled everybody, including himself, by becoming the strong man and extremist of the Church of England'. This put him directly in conflict with the Bishop of London, who was chairing the Board of Social Responsibility, to which the working party had first to report. He, said Judd, 'has shocked Christian nuclear disarmers by saying that nuclear weapons are morally acceptable'. For the record, the Bishop of London outlined his position in an address that was later published:

While recognising the utterly appalling prospect of the use of nuclear weapons, I believe that their possession and use can be morally acceptable as a way of exercising our moral responsibility in a fallen world. I do not believe that we can ever say that their possession or use can be morally good. At best we can say that they may be morally acceptable.[11]

As for Archibishop Runcie, he was described by Judd as a multilateralist opposed to the conclusion of *The Church and the Bomb*: 'The Archbishop, holder of the Military Cross, will weigh his words with customary care.'

FRAMING AND LINKING THE DEBATE: TWO ILLUSTRATIONS

We give now two illustrations from the quality press of the way the 'Church and the Bomb' debate was contextualised. The examples are drawn from the *Sunday Times* and the *Guardian* and form something of a contrast with TV news coverage, which we examine later.

On consecutive Sundays, one before and one after the debate, the *Sunday Times* featured pieces by its religious affairs correspondent, John Whale. As the son of a former Bishop of London, he was perhaps particularly well placed to comment on the organisation and politics of the Church of England. His prediction of the outcome of the debate was accurate: 'The Church of England will this week distance itself from the government's policy on nuclear weapons.' He outlined the three main positions in the debate represented by the Bishops of London, Salisbury and Birmingham and forecast, again correctly, that Salisbury would lose but that Birmingham's amendment, which argued for no-first-use of nuclear weapons, would carry the day and hence create a gap between the Church's position and the government's. What Whale also did was to draw attention to a well-attended conference of Christian Conservatives (mostly Anglican) which had just taken place and to the rapturous reception accorded to the journalist Paul Johnson, who had stated that the evil of nuclear weapons was outstripped by the evil of possible Soviet domination.

On February 13, Whale had a centrepiece article entitled 'The Church political'. He suggested that the vote went the way it did because the Church remains deferential to its hierarchy: 'Unilateralism went down heavily – the vote was three to one – because the Archbishop of Canterbury strongly resisted it; no-first-use scraped through because a figure of almost equal seniority and weight, the Bishop of Durham, spoke up for it.' At the heart of Whale's article, however, was a statement about the relationship between moral judgements and specific recommendations. He supported the view that Church leaders had to get down to specifics. The effect of doing so is that two different kinds of discourse intermingle. The Bishop of Birmingham had said in the debate that there could never be a moral justification for a first nuclear strike: 'The intention is not defence but naked aggression in the form of preemptive action. The nature of the act is evil. It is deliberately to loose hell on earth.' Yet, as Whale points out, this is current NATO strategy for stopping a Soviet tank attack on West Germany, so the moralist becomes a strategist whether he wants to or not. Whale's conclusion is that if Michael Heseltine can come into the Ministry of Defence and express his opinions, without any specialist experience, then the Bishops of Birmingham and Salisbury, with a good knowledge of defence issues to call on, certainly have the right to offer guidance and advice on such matters.

The *Guardian*'s coverage of the debate merits comment for several reasons. On both the day of the debate and the day after the leading editorial was devoted to the issue. 'What binds the Synod and Mr Bush?' asked the *Guardian*, referring to the American Vice-President's current tour of Europe for discussions on defence policy. The article pointed to the widespread anxiety in Europe and the United States about the adequacy of received theories of nuclear deterrence and the increasing concern about the growing stockpile of nuclear weapons. This was linked to a lack of confidence in President Reagan, doubts about the intentions of the US to negotiate seriously with the Russians on arms reductions, and a feeling that policy in the West lacks substance. The last paragraph of the editorial sought to connect the two concurrent events, the Bush visit and the Synod debate, as a way of symbolising the policy dilemmas of the West:

> It is that void [in Western policy] in their own humble way, which the Salisbury team sought to fill. They seek (in a rather more measured way than Mr Foot) to dispose of Britain's own small segment of nuclear armoury. It is – and this should be clearly understood – only a small beginning in their terms. It is giving away something that does not much matter: something that could not be used independently in any remotely foreseeable combat, something which if considered one-to-one (the doughty US alone against the USSR) automatically undercuts all NATO's case about the importance of the nuclear balance to deterrence. The question, of course, is what one would get in return for the gesture: and the sad answer, alas, is probably very little. But the context – displayed clearly enough in all the Synod's likely amendments today – is not any longer one where that single, sad answer suffices. We have reached a point where the obscenity and finality of the holocaust in waiting must be made to retreat by one means or another rather than allowed inexorably to advance. That is the message Mr Bush must take home with him: by one means or another.
>
> (*Guardian*, 10 February 1983)

Next day, the first editorial declared: 'The Synod declines to stand pat'. It took the view that the Conservative Party, while no doubt very pleased that the recommendations of the 'Church and the Bomb' report were rejected (it obtained 23 per cent support from the Synod), would be unhappy with the

Bishop of Birmingham's amendment 'which plainly repudiated the first use of nuclear weapons in any circumstances'. The whole decision is interpreted within the wider context of the Geneva arms control talks. If they failed, the likelihood was, it was argued, that the Bishop of Salisbury's warning that the balance of terror can no longer be regarded as a stable force would gather support. The editorial concluded:

> The message from Church House is thus sharply different from that which Mr George Bush came to Britain hoping to hear; it is also, no doubt, sharply different from that which he will have heard in Downing Street. But it was the product of the same kind of doubts and uncertainties which now agitate the country as a whole. And they much more certainly reflect the mood of ordinary people in Britain that the proclaimed certainties emanating from high places.
>
> (*Guardian*, 11 February 1983)

On the same day the paper carried a half-page report from Martyn Halsall of the Church debate, with a photograph of the Synod in session under the heading: 'Compromise decision rejects any NATO first use of nuclear weapons. Synod throws out unilateralism by three to one'. Extracts from a number of speeches were given, the most extensive being that of the Archbishop of Canterbury. His opposition to the report was explicitly linked to his fear that its recommendations would undermine the Geneva negotiations, put the NATO alliance in disarray and strengthen United States isolationism.

In addition, there was a front-page story from Halsall headed 'Church rejects unilateral stance and favours no-first-strike'. There were photographs of the Bishops of Birmingham, Durham and Salisbury at the top of the page. Alongside the Halsall story and also under the photographs, David Fairhall, the defence correspondent, had written a piece headed 'Heseltine begins peace assault'. This referred to an address given to Tory women at the Conservative Central Office:

> he outlined the government's fundamental approach to nuclear deterrence and disarmament, reiterating its commitment to Trident, to NATO's 'duel track' decision on Cruise missile deployment and its continued refusal to yield to Opposition demands for a 'dual key' or British safety catch on these new weapons.

He also restated his refusal to debate the issues on a public platform with CND. In this respect the distance between the government and the Church of England was signalled. At the same time, the government's opposition to peace campaigners generally is indicated, a matter which is connected with a wider campaign initiated and co-ordinated by the government.

THE CHURCH AND THE BOMB: DEBATES ON TV NEWS
10 FEBRUARY 1983

It's been a long time since the Church of England found itself at the centre of so much attention. Queues for the public gallery were forming two hours before the debate began. Teams of police, unneeded as it happened, were on hand in case anti-nuclear demonstrators should disrupt proceedings. The debate was covered live by radio and television in Britain, and attended by thirty overseas broadcasting organisations. The issue – whether to back the recommendations of the report *The Church and the Bomb*.

(BBC1, 21.00, 10 February 1983)

What exactly was the Synod of the Church of England debating? The Chairman of the Church's Broad for Social Responsibility, the Bishop of London, put a motion to the Synod concerning Britain's nuclear weapons policy. An amendment was tabled by the Bishop of Salisbury in support of the working party's report, *The Church and The Bomb*, which he had chaired. In the event of that amendment falling, as it did, the Bishop of Birmingham had tabled another amendment, proposing Britain adopt a no-first-strike policy. This amendment was carried. The motion and the two amendments are detailed in Table 8.10.

The debate had been signalled in advance as a potential clash with government policy. Perhaps the Church of England, sometimes caricatured as 'the Tory Party at prayer', was moving leftwards and was going to embrace the Labour Party's policy on disarmament. Was the established state church going to speak with a different voice from that of the government?

The headlines of the main evening bulletins on the four channels put it this way:

Hello, good evening. First the main news of the day. The Church of England has voted to reject the policy of unilateral disarmament.

(Channel 4)

The Church of England's governing body, the Synod, has firmly rejected the idea of unilateral disarmament by Britain.

(BBC1)

The Church of England has voted overwhelmingly against Britain banning the Bomb.

(ITN)

Here at home the Church of England has had its most important debate of the week, some say its most important since the war, on the issue of nuclear policy. As predicted on *Newsnight* two nights ago, they voted against unilateralism.

(*Newsnight*, BBC2)

Table 8.10 The Church and the Bomb debate

Bishop of London's motion	Bishop of Salisbury's amendment	Bishop of Birmingham's amendment
15 That this Synod recognising:	34 Leave out all words after 'HM Government' and insert:	55 Leave out all words after 'international situation' and add:
(a) the urgency of the task of making and preserving peace; and	(a) to announce the UK's intention of carrying out, in consultation with its allies, a phased disengagement of the UK from active association with any form of nuclear weaponry, involving:	and (c) that it is not the task of the Church to determine defence strategy but rather to give a moral lead to the nation;
(b) the extreme seriousness of the threat made to the world by contemporary nuclear weapons and the dangers in the present international situation,	(i) bringing to an end the Polaris strategic nuclear system, and cancelling the order for proposed Trident replacement;	(i) affirms that it is the duty of Her Majesty's Government and her allies to maintain adequate forces to guard against nuclear blackmail and to deter nuclear and non-nuclear aggressors;
calls upon HM government, together with our allies NATO,	(ii) discontinuing all nuclear weapons wholly or mainly of British manufacture;	(ii) asserts that the tactics and strategies of this country and her NATO allies should be seen to be unmistakably defensive in respect of the countries of the Warsaw Pact;
(i) to reduce progressively its dependence upon nuclear weapons in its programme for defence; and	(ii) discontinuing all nuclear weapons wholly or mainly of British manufacture;	(iii) judges that even a small-scale first use of nuclear weapons could never be morally justified in view of the high risk that this would lead to full-scale nuclear warfare;
(ii) to work to strengthen international treaties especially as they apply to the possession and use of such weapons.	(iii) negotiating Britain's withdrawal from the manning of nuclear weapons systems manufactured by others;	(iv) believes that there is a moral obligation on all countries (including the members of NATO) publicly to forswear the first use of nuclear weapons in any form;
	(iv) negotiating an end to agreements for the present or future deployment of nuclear weapons systems on British soil;	(v) bearing in mind that many in Europe live in fear of nuclear catastrophe and that nuclear parity is not essential to deterrence, calls on Her Majesty's Government to take immediate steps in conjunction with her allies to further the principles embodied in this motion so as to reduce progressively NATO's dependence on nuclear weapons and to decrease nuclear arsenals throughout the world.
	(b) to invite other governments to make positive responses to the British initiative by comparable measures either of renunciation or restraint;	
	(c) to continue to prosecute vigorously disarmament negotiations of all kinds; and	
	(d) to devote resources to positive programmes for the building of peace and the fostering of international confidence along the lines indicated in the remaining recommendations of *The Church and the Bomb* (namely nos 2–17 and 21–22).'	

So the inference was clear:

> The Church of England, the State Church, pillar of the establishment, today firmly ended speculation that it was flirting with the defence policy of the Labour Left.
>
> (Channel 4)

> Mrs Thatcher will no doubt be relieved that the Church has voted down the Bishop of Salisbury and his unilateral report *The Church and the Bomb*.
>
> (*Newsnight*, BBC2)

The word 'Left' in the sentence is redundant in the sense that the amendment was consistent with the policy of the Labour Party. To refer to the Left is a coded way of speaking about 'extremism' in this cultural context. It diminishes the strength of the unilateralist position in the Labour Party. Of course, as the Bishop of Salisbury's motion made clear, the unilaterism in the proposal was not seen as an alternative to multilateral disarmament, but was seen in the context of multilateralism. Channel 4 reported the Bishop of Salisbury as having made 'an impressive speech, surely one of the most cogent marshallings of the arguments for unilateralism ever assembled' but it is the dichotomy between unilateral and multilateral that is typically reinforced.

In the Channel 4 news, moreover, the opening statement about the Church debate and the later developments of the story is separated by references to the British Secretary of Defence, the Prime Minister and the visiting American Vice-President all commenting on disarmament. Since the statements they make are left without comment or challenge, they serve to contextualise our understanding of the Church debate. This section of news is linked with the word 'meanwhile':

> Meanwhile down the road from the Synod, Michael Heseltine has been talking about the Bomb to a group of Conservative women. He opened his speech by stressing that he was Secretary of State for Defence, not Attack, and went on to explain the government's stance on disarmament: 'No sane person could hold my job for a moment without becoming preoccupied with how to achieve negotiated arms control and arms reduction. I believe that if we are to do this, we must maintain forces strong enough to deter aggression, while at the same time pursuing security at low levels of force on both sides. The so-called 'peace campaigners' present these as opposites, but in negotiating with a hardheaded power like the Soviet Union they must go hand in hand.'
>
> NEWSCASTER: In the Commons the Prime Minister affirmed that President Reagan's zero option is not a 'take it or leave it' option, but she went on to stress that it is the ultimate goal, because it would provide the very best possible result for those who believe in safeguarding our way of life. The United States Vice-President George Bush left London today

at the end of his seven-nation European tour. Before he went he stressed that his attitude on disarmament had changed little:

BUSH: I have heard only one argument, only one, against our proposal. You know what it was? The Soviet Union doesn't like it. It's not good to negotiate, but again it takes a united strong alliance to stay firmly together and that's what I think we've got as I leave after this eleven-day trip.

Meanwhile, as they say, back at the Synod the Church had actually passed the Bishop of Birmingham's amendment. This endorsed the view that all countries should publicly forswear the first use of nuclear weapons in any form. This was only very briefly referenced on BBC1 and ITN's main evening news bulletins. These programmes have the largest news audiences. Yet this position is quite at variance with British government and NATO policy, and was identified as such on BBC2's *Newsnight*. No bulletin pointed out, however, that the no-first-strike pledge had been publicly made by the Soviet Union at the UN Special Session on Disarmament 1982.

The example we have used of special-event news leads us to suggest that the arrangement and juxtaposition of news information is a form of impression management. After all, the positive decision of the Church on the no-first-strike issue could have been the focus of attention and it would presumably have been somewhat more embarrassing to the government had that been the case. Even when it is mentioned in the account, there are also techniques that may be deployed to diminish its significance. The conclusion of the Channel 4 bulletin illustrates both the sustaining power of the 'anti-unilateralist' story and the discounting of the other issues raised:

Bishop Montefiore's amendment was passed by 275 votes to 222. So the debate ended with the Church of England firmly opposed to unilateral disarmament, but opposed, too, to a central plank in NATO doctrine, the commitment to be the first to use nuclear weapons if conventional forces can't contain a Russian advance. But does any of it matter? If the Church had joined the unilateral disarmers it would have been a huge embarrass-ment to the Tory Party, the government, especially in election year, and probably the Head of the Church, The Queen herself. It could have cost the Church dear in cancelled covenants from wealthy right-wing supporters, but that was avoided, even though Synod decisions like these aren't actually binding on anybody.

(Channel 4)

A day in the life of the Church became a day in the life of the media. Did it really matter? Did we really want to hear a group of serious-minded people calling the nation and the government to a position of no-first-strike? We would have to have been very attentive to tease out the potential significance of that message.

It would be a mistake to suppose that the concern of the Churches with the issue of nuclear war is to be equated with the presence or absence of media coverage. In this respect it is worth recalling the observations of two Church groupings which met later in 1983. The World Council of Churches at its Vancouver Assembly, July/August 1983, came out with a statement that is at variance with the kind of assumption typically enunciated on television news bulletins:

> Nuclear deterrence can never provide the foundation for genuine peace. It is the antithesis of an ultimate faith in that love which casts out fear. It escalates the arms race in a vain pursuit of stability. It ignores the economic, social and psychological dimensions of security and frustrates justice by maintaining the status quo in world politics. It destroys the reality of self-determination for most nations in matters of their own safety and survival, and diverts resources from basic human needs. It is the contradiction of disarmament because it exalts the threat of force, rationalises the development of new weapons of mass destruction, and acts as a spur to nuclear proliferation by persistently breaking the 'good faith' pledge of disarmament in the Non-Proliferation Treaty, thus tempting other governments to become nuclear weapon states. It is increasingly discredited by first-strike and warfighting strategies which betray the doubts about its reliability.

Not surprisingly, in the light of that statement, the World Council of Churches went on to recommend a mutual and verifiable freeze on the development, testing and deployment of nuclear weapons and delivery vehicles. We may pause to wonder what would be the significance of information that was structured on those assumptions, with alternative views being treated as misguided, as opposed to the dominant notion of deterrence as a regrettable necessity for keeping the peace.

In November 1983, the British Council of Churches produced its statement 'On making peace in a nuclear world'. There we read:

> This Council does not question the right of every nation to self-defence. It recognises that this and all nations have legitimate security interests. In view of the present threat to survival, however, it is becoming increasingly clear that traditional understandings of security are no longer adequate. It is now necessary for nations to move (if possible in a United Nations context) towards a framework of common security, an expression of rational love for our enemies, a love that is both in their interests and ours, a love that seeks to avoid steps that they will perceive as threatening.

The Council went on to support an agreed and verifiable freeze between the United States and the Soviet Union. It also urged that the United Kingdom, while remaining within NATO, should phase out British nuclear weapons and should not replace Polaris with Trident missiles. It also supported the view that Britain should support a no-first-use policy and posture within NATO, thus adding its collective weight to the view that prevailed in the Church of England Synod a few months earlier and on which this section has focused.

NOTES

1   Cmnd 6753, London: HMSO, 1977, p. 273.
2   Sometimes there seems to be a reluctance even to mention women. The report on Greenham Common on BBC1, 17.45, 11 December 1983, uses the word 'women' only once, substituting 'people' twice and 'demonstrators' three times. Other TV news coverage reveals a stereotyped approach to women and their role in the family.
3   This is not to say that their analysis of political parties is adequate. See the chapter on TV coverage of the Labour Party in *Really Bad News*, London, Writers & Readers Cooperative, 1982.
4   Beeban Kidron and Amanda Richardson, *Carry Greenham Home*, NFTS, 1983. This film has now been shown on Channel 4.
5   John Austin Baker, Bishop of Salisbury, 'People and the bomb', in David Martin and Peter Mullen (eds), *Unholy Warfare. The Church and the Bomb*, Oxford: Blackwell, 1983, p. 221.
6   *Ibid.*, p. 81.
7   *Ibid.*, p. 154.
8   *Ibid.*, p. 155.
9   *Ibid.*, p. 156.
10 Paul Abrecht and Ninian Koshy (eds), *Before It's Too Late. The Challenge Of Nuclear disarmament*, World Council of Churches, 1983.
11 Graham Leonard, Bishop of London, 'The morality of nuclear deterrence', in Martin and Mullen, op. cit., p. 193.

Chapter 9

The current affairs prism*

INTRODUCTION

What part have current affairs programmes played in the area of peace, defence and disarmament questions? We take as our point of departure two short articles by Peter Fiddick: 'Is TV properly reflecting the public concern with nuclear weapons?' and 'Doomsday debates that fit their pigeonhole'. The second of these is essentially an updating and amplification of the first. Fiddick reviewed the way in which the nuclear issue has come back on to the agenda of television since 1979 and raised a number of questions as to what it all signified. We take matters a step further by considering some more recent current affairs programmes and the formats and formulae within which they tend to operate.

Fiddick reminds us that in addition to treatment of the nuclear issue on regular current affairs programmes such as *Panorama*, *Weekend World* and *World in Action*, there is evidence of additional coverage. Among the examples he cites are *QED*; the BBC's popular science programme showed Mick Jackson's film *A Guide to Armageddon*. This sought to demonstrate what would happen if a one-megaton bomb was exploded above St Paul's Cathedral, and thereby give some appreciation of the power of today's nuclear weapons. Channel 4's all-women current affairs programme *Broadside* opened with a film on Greenham Common and the women's peace movement; it later looked at the effects of exposure to nuclear contamination on British servicemen and Australian Aborigines as a result of the weapons test programme in Australia during the 1950s. *Everyman*, the BBC's religious affairs programme, also looked at the Greenham peace protest. Although Fiddick does not mention it, *Everyman* also produced a film report by Peter France entitled 'What's wrong with the Bomb?' This was an account of the World Council of Churches' hearing on nuclear weapons and Christian conscience, which took place in Amsterdam in November 1981. There have

*First published in Glasgow University Media Group, *War and Peace News*, Milton Keynes, Open University Press, 1985, pp. 277–94.

been presentations of the defence debate made by Jonathan Dimbleby – his documentaries on *The Bomb* and *The Eagle and the Bear* – by John Pilger in *The Truth Game* and by Max Hastings in *The War about Peace*.

Fiddick comments in his *Listener* article:

> On the face of it, all this adds up to not a bad record of television, the main national communication medium, dealing with one of the most pressing subjects of national concern. If some researcher were to ferret out all the reports, discussions and documentaries, the list would seem quite long, I do not doubt, and the approaches suitably various, exposing different facets of a complicated and changing bundle of issues.
>
> (*Listener*, 21 April 1983)

Before touching on Fiddick's doubts and questions as to what this signifies, let us look at some examples of programmes that have been screened since May 1983. Most of this is within the current affairs framework, although we also make brief reference to other kinds of coverage, notably Channel 4's Nuclear Week in May 1983, which took on added significance since it was in the middle of the British General Election campaign.

As far as current affairs programmes are concerned, there are three main formats: (1) the structured debate; (2) the film report plus studio discussion; (3) the film report without studio discussion.[1]

MAIN FORMATS

The structured debate

The debate format is not uniform. Different programmes may operate different ground rules relating to turn-taking, the use of witnesses, the possibilities of cross-examination and ways of evaluating the outcome. For example, on 4 May 1983, BBC2 featured *The Great Nuclear Arms Debate*. This was in fact an American CBS programme, briefly introduced for a British audience by Charles Wheeler but chaired by CBS's Walter Cronkite. Four contributors in London, New York, Florence and Bonn respectively were linked up by satellite. These were Michael Heseltine, the British Secretary of Defence, Henry Kissinger, a former US Secretary of State, Paul Warnke, formerly a US SALT negotiator, and Egon Bahr, the chief opposition spokesperson on arms control for the Social Democratic Party in West Germany.

The debate lasted ninety minutes and was on the subject of the deployment of Cruise and Pershing II missiles in Europe. Cronkite soberly told his audience that there would be no concession to entertainment. The debate was preceded by a short film with voice-over commentary. This referenced the post-war growth in the arms race with long- and short-range weapons, the signing of SALT I and the refusal on the part of the USA to ratify SALT II in the aftermath, it was said, of the Soviet involvement in Afghanistan. The Soviet refusal to accept President Reagan's zero option was noted. The growth of the peace movement in Europe and the USA including the proposal for a nuclear freeze was also presented as part of the climate in which the current Geneva arms talks were taking place. A formal resolution was then put for debate: 'The United States should proceed with its scheduled deployment of nuclear weapons in Europe.' There was to be no formal voting on the resolution; at the end of the debate, which concluded in the early hours of 5 May in Britain, although it occupied prime time on American TV, Cronkite simply said that he would leave the outcome of the debate to the audience 'and perhaps to history'.

The procedure for the debate was elaborated at the outset: each speaker had 5.5 minutes to begin with; they then had 4 minutes each to reply to points that others had made; each then had 4 minutes' summary time; and finally there was time for a less rigidly organised exchange of views. Cronkite simply facilitated the turn-taking. Essentially this was a discussion about the strategy and tactics of arms control negotiations, especially the Geneva INF talks. As such the language of the debate was couched in political and military terms. Heseltine and Kissinger supported the dual-track position of NATO and its timetable, whilst Warnke and Bahr expressed reservations. Bahr appeared the most sceptical and suggested that fruitful discussions and negotiations were not possible on the basis of present positions and that both sides needed to negotiate seriously. There was, however, no account of how NATO arrived at its dual-track strategy and why its modernisation programme had been linked to the deployment of SS 20s by the Soviets. Was the rationale primarily military or political? Nor, as Cronkite mentioned at the end of the programme, was there a contribution from the nuclear freeze lobby, which would have produced an alternative perspective on what was a narrowly defined arms control debate.

The restricted terms within which this debate was conducted led to criticism from Professor Michael Pentz, a leading figure in CND. In a letter to the *Guardian* he challenged the accuracy of the figures relating to nuclear weaponry cited by Kissinger and Heseltine. He concluded:

This non-debate showed yet again that the exclusion of serious critics of NATO policy from 'the nuclear debate' is depriving the public of its right to know about and to judge an issue of vital importance to its security and survival.

(*Guardian*, 27 April 1983)

Such critics are not always excluded on current affairs as we shall show; nevertheless this objection reminds us that, even when the chairman of the debate was non-interventionist, the selection of the participants was a crucial editing decision. It remains possible that relevant and considered views on the topic in question may be omitted even when a large amount of time is allocated, as on this occasion.

In a debate screened on 29 May 1983, as part of Channel 4's Nuclear Week, CND did play a leading role. The resolution was: 'Nuclear weapons are immoral and serve no military purpose. Britain should give them up unilaterally'. This was chaired by Peter Jay, an experienced journalist and a former British Ambassador to the United States. The resolution was proposed by Monsignor Bruce Kent, General Secretary of CND, and opposed by Keith Ward, Professor of Moral and Social Theology at King's College, London. Each side was given 30 minutes to put forward their case. They were allowed to call two witnesses to support their case, who were also subject to cross-examination by the opposing side. This gave something of a court room atmosphere to proceedings, which was added to by the fact that a panel of twelve people, selected by a market research company 'because they have an open mind on this issue', was present to vote on the issue. In the event seven supported the motion, four opposed and one abstained. At the end of the programme Jay asked a number of the panel why they voted the way they did.

Given the title of the debate it was not surprising that the arguments were couched in both moral and military terms. Bruce Kent referred to just war theory, arguing from the principle of proportion that the use of nuclear weapons is wholly disproportionate to any objectives imaginable and therefore was immoral. He argued that first use of nuclear weapons was part of NATO's doctrine and that first-strike capacity was now more feasible with the advance of technology. In consequence, he maintained, the modernisation of nuclear weapons was destabilising in its effect and that, moreover, in military terms Britain's possession of nuclear weapons was senseless since their use against the Soviet Union would be suicidal. He used as his witnesses Dr Paul Rogers, Senior Lecturer in Peace Studies at Bradford University, and Ms Sheila Oates, General Secretary of the National Peace Council.

Keith Ward based his case on the right to self-defence in a violent world, arguing that the possession of nuclear weapons served to defend the values of the rule of law, democracy and civilisation. There are, he maintained, no self-evident absolutist truths in this situation and the realist has to think about the likely consequences of proposed actions. The possession of nuclear weapons was therefore not immoral in itself and could defend Britain against nuclear blackmail. He concluded that his view took better account of the complexities of the matter. As witnesses he used two colleagues from King's College: the Professor of War Studies, Lawrence Freedman, and the Principal, General Sir John Hackett, formerly of NATO High Command. The arguments used by both sides covered very similar ground to that of the Church and the Bomb debate, which we have already discussed.

The film report plus studio discussion

We take three examples of this format. The first is *Weekend World's Inquiry on the Bomb*, shown on 22 May 1983, on Channel 4. Brian Walden provided the voice-over to the film and interviewed the studio participants in an unusually long programme lasting 1 hour 40 minutes. He introduced the programme by telling us that the Bomb was second only to unemployment as an election issue. The film that followed sought to pursue the question: How and why did we get to our present predicament?

In his voice-over commentary, Walden started from the Second World War. He proceeded to reference Hiroshima, the post-war European settlement, the formation of NATO, Britain's decision to go nuclear, the development of Soviet nuclear weapons, and the movement of the USA's position from one of mutually assured destruction (MAD) to flexible response. This was the story, said Walden, of how we developed nuclear weapons to defend against foreign tyranny but today doubts are expressed about its wisdom. The story he told with the aid of archive film was elaborated and assisted by comments from military and strategic experts including Professor Margaret Gowing, Colonel Jonathan Alford, Professor Lawrence Freedman, Philip Windsor, Philip Williams, Professor Michael Howard and David Bolton. Institutional affiliations of these people included Oxford University, the LSE, the Institute for Strategic Studies, the Institute of International Affairs, and the Royal United States Institute.

Walden then interviewed three senior representatives of the main parties: Michael Heseltine (Conservative) John Silkin (Labour) and David Owen (SDP Alliance). The programme was in the run-up to the election and Walden as interviewer centred his questions on what he regarded as problematic in each party's position. Heseltine is asked about how a Tory government will handle a continuing protest movement. Silkin is questioned about the 'realism' of Labour's unilateralist position on nuclear weapons, and Owen about the niceties of no-first-use and no-early-use policy in relation to NATO's nuclear strategy.

The position of the presenter in this kind of format is very powerful and in a sense the more so since he is not ostensibly offering us a 'personal view'. He tells us at the beginning of the programme that we are dealing with complex military and diplomatic matters but claims that the film will set out the facts. Yet the selection of facts and their interpretation is fraught with methodological problems. The presenter is also an interpreter. In that respect Mr Walden's own political background as a former Labour MP opposed to unilateral nuclear disarmament over an extended period should be recalled. The choice of 'experts' to reinforce the implicit line in the programme is also crucial and simply nuances aspects of the philosophy of deterrence. In a strong attack on the programme, E. P. Thompson of *END* wrote:

What was offensive about this operation was the fact that anyone familiar with the literature will know that these 'experts' were hand-picked and rehearsed by Mr Walden to confirm the prejudices which Mr Walden has long held, and that for every 'expert' offered the presenter could have (if he had wished to be objective) found an expert with equal or greater authority to offer a contrary view. And most of the questions proposed by Walden to these experts were not matters of information at all, which require expert research, but were matters of political choice and value as to which these gentlemen have no more right to claim authority than any other citizen.[2]

In the studio interviews that followed, the initiative is also very much with the interviewer. The participants were segregated from each other in the conventional arrangements and the presenter becomes the mediator of the message through the questions he chooses to ask.

The second example of this format is the BBC programme *A Matter for Joint Decision*, screened in November 1983. This was presented and chaired by John Tusa, when Heseltine, Silkin and Owen as political adversaries and party spokesmen were again involved in the studio discussion. Was there, could there be, should there be, dual control over the use of American nuclear weapons based in Britain? This issue was explored in a film report by David Henshaw. The reason for taking up the issue was anchored to an opinion poll which indicated that 55 per cent of the population was against the installation of Cruise missiles and 45 per cent for it. At the same time 82 per cent as against 18 per cent were reported as being in favour of the presence of nuclear weapons in Britain. In the case of Cruise, however, only 4 per cent of the population thought that the USA should have sole control, whilst the overwhelming 96 per cent supported dual control if the missiles were to be installed.

The film report was designed to show, mainly through interviews with US politicians and military people, that despite declared 'understanding', dual control was not a serious reality and over the past thirty years never has been. The US airforce has been in Britain continuously since 1948, when it first arrived for what were described as goodwill and training purposes. General Len Johns of the USAF, who was in Britain between 1948–52, pointed out that the alert could have been activated if necessary. Professor Margaret Gowing took the view that the then Prime Minister, Clement Attlee, did not realise the implications of what he was doing and made no agreements about the use of the bases. Dean Acheson, then US Secretary of State, had taken the view that the British could not interfere with the United States' constitutional right to declare war. He would accept, therefore, no agreement on the use of the bases, which none the less increased in number under Attlee and other post-war Prime Ministers. The position essentially taken up in the film report was summed up in the response of the US arms control negotiator Paul Warnke – that the country which physically controls weapons makes the decision and that therefore joint controls are effective until it counts! This view was also expressed by former Secretary of State Robert MacNamara. A definite line is taken in the film report even though it is not billed as a 'personal view'.

The subsequent studio discussion with the politicians was not segregated as in the previous example but involved some interchange. Heseltine claimed that the film misrepresented the position, which was that joint control was a reality. Silkin said it was all very disturbing and that there were a number of occasions when American bombers had flown off on an alert without consultation. Owen said that dual control was possible and that the film was ridiculous because it had omitted to mention the period of the Thor missile, 1959–62, when joint control was a reality. It was, he said, safer for this country to be involved in the launch mechanism and that was why the then Prime Minister, Harold Macmillan, had been prepared to pay for it. The concluding part of the programme then allows a turn of the political wheel in which we hear: (a) that we actually have dual control, (b) that we do not and cannot, (c) that we do not but could and should.

A final example of this format is the *Panorama* programme of 21 November 1983. Fred Emery, a regular presenter, opened the programme by referring to the fact that the film *The Day After* had just been shown in the USA and that in Britain we were facing the advent of the Cruise missile. He poses two questions: Are we on the verge of a hair-trigger strategy with no time for second thoughts? And are we making the world more dangerous? As with the previous example, use is made of public opinion polls, in this instance a specially commissioned *Panorama*/Marplan poll. Four questions and responses were reported (see Table 9.1).

Table 9.1 Panorama/Marplan poll results on nuclear weapons in Britain, 1983

1 Should Britain accept American Cruise missiles?			
	Nov. 83	*Oct. 83*	*May 83*
Yes	42%	37%	34%
No	47%	48%	54%

2 Has American action over Grenada made you more or less likely to trust the Americans?	
More likely	17%
Less likely	58%

3 There should be a physical device to prevent firing without British consent	76%
No such safeguard is necessary	17%

4 Britain should not keep any nuclear weapons	29%
Britain should keep nuclear weapons	64%

Whereas in the previous example the responses to the questions aggregated to 100 per cent, here they do not. In the first case the 'don't know' category is ignored, whereas in this case the 'don't knows' are not listed but are implicitly taken into account. But in both instances we can see that from the interpretation of a perceived concern based on poll findings the programme identifies an issue and then proceeds with a film report.

In his film report Peter Taylor explores how it was that the West developed the 'dual attack' approach to arms control and the problems this has brought in its train. The case developed by Taylor was that the reasons for the decisions on Cruise and Pershing II deployment were political and not military. This was prompted by Herr Schmidt, then West German Chancellor, who feared that the strategic parity of the USA and the USSR, as he saw it, might lead to a refusal on the part of the USA to support Western Europe, and especially West Germany, in the event of a Soviet attack. This anxiety that the USA might 'decouple' from the Western European alliance was all the greater since Schmidt feared that the other members of the alliance might not come to West Germany's aid in that event. Hence the deployment of United States land-based nuclear theatre weapons, in Schmidt's view, could be seen as a guarantor against decoupling. He successfully argued for this policy within NATO and this was approved in December 1979. According to Raymond Garthoff, a former SALT negotiator, the development of SS 20s was seen as part of the Soviet modernisation programme and in military estimations did not call for additional requirements of deployment or a special necessity to deter the Soviets from deploying SS 20s. Taylor also cited a secret discussion document – 'Theatre modernisation and arms control' – prepared by the Americans before the Schmidt initiative which supports this view. This could of course provide a context in which President Reagan's subsequent zero option offer would not be regarded as a serious negotiation by the Soviets. Garthoff suggested that there was nothing surprising about the Soviet rejection of the zero option.

In this report Taylor counter-balances the views of Garthoff with those of Kenneth Adelman, the United States arms control negotiator, who argued that NATO must keep up its deterrent strength. He also contrasted in interviews the differing positions of Helmut Schmidt and Willy Brandt. Brandt, a former Chancellor, now represents the majority view in the SDP, which regards the deployment of Pershing II in West Germany as undesirable.

Two themes emerge in the film: first, that the hearts and minds of the people in the Western alliance have been disaffected by a clumsy policy which has raised many worries; and second, that the effects of deployment will be profoundly destabilising. In particular, Professor John Erickson, an Edinburgh University defence specialist, argued that Pershing II has 10–11 minutes' flight time from launch to target. The Soviets believe, he said, that their command and control centres are under threat by the new weapons and that this severely restricts their military options. Launch on warning becomes their most workable option.

Following the film report, Emery chaired a studio discussion with Michael Heseltine and Denis Healey, representing the government and the opposition. This hinged on the issue of how far the dual-track policy, if it led to the deployment of Cruise and Pershing II, enhanced or diminished collective security. On all aspects of the issue the two men were opposed: the necessity of the policy; its effect on decoupling and destablisation; and the dangers inherent in it as an element of flexible response strategy. Heseltine supported the policy and the position of Helmut Schmidt. Healey did not and also cast doubt on the good faith of the US negotiators. He pointed out that Adelman, the man in charge of negotiations, had gone on record at one time as saying that arms control negotiations are a sham, whose only purpose was to soothe public opinion at home and abroad.

The film report format

Here we cite three examples taken from late 1983. We see that this format can take the character of investigative journalism.

On *Panorama* (5 September 1983), Tom Mangold, following a brief introduction from Fred Emery referencing the Korean airliner which the Russians shot down, gave us a report entitled 'Beyond deterrence'. This was filmed in the United States and the interviewees comprised military men, strategic specialists and scientists. Mangold referenced President Reagan's endorsement of the militarisation of space (23 March 1983), the ultimate goal of which was to eliminate the threat posed by strategic nuclear missiles. He cites this as an example of the extension of the arms race and as a concomitant to the doctrine of flexible response, which has taken the place of the earlier deterrent doctrine of Mutually Assured Destruction. Mangold proceeds to bring forward specialist witnesses such as Dr John Steinbruner, Director of Policy Studies at the Brookings Institute, to suggest that with or without extensions into space the whole defence system is vulnerable. Because of this central vulnerability of the command posts and communication networks there is tremendous pressure on both sides (although they deny it) to go for a pre-emptive strike. This can create great tension between political and military decision-makers. Even the President of the USA is viewed as a poor command and control risk. Whether he would reach his jumbo jet in the eight minutes required is doubtful and in any case he would then have no means of communicating with Moscow. Thus the pre-emptive strike would cause very great confusion as a result of the vulnerabilities of the system.

It is in this context that the planned deployment of Cruise and Pershing II is set. The Soviets see them as targeted on Moscow and their command posts. Given the short flight times of Pershing II, the options open to the Russians are very limited. The argument followed is that they will be constrained to follow a launch on warning policy and that this is a very risky situation. The extension of defence into space to deal with pre-emptive strikes constitutes the strategic defence plan which goes 'beyond deterrence'. Mangold draws attention to critics who see this as further contributing to the arms race and causing greater instability. Dr Sidney Drell, Professor of Physics at Stanford University, described the whole approach as 'the fallacy of the last move'. Since the time-scales for decision have become so short, we are living in a hair-trigger situation where human decisions are heavily constrained by computers. Hence computer errors can precipitate the fateful exchanges. In a similar vein Dr Desmond Ball of the Department of Strategic Studies at the Australian National University concluded that the question of control is central and that the political control of such technical systems is the most difficult one can possibly envisage. People are deluding themselves if they have confidence in such arrangements.

We can see in this example that Mangold is questioning the rationality of the arms race and the direction it is taking. To do so he employs a combination of scientific and strategic specialists to expose what he sees as the contradiction and dangers implicit in the developing tendencies. Even though he interviews those who support the arms race into space, such as Edward Teller and the head of the Pentagon's Defence Advanced Research Projects Agency, Dr Robert Cooper, it is clear where Mangold's sympathies lie. This comes out in the programme and also in articles in the *Listener* based on his investigation. There he writes of a new instability which could lead to a witting or unwitting pre-emptive strike:

> Even if both superpowers were to develop these new systems in roughly equal time-scales and achieve rough parity, the technological time-scale of warfare will have been changed by several orders of magnitude. Today, we still have a precious few minutes – not many, but perhaps enough – to think, reason, cool down and judge against the destruction of the Northern Hemisphere.
>
> In President Reagan's brave new world of strategic defence, those minutes will have been replaced by milliseconds; and human judgement and compassion by the circuits on a silicon chip.
>
> How can that prospect enhance international security?[3]

The second example is a BBC *Newsnight Special* presented by John Tusa in November 1983. This is introduced by an anonymous announcer: 'John Tusa talks to leading defence experts about new ideas on NATO's strategy that could lead to a nuclear-free Europe.' Tusa, in his film report, records the views of senior politicians and military commanders who regard NATO's current policy as 'suicidal, misguided and unnecessary'. They include Robert MacNamara, General Jochen Loser, a former West German NATO chief and Admiral Noel Gaylor. The opinion of Lt General Mikhail Milstein, Senior Researcher at the US–Canada Institute, was also obtained. The overall argument was that the deterrent strategy of NATO was not credible and that a system of defence based on conventional weapons was an available alternative to deal with the Soviet 'threat' in Europe. This was both possible on the basis of new anti-tank weapons and financially credible. And there is no good reason to suppose it would lead to a decoupling of the United States from Western Europe. To move in this direction would take away the need for tactical nuclear weapons and possibly in time go beyond that. So Tusa interpreted his role as presenting the early stages of a debate within NATO of an alternative defence policy that would diminish the reliance of both East and West on nuclear weapons and with it the possibility of judgemental mistakes that could lead to nuclear war.

The third and final example of this kind of investigative journalism is *TV Eye*'s programme in November 1983, 'Here comes Cruise'. After a brief introduction from Alastair Burnett, who described Cruise as the most controversial weapon in the present nuclear debate, Peter Prendergast gave his film report. This consisted of a simulation of what was involved in moving Cruise out of Greenham to an appropriate launching-base. A convoy of the exact size and dimensions with replica missiles on board was moved from Greenham some twenty-two miles away to a place just outside the village of Whitchurch in Hampshire.

Air Vice-Marshall Stuart Menaul described the weapon in positive terms as very efficient, small, flying subsonic but at reasonably high speed, difficult to detect and not easy to shoot down. Colonel Jonathan Alford said the purpose of moving the weapon out of the base was to keep the other side guessing. Three *vox pop.* interviews were conducted at Whitchurch. Their responses ranged from 'It's got to come. You can't stop progress', to 'They won't work anyway' and 'We can't have peace and destruction at the same time'.

But what is Cruise for? Prendergast outlined the scenario for possible use in relation to a Soviet conventional attack on West Germany where they had obtained the upper hand. Colonel Alford saw the missile as primarily a deterrent but noted that it could be directed at Soviet military bases, which of course implies first-use possibility. Frank Barnaby, a former Director of the Stockholm Peace Research Institute, claimed that the missile was accurate to within 50 metres and since it carried very large warheads could destroy military targets. But it was slow and he questioned the usefulness of its strategic and tactical role. Later in the programme the disarmament analyst Dan Smith claimed that if Cruise was used, or the Russians thought it was about to be used, the consequence would be a massive retaliation. Furthermore, although he thought the concept of parity was a ludicrous idea, the Russians work with it. They are behind at present and will want to catch up.

Some doubt was cast upon the usefulness of moving Cruise about the English countryside. Defence analyst Owen Greene pointed out that there are so many defence sites in central and southern England that there are considerable limits as to where the convoy could end up if these were to be avoided. He argued that the Russians would follow the same logic and have all these possibilities targeted. Therefore the weapon was very vulnerable to attack.

Prendergast brought two senior politicians, Denis Healey (Labour) and Francis Pym (Conservative), down to the site at Whitchurch and interviewed them separately. Healey claimed the weapon was militarily useless because vulnerable to attack; that it raised the risk of a nuclear attack on Britain; that it made disarmament more difficult, and that it weakened public support for NATO. Pym argued that it would convince the Kremlin that, even though they are stronger than us, the price for attacking us was too high to pay. Cruise filled a gap in the West's deterrence strategy, he maintained. It would not be a British finger on the button, however. Professor Lawrence Freedman took the view that despite talk of a British veto, in the end it was an American decision. The programme concluded that arguments over whether Cruise is the price of peace or the height of folly will go on.

SATIRE AND OPINION

In the last week in May 1983, Channel 4 produced a cluster of programmes on the issues of defence disarmament. These had been scheduled before the announcement of the General Election and therefore were additional to the discussion of these matters which the forthcoming election was provoking. The programmes represent a variety of styles, formats and emphases which take us beyond the current-affairs mode in some instances.

One new approach to the presentation of the topic of nuclear war was *It'll all be over in half an hour*. This consisted of three late-night programmes on successive evenings in which Jonathan Dimbleby explored a number of questions, which were illustrated by songs and sketches. With a mixture of satire and black humour, the programmes questioned the rationale for the arms race.

The first programme focused on the in-built momentum of the arms race. It elaborated the significance of President Eisenhower's warnings about the need to control the military-industrial complex. It looked at the ways in which modernisation of weapons systems took place, often in secret as in the case of the Chevaline programme to update Polaris. The role of deterrence theory was then questioned in the light of modernisation programmes since, it was said, new weapons can create new rules and in particular there was now talk of winning a nuclear war. Consequently, nuclear deterrent theory was turned on its head.

The second programme looked at the issue of civil defence. It suggested that we tend to live with images of past wars which are totally inappropriate to a nuclear war. It criticised the government for its unwillingness to give adequate information about the impact and effects of nuclear attacks. It suggested that *Protect and Survive* was thoroughly unsatisfactory as a guide to citizens as to what to do in the event or nuclear war and that there is no coherent civil defence policy except that, in David Owen's words, 'The governors will go underground, the governed will stay on top.' Civil defence, nevertheless is portrayed as being inextricably linked with military strategy. To provide adequate civil defence for all the people would be enormously costly and could sharpen the fear of war, whereas for the deterrence threat to remain credible it is necessary for us to appear resolute and not fearful of war. Against this, Dimbleby suggested, perhaps the less you fear war in the present circumstances the more likely it becomes.

The third and last programme looked at the position of Europe in the context of current nuclear strategic thinking. This considered the doctrine of flexible response, argued that the concept of a limited nuclear war was a dangerous fallacy, and encouraged strategists to think of Europe as a principal battleground. Scepticism was expressed about the conduct of arms negotiations in so far as disarmament talks are actually accompanied by increases in nuclear weaponry, in the name of the modernisation. It was argued that the real debate about disarmament must go beyond simplistic labels of unilateralist and multilateralist. Attention was drawn to the views of Lord Mountbatten, Lord Carver and Sen. Edward Kennedy as departures from orthodoxy. The conclusion was drawn that there is no longer a consensus on nuclear strategy in Europe, and that is partly a result of the growth of the peace movement in Europe and its impact on the political parties. Consequently, we have reached a critical moment in a critical debate.

These programmes could be described as anti-establishment in their general thrust. Nor did they ignore the position of the Soviet Union and its responsibility to promote peace through disarmament. They were a new departure in style. With the memorable exception of the comedian Jasper Carrot reading out portions of *Protect and Survive* in the course of one of his programmes, it is difficult to think of nuclear defence issues being handled in this format. The songs were reminiscent of those of Tom Lehrer first heard some two decades or more earlier.

For the three days in which *It'll all be over in half an hour* were shown, there were also three *Opinion* programmes. In each case these were shown directly following the anti-nuclear satirical programme; in each case also the chosen spokesman defended the policy of nuclear deterrence. These were straight to the camera talks with only slight camera movements around a head and shoulders focus. The sequencing of these programmes could be interpreted as an attempt at balance.

Michael Howard, Professor of History at Oxford University, spoke on the case against unilateral nuclear disarmament. His argument was that we cannot disinvent nuclear weapons and return to the garden of nuclear innocence and that the concept of deterrence was the worst system for keeping the peace except for all the others. Policy should be based on the attempt to maximise the deterrent effect while minimising the chance of use. The realistic approach, he argued, to keeping peace was through arms control agreements. Alternatives such as nuclear-free zones in Europe, or absolute moral positions such as pacificism, would, he judged, have the unintended consequence of destabilising the world and creating terrible uncertainty. We have to take account of the consequences of our actions rather than having utopian views about world government or bringing about a new international order. We can stabilise the peace if we are clear headed. He concluded with the observation that it is unwise in a minefield simply to get up and run.

Lord Cameron, a former Chief of Defence Staff, argued the case for a nuclear defence policy for Britain. He started from a similar position to Professor Howard: nuclear weapons cannot be disinvented. Millions of people did not take the Nazi threat seriously; it would be just as mistaken to ignore the Soviet threat today. Lord Cameron described the Soviet arms position as representing a real but marginal advantage over the West, and justified the NATO doctrine of flexible response. He went on to justify from his standpoint the deployment of Cruise and Pershing, NATO's first-strike position, Britain's independent nuclear deterrent, and the decision to install Trident as a replacement for Polaris (preferring the larger D5 to the C4 system).

Roger Scruton, Reader in Philosophy at Birbeck College, London, entitled his talk, 'The Illusions of Disarmament'. This was a very explicit attack on CND. He likened this 'so-called peace movement' to Hitler's Nuremberg pre-war rallies, where crowds supported him with a mystical enthusiasm for a cause they did not understand. He likened the CND movement to a millennarian religion with an apocalyptic longing to be rid of the dilemmas of the real world. CND's concentration on the horrors of nuclear death, he suggested, were the equivalent of hell-fire sermons, yet their solutions were ludicrous and irrational. The emphasis of his talk was to categorise CND as irrational, a term which recurred. Against this he set his assessment of the Soviet threat, and its disposition to overrun its neighbours. Therefore, we are bound into a system of deterrence through circumstances beyond our control: without this power to repel and deter Soviet leaders, we would be subjected to moral blackmail.

The *Opinion* programmes were very different in style to the cabaret satirical programmes that preceded them. They give the speaker the opportunity to state a position and then develop or seek to justify the grounds for that view. They are in effect visual radio talks.

CONCLUSION: GESTURE WITHOUT MOTION?

While the role of nuclear weapons in defence has clearly come on to the agenda of television, the extent of the initiative should not be overstated. In Fiddick's view public concern has run ahead of the media. It is relevant to observe how public opinion polls are themselves used and even commissioned by current affairs programmes. These can then serve to legitimise the case for examining the topics as being a matter of public concern. There is,

Fiddick suggests, a general awareness of the sheer killing power of the new generation of nuclear weapons. Hence the internal contradictions of poll findings – with strong support for Britain remaining in NATO and retaining a nuclear capability, but strong opposition to Cruise and Trident – make some kind of sense. If this assessment is deep rooted, then it will not easily go away. Moreover, since 1979–80, with the advent of the Thatcher and Reagan administrations, the nuclear question has more sharply divided political establishments. The working consensus that existed for over a decade, such that in Britain it was not even a subject for parliamentary debate, has dissolved. To this extent, as Fiddick observes, television was knocking on an open door. Once the issue had become controversial and a source of dissent, politicians and defence experts would be ready to express their point of view on current affairs programmes. As we have seen from the examples discussed, some of them appeared on several occasions. Current affairs programmes tend to operate in the responsive rather than the initiating mode so far as public discussion is concerned.

Yet some programmes do come to be defined as problematic and not only in the current-affairs framework. In such cases controversy may precede the showing of the programme, if indeed it is shown. Peter Watkins' film *The War Game* has become a *cause célèbre*. Originally made for the BBC in 1965, it had still not been shown on television by 1985. Lord Normanbrook, the then Chairman of the BBC, held the view that it risked swinging public opinion against the government's defence policy. It seems that oppositional arguments are more likely to be seen as problematical. The dropping of the proposal to give E. P. Thompson the floor for the Dimbleby Lecture in 1981 is a well-known example (although the Reith Lectures shortly afterwards were given over to the thoughts of a NATO strategist). Nicholas Humphrey, the psychologist, did manage to deliver his Bronowski Lecture, in which he argued the case for nuclear disarmament, but the Bronowski Lectures have been discontinued. His was the last to be delivered. 'I could have told you five minutes after the lecture that there'd never be another one. I think it's basically a political thing,' said Mrs Bronowski (*Guardian*, 17 July 1982). More recently there were delays to the screening of John Pilger's *The Truth Game* until another programme could be made to 'balance' it. Pilger's 'personal view' had to be balanced by Max Hasting's 'personal view', *The War about Peace*, although how many people watched both programmes is a matter for speculation. If *The War about Peace* had been made first, would there have been a mirror-image controversy? If so, would it have been resolved in the same way? We cannot think of an instance where a 'safe' programme has been balanced by a 'provocative' one.

This suggests that TV current affairs, documentaries and opinion programmes are the site of considerable cultural and political struggle. There are very able people working in this area of television and they have been able to probe some aspects of government and NATO policy. But there are programmes which get knocked back or delayed and are defined as problematical. Such disputes and their outcome help to define the limits of pluralism in a democratic society. From time to time, erratically but not randomly, intended programmes are identified by senior administrators within the BBC or the IBA as risky. The ensuing rows, if the dispute becomes public, may be embarrassing to those administrators since they may be accused of political censorship; but from another point of view, for example, the government's, it may be regarded as a sign that they are taking a responsible view of their duties. Nevertheless the positions taken up by the senior authorities in broadcasting do not have to be predetermined – as the IBA's screening of *The Day After*, whilst refusing Secretary of State for Defence Michael Heseltine an official right of reply, demonstrates.

In a *Times* article (14 November 1983), 'Balance: TV's eternal victim', David Hewson asked: 'Is there not good reason to believe that television as a medium is chronically unsuited to the notion of impartiality altogether, except in the rigid form of editorial *diktat*?' The artificiality of the concept, supported as it is by *ad hoc* or mechanistic notions of balance, should be stressed. It is not only a question of supposedly setting one 'personal view' against another – Pilger versus Hastings – but of recognising that in programmes with experienced journalists such as Tusa or Mangold, personal views are also being presented; or at the very least a line of thought with references and implications is developed. Hewson's concluding question is worth repeating: 'If there can be a free-for-all in the market place of television drama, which makes up the most popular part of the broadcasting constituency, can a loosening of the reins on news and current affairs be long delayed?'

NOTES

1   Attempts to look at a number of current affairs programmes rather than individual instances are still rare. One recent study which attempts to classify and analyse them as a form of actuality television (in which are included news bulletins, topical, current affairs and documentary programmes) is Philip Schlesinger, Graham Murdock and Philip Elliott, *Televising 'Terrorism': political violence in popular culture*, London: Comedia, 1983.

2   E. P. Thompson, 'Gatekeepers to the nation's politics', *END*, Aug.–Sept. 1983, pp. 20–21.

3   Tom Mangold, 'President Reagan's arms race into space goes beyond deterrence', *Listener*, September 1983.

Chapter 10

Ritual tasks*

We have an almost ritual task. When I read the news, I am The Messenger. I am the Town Crier. I am there to express a communal sentiment.

(Richard Baker, *Listener*, April 1976)

IDEOLOGY AND NEWS VALUES

The response from both broadcasters and critics to the first volume of our study (*Bad News*) included arguments mounted against the overall strategy of our work but, significantly, not against its evidential detail. The broadcasters tended to respond unacademically and on occasion almost hysterically from a standpoint which appears to us to be firmly on the Right. The critics with greater care and a clearer understanding of our purpose seemed to be largely of the centre or the Left. It would be possible, but obviously ironic, for us thereby to claim, as do the manufacturers of news programmes, that this range of criticism is a testimony to our own objectivity and neutrality. But of course this is no more true in our case than it is when used as a professional defence of their output by the broadcasters.

We began *Bad News* by observing that:

> Contrary to the claims, conventions and culture of television journalism, the news is not a neutral product. For television news is a cultural artefact; it is a sequence of socially manufactured messages, which carry many of the culturally dominant assumptions of our society. From the accents of the newscasters to the vocabulary of camera angles; from who gets on and what questions they are asked, via selection of stories to presentation of bulletins, the news is a highly mediated product.[1]

In this we were doing nothing more than following a majority opinion among media scholars. Anthony Smith in *The Shadow in the Cave* puts it thus:

---

*First published in Glasgow University Media Group, *More Bad News*, London, Routledge & Kegan Paul, 1980, pp. 398–41.

News tends to lay out the order of 'Priorities' among the issues which confront society: it creates some of the doubts and fosters the certainties of that society, placing them all in a context of its own. Yet in every society which contains broadcasting on any scale the news is under instruction to be 'objective'.[2]

Our justification in stressing the manufactured quality of news broadcasts can best be summed up by a phrase used in an otherwise hostile review of *Bad News*: 'All this is true and cannot be shouted too often into the ears of the broadcasters'.[3] Yet professional opinion still seems to reject this position. As the Annan Committee reported: 'such analyses of the agenda-setting activities of journalists naturally raised resentment, not to say bewilderment, among the journalists in broadcasting with who we discussed this outlook'.[4] The Committee quoting the Editor of ITN said news 'was dictated primarily by events that had happened that day'.[5] This viewpoint begs considerable questions as to what events and what interpretations are placed on them. We can only endorse Stuart Hall's assessment of Annan's response to what Hall calls 'a well-established conventional wisdom of broadcasting research'. He states:

But here, at the very centre of the issue, Annan's thinking dissolves into pious platitudes. It raises the critical issue of the power of the media to 'set agendas and define reality' . . . only to find it unproven. What seems to have persuaded Annan against it was the 'bewilderment' with which the very idea was received by professional broadcasters! But the concept of the 'agenda-setting' is a *structural* concept. It deals with the relationship between a highly concentrated system and its professionals (the latter, precisely insulated from larger imperatives of the work they perform by the professional ideologies), which reports on and communicates with, but is not operated by the great mass of the public outside who are 'consumers'. It cannot be reduced to the 'recognition' of this journalist or that.[6]

The refusal of the broadcasters to recognise the basic constraints of their professionalism cannot be taken as a refutation of their power to set agendas defining the perimeters of social issues. Here our evidence is overwhelming.

In *Bad News* we presented a mass of evidence culled from a large sample of recorded news bulletins to illustrate the basic agenda-setting function of the news. We demonstrated that the bulletins of competing services did not really compete as to the stories they were reporting, or the style in which they reported them. We showed a predictability in the ordering of news items and the limited range of presentational devices available to the broadcaster. We further demonstrated that regularities in the area of industrial reporting lead to a consistent failure to cover the area thoroughly; that major factors in industrial life were systematically underreported (e.g. industrial accidents), whilst others which were reported (e.g. strikes) were reported unsystematically.

We further demonstrated in the case studies in that volume how the basic inferential frames regularly used by the news producers conditioned the reporting of strikes and did so in ways that were quite clearly skewed against the interest of the working class and organised labour – if only in that the inferential frames accepted uncritically narrow consensus views of the nature of strikes in particular and the realities of industrial life in our economic system in general. And we revealed that these frameworks were, because of their uncritical nature, skewed in this area in favour of the managers of industry. This is without prejudice to the charges laid at the broadcasters' door by those managers. The level and range of industrial reporting on television does not give them access or allow proper explanatory material to be laid before the public as they might wish. But it is our finding that what news there is is based on premises (inferential frames) sympathetic to their point of view.

In our work we have demonstrated, for example, that a narrow view, in this instance one based on Treasury policy and interpretation, was used systematically to foreclose on alternative views whatever their source. In detail this meant that as far as the news was concerned, wages were the prime source of inflation and wage demands the main cause of the crisis. And that in so presenting the issue, media personnel across a wide range of stories throughout the period under study actively embraced these points of view in a way that it would be hard to justify as impartial. The public thereby were never presented, as part of the media institutions' interpretation of these events, with the possibility that causes other than wages and solutions other than the moderation of wage demands could relate to the crisis. And the processes of selection leading to this result include not only the agenda-setting functions we have described, but also a systematic partiality in the reporting and interpretive use of government statistics.

As regards the language of the bulletins, we have shown that in many respects it conforms to the restricted and redundant usages of the popular press and that news talk in the area of industrial reporting relies on the assumption that industrial disputes are about 'trouble' – trouble for us as consumers, commuters and members of the public, trouble for the managers of industry, trouble for the nation; but never trouble for the workers involved. In the detailed examination of the vocabulary used we have demonstrated that in disputes the traditional offers of management are inevitably countered by the demands of the workers – to the point where nouns and verbs describing management actions are generally positive while the matching vocabulary for workers' actions is negative. In demonstrating this, we have not relied on an examination of what some might consider exotic or provocative terms, but rather the constant repetition of the small stock of descriptive terms which form the meat of the bulletins' language.

We have continued to demonstrate this cultural skewedness against one particular class in our examination of the visual elements of the bulletins. We have found in particular that there is a measure of isomorphism between a person's status and how that person will be presented in the bulletins. We have also more generally demonstrated that the lack of competitiveness between the services extends down to the most minute examination of technical inputs; that not only stories but the ways in which they are covered, the graphics they generate, the locations and interviewees they bring forth, are extraordinarily similar from channel to channel.

In doing all of this we have not explicitly suggested that corrections to the above are beyond the reasonable, not to say conservative, expectations of professional practice since much of our evidence as to what could have been done is culled from the so-called quality press. Given the privileged nature of these forms of electronic news transmission, we have shown that in other areas other journalists, whatever their faults might be, do better at reporting the range of opinion and facts in industrial life.

To suggest that in some way we conditioned by our own prejudices the phenomenon we have here documented is to say in effect that we failed to see the high-status supercaptioned interview with the rank-and-file worker, the considerate and extended interview with the monetarist economist, the language that claimed that a management was by its actions threatening us, the nation or the workforce.

It is significant that little attention has been paid thus far to the evidence on which we based these conclusions. The broadcasters especially have largely sought to counter the criticisms outlined above by attacking what they call our 'bias'. Of course, having argued that the ideology of neutrality is impossible of performance in their case, we would not claim to exercise it ourselves. Our very interest in this area of broadcasting might be seen by some as clear evidence of a host of other attitudes and beliefs which can be attributed to us. But although we would deny little of this, the facts still remain. We did not anticipate the possible production of 'neutral' news, and still less would we in some way welcome such production: on the contrary we were arguing and demonstrating that the ideology of news which requires it to be neutral, unbiased, impartial and balanced merely leads to a 'naturalism' on the level of stylistics which hides its ideological components. How we stand as regards that ideological component is irrelevant, given the weight of our findings. Just as attention must be directed at the evidence we present rather than at assumptions as to our ideological stance, so, too, we would not argue that the broadcasters are engaged in simple-minded conspiracy to distort or bias their work. The prevailing professional ideology encompassed by the myths of impartiality, balance and objectivity allows the broadcasters tacitly to trade upon the unspoken and dominant ideology of our society – the liberal notion that there is a fundamental consensus. Our use of the term 'ideology' in this context and throughout refers to sets of ideas that represent or serve the interests of social groups or classes. It is not intended to convey the meaning of merely illusory or false thinking.[7]

News and the ideologies of the larger society are integrally related. As Gouldner states, 'news is defined against the tacit background of unspoken premises, and by the bench marks these provide'. Gouldner's theoretical point, which we are empirically substantiating, is that ideologies are the connecting link between the so-called 'facts' of the news and the background assumptions which enable us, the audience, to understand those 'facts'.[8]

Depending on the kind of ideology we hold about the nature of society, the ideologies speak to the 'events' by the news; and, on the other hand, they may refer to certain news-censored aspects of everyday life, 'recovering' certain underprivileged elements within it. Ideologies are thus a 'background' to the news – e.g. 'The News Behind the News', or 'The Big News' – that premises the reading of certain news-reported events.[9] In attempting to refute the above position, broadcasters reply centrally on the twin notions of actual 'events' occurring in the real world and the 'newsworthiness' of those events.

One can see that, at the centre of this controversy, as in others, the professional response is to hold up the shield of such values, in this case, news values. When this is challenged various responses are possible. The efficacy of the challenge can be denied; the terms of the debate can be changed; or the values themselves may be in part questioned, to give ground, as it were, in order to maintain the central position.

A clear example of this last position occurred when Jeremy Potter, the then Managing Director of Independent Television Publications, suggested in an IBA public lecture:

It used to be said, rather smugly by us British at the time of Goebbels, that you cannot get away with propaganda unless you have proper geese. But we have since learned that all communication is propaganda. There is no such thing as due impartiality on the screen despite the exhortation of successive Television Acts and the earnest endeavours of the IBA, and the BBC and the companies. There is selection in every news bulletin.[10]

Potter went on to suggest that 'unavoidable partiality and involvement are common to all media, not characteristics peculiar to television'.[11] Here we have a clear illustration of the professional rejection of a position because it is thought to be inherently untenable. But in responding to the difficulties of admitting television to be partial and involved, Potter adheres to another professional value, that of balance. This for Potter appears to mean making judgements on such things as how much violence to show on news bulletins and at what times. Although balance might normally be seen as having to do with the internal organisation of a programme or, perhaps, a channel. Potter seeks a check against any channel having a monopoly of control and hence in effect determining balance. A diversity of control provides a check against particular viewpoints predominating:

All television is subliminal advertising and the responsibility of producers correspondingly immense. Whatever their standards, they cannot avoid a viewpoint. The viewer is continually registering in his mind situations which he may not realise that he has seen: women always in kitchens, coloured men always outsiders. We viewers are being got at all the time. This is the strongest of arguments in favour of diversity of control.[12]

But if news is the presentation of balanced viewpoints (which our evidence would deny), what becomes of 'objectivity'? It becomes difficult to hold on to a notion of objective news in terms of the honest and accurate reporting of facts and events. Perhaps the attempt to hold on to it has something to do with the feeling that to depart from it in the name of a plurality of perspectives is to move towards a view of news as 'subjective'. This invites one to doubt the credibility of news and to question the authority of those who deliver it. Of course all the multiple subjectivities in the world would not add up to a new objectivity transcending these partial viewpoints. It is precisely this point to which Anthony Smith seeks to attend in *The Shadow in the Cave*:

> News is founded upon the idea of a homogeneous mass audience (in the sense that it has a common frame of reference for what constitutes a news 'event') listening to an account, as accurately ascertained as can be, of actual daily events. The whole idea of news is that it is beyond a 'plurality of viewpoints'. The fact that the world has to a great extent ceased to believe in the intellectual possibility of such objective facts does not mean that one can quickly devise a new set of organisations in which new, 'pluralist facts' can be gathered and disseminated.
>
> Ten separate news bulletins would not provide a more *accurate* picture even if we listened to all of them. A society which demanded its news from ten separate perspectives would not be receiving *news*. Ten views of reality do not between them add up to a new 'objectivity' to exchange for an old one.[13]

Smith's own practical solution to this dilemma is merely to suggest that the crisis of credibility can be resolved, first, by mopping up areas of criticism (say coverage of trade-union affairs) into a revised national news; second by supplementing the news presentations of reality with documentary interviews and discussion programmes operating from varied perspectives. In place of news from a plurality of perspectives, we are offered 'reality' from a plurality of 'genres'. It is a defence of a news genre (albeit sensitive to criticism) not a defence of objectivity that is proposed. This position is somewhat quiescent, since it does not address the homogeneity of the current news services with their shared and largely non-competitive reliance on a narrow range of views. Yet Smith does make it clear that a 'news' view of the world cannot in its nature be an 'objective-realistic' view:

> News is a cultural discipline, choosing it an intellectual skill, collecting it

a profession. Within the confines of the broadcasting institution the news organisation absorbs the institution's picture of the society and inherits the professional assumptions and methods of newsmen in other media. News is only one vessel in which broadcasting strives to catch reality. The answer to the problem of in-built 'distortion' in the disseminated picture of society must be to encourage other parallel 'genres' for the representation of reality.[14]

The representation of reality in television news has come under more severe criticism in a series of articles in *The Times* by John Birt and Peter Jay.[15] News was held to be not simply incomplete or necessarily partial because selective. It was positively misleading and unhelpful because it created a 'bias against understanding'. Birt and Jay argued that television news carried a large number of stories in a thirty-minute bulletin, but in a narrow and limiting way which inhibits rather than aids appreciation of the issues presented:

> Our economic problems, for instance, manifest themselves in a wide variety of symptoms – deteriorating balance of payments, a sinking pound, rising unemployment, accelerating inflation and so on. The news, devoting two minutes on successive nights to the latest unemployment figures or the state of the stock market, with no time to put the story in context, gives the viewer no sense of how any of these problems relate to each other. It is more likely to leave him confused and uneasy.[16]

Birt and Jay argue that television journalism can be differentiated in terms of news, feature and issue journalism. These vary in terms of the generality of context in which information is communicated. The news context is superficial, the feature context focuses upon particular instances (say, a famine in Ethiopia) and not on the general problem (in this case, world food resources). Issue journalism seeks to come to terms with the complexities of industrial and social problems. It is desirable but difficult to accomplish. It does not abandon the notion of a real world to be analysed and in that sense is not a matter of subjectivity: 'The realities one is seeking are abstract – macro-economic mechanisms, political philosophies, international strategies – and cannot be directly televised like a battle zone or a demonstration.'[17] In their view, news is not organised to give accounts of this reality. Instead of recognising the world as being one of interacting processes, news splits it into innumerable atomised facts and millions of tiny, discrete stories.

Yet, the *reductio ad absurdum* is not that we are offered a continuous stream of unrelated facts. Despite the maxim that news should separate fact from comment, this is not possible. It is an empty myth. The news journalist does implicitly and explicitly blur the line between fact and interpretation. There is selection, compression, simplification of reported events. There are connecting links between statistical information, the events to which they purport to relate (say unemployment) and government policy and future prospects. Moreover there is the inherent problem of the relationship between language and reality:

> Even if selection [of stories] were random or could be based purely on market analysis of reader/viewer interest, the journalist would still face the difficulty that every sentence and every word carries connotations which go beyond what he can see, hear, touch, smell and feel. Interpretation is implicit in any use of language at all to describe the world.[18]

Birt and Jay in writing of 'the bias against understanding' lay down the challenge to journalists to make the 'real world' more intelligible. The paradox they appear to embrace is that in the name of 'hard facts' about the real world, television news is peculiarly uninformative and unreal. And yet there is another kind of bias which suggests itself to them as a consequence of actual news practices. It is a bias in favour of the powerful:

> Most current broadcast journalism is partial – it favours the views of one group at the expense of those of another. This is because, lacking a clear sense of its obligation to society as a whole, most journalism lives under the shadow of the state and the other main repositories of power in our society: the political parties; business; the trade unions; and so on. It might almost be called 'corporate journalism'.[19]

If that is so, then while Birt and Jay might go on to write of news values as restrictive, simplistic and highly prejudicial, it is a picture of the world that is being conveyed. If this picture turns out to be one that continually favours some interest-groups at the expense of or to the relative exclusion of others, we may wonder whether the bias against understanding turns out to be a bias towards the powerful. The question might have to be put again: what kind of understanding is on offer? For it would not be true to suggest that no understanding is on offer. The ideological underpinnings of news production do in fact create a coherence which Birt and Jay are unwilling to acknowledge. It is not that the news programmes leave the audience bewildered. On the contrary, the agenda-setting function works to limit the range and density of information just so that it can be comprehended within a narrow consensus. As has been observed:

> Media neutrality and independence are therefore quite 'real' in the sense that their function is essentially to try to *hold the ring*, to sustain an arena of 'relative independence', in order that this *reproduction of the conditions* of political power can take place.[20]

CONTENT ANALYSIS

It has been a basic contention of our approach that the detailed examination of the output of television journalism can be used to demonstrate its ideology and practices. Some have suggested that this is not the case; that we have made assumptions as to the audience's inability to view the output critically; that we have ignored and indeed have no way of knowing what goes on in the newsrooms; even that we are intending to create a statistical measure as a substitute for the editorial control of news decisions.

To tackle the last of these first, it has been claimed that in deciding what to cover there are a range of factors and values 'which an industrial editor must weigh in his mind, in general though not in statistical terms'.[21] This might seem to suggest that news values are unfathomable, locked as they are in the minds of news editors. If that is so, then no amount of research would suffice to refute the claims by broadcasters that news is impartial and balanced. But by the same token the claims would simply be rhetorical, capable of neither confirmation nor denial. But this view misunderstands the whole nature of content analysis. We are not in undertaking such work implicitly suggesting that the broadcasters should abandon rule-of-thumb decision-making (whatever professional rhetorics are used to justify such internal critica) for higher mathematics. The point of such counting is that while, for instance, checking whether there is parity in the number of interviews given to antagonists might only tap the surface of any distortion that may occur, yet where it does occur it is still worth drawing attention to. If there is imbalance at this crude level (as we showed to be the case in the Glasgow dustcart drivers' dispute) then the credibility of news coverage is challenged, so to speak, at the first line of defence. We are thereby demonstrating that although we would not expect the newsmen to measure their output in more refined sociological terms, yet the rule-of-thumb can sometimes lead them into major distortions. As the Annan Committee reported:

> the broadcasters were not guilty of deliberate and calculated bias. But that the coverage of industrial affairs is in some respects inadequate and unsatisfactory is not in doubt. Difficult as the reporting of industrial stories may be, the broadcasters have not fully thought it through. They too often forget that to represent management at their desks, apparently the calm and collected representatives of order, and to represent shop stewards and picket lines stopping production, apparently the agents of disruption, gives a false picture of what strikes are about. The broadcasters have fallen into the professional error of putting compelling camera work before the news. Furthermore, the causes why people come out on strike are often extraordinarily complex. No reporter does his job adequately if he interviews only the leading shop steward or union official. The fact that a strike is not backed by the union does not exonerate broadcasters from discovering why the work force is out.[22]

In other words, the time-honoured notions of journalistic practice do not seem to be working too well in this area.

While the main thrust of our work has been to look at the deep structure and agenda-setting function of the bulletins, we were also interested in devising ways of checking news coverage against other bases of information on what was happening in the world. Commenting on this approach, Professor Elihu Katz has recently said that one of the functions of tracking social trends:

> is to create certain external criteria to use as a guide in the selection of stories and in assuring adequate coverage. Such indicators cannot be allowed to dictate to journalists, no more than audience measurements should do, but they are worth having around as a basis for professional judgments.[23]

The point is that the tripartite division of the research tradition, between the sociology of broadcasting institutions, the sociology of audience response and content analysis, is basically unsatisfactory. Ideally, participant observational studies of the production offices should be matched to content analysis and audience research relating to the same period. This has not yet been done. Our justification for concentrating on content analysis in the light of this tradition is simply that of the three branches it has been the most neglected. Without a body of content analysis research the other two divisions are in danger of addressing a vacuum – for what is it the studied producers produce? And what is it the audience reacts to?

The criticism that nothing can be learnt of real social relations from the screen is so palpably absurd as scarcely to warrant responses. If that were true: then in some sense the output would have no semantic component; it would in fact be meaningless. For when it comes to the use of language and the visual treatment of news, we do not argue that these are to be dismissed as surface phenomena. For us they are central to any attempt made to discover whether there is systematic distortion of news information. The spoken and visual vocabulary of news may be regarded as the outward and visible expression of newsroom codes and conventions and not as separate from them. Since the output clearly has meaning, then the production of that meaning can as clearly be studied on the screen as it can be by interviewing either producers or audiences.

We further take the view that an analysis of news output over an extended period should enable us to discover some of the rules governing the presentation, ordering and frames of reference which guide newsmen as they scan the world day by day. Just as newsproducers argue that they cannot be expected to understand and work to these latent structures (and thereby hope to deny their very existence), so it is argued that the audience, too, is unaware of them. This last can then be made the basis of a critique of all broadcasting research which does not focus upon the decoding abilities of the audience. It is true, of course, that a variety of readings or viewings of any given piece of the output are possible, but before proper work on audience comprehension can be undertaken there has to be systematic documentation and mapping of the dominant modes of presentation and framing. Otherwise how can the study of the audience be made to address precisely the issues of routine absences and presences in the coverage?

Given the current state of knowledge of the audience, it is possible both to argue that they do not truly comprehend the bulletins and that if they do, the bulletins are not the sole influence upon them.[24] Such critics see our methods as implying a low assumption on our part of the audience's ability to resist or renegotiate the preferred ideology offered up in the output. But the contrary is true. The argument outlined above is nothing more than a restatement of the classic reinforcement view. And, as in the case of those who argued reinforcement as the dominant effect of the media, it leaves aside the whole question of agenda-setting and itself hides behind notions of the overall unimportance of television to the viewers. For us this is nothing more than a failure of methodology. If researchers can show that little information is passed by the medium, then it could be the case not that little information is actually passed, but that what is passed cannot properly be measured. We obviously take the latter view, at least for the present, and therefore stand by the need for as sophisticated and systematic a method of content analysis as can be devised. The fact remains that, despite recent developments, the history of sociological research of the audience concentrates on the audience's ability to decode without paying concomitant attention to the encoding of the messages. We believe that the work offered here is an essential step in tackling this problem.

FRONT PAGE

While the longitudinal dimension of the study was on the whole regarded as unproblematic, a number of our critics hastened to point out the lack of a regional dimension. The bulletins, it was suggested, are like the front page of a newspaper and the regional magazines like the inside pages. It is argued that concentration on the national bulletins cannot give a true picture of the news because regional bulletins are complementary to network news. This view is espoused particularly by professional broadcasters who maintain that an apparent lack of depth at the national level will generally be made up for in regional bulletins, especially in those regions in which the stories occur. Such a view ignores the vital fact that national news by definition is the news that the large majority of people see and listen to for information on national issues.

While we do not agree that such complementarity can be maintained given the division between news and current affairs, nevertheless, during the period of our study we did collect the local broadcasts of both STV and BBC

Scotland. Basically we found that the similarity of professional practice between national and local newsrooms counters the argument that the latter deal with the news in markedly different ways (by using different inferential frames or reporting in greater depth).

It could further be argued that the considerable debate about the television news and the changes made in the bulletins since the period of our study have rendered our findings obsolete. We felt that another week's output would therefore provide us with a check on the scale of the alterations which had been made in bulletin formats, running orders, visual inputs and styles of presentation. The profiles which emerged tended in every major respect to strongly confirm the patterns described in *Bad News*. In particular, ITN's main innovation, the *News at 5.45*, varied from the previous early bulletin in the predicted direction.

CRITIQUE

There is another level of criticism of our approach which casts doubts on the value of content analysis that is not grounded in, or developing, some particular theory or another. Gouldner perhaps sums up the basic attitude of such critics when he writes: 'Given a commitment to protect understanding of the social world from the biasing interests of dominant societal groups, there is a tendency to surrender and sneer at primary research.'[25] These critics fall into two groups: those who hold that a general theory of the media is a prerequisite for doing any analytic work and those who argue for particular positions in cultural analysis (currently within semiotics or a variant of it).

The first of these positions suggests that analysing the dominant codes governing cultural production (in our case, news bulletins) is merely dealing with the surface phenomena of our society. The task of a general media theory is, in contradistinction, to begin to spell out the structural relationships which hold between given institutions and the rest of society. The aim in our area would therefore be to contextualise news production as merely one part of the larger structure of power and domination within our society. It is assumed that some general theory can be developed that allows the specification of such relationships within which detailed study of the output would fit.

The crudest version of this position appears to believe that the market forces, in economic terms, coupled with the institutions of the capitalist state operate so forcefully upon the media institutions that the reproduction of culture is almost a perfect mirror image of the mythic relationships of bourgeois society (e.g. sanctification of the family; the special position of the Church; notions of law and order; and a central cultural commitment to competition). While this simple 'base/superstructure' view of broadcasting might account for a small part of the output, it can in no way explain and analyse the inherent contradictions and varieties of permitted views and the surface openness which exists across the range of broadcasting output. For instance, the view would be hard pressed to offer a reasonable account of the sophisticated processes at work whereby a play by Dennis Potter, say, will be elaborately produced at considerable expense by an organisation replete with managerial and editorial control levels, which then shelves it.

Of course it does at times appear that nothing more than a crude ruling-class viewpoint is at work. From the minutes of the most senior policy-making committee of the BBC in the news and current affairs area in 1976 (as published in *The Leveller*)[26] we learn that the editor of news and current affairs (albeit 'for the first time in his career') suggests that:

> at the present juncture stories about this country's currency needed careful handling.... He was inclined to suggest that they should always be checked first with the Treasury. It would be wrong in the present circumstances to put out a major news story of which the Government had no warning.[27]

In the light of this sort of information it is difficult to break totally with the notion of some kind of reflexive, ideological bias at least in the upper echelons of the media institutions. But it seems to be becoming fashionable to suggest that since the phenomenon of broadcasting ideology is so deeply embedded in the society, it is unforgivably crude to suggest any single person capable of biased decision-making within that ideology, even in meetings such as the one quoted. This view seems to us to have all the makings of the sort of liberal double-bind that characterised the debate about the reinforcement effects research of some decades ago which we mentioned above. it was argued that since the only observable effect of broadcasting was to reinforce the audience's previous points of view and attitudes, there was thus no basis for mounting critiques of broadcasting power.

It seems a pity for instance that Stuart Hall and his group in their concern 'to demonstrate how the television discourse could not be "read back" either to its class origins or – worse – to class interests' should suggest that their work seeks 'to break with any simplistic notion of television "bias" (still to be found residually in *Bad News*) as though simply directed by "the ruling class".'[28] Yet as they themselves suggest, their own analysis 'could have been faulted for underplaying the connections and relations between the ideology of the television discourse and the ideologies of particular class fractions'.[29] It is apparent that our work rejects any crude notions of 'bias' and reductions to class interests. Yet the relative autonomy of senior managers within the television institutions means at times that they must be able to act. To deny this is to consider them automata; and in this sense any general position must accommodate some notion of classes of actions on their part which systematically bolster one view of society rather than another. However, any work in this area which treats our detailed evidential documentation of television discourse as merely an exercise in spelling out 'bias' fails to grasp its major direction. We have empirically established that, at least with regard to industrial and economic stories, the overwhelming use of inferential frameworks, routines and presentational techniques that favour one side of industry rather than the other does exist. In this sense, for whatever reasons, the ideology of one particular class, despite contradictions in the output, is dominant and preferred. Yet we would agree with Hall and others that those who wish to push a reductionist analysis to include all areas of output at all times somehow want a theory which, in Sartre's words, 'tells us everything and gives us nothing'. For such a general theory of the media turns out on examination to be a general theory of society.

Whilst agreeing that some general theories of society, especially those that stress the role of class structure and conflict, are more feasible than others, we cannot agree that such theories at present offer us the concepts to analyse the manifold variations of cultural reproduction in our society. Perhaps the most sophisticated exponents of such a general position are Murdock and Golding, who in their article 'Capital, communication and class relations' move uneasily between asserting that 'control over material resources and their changing distribution are ultimately the most powerful of the many levers operating in cultural production', and the argument that:

> if news coverage of industrial relations is cumulatively unsympathetic to militancy, radicalism, or union activism in general, is it simply because of the hostility of the capitalist media entrepreneurs or even anti-socialist sentiment among industrial relations correspondents?[30]

As they suggest:

> A fuller explanation must look for the complex of interrelationships between pervasive definitions of industry, the Nation, responsibility and the like, with trends in industrial news practice, the conventions of interview, film and narrative and so on.[31]

It is just these later trends and conventions that we have addressed in our work. At this time it seems that moving from the macro-level successfully articulated by Murdock and Golding in their detailed examinations of the patterns of ownership and cultural monopoly to the micro-level of close content analysis such as we have undertaken is difficult. But however sophisticated such an analysis becomes, there is a fundamental difference of levels between institutional and societal forms and the routine content of particular genres. Any method which relies at base upon economic reductionism will be unable to explain the routine presences and absences in content. Yet the basic assumptions at work in both are the same. Neither approach needs to rely on any crudity in its understanding of the patterns of cultural power in this society.

SEMIOTIC CRITIQUES

Aside from the general problem of economic determination, another critique of our work can be mounted from the position in cultural analysis of those who consider themselves structuralists or semioticians. Initially this work is grounded in the linguistic studies of de Saussure, who pointed out that language was coded in an arbitrary fashion; that in fact the sound 'd-o-g' or 'ch-i-e-n' had little to do with the animal meant (or signified) when those sounds are uttered. This is a general point; the relationship between the sounds and the concepts of any language are arbitrary – the sound is, as it were, an arbitrary sign. De Saussure saw this basic distinction between the thing signified and the signifier as being the crucial concept in a new analytic. 'I shall call it', he announced, 'semiology' (from the Greek for sign). He further suggested that 'linguistics is only part of the general science of semiology'; which was the view of the American logician Peirce, who called the science semiotics,[32] and who refined the basic notion of the arbitrariness of the sign and extended it beyond linguistics, by distinguishing a tripartite possibility in the relationship between thing signified and signifier. For Peirce the three divisions are *symbolic* where the relationship is arbitrary, as in language on the Saussurian model; *indexical* where the relationship is not arbitrary but related, as for instance with a sundial signifying time, or a weather-vane; *iconic* where the arbitrariness is further reduced and the signifier agrees most closely with the thing signified, as in a photograph. For Peirce any sign could contain elements of all these categories.

In recent years a large body of work has grown up from such beginnings. Roland Barthes is probably the best-known of semiologists, in popular terms, whose work, together with that of other European structuralists, has come to play an influential role in the attempt to decode and recover the hidden relationships which we take for granted in everyday communications, verbal and non-verbal. Barthes suggests, for instance, that in our society visual images rarely appear without accompanying text which tends to foreclose on a range of possible connotations that the image by itself might have.[33] Others have developed ever greater refinements of the tripartite division of Peirce, relying on a distinction between denotation and connotation in attempting to show that varieties of signifying practices do not merely reproduce varieties of meanings but systematically foreclose on such ranges of meanings. The object of this analysis is to open up the flexibility of structuralist accounts of cultural production and reproduction so that they are not reduced to some mirror image or homology of some other level of analysis. One such contemporary account is articulated by Rosalind Coward, who argues that present usages of the notion of ideology, no matter how sophisticated, fail to grasp that the processes of signification are themselves autonomous and have no necessary correspondence to other levels of structural analysis. In *Language and Materialism* by Coward and Ellis, it is suggested that the way forward for cultural analysis is to accept the insights of Lacan: 'The analysis of the proper relations of the signifier leads to the conclusion that no meaning is sustained by anything other than reference to other meaning.'[34] This seems for all practical purposes to be approaching a *reductio ad absurdum* wherein the promise of semiotic analysis to open closed areas is itself reduced to the mere documentation of a constantly fluid cultural process. But we may ask what is the point of such analysis? Ought it not to illuminate the larger structural relationships which allows closings and thus allow those using the dominant ideologies of our society to trade upon the weaknesses of routine perceptions? Even if it is the case that all the relationships between signifier and the thing signified are arbitrary in the sense of having no necessary or natural connection (which thereby destroys the validity of the basic Peircean divisions), nevertheless to suggest that all signifying practices are of themselves arbitrary and autonomous is to mistake the issue at hand. As Eco points out, 'the core of the problem is obviously the notion of convention which is not coextensive with that of arbitrary link but which is coextensive with that of *cultural* link.'[35] Because the production of signs is arbitrary, it in no way means that the cultural practices of signification which take place *within a code* are also arbitrary and autonomous. For, to take this position, as Coward and Ellis seem to do, would be to assume that there is no meta-language at all and that cultural analysis is empty except for the absolute autonomy of signifying practices. The point of engaging in television analysis, or any other cultural analysis, is to reveal the subtleties and refinements of ideological closure and imbalance by revealing the various codes in operation. In doing so, one shows how much broader than particular ideologies is the shifting of 'the semantic universe', to use Eco's phrase. However, the purpose remains clear – to open up significant closures: 'semiotics in its double guise as a theory of codes and a theory of sign production is also a form of social criticism, and therefore one among the many forms of social practice.'[36]

Thus in the work of visual analysis undertaken above we continued to rely on the simple Peircean division of the relationship between signified and signifier. We did this not because we felt that the problems of so doing could be avoided, but because in the particular field of empirical analysis, such a use reveals cumulative examples of the codes with which the dominant ideology works in the production of television news.

AN ADVERSARY RELATIONSHIP

The history of this project has been one in which considerable hostility and attempted interference has characterised the reactions of the broadcasters. While it is flattering to be the object of such activity (sustained as it has been and undertaken at the high levels it has been), it is perhaps important at this point that the more general history of the relationship between broadcasters and broadcasting researchers should not be forgotten. It is in fact the case that even more than with most professional groups coming under the scrutiny of academics, broadcasters have not hitherto in any way welcomed such attention. But we are only the inheritors of this poor tradition, not its creators.

Tom Burns recently described the difficulties he encountered as a researcher studying the BBC. These included a veto on the publication of his work on the Corporation, a ban that was lifted only after many years. He points out that this kind of experience is not uncommon for social scientists studying the media. he cites Paul Lazarsfeld's 1948 article in *Journalism Quarterly* on 'The role of criticism in the management of mass media'. In the light of our more recent experience, Lazarsfeld's comment still sadly stands:

> If there is any one institutional disease to which the media of mass communications seem particularly subject, it is a nervous reaction to criticism. As a student of mass media I have been continually struck and occasionally puzzled by this reaction, for it is the media themselves which so vigorously defend principles guaranteeing the right to criticise.[37]

In the light of Lazarsfeld's comments on the broadcasters' espousal of the right to criticise, we can only wonder what world view, what institutional ideology led to the following sort of debate in one of the highest councils of one of the world's leading cultural organisations:

> DG said there would be no sense in attacking *Bad News* in detail ... he thought however that the ideology of sociologists was a subject which would repay a little study and hoped that it would be possible for a programme like 'Analysis' to tackle it. ... Desmond Wilcox felt it would be dangerous to launch a widespread attack on the discipline of sociology, which included some perfectly responsible practitioners. It should attack, where necessary, particular arguments and ... the standpoint from which they were presented. Michael Bunce repeated his view that the BBC should counter-attack spurious communicators and academics ... DG agreed that the BBC could examine the aims and politics of sociology.[38]

That a basis for a sociological critique of broadcast news might exist seems at no time to have entered the apparently fevered discussion of the editor of news and current affairs' fortnightly meetings in the BBC.

What has been offered up here is not a contribution to an unnecessarily small-minded debate, but a detailed and documented critique of the ideology and practice of current television journalism – a first step in the decoding of the all-pervasive messages of the electronic media.

NOTES

1 *Bad News*, London: Routledge, 1976, p. 9.
2 Anthony Smith, *The Shadow in the Cave*, London: Quartet, 1976, p. 143.

3 Richard Collins, *Screen Education*, winter 1976/77, no. 21, p. 80.
4 The Annan Committee, *Report of the Committee on the Future of Broadcasting*, Cmnd 6753, London: HMSO, 1977, p. 276.
5 *Ibid.*, p. 277.
6 S. Hall, *The Report of the Committee on the Future of Broadcasting*, NUQ, summer 1977, p. 272.
7 There is a useful summary of the history and meaning of the word in R. Williams, *Keywords*, London: Fontana, 1976, pp. 126 ff.
8 A. Gouldner, *The Dialectic of Ideology and Technology*, London: Macmillan, 1976, p. 111.
9. *Ibid.*, p. 112.
10 ITV, 'Critics and Viewers', *Independent Broadcasting*, May 1975, p. 17.
11 *Ibid.*, p. 17.
12 *Ibid.*, p. 17.
13 Smith, *The Shadow in the Cave*, London: Quartet, 1976, p. 176.
14 *Ibid.*, p. 174.
15 Peter Jay and John Birt, *The Times*, 28 September 1975, 30 September 1975, 1 October 1975, 2 September 1976, 3 September 1976.
16 'Can television news break the understanding barrier?', *The Times*, 28 February 1975.
17 *Ibid.*
18 'Why television news is in danger of becoming an anti-social force', *The Times*, 3 September 1975.
19 *Ibid.*
20 Curti, Hall, Connell, 'The unity of current affairs television', in *Cultural Studies* 9, University of Birmingham, spring 1976, p. 92; italics in original.
21 Cox, 'Bad News – or poor Scholarship?', *Independent Broadcasting*, December 1976.
22 Annan Report, p. 272.
23 *Social Research on Broadcasting: Proposals for Further Development*, London: BBC, 1977, p. 67.
24. Findahl and Hoijer, 'Fragments of reality', Swedish Broadcasting Corporation, 1976, p. 48. Even this work reveals that careful presentation can heighten viewers' perception and memory of causes, for instance.
25 Gouldner, *The Dialectic of Ideology and Technology*, London: Macmillan, 1976, p. 116.
26 *The Leveller*, London: January 1978, pp. 14 ff.
27 *Ibid.*, p. 15.
28 Stuart Hall *et al.*, 'Debate', *Screen*, London: winter 1977/78, p. 113.
29 *Ibid.*
30 Murdock and Golding, 'Capitalism, communication and class relations', in Curran, Gurevitch and Woollacott (eds), *Mass Communication and Society*, London: Arnold, 1977, p. 20.
31 *Ibid.*
32 B. Winston, *Dangling Conversations*, vol. 2, London: Davis-Poynter, 1973, p. 42.
33 R. Barthes 'Rhetoric of the image', in *Image, Music, Text*, London: Fontana.
34 R. Coward and T. Ellis, *Language and Materialism*, London: Routledge & Kegan Paul, 1977, p. 3.
35 U. Eco, *A Theory of Semiotics*, London: Macmillan, 1977, p. 191
36 *Ibid.*, p. 298.
37 Cited by T. Burns, *The BBC*, London: Macmillan, 1977, p. xv.
38 *The Leveller*, p. 17.

Coda

'Isn't the news terrible?'*
Raymond Williams

'I see the news is bad again.' The banal phrase punctuates my memories of the late 1930s. I remember an adolescent anger that people would not name the things that were happening: the invasion of Austria; the cession of the Sudetenland; the invasions of Czechoslovakia and Albania – all packaged as 'the news'. While in London it no doubt seemed ridiculous that Chamberlain referred to Czechoslovakia as a far-off country of which we knew little or nothing, I could see, there in Wales, that what he said was true for these railwaymen and farmers, whose gravity and abstraction, at this level of affairs, at once puzzled and irritated me.

This situation is still, in general, too little understood. The banal phrase of our current years is a rhetorical question: 'Isn't the news terrible?' I still sometimes make the mistake of trying to answer it, since when I have taken off the packaging some of it is not at all terrible to me; indeed, some of the most officially outraging events are positively welcome. Yet the structural problem persists, and has become more acute. In the late 1930s, after all, the wireless news of these European convulsions came only after a steady reading of the fat-stock prices. Now the bumptious arresting music, the spinning image of the world, the celebrity reader, induce forms of attention and of stress which are often justified, though the signals occur whether there is anything of substance to follow them or not. And then what we can observe, past the apparent sophistications, is a lack of human fit between exposure to reports of world-wide events and either effective knowledge, through which to try to assess them, or any effective possibility of response – some action even if it is as occasional as a vote: anything practicable, that is, beyond either spectacle or worry.

The official answer to this problem is at once easy and beside the point. It is factually true that some of these reported events could signal, through a chain of relationships, the most immediate effects, from a nuclear war through

*First published in R. Williams, *What I Came To Say*, London, Hutchinson, 1982, pp. 113–19.

the more imaginable scales of disaster, disturbance and nuisance. Thus the public must be informed. If they do not know these connections, they must be made aware of them, or have them pointed out by our diplomatic, defence or industrial correspondents.

But this is an abstraction less forgivable than the more mundane blocking of all events as 'the news'. These railwaymen and farmers did not need to be told that distant events could end in their own bodies. Some of them, including my father, still carried in their flesh the wounds of the wanton metal that had attended the last demonstration of relationships and consequences. It was not, then as now, the gravity of generalised attention that was lacking. Instead, now as then, the news was received, accurately if too simply, as alien: not just because it was coming from places and peoples of which there was no direct knowledge, beyond these isolated reports, but also because its mode of communication was not that of people talking, questioning, moving across to talk or listen to others, as in everyday practice and knowledge, but was this authoritative transmission – an authority without rivals and beyond effective challenge, imposing itself professionally, in every signal, accent and tone, upon the near and the far.

Let us face it then: the news has been very bad lately. But it is very difficult to be sure how much of this badness has been in the events themselves, and how much in their intense and relentless interpretation by the authorities: a one-sided polemic which I cannot remember being at this pitch since the late 1940s. Some of us, at least, must be ready to appreciate the verbal joke by the Glasgow University Media Group, whose *Bad News* and now *More Bad News* indicate the faults of news presentation rather than the import of the actual events.

To be sure, we cannot draw any firm line between events and their presentation. A very large number of the events now presented are in fact interpretations, by a small group of highly privileged voices, directly transmitted or read out by the hired celebrities. The privilege of such voices would matter less if it were not also, in the leading cases, the privilege of command of men and resources. Such privilege, now quaintly known as a 'mandate', even where it refers to unforeseen events on which no wider opinions have been canvassed, has to be distinguished, of course, from that of the voice alone. But then it is a very long time, in British broadcasting especially, since we heard any voice of this kind that sounded as if it were speaking quite for itself, from its own knowledge and experience. An institutional definition encloses this absence. Discussion and argument occur elsewhere, but meanwhile, here is the news.

It is, then, a major intellectual gain, in recent years, to have found ways of seeing the news as a cultural product. There is still a central difficulty. On the one hand, it is true that in some respects we have to read the news as if we were reading a novel. Until the early eighteenth century the word 'novel' carried two senses – of a tale and of what we now call the news. Spenser had written, in a sense that we might now echo, observing the arranged features of a newsreader: 'You promise in your clear aspect, some novel.' 'Novelist', in the eighteenth century, meant a newsmonger as well as a writer of prose fiction. But a distinction was forming between 'fiction' and 'fact', and this had serious effects, both ways, on what appear at first sight two distinct kinds of narrative. At its most confident, this assigned all novels to 'fiction' in the sense that the events had not occurred, but had been imagined or created: a definition that not only makes for many difficulties with the reading of certain novels of the past, from *Romola* to *War and Peace*, but is now in trouble with the arrival of the important contemporary form of the 'novel based on a real-life event', or 'faction'.

Yet the worst effects were at the other end of the scale. The fact that certain events have undoubtedly occurred – have happened to people, have been observed, have been reliably reported, have been tested from the evidence of participants and witnesses – has been used to conceal or to override the equally evident fact that as they move from events to news they are being narrated. Therefore certain longstanding problems of narration – the identity of the narrator, his authority, his point of view, his assumed relationship to his readers or hearers, his possible wider purposes in selecting and narrating these events in this way – come inevitably into question. Most experienced adults get used to having to ask these questions, however politely or tacitly, when they hear stories and reports in everyday talk. Yet it seems that we have only to ask them about a broadcasting service or a newspaper to produce outraged cries about an assault on professional competence and independence, or to provoke dark hints, which at least sometimes are surely projections, about a conspiracy to interfere with freedom of news and indeed to manipulate or censor it.

Thus it would be reassuring to know that the minute of a high-level discussion in the BBC (quoted in *The Leveller* of January 1978) was inaccurate: the Director-General 'said there would be no sense in attacking *Bad News* in detail ... he thought however that the ideology of sociologists was a subject which would repay a little study and hoped that it would be possible for a programme like *Analysis* to tackle it.' What *Analysis* or some other programme might equally have tackled, down to that level of detail, which is one of the surest means of testing accuracy, was the body of evidence about actual news presentations which *Bad News* had presented. The 'ideology' (ideologies) of sociologists would have been a wholly proper matter to include, not least because it would have helped to promote a genuinely critical attitude to sociological 'findings', which in other, happier cases – this or that poll or survey – make their unproblematic way into the news. Moreover, once discussion had begun, the problem of the 'facts', and the related problems of selection and interpretation, could have been rationally addressed over the whole range, in and out of university and newsroom.

There are at least two reasons why this has not happened. The first, undoubtedly, is that this kind of independent criticism is taken, almost instinctively, as a challenge to authority, of a piece with all those other challenges to authority which sociologists (by those who do not know them, but have heard the ugly word) are supposed in recent years to have been making and inciting. Yet I do not find this response, however hasty or muddled, unreasonable. What is at stake is indeed authority at its deepest level: that deep sense of propriety and legitimacy which has assigned both authority and responsibility to certain public sources of news and inter-pretation. These qualities are tested over the years, and over a range of events are proved to have certain reliabilities. It is then easy to move from that kind of public record to an assumption of more general authority, in which the institution comes to see itself, and to be widely seen, as an organ of the 'national interest', a warrant of independence and fairness, standing above the mere ideologies which this or that minority might indulge. Anyone question-ing this identity, backed as it is by a centralised and very powerful technology, and by the symbols, rhythms and timed regular occasions of public address, can rather readily be seen as a small boy throwing stones. And if he has written a fat book, full of tables and referenced details, he does not cease to be an unruly small boy: it is only that he has provided himself, for his own questionable purposes, with even more stones.

The second reason, an outraged professionalism, needs to be carefully considered. It is true that the same kind of defence is rather often rejected, by news-gatherers, when it is made by other professions. 'What evidence do you have for saying that?' 'Don't other experts disagree with you?' 'Doesn't this go against what most of us believe?' These are the regular and admirable questions of the most persistent reporters, and at their best they are asked of the most as well as the least privileged. It seems then reasonable that they should be asked, with the same persistence, of reporters, correspondents and editors themselves. And indeed it is noticeable that when a reporter has delivered a certain kind of story – when he has, say, interviewed a representative of the IRA, or a Welsh republican, or has what he takes to be secret or confidential information about some national body – he is often quite sharply interrogated, within his profession and in other ways. These are indicators of situations in which reporters have broken the consensus of 'responsible' news-gathering. The professional defence, of the right to establish and publish the facts, is then qualified or overridden by other criteria.

Yet what this situation most illuminates is the underlying structure of communicative relationship, within a particular social order. For there is no normal space in which news reports can be examined and interrogated, unless the consensus has been broken and other social forces move through and take it into a public, administrative or legal domain. In the ordinary rush of news reports, within the consensus, this does not often happen, though the need is as great for events within the consensus as outside it.

It is at this point that the 'sociologists' announce themselves. The growth in media studies and cultural studies in the last twenty years has been remarkable. A space that does not exist, to any effect, within the major news-and-opinion institutions is carved out in other institutions, mainly educational. Hence books like *Bad News* and *More Bad News*. But it is then obvious that the conditions under which such work is done are radically different from those in which the work being studied is and in most cases has to be done. It is understandable that reporters and editors, who work under considerable pressure, especially of time, are impatient when confronted by analyses of their work made by researchers who seem to have all the time in the world. I remember a related exchange between a gifted analyst of television and a gifted producer. The analyst had indicated a particular effect through a particular use of shot. 'Tell me that,' said the producer, 'next time I'm filming in the rain on Liverpool Docks at five in the morning.' But then neither position, as it stands, can be quite accepted. The effect, after all, was there, and so were the real and difficult conditions of practice. When Annan found that editors and reporters were 'bewildered' by the findings of *Bad News*, it should not have been the end of the matter. The point is to investigate the social conditions of such bewilderment.

It is just because of the immediate pressures, the difficult moment on Liverpool Docks, that a detached analysis of methods and conventions is necessary. What we do, under pressure, and especially what we do as professionals, is what we have been trained to do, what we have got used to doing, what at deep levels we can take for granted so that we can get on with an immediate job. And there is no profession that can fail to learn from someone making explicit just the training, the usage, the taking for granted, that underlie all practice. These can then be consciously affirmed, or consciously amended. This is how all rigorous professions work.

The special problem of communications is not only the relative absence of fundamental as distinct from on-the-job training. It is also that the fundamental analyses of method – for example, the quite new problems of *visual* presentation – are being carried out in one place, and the practice in another. Yet nothing can be understood if it is not recognised that both these real levels exist. I do not see what more the *Bad News* group could have done to show the intricate practical problems (highlighted, of course, by the many practical failures) of the 'objectivity' and 'balance' which the professional broadcasters claim. The greater relative monopoly of broadcast news has at least this advantage: that the greater relative diversity of the press (for all its own tendencies to monopoly and shrinkage) provides accessible evidence to test 'objectivity'. This is well demonstrated in the reporting of the Price Commission's calculations of the contribution of wage rises to inflation (*More Bad News*, pp. 19–22), where, in complicated ways (professionally traced by the *Financial Times*), an estimated 20 per cent contribution became, through various hands, a 'between 60 and 75 pence in the pound' contribution in a BBC news item. Given the importance of such issues, and the genuine difficulties of interpreting such statistics, within different theoretical frameworks, there is really no case at all for saying that the exigencies of practice must override fundamental questions of method. Thus, on so contentious and professional an issue, there is no defensible practical reason for leaving interpretation to the single voice of 'our correspondent' or to the demotic skills of a particular newswriter. Why could there not be two 'correspondents', deliberately chosen for their theoretical differences? Because that would be discussion? But the whole problem is the selection of one interpretation as *news*.

Are we then asking for the impossible, a neutral news service? The *Bad News* team argue that neutrality is impossible and undesirable; indeed, that it is the claim of the existing organisations that what they offer is 'neutral, unbiased, impartial and balanced' which is at the heart of the problem, since what happens in practice is a demonstrably ideological presentation, at many levels, which at once presumes and helps to form an effective consensus of news and other values. There can be little doubt that they have, in general, made out their case, yet where, theoretically and practically, do we go from there?

It is a further effect of the institutional division of labour that professional researchers follow the rules of their own profession, presenting and commenting on evidence, but not otherwise, except implicitly, declaring themselves. I do not blame the *Bad News* team for this, but I notice the contrast with, say, Todd Gitlin's *The Whole World is Watching*, where a comparable but more committed analysis is made of the American media on a specific set of issues. There the focus is on the definition and characterisation of the American New Left, and the fact that it is written by one who actively participated in the events reported, and saw not only their slanting by the media but the complex results within the movement itself, adds a welcome sharpness. I think we do have ultimately to say that the practices in question are matters of fundamental social and political conflict, the integrity of information and the actual diversity of opinion can be reasonably assured, and that we should all be looking for ways to enlarge that space to its still distant limits.

One notable opportunity for such enlargement now exists in the new communications technology, especially in the common-carrier and interactive versions of teletext. It may well not be taken, given the pressure to adapt the technology to current forms of news and marketing. But there would be immediate gain if broadcast news could be, in effect, footnoted, given the developing teletext services which can both handle and recall complicated information and necessary context. Moreover, here as more generally, an enlarged space requires that diversity of channels and voices which all existing systems and their ideologies seem determined to limit, in the name of their own irreplaceable excellence. This looks like being a very long struggle, but it is worth saying, finally, that a considerable amount of that 'terrible news' – the events, not the reports – occurs and will continue to occur because too few people are speaking to and for too many, in conditions in which, increasingly, they nevertheless cannot prevent others from acting and failing to act. That, more than anything, is now the welcome and terrible news.

Index